# Welcome to THE EVERYTHING Family Guides

THESE HANDY, PORTABLE BOOKS are designed to be the perfect traveling companions. Whether you're traveling within a tight family budget or feeling the urge to splurge, you will find all you need to create a memorable family vacation.

Use these books to plan your trips, and then take them along with you for easy reference. Does Jimmy want to go sailing? Or maybe Jane wants to go to the local hobby shop. *The Everything® Family Guides* offer many ways to entertain kids of all ages while also ensuring you get the most out of your time away from home.

Review this book cover to cover to give you great ideas before you travel, and stick it in your backpack or diaper bag to use as a quick reference guide for activities, attractions, and excursions you want to experience. Let *The Everything® Family Guides* help you travel the world, and you'll discover that vacationing with the whole family can be filled with fun and exciting adventures.

 **TRAVEL TIP**

Quick, handy tips

 **RAINY DAY FUN**

Plan ahead for fun without sun

**FAST FACT**

Details to make your trip more enjoyable

 **JUST FOR PARENTS**

Appealing information for moms and dads

# THE
# EVERYTHING®
## — Family Guides —
## Coastal Florida

Dear Reader,

Thanks for picking up this copy of *The Everything®
Family Guide to Coastal Florida*. I've written this book to
help you and your family get the most out of your trip to
Coastal Florida, no matter whether it's your first time or one
of many visits. As one of the few family guides to Coastal
Florida on the market, it's an important tool in helping your
family experience Coastal Florida to its fullest and bring
back memories to cherish forever.

It's hard to keep information current about any destination, and Coastal Florida is no exception. Phone numbers
and Internet addresses change constantly. I've made sure all
of these phone numbers and Web sites are up-to-date, but as
time passes, please be aware that you may have to double-
check with a hotel concierge or local phone book.

In order for you to keep up with the latest information
on Coastal Florida, please visit the Web sites listed in this
book, including *www.visitflorida.com*. If you'd like to share
your Coastal Florida experiences with me, drop me a line
at *bobbrooke@bobbrooke.com*. To learn more about me,
visit my main Web site at *www.bobbrooke.com*. My goal
has been to provide a comprehensive and informative
book on Coastal Florida. Only after you've returned with
suitcases full of happy memories will I be able to know if
I've succeeded.

*Have a great trip!*

*Bob Brooke*

# THE
# EVERYTHING®
## FAMILY GUIDE TO
# COASTAL
# FLORIDA

A complete guide to Jacksonville,
Miami, the Keys, Panama City—
and all the hot spots in between!

Bob Brooke

Avon, Massachusetts

*I'd like to dedicate this book to my close friend Michael, who encouraged me to do the best that I could throughout the writing of this book.*

• • •

Innovation Director: Paula Munier
Editorial Director: Laura M. Daly
Associate Copy Chief: Sheila Zwiebel
Acquisitions Editor: Lisa Laing
Development Editor: Meredith O'Hayre
Production Editor: Casey Ebert

Director of Manufacturing: Susan Beale
Production Project Manager:
Michelle Roy Kelly
Prepress: Erick DaCosta, Matt LeBlanc
Interior Layout: Heather Barrett,
Brewster Brownville, Colleen
Cunningham, Jennifer Oliveira

An Everything® Series Book.
Everything® and everything.com® are registered trademarks of F+W Publications, Inc.

Published by Adams Media, an F+W Publications Company
57 Littlefield Street, Avon, MA 02322 U.S.A.
*www.adamsmedia.com*

ISBN-10: 1-59869-157-0
ISBN-13: 978-1-59869-157-3

Printed in Canada.

J I H G F E D C B A

**Library of Congress Cataloging-in-Publication Data**
Brooke, Bob.
The everything family guide to Coastal Florida / Bob Brooke.
p. cm. – (The everything series)
ISBN-13: 978-1-59869-157-3 (pbk.)
ISBN-10: 1-59869-157-0 (pbk.)
1.Florida–Guidebooks. 2. Atlantic Coast (Fla.)–
Guidebooks. 3. Gulf Coast (Fla.)–Guidebooks. 4. Family recreation–Florida–Guidebooks. 5.
Family recreation–Florida–Atlantic Coast–Guidebooks. 6. Family recreation–Florida–Gulf
Coast–Guidebooks. 7. Children–Travel–Florida–Guidebooks. 8. Children–Travel–Florida–
Atlantic Coast–Guidebooks. 9. Children–Travel–Florida–Gulf Coast–Guidebooks. I. Title.
F309.3.B758 2007
917.5904–dc22
2007015757

*This book is available at quantity discounts for bulk purchases.
For information, please call 1-800-289-0963.*

**Visit the entire Everything® series at *www.everything.com***

# Contents

## Top Ten Family-Friendly Activities to Experience in Coastal Florida

1. Beaches: Soak up some sun on Coastal Florida's fabulous sparkling white sands.

2. Exploring the Florida reef.

3. The mysterious Everglades: Explore the "river of grass," the only ecosystem of its kind on Earth.

4. Playing the links.

5. Mother Nature's best: Discover a natural world just waiting to be explored.

6. Soaring into virtual space: Visit the Kennedy Space Center, Coastal Florida's number-one attraction.

7. Visiting museums: No longer dark and boring places, Coastal Florida's museums help you to understand her culture and people.

8. Theme parks.

9. Baseball rendezvous: See your favorite baseball players warm up for the season in Spring Training.

10. Shopping.

# Acknowledgments

Thanks to all who made this book possible. Special thanks go to all the state and local tourism offices throughout Coastal Florida for their help in gathering information about their destinations.

# Introduction

For the last four decades or so, Florida has become known as the land where fantasy is reality. Yet so many of its visitors miss the real Florida—the beauty and mystery along its coast. With so many miles of spectacular shoreline, it's hard to choose where to go. The sheer scope of coastal vacation possibilities will astound you. There's far too much to see and do in one day, one week, or one visit. To make the most of your vacation time, you'll want to pinpoint the places and activities that appeal to you and your family.

Even Florida's name suggests a wealth of tropical beauty: waving palms, fragrant orchids and bromeliads, emerald green waters, and sparkling white sands. Colorful birds wade through the waters and fly overhead as alligators doze in the sun on the banks of tropical rivers and swamps. Mother Nature populated this green peninsula with a variety of creatures and plants, all for you to discover.

Since the first railroads carried wealthy vacationers to the region in the late nineteenth century, Coastal Florida has been touted as a paradise. And though parking lots are paving over much of it, you can still find coastal areas where your family can have fun and commune with nature, too.

No two days of your vacation need be alike. You can walk in the footsteps of conquistadors and pirates one day, then canoe along a river little altered by time or man the next. You can eat seafood fresh from the ocean or sample local delicacies such as alligator tail. Though no place of interest lies more than 60 miles from the sea, this book covers only what's along the coast. Beginning in vibrant Miami, it heads northward up Florida's Atlantic coast to Fort Lauderdale, Palm Beach, and Cocoa Beach, then on to historic Saint Augustine and Jacksonville. Next, it focuses on the south, covering the magnificent Florida Keys and Key West before exploring the mysterious Everglades. Traveling up the Gulf coast to cultural Sarasota and urban Tampa and Saint Petersburg, it finally makes a journey across the Panhandle from beachside Panama City to genteel Pensacola. Each destination is intended to be used a base to explore the area around it. Each is distinctive, but combined they create a tapestry of beauty and history that's Coastal Florida.

You'll find both the old and the new celebrated here. The region's colorful past comes alive through exhibits of Spanish treasures, historical recreations of Native American settlements, re-enactments of buccaneer invasions, and state-of-the-art tours into the future at the Kennedy Space Center. But to discover the real treasures of Coastal Florida, you have to look beyond this book, meandering down narrow streets, hiking along wilderness trails, and visiting small towns and villages.

Through this book, you'll also become acquainted with Coastal Florida's natural habitats and human-made wonders. Each river, stream, and tropical lagoon has its own character. Each waits to be explored. Each offers a setting of peace and beauty found nowhere else in the country. You'll discover animals and plants here that exist nowhere else in the world. But even Coastal Florida's cities have their own personalities, from Latin Miami to commercial Jacksonville to Old South Pensacola.

If you already have an itinerary in mind—lying on a beach working on your tan, visiting a museum or two, watching silhouetted palm trees sway in the breeze at sunset, or perhaps encountering an alligator, a dolphin, or a tarpon—this book will help you fill it out. If not, you'll find a wide selection of recommended tours to use singly or in combination. Each chapter also offers recommendations for places to stay, to eat, and to play, all selected with your family's enjoyment in mind.

Whatever you choose to do, leave your watch at home and follow the sun. Bring along plenty of sunblock and a sense of wonder and curiosity that will allow you to discover the magic of Coastal Florida, and you'll go home wondering how soon you can return. Floridians say, "Once you get Florida sand in your shoes, you'll always return." And when you do, you'll have *The Everything® Family Guide to Coastal Florida* to help you have a great time.

# CHAPTER 1

# Welcome to Coastal Florida

A WORLD OF FUN and history awaits you in Coastal Florida. You've probably imagined lying on a sandy beach while palm trees rustle in the breeze. Or maybe you prefer to wrestle a mighty tarpon or run across an alligator on a walk through a tropical forest. You'll find much more in Coastal Florida than sun, sea, and sand. You and your family can go back in time to the days of the buccaneers or forward to outer space. In between, you'll find a land with so many diverse attractions, you'll barely have time to sleep.

## Getting to Know Coastal Florida

Over forty million tourists come to Florida each year, and although a great many visit Central Florida's theme parks, many more visit the resorts and towns of Coastal Florida. With nearly 1,200 miles of coastline, the second longest coastline of any state, the coast of Florida is probably one of the least tapped resources in the United States. Beyond its beaches, you'll find fascinating historical sites, hikable tropical forests, canoeable rivers, and enough golf courses to play a different one every day of your vacation.

The first place that most people think of when someone mentions Coastal Florida is Miami Beach. Its glamorous notoriety through much of the twentieth century has made it Florida's premiere beach resort. But there are so many more—lively Fort

Lauderdale, sedate Jacksonville Beach, historic Saint Augustine, elegant Naples, cultural Sarasota, family fun land Panama City, nautical Pensacola, artsy Key West, plus many others. Each has its own personality, its own lifestyle, and its own attractions. All have a laid-back feel—an "I'll get to it sooner or later" attitude found nowhere else in the country.

And maybe that's what endears Coastal Florida to so many return visitors. They're looking for a place to escape the hectic pace of life. In the northern cities in particular, they can hang back and enjoy life by just lying on the sand and looking up at the rolling blue sky above.

## A Brief History of Coastal Florida

When Juan Ponce de León arrived in what's now Florida in 1513, he met Indians whose ancestors had harvested the waters, roamed the hills, and waded the swamps of Florida for at least twelve centuries. Little remains of these early wanderers except artifacts and mounds of discarded oyster shells. The Apalachees roamed the western regions, the Timucuas spread from Tampa Bay, and the Calusas roamed the southern swamplands.

### ≡FAST FACT

English explorers Sebastian and John Cabot may have been the first Europeans to see Florida in 1498 through an error in latitude readings. When John Cabot stepped ashore on what's now known as Cape Florida on Key Biscayne, he supposedly called it *Baccallaos*, the name the Indians gave to tuna that swam in the offshore waters.

Ponce de León came to America looking for a legendary fountain of youth that he had heard about from the Indians on the island of Puerto Rico. He landed near present-day Saint Augustine and claimed the land for Spain. He and other Spanish explorers had also heard tales of great caches of gold just waiting to be taken. Unfortunately, Ponce de León never did find his fountain of youth, but he did name the new land *La Florida* in honor of Spain's Festival of Flowers, *Pascua Florida,* or the "feast of flowers."

After exploring Florida's eastern coast, he returned again in 1521 to set up a colony on the southwestern side of the peninsula. The Calusa Indians fiercely defended their territory, wounding Ponce de León with a poison arrow, sending him scurrying for Cuba where he died of his wounds. Following his accounts of the new land, fellow explorer Hernando de Soto explored around Tampa Bay before dying of fever. In 1559, Tristán de Luna tried to set up a colony on Pensacola Bay, but hurricanes and hardships put an end to it two years later. Undaunted, the Spanish king sent Pedro Menéndez de Avilés to Florida in 1565. After arriving on the northeast coast and establishing what would become the first permanent settlement in America, he went on to establish forts and missions to convert the Indians to Christianity. Since the Spanish had a hold on Florida, the English headed north to found their colonies.

English colonists from what's now Georgia began harassing the Spanish colony in the early eighteenth century, eventually destroying it. At around the same time, the French captured Pensacola in 1719. England's hold grew stronger as Spain's grew weaker. Finally, in 1763, following the devastating Seven Years War, Spain traded Florida for Cuba, which the British had captured, thus ending her dreams of riches.

The British divided Florida into East and West, with capitals at Saint Augustine and Pensacola. Though they promised colonists land grants, they couldn't follow through on much else because the Revolutionary War in the northern colonies had begun. Though East and West Florida remained loyal to the British, Spain once again won the two territories after the war, offering generous land grants both to potential Spanish colonists and those from America. And slaves escaping from the American colonies found a safe haven in Florida.

By the late eighteenth century, most of Florida's original tribes had been killed or scattered, victims of European exploration, raids, and wars, but as the eighteenth century progressed, more Creek Indians from Georgia moved in to fill the void. They called themselves Seminoles, from the Creek word *siminoli*, meaning wanderers or exiles. Andrew Jackson invaded northern Florida in 1814 supposedly to squelch an Indian uprising in what was then Alabama, but his actual mission was to roust the British troops from Pensacola. Instead, he attacked Indian settlements, which started the First Seminole War.

## ≡FAST FACT

President James Monroe sent Andrew Jackson the Rhea Letter in 1818, which Jackson understood to be his official authorization to march into Florida on the pretext of subduing the Seminoles, but in actuality ordered him to take control of the region for the United States.

After the war began, Spain decided to sell Florida to the United States in 1821. Andrew Jackson became the first territorial governor over united East and West Florida, governing from the new capital, Tallahassee.

Just like their brothers and sisters across the country, Florida's Indians struggled hopelessly to hold onto their homeland. Settlers pressured Jackson to remove the Indians to territory set aside for them west of the Mississippi. When Andrew Jackson became president in 1835, he declared the Second Seminole War. But he underestimated the Seminole's resolve to fight for what was theirs. Seven years and 1,500 lives later, Jackson declared a victory and sent the surviving Seminoles to the Indian Territory. But several hundred escaped into the Everglades to live and hide in the swamp. Their descendants, 500 Miccosukees and 1,500 Seminoles, live there today.

Florida became a state in 1845. Most of its people lived in the northern part of the state, growing cotton, sweet potatoes, and rice on large plantations. Soon after the Civil War broke out, Florida joined the Confederacy. Spared from any major battles, it was able to recover faster than other southern states. Georgia farmers, later known as "crackers," immigrated into northern Florida to work on farms.

Southern Florida dozed in the sun until millionaires Henry Flagler and Henry B. Plant built railroads down each coast in the 1880s. These brought not only visitors to luxury seaside resorts catering to the well-heeled that each built, but also thousands of workers to build them. Not accessible to the rest of the country, southern Florida opened up to new industries such as cigar-making, sponge-fishing, and citrus-growing. Immigrants, eager to work in the new industries, began to arrive by the boatload. Greek sponge-fishermen settled in Tarpon Springs. Cuban cigar-makers first settled in Key West, then later moved north to Ybor City in Tampa. Scots joined them soon after.

Additional rich farmland opened up as workers drained swamps. Real estate boomed. Then it fell in 1926. Violent hurricanes, the Great Depression, and the Mediterranean fruit fly decimated Florida's economy. All seemed lost until World War II broke out, and Florida became a major military training ground. The good times came back.

Postwar America boomed. And Florida was no exception. A new industry with its eye on the far reaches of the universe set up shop on several desolate barrier islands halfway down Florida's east coast, while an entertainment conglomerate set up shop in Central Florida. NASA and a little mouse named Mickey changed Florida forever.

## Who Are the Floridians?

During the past two decades, over two million people have settled in Florida, either through immigration or retirement, making it the fourth most populous state in the country. Often called "God's Waiting

Room," the perception held by many is that Florida is a land of senior citizens. But the fact is that the average age is just thirty-six.

Florida has become a true melting pot, a symbol of what America stands for. Native Americans, Cubans, Greeks, Scots, Slavs, Mexicans, Minorcans, Asians, African-Americans, Jews, and many others have contributed their skills and traditions to make Florida what it is today. Miami, where more than 130,000 people speak eighteen languages other than English or Spanish, has become a truly ethnic metropolis.

## Ethnic Groups

In order to have some political clout, the Big Cypress, Brighton, and Hollywood Creek Indians joined together as the Seminole Tribe of Florida in 1957. The Miccosukee tribe broke away and formed their own group in 1962. The former live on the Big Cypress Reservation, the Brighton reservation, and in Hollywood, Florida. The latter live on the Tamiami Trail and Alligator Alley reservations north of Everglades National Park. Both continue to battle with the federal government over land rights and compensation.

Since 1959, nearly half a million Cubans, fleeing Castro's communist government, have reached Florida's shores. By the early 1960s many of Cuba's doctors, lawyers, politicians, and civil servants arrived with nothing but their skills and a willingness to endure whatever hardships were necessary to build a better life. Today, over half of Greater Miami's population is Hispanic. With so much Spanish spoken, other Latin American immigrants from Central and South America have joined the Cubans in Miami.

Nearly one-third of the population of Tarpon Springs, the oldest city on Florida's west coast, are descendants of Greek sponge-divers.

Also on the west coast, in 1870 Scottish immigrants opened a general store and petitioned the U.S. Post Office to name their town Dunedin, a Gaelic word meaning "peaceful rest." Count Odet Phillippe, a surgeon, introduced grapefruits to Florida in the 1830s and the citrus industry began. Though the area no longer produces citrus fruit, the Scottish heritage lives on in the annual Highland Games.

Runaway black slaves began arriving in Florida in the early nineteenth century. Over 1,400 lived alongside the Seminoles in the swamps. Plantation owners in Florida had their own slaves as well.

## Appreciating Local Culture

Many immigrant groups have contributed to Florida's culture. Each, in its own way, has infused its traditions into the melting-pot Floridian culture you'll experience today.

The most obvious and conspicuous is the Cuban culture of Miami. Cubans brought with them their cuisine, music, traditions, and language, all of which have dramatically affected life in their adopted city. Little Havana, the Cuban neighborhood of Miami, feels more like Cuba than America. The aroma of rich Cuban coffee mixes with that of black beans and rice. Hispanic arts and music festivals carry on their traditions.

On the other side of the peninsula, the fragrant aromas of moussaka and baklava spill out from Greek restaurants and bakeries in Tarpon Springs, as Greek spongers sit and talk at sidewalk cafés. Today, Tarpon Springs is the largest sponge market in the world. The beautiful Byzantine-style Saint Nicholas Cathedral, built in 1943, serves as a focal point of this lively Greek community. Every year on the sixth of January, more than 30,000 residents and visitors take part in Epiphany, a day of Greek tradition and culture commemorating the baptism of Christ by John the Baptist.

The Scottish community of Dunedin keeps its heritage alive with the Highland Games and Festival, held in April, where bagpipes, drums, highland dancing, and athletic games turn the town into a huge celebration.

Native American tribes like the Miccosukees sustain their way of life by sharing it with visitors at the Miccosukee Indian Village, a re-creation of one of their settlements offering alligator wrestling shows, a restaurant, a soda stand, and souvenir shops selling fiber dolls, baskets, bracelets, and colorful wooden tomahawks. There's also a model of their old homestead, called *chickee*, from the days when they had to camp in the Everglades swampland, hiding from government officials trying to evict them.

By the 1940s, Miami's black Overtown neighborhood had become well known for its major nightclubs. Great performers like Cab Calloway, Nat "King" Cole, Ella Fitzgerald, Billie Holiday, and Louis Armstrong put Overtown's Northwest Second Avenue on the map.

# What Does Coastal Florida Have to Offer Your Family?

Florida is a wonderland for families. Unfortunately, the theme parks have given everyone the impression that that's all there is to do here. And that can't be further from the truth. When traveling as a family, you want to make sure that everyone has a good time—that everyone gets to do what interests them. And at every coastal destination, you'll have plenty of opportunities to do that.

### Outdoor Activities

Wherever you go in Florida, there's someplace to cast a line, cruise a craft, or hike a trail. Coastal Florida offers so many opportunities for outdoor fun that it's a wonder anyone stays inside. Water activities dominate the outdoor scene of Coastal Florida, where you're always less than 50 miles away from water. Fishing and boating are the major activities, with opportunities to hook prize-winning game fish or just some trout for dinner. Second to that is surfing and windsurfing along Florida's Atlantic coast beaches. The Intracoastal Waterway provides not only a means to travel the coast by boat, but also calmer waters on which to water-ski or Jet-Ski.

Golf and tennis join fishing as Florida's top recreational activities. There's a joke going around Florida that says if anyone finds an extra tract of land in Florida, it more than likely will turn into a golf course or tennis court with an accompanying residential development before too long. Currently, Florida boasts hundreds of golf courses. In fact, if you traveled around the state, you probably could play a different course every day.

## Cultural Activities

If you're like most of Coastal Florida's visitors, you're unaware of its fascinating historical sites and districts. Pensacola's North Hill Preservation District, for example, has restored homes built during the timber boom of the late 1890s and early 1900s. Its Seville Square Historic District offers restored eighteenth and nineteenth century buildings containing specialty shops and restaurants.

And then there are the old forts constructed to defend the coast, first by the Spanish and then by the English and Americans.

When you're not sunbathing on Florida's white sand beaches, you can visit countless museums with thousands of pieces of historic memorabilia, photographs, documents, and artifacts on display. Some, like the Ringling Museum complex in Sarasota, house priceless works of art. Others, such as the Edison Home and Gardens in Fort Myers, tell the story of inventions that we take for granted today.

## Nature Activities

If you're looking to commune more with nature, you can rent a canoe and paddle the many state trails through miles of undisturbed scenic beauty in many state parks on or near the coast. You'll find opportunities for canoe rentals plentiful at all Florida state recreation areas.

There are plenty of places to hike, also. Unlike its northern neighbors, Coastal Florida offers tropical hammocks through which you can hike to see unique wildlife and vegetation. You'll find the country's largest remaining stand of virgin bald cypress, the oldest trees in eastern North America, in Corkscrew Swamp Sanctuary, near Naples. Maintained by the National Audubon Society, the entire preserve is a must if you're a nature buff.

## TRAVEL TIP

The best time to hike is from late fall to early spring, avoiding the heat of summer and the worst of the mosquitoes. You'll also see more variety of wildlife. Be sure to carry plenty of drinking water and wear comfortable hiking shoes.

And along those same lines, Coastal Florida is a birder's wonderland. With over 400 species of birds in the area, you'll find that carrying your binoculars at all times is a must. State recreation areas all along Florida's coasts provide a myriad of opportunities to observe herons and egrets, plus hundreds of migrating birds. You can also go for a swim and have a picnic.

One of the most extraordinary natural areas in the world exists in southern Florida. The Everglades sprawls over 5,000 square miles of land and water. It has been called the wildest, shallowest, strangest river in the world. Spending a day here is like going back in time to a primordial age.

And Collier-Seminole State Park, a 6,423-acre park south of Naples, where Big Cypress Swamp joins the Everglades, is the last refuge of the Seminole Indians. Walking the nature trails will give you an idea of what they had to endure to live in the swamp.

## When Should You Visit?

Florida is called the Sunshine State—and why not, for the sun shines brightly nearly every day in some locations. While Florida can also get both colder and hotter from time to time than you might expect, it justifiably claims year-round weather nearly as perfect as can be found anywhere in the continental United States.

Generally, the "shoulder seasons," spring and fall, offer the most pleasant days and nights in all but the southernmost regions of

Florida, where you'll find winter the favored time to visit. Throughout the state, summers tend to be wet, hot, and humid. Winters are drier, mild and sunny with moderate readings, though in the northern regions there can be periods when temperatures drop into the 20s and even occasional snow. From Central Florida southward, freezing can occur occasionally in all but the most southerly regions.

Hurricanes, though they can be devastating, shouldn't keep you from visiting in the fall. Usually developing in September, they have also occurred much later. In recent years, Mother Nature has stretched out hurricane season, beginning earlier and ending later with many more violent storms. Unlike many other weather phenomena, they come with plenty of warning, allowing visitors either to batten down or depart for inland locations.

All in all, you'll discover that temperate seasons, refreshing cold springs, breezy beaches, and lots of air conditioning all contribute to making Coastal Florida a good year-round destination.

# The Climate of Coastal Florida

Coastal Florida's year-round mild temperatures and almost constant sunshine lure families weary of the gray skies and cold of the north. The Gulf of Mexico and the Atlantic Ocean alternately provide cool breezes in summer and warm ones in winter. Winters are usually dry and mild while summers are wet. Sea breezes help to alleviate the summer heat and humidity. Florida's coastal areas remain slightly warmer in winter and cooler in summer than inland destinations. The Gulf Stream, flowing around the western tip of Cuba through the Florida Straits and northward along the lower East Coast, makes southern Florida one of the warmest places in the continental United States during the winter.

Frequent afternoon thunderstorms temper the summer heat. In fact, Florida has more thunderstorms than any other state. On the positive side, thunderstorms can lower temperatures as much as 20°.

You'll find that these summer thunderstorms most frequently occur in an area from Tampa east to Daytona Beach, then south to Cape Canaveral and west to Fort Myers, which averages 100 days of lightning per year. Overall, Florida receives 50 to 65 inches of rain per year, but that amount can vary from 80 inches in Pensacola to 40 inches in Key West. The Panhandle has two rainy seasons, one from late winter to early spring and another during summer. Statewide, April and November are the driest months. Generally, more than 50 percent of the total annual rainfall for the state falls between June and September. Add to that the average of thirty tornadoes that touch down each year from April to June.

## Average Temperature Range

The hottest months along Florida's coasts are June through August, when the daytime temperature can soar to 95°. Daytime winter temperatures average between 45° and 70°, dropping to as low as 40° in northern Florida and 70° to 80° in the southern half. Springtime has the lowest relative humidity, between 65 and 70 percent. Summer temperatures are more or less uniform throughout the state, with average highs around 90°. and lows seldom falling below 70°. While summer can bring hot afternoons, offshore breezes keep life comfortable in most regions near the coast.

## Hurricanes

The hurricane season lasts from June through October, with most of the hurricanes occurring in September or October. As this could put a damper on your vacation plans, you should check the Weather Channel (*www.weather.com*) or the National Weather Service (*www.nws.noaa.gov*) before your departure in case you have to reschedule your visit. Miami's National Hurricane Center tracks storms by radar and satellites. If you're already in Florida, tune in to local radio or television stations for up-to-the-minute advisories and evacuation warnings. Most storms that enter Florida approach from the south or southwest, entering the Keys, the Miami area, or along the west coast.

# Deciding How to Get There

Using the discount and promotional fares offered by various airlines, flying to Coastal Florida is probably your best bet. The major flight hubs of Miami and Tampa, plus many smaller airports with good air service, such as Jacksonville, West Palm Beach, and Pensacola, make getting to your destination easy.

With the price of gasoline what it is today, traveling by car to Coastal Florida isn't the value it once was. Unless you live close by, you'll pay less flying. In most cases, flying also beats traveling by train. Amtrak (Toll-free 800-872-7245, *www.amtrak.com*) trains only connect to the coastal cities of Jacksonville, Fort Lauderdale, Tampa, and Miami. A train trip from Philadelphia to Jacksonville will cost you nearly $300 and take over sixteen hours one-way. Unless you're afraid of flying or have a long vacation time, traveling by train isn't an option.

Many tour operators and airline tour desks offer packages combining plane tickets and hotel accommodations with sightseeing and dining. If you think a package will be inflexible, think again. Though you may have to stay over a Saturday night or stay at least seven days, the money you save by using a package will more than offset any inconvenience.

# Getting Around

Since distances in Florida are relatively short, driving from the west to the east coast takes a little over two hours. And traveling from Miami to Pensacola can take about six hours. If you're taking a bus, the trip will take much longer. Flying is probably your best option if you plan on visiting several areas on your vacation.

By traveling early or later in the day and midweek, you can fly between cities in Florida for about what it costs to travel by bus. A one-way flight between Miami and Jacksonville, for example, will cost about $99 and take under two hours. The same trip by bus will cost $60, but it will take over eleven hours, while a similar trip by train will cost $49 and take nine hours.

Though buses used to be the least expensive method of travel within Florida, they aren't anymore. Greyhound is the only long-distance service, linking all major cities and many smaller towns. Buses connect the major cities 24-7, stopping only for driver changes and meal breaks. If you're traveling through the Florida Keys, you can flag down a bus anywhere along the Overseas Highway or board at scheduled stops. As with airline fares, you'll pay less if you travel on weekdays and use special companion, military, or student discounts.

Traveling by train between Florida's coastal cities takes time and may limit your itinerary. Though Amtrak links major coastal cities, service is limited to one or two departures a day.

Taxis in Florida's coastal cities are relatively expensive. For the most part, travel here is more suburban than urban, except in the largest cities. Because of this, rental car rates are often low.

### Renting a Car

Renting a car to get around a particular area is probably your best option. All the major companies—Hertz, Avis, Budget, National, Alamo, and Thrifty—have rental locations at airports. Others, like Dollar and Enterprise, have locations nearby. If you plan to rent a car anyway, check for fly-drive packages that offer discounted car rental rates when you buy an air ticket. They're usually cheaper than renting on arrival and often give you unlimited free mileage. But you may do better if you buy a cheap air ticket and combine it with a holiday or weekend car-rental package that includes unlimited mileage. If you plan on renting a car for a week or more, you should use the fly-drive option, as the cost of mileage could be as much as the car rental itself. Remember, if you plan to drive a car to a different city and drop it off, you'll might have to pay a drop-off charge that's often as much as a week's rental. The following companies offer car rentals in Florida:

- **Alamo:** ☎Toll-free 800-462-5266, ✍*www.alamo.com*
- **Avis:** ☎Toll-free 800-331-1212, ✍*www.avis.com*
- **Budget:** ☎Toll-free 800-527-0700, ✍*www.budget.com*
- **Dollar:** ☎Toll-free 866-434-2226, ✍*www.dollar.com*
- **Enterprise:** ☎Toll-free 800-261-7331, ✍*www.enterprise .com*
- **Hertz:** ☎Toll-free 800-654-3131, ✍*www.hertz.com*
- **National:** ☎Toll-free 888-501-9010, ✍*www.nationalcar .com*
- **Thrifty:** ☎Toll-free 800-847-4389, ✍*www.thrifty.com*

 **TRAVEL TIP**

Check with your auto insurance carrier to see if you're covered while driving a rental car. If yes, check "No" for the Collision Damage Waiver on your car rental agreement of insurance. This waiver often isn't included in the initial rental charge, but you should take it out. At $10 to $12 a day, this can add substantially to the total cost, but without it you're liable for every scratch to the car—even if none was your fault.

## Driving in Florida

To make the best time, ride the interstate highways—odd-numbered ones run north and south and even-numbered ones run east to west. Some of these are toll roads, such as the 318-mile Florida Turnpike. Usually you'll pay a toll according to how far you've driven. Also, along Florida's coast you'll have to pay tolls to cross a number of bridges and causeways.

**TRAVEL TIP**

Whenever possible, park in the shade. If you don't, you may find your car too hot to touch when you return. Temperatures inside cars parked in the full force of the Florida sun can reach 140°F. Purchase an inexpensive cardboard windshield screen at a discount or auto store. It will keep your parked car a lot cooler.

To really see Coastal Florida, amble along scenic roads like Highway A1A, which runs parallel to U.S. Route 1 along Florida's east coast. But be aware that back roads are often just two lanes.

The official speed limit in Florida is 55 miles per hour, raised to 65 miles per hour on interstate highways. The speed drops to about 35 miles per hour on roads through smaller towns. Keep an eye out for speed traps, since the speed may change within a few yards, not enabling you to slow down fast enough. Fines for speeding can start at $75. And make sure your front-seat passenger fastens his seat belt—it's the law in Florida.

### Bicycling

Bicycling around Coastal Florida's major cities can be dangerous because of heavy traffic and lack of bike paths. However, you'll find it a great way to explore smaller towns and villages using marked cycle paths along the coast. You can rent a bicycle for $8 to $15 a day or $30 to $55 a week from many beach shops and concessionaires in some state parks. You'll find the best cycling areas in the Panhandle and along the northeast coast.

For safety and visibility, wear a brightly colored helmet and cycling gloves. And always keep your water bottle filled and drink from it frequently to avoid getting dehydrated in the hot Florida sun. For free bicycle touring information and detailed maps of cycling routes, contact the Florida Department of Transportation (605 Suwanee Street, Tallahassee 32399-0450, 850-414-4100, *www.dot.state.fl.us*).

# CHAPTER 2

# The Land of Coastal Florida

WHEN MANY PEOPLE THINK of Florida, images of theme parks and sandy beaches come to mind. But you'll be surprised to discover that Coastal Florida is a world of natural wonder and mystery with extraordinary land and wildlife. Though much contributes to the diversity of ecosystems found here, latitude and elevation top the list. Florida straddles both the temperate and subtropical zones, allowing for a wide variety of plants and animals. And though much of the coast is flat and low-lying, just a few inches in elevation drastically affects what grows and lives there.

## The Lay of the Land

Hundreds of millions of years ago, what's Florida today was just a string of volcanic islands. Its landmass, a huge, mostly submerged projection known as the Floridian Plateau, separates the Gulf of Mexico from the Atlantic Ocean. Over time, the magma of these ancient volcanoes hardened, and erosion and deposits of silt and sand buried them beneath the sea. Like Venus from the sea, Florida first emerged as a sandy bar thirty million years ago. For eons its bedrock had lain beneath the warm ocean, slowly collecting sediment and forming limestone deposits that would one day become new land. Washed by pounding waves, worn by wind and rain, the mass enlarged and shrank as Ice Age glaciers to the north formed and reformed, intermittently raising and lowering the level of the sea. The tides carved out stone bluffs and terraces.

Following the Ice Age, centuries of heavy rain filled scars and caves created in the limestone crust by the changing seas. Springs burst through the surface, transforming sinkholes into marshes and lagoons. The limestone foundation became covered with sand and red clay that in some places has mixed to produce a rich sandy loam fertile enough to grow a variety of fruits and vegetables. In the extreme southern portion of Florida, peat covered the limestone, enabling lush jungle-like areas to form.

Large reptiles, mastodons, and other creatures began to roam over this new land one million years ago. And as the last Ice Age retreated in North America, the Florida peninsula took the shape it has today.

# The Regions of Coastal Florida

The eight major tourism areas discussed in this book—the Northeast Coast, the Space Coast, the Southeast Coast, the West Coast, the Northwest Coast, the Florida Panhandle, the Florida Keys, and Southern Coastal Florida—all fall into one of four geographical regions: coastal plains, lowlands, the Everglades, and the Keys.

### Coastal Plains

Like a watery fringe, the Atlantic and Gulf coastal plains surround the state, extending inland as far as 60 miles in some places. Mostly quite level and low, they are often wooded and dense; offshore they take the form of sand bars, coral reefs, lagoons, and islands.

The Atlantic Coastal Plain is a low, level plain ranging in width from 30 to 100 miles, covering the eastern part of the state. Just beyond the mainland, there's a narrow ribbon of sandbars, coral reefs, and barrier islands. Between this ribbon and the plain are shallow lakes, lagoons, rivers, and bays. This plain includes the Big Cypress Swamp and the Everglades at over 1.5 million acres. Also within the Atlantic Coastal Plain are the Florida Keys, a chain of small islands that curve 150 miles off the southern end of the main-land from Miami.

The East Gulf Coastal Plain has two sections: the southwestern part of Florida and the curves around the northern edge of the Gulf of Mexico across the Panhandle to the western border. Here are also long narrow barrier islands and coastal swamps.

## Lowlands

The Gulf Coast lowlands, formally known as the Marianna Low-lands, along the coast of Florida's Panhandle are a flat sandy area with many sinkholes, which have been filled in by the dissolution of the limestone foundation to form numerous marshes and ponds. Shaped by the seas during the Pleistocene period, they rise no more than 100 feet. Here, streams and clear rivers like the Apalachicola, the largest in Florida, meander between gently rolling hills on their way to the Gulf of Mexico.

## Everglades

The southernmost region, the Everglades Basin, contains Florida's largest swamp area, though today large sections of it have been drained and converted to farmland. The great Everglades, a giant "river of grass" flowing from Lake Okeechobee through the Big Cypress Swamp, dominates this area. Here, small pockets of trees poke their heads above an endless flat expanse of sawgrass stretching to the horizon. The water from a 50-mile-wide river replenishes the sawgrass, which produces algae that feeds a myriad of creatures, including alligators.

## Keys

The farthest bit of fringe, the 100-mile-long string of small islands known as the Florida Keys, stretches southwest from Key Biscayne to Key West. The Upper Keys have a base of coral rock, an extension of the only living coral reef in the continental United States, lying due east. Dense woodland covers the Lower Keys, with a foundation of oolitic limestone, once part of the seabed.

## The Coast

Florida has 1,197 miles of coastline, more than any state except Alaska. The Gulf Coast stretches for 798 miles while the Atlantic coast is 399 miles long. Of the total length of Florida coast, beaches lie over 800 miles. Add to that Florida's 4,424 square miles of water—nearly 10 percent of its total area—and you can see why Coastal Florida is a fishing and boating paradise.

## ≡FAST FACT

Florida's Gulf coastline has a low ocean floor 60 feet deep, from 3 miles out near Panama City to 40 miles out off Cedar Key. On the east coast the low area begins at West Palm Beach, widening toward Jacksonville Beach. However, off Miami Beach the ocean floor drops from 600 to 6,000 feet, making this the closest area to the continental shelf.

Tucked into Florida's coast are a myriad of estuaries, inlets, bays, and islands. The state's eastern shore from Fernandina Beach to Miami Beach is one long string of sandy beaches, some extremely wide, like Daytona. On the Gulf side, sandy beaches run from Pensacola east to Saint George Island in the northwest and from Honeymoon Island south to Marco Island along the west coast. Florida's Big Bend, as the peninsula curves into the Panhandle, has shorelines consisting of mostly salt marshes. Around the state's southern tip lie 96 miles of mangrove islands and another 438 miles of coastal marshes and lagoons.

But Mother Nature frequently remodels shorelines. Through wind and wave action, sands move from one side of an island or inlet to the other. Storms and hurricanes can drastically alter the coastal landscape, creating channels where before there were none and filling in those created previously. These high-energy shorelines have natural sand dunes, built up over time around stands of wild sea oats. This particular grass is so important to dune protection that Florida law prohibits anyone from picking, breaking, or trampling it. Beach erosion is a natural thing, but the State of Florida has undertaken extensive beach restoration to preserve its major tourism resource.

##  TRAVEL TIP

Of the seven species of sea turtle, five nest on Florida's sandy beaches—green, loggerhead, leatherback, hawksbill, and olive ridley. The best time to view them is in June during peak nesting time. Take one of the ranger-led turtle walks offered at state parks and national seashores along the southern portion of the northeast coast.

When you think of sandy beaches, you naturally think of sunbathing and swimming. But there's so much more going on along Florida's coasts. Beaches provide a habitat for many species of animals and birds. By day, shore birds prowl the break line—that line where the waves break on the sand—searching for a tidbit. By night, sea turtles creep ashore to lay their eggs along some beaches. And where you don't find sand, you'll find mangrove forests, salt marshes, and estuaries. Offshore, coral reefs provide you with another exotic ecosystem to explore.

### Beaches

Beaches are probably Florida's prime natural assets. Of the twenty-five state beach parks, Little Talbot Island, off the coast of Saint Augustine, is the largest while Cayo Costa Island is one of the most unspoiled. In recent years, the State of Florida has undertaken a "Save Our Coast" campaign by purchasing natural beach property for recreation while at the same time preserving it. In addition, the federal government has established national seashores, one encompassing 26 miles of shoreline at Cape Canaveral on Florida's east coast and another encompassing 50 miles of shoreline among the Gulf Islands of the Panhandle.

## ≡FAST FACT

Since Portuguese man-of-wars have no means of locomotion, their floating, sail-like bodies often wash ashore. Their tentacles, sometimes up to 60 feet long and often buried just under the sand's surface, can deliver a painful sting. Be aware of their purplish bodies with far-reaching tentacles.

One of the major activities along Florida's beaches, especially those along the west coast, is shelling. Sea waves toss many interesting creatures onto Florida's beaches. Horseshoe crabs lie waiting for the next tide while sponges and seahorses dot the sands. The variety of Florida's shells will boggle your mind—conches, fig shells, moon snails, whelks, red and orange scallops, cockles, turban, and pen shells, to name only a few.

### Mangroves

Nearly 470,000 acres of tropical mangrove swamps dot the shores of southern Florida. Some occur even as far north as Cedar Key, north of Saint Petersburg on the Gulf Coast. Botanists call them "walking" trees because their knee-like roots make them look as if they're ready to walk away. They're a necessary part of the coastal ecosystem because they create a protected nursery for shellfish, crustaceans like lobsters, and some fish. And along Florida's hurricane-prone coastline, they also protect the mainland from storm winds and floods.

Three species of mangrove grow in the brackish waters around the Florida Keys and the southwest coast. Unlike other trees, mangroves produce live young. Their seeds germinate while still attached to the tree. After dropping from the parent, the young seedling can float for weeks or months until it washes up on a suitable shore, where its sprouted condition allows it to quickly send out roots. Mangrove trees have difficulty extracting oxygen from the muddy soil, so they send out a system of aerial roots, which dangle from branches or twist outward from the lower trunk. Crocodiles, frogs, river otters, mink, and raccoons love to hide beneath them.

## Islands

Florida's territorial boundaries also include thousands of islands. In fact, locals call the coastal area south of Naples and west of the Everglades "the Land of Ten Thousand Islands." Second in number only to Alaska, these islands rise from Biscayne Bay to Pensacola Bay. Others occur in rivers, lagoons, inlets, and harbors. At least 4,500 of them cover 10 acres or more.

## Coral Reefs

Florida's living coral reef, the only one in the nation, frames its southeastern corner. Coral comes in a rainbow of colors—orange (elkhorn coral), red (brain coral), and green (star coral). Though to a diver, coral lying on the ocean floor may seem huge—and some is gigantic—it's actually made of millions of small, soft animals called polyps, related to sea anemones. The polyps secrete limestone to form a hard outer shell. At night they extend their feathery tentacles to filter seawater for microscopic food. This provides only a fraction of the coral's nutrition. They gain the most from the photosynthesis of algae that live within their cells. When warmer water kills off large numbers of these algae, the weakened polyp succumbs to disease and dies. While this may sound severe, the damage from tourist activities in Florida has had much more of an impact on the reef. Fortunately, it's against the law to take any live coral to sell or as souvenirs.

Hundreds of colorful fish, including parrot fish, porkfish, grunts, and blennies, swirl about in dazzling schools or lurk between coral crevices. Sponges, sea fans, crabs, spiny lobsters, sea urchins, and conches all make their home on or around the reef.

# Woodlands

Normally, when you think of Florida, you don't imagine forests and woodlands. Once there, however, you'll discover a wide assortment, ranging from the upland pine forests of the north and northwest to the tropical foliage of southern coastal hammocks.

 **TRAVEL TIP**

For general hiking information, write or call for the free pamphlet *Backpacking in Florida State Parks* from the Florida Department of Natural Resources at 3900 Commonwealth Boulevard, Tallahassee, Florida 32393 (☎904-488-7326) and to the Florida Trail Association at P.O. Box 13708, Gainesville 32604 (☎Toll-free 800-343-1882).

Did you know that mahogany trees grow in Florida? Though they're not as large as their South American cousins, they grow alongside cypress, magnolia, and various kinds of oak. You'll also find cabbage palmetto in coastal regions throughout the state. Because lumbering was one of the state's earliest industries, few virgin forests remain.

Forests cover half of Florida's territory, with 75 percent of northwest Florida forestland, 70 percent in the northeast, and 25 percent in the central coastal area. You'll find upland pine forests covering the rolling hills of northeastern Florida and the Panhandle. They tend to be drier and more open than the flatwoods to the south because of their dense groundcover of wiregrass and mostly tall longleaf pine trees. Eastern bluebirds and redheaded woodpeckers alight on the branches while pocket gophers and gopher tortoises burrow under the grass.

Pine flatwoods cover over half of southern Florida, with most growing from Miami around to the Everglades. These slash, long-leaf, and pond pines rise tall and straight. Open and airy, with abundant light filtering through the upper canopy of leaves, they allow thickets of shrubs like evergreen oaks, saw palmetto, and gallberry to grow beneath them. White-tailed deer, fox squirrels, and eastern diamondback rattlesnakes are among the wildlife that lives in their cover.

Elevated areas in the Everglades and along the Florida Keys also harbor pines or tropical hardwood hammocks on limestone outcroppings commonly called "rocklands." They support over forty plants and dozens of animals found nowhere else on Earth, including such strange creations as the Key tree cactus and creatures such as the diminutive Key deer and the Miami black-headed snake. Scraggly looking slash pines grow in the pine forests. Here, elegant-looking black and yellow butterflies glide from tree to tree on long paddle-shaped wings as raccoons scamper in the thick tropical foliage.

 **TRAVEL TIP**

Although most of Florida's state parks have nature trails intended for a pleasant walk, any hiking trail, which you'll find in national parks and forests, requires more planning. The best time to hike is from late fall to early spring, thus avoiding summer's intense heat and humidity and fierce mosquitoes and enabling you to see more wildlife.

# Wetlands

Wetlands—prairies, cypress ponds, river swamps, hammocks, freshwater and saltwater marshes, and mangrove swamps–cover a large area of Coastal Florida. Cypress ponds stay wet throughout the year. Here, Mother Nature maintains a delicate balance between the wetlands, and the animal and plant life that survive within them.

Within the wetlands, you'll see tropical hardwood hammocks, home to much of Florida's wildlife, dotting the monotonous landscape. More jungle-like than their northern neighbors, they grow as "tree islands" surrounded by tall grasses. In fact, *hammock* is a

Seminole word meaning jungle. Because the soil is so rich, it supports a thick tangle of vegetation, including cypress, live oaks, hickory, and magnolia trees intertwined with vines and ferns, topped off with colorful orchids. Coastal hammocks, with cabbage palms, red cedars, and oaks, lie near the shore. Hammocks containing live oaks, draped with Spanish moss, grow throughout the state. And in tropical hammocks in southern Florida grow magnificent royal and pigeon palms and mahogany and gumbo-limbo trees interspersed with ferns, forming dense thickets. The Corkscrew Swamp Sanctuary near Naples and the Fakahatchee Strand near Sarasota, both diffused streams known as cypress strands, contain trees soaring over 100 feet tall. Wet prairies or mangroves surround the hammocks.

## ═══FAST FACT

Florida swamps also have many species of insectivorous plants, with sticky pads or liquid-filled funnels that trap small insects, which are then digested by the nitrogen-hungry plant. The highest diversity of carnivorous plants, including bladderworts and pitcher plants, grows around the Apalachicola National Forest in Florida's Panhandle.

The Everglades consists mostly of freshwater marsh or wetlands with few trees. During the winter months, the sawgrass, a favorite haunt of alligators and water birds, turns brown from lack of rain, but once rainfall begins in the spring, it returns to a brilliant green. White-tailed deer mingle with bullfrogs, egrets, herons, and panthers. Unfortunately, the numbers of all of these have diminished following the draining of marshes for farming and flood control. So far, 65 percent of the Everglades has been irreversibly drained.

## 🧳 TRAVEL TIP

From June to November, mosquitoes are virtually unavoidable in any area close to fresh water. Through these months, it's absolutely necessary for you to wear long-sleeved shirts and long trousers, plus wear insect repellent.

Salt marshes, on the other hand, are coastal wetlands rich in marine life. Also known as tidal marshes, they form along what's called "low-energy" shorelines—that is, shorelines lacking significant wave action—such as you'll find in the Big Bend area between Apalachee Bay and Cedar Key. Like the mangrove swamp, the salt marsh provides a nursery for many types of fish, which provide food for larger fish, as well as water birds like egrets and herons. In a few southern Florida salt marshes, you might even see a rare great white heron.

Where fresh water from springs and salt water from the ocean combine is known as an estuary. As the spring water flows toward the Gulf of Mexico or the Atlantic Ocean, it becomes saltier, forming different habitats for a variety of wildlife. While frogs and water insects prefer fresh water, jellyfish and barnacles prefer salt water. When the water achieves a half-salt and half-fresh ratio, it's termed "brackish." It's here that you'll likely see turtles and crabs, as well as egrets standing in the tall grasses.

## Rivers and Lagoons

Of thirty-four major rivers in Florida, all except seven tributaries flow to the east or west coast. The Saint Johns River, running through Jacksonville, is the only major one to flow north. It's also the longest, traversing 273 miles to the Atlantic, as well as the most historic, for it was at its mouth that Ponce de León first landed in 1513.

Lagoons fill in the areas between barrier islands and the mainland. Some—like the Indian River, along the coast south of Cocoa Beach—while technically lagoons, flow north to south like a river.

Manatees inhabit the mouths of rivers, bays, and shallow coastal waters. They eat only aquatic plants and cannot tolerate cold conditions; they sometimes swim upriver during the winter to bask in the warm water discharged by power plants.

## Plants

Florida has some 3,500 plants, and of 344 trees, 80 percent are native to the United States. Many are sensitive to subtle changes in moisture, resulting in river bottoms and low water-filled hammocks containing oaks and varieties of gum, riverbanks abundant in cypress, and high, dry regions supporting pines.

As you walk on nature trails in Florida, you'll notice hundreds of different species of wildflowers—among them wild orchids, such as the rare spider orchid that blooms during the winter, spring, and summer—within the hammocks of the Everglades. Meanwhile, azaleas and camellias burst into bloom. Oleanders, hibiscus, poinsettias, gardenias, jasmine, trumpet vine, and morning glory thrive almost everywhere. For brilliant floral displays, nothing can match a blooming royal poinciana or a colorful shower of bougainvillea along the southern shores.

## ≡FAST FACT

You'll see a variety of epiphytic plants—those that use another plant for physical support but don't depend on it for nutrients–in tropical hammocks. Orchids and bromeliads such as Spanish moss hang from tree branches. The most aggressive is the strangler fig, which sends out aerial roots that soon bind the host, preventing growth of its trunk and eventually choking out the host's foliage with its own.

Just about everywhere you go along Florida's coasts you'll see all types of ferns, among them the Boston, mosquito, bracken, cinnamon, royal, and resurrection varieties. Plus there are about 100 species of palms. You'll see the cabbage palmetto and the saw palmetto most frequently, and the classic royal palm more near Fort Myers and in the Fakahatchee Strand. The coconut palm, the one most people associate with palm trees, thrives in the warmer temperatures of South Florida.

# Wildlife

Large numbers of animals once roamed the forests and coastlines of Florida. Early explorers saw them wherever they traveled. While you'll still see a good number today, they're mostly limited to wildlife refuges, preserves, and parks. Of all of Florida's wild creatures, alligators and snakes may cause you problems if you provoke them.

Of the eighty-four land mammals still found in Florida, only the gray fox, black bear, puma, and wildcat are rare. Though you'll see white-tailed deer in many areas, you'll only find Key deer on one of the Florida Keys. Squirrels, rabbits, raccoons, and opossums are as common as elsewhere. However, the numbers of otters and minks have fallen after years of being trapped for their pelts. In many woodlands, you can hear armadillos noisily poking around for insects. Because of their poor eyesight, they won't know you're close by until you're almost next to them; then they'll leap up and run for cover. It's a good idea to steer clear of feral hogs and wild boar should you encounter them while hiking.

While you may not knowingly provoke a snake attack, you could accidentally step on one. Watch out for the deadly coral snake, with its black nose and bright yellow and red rings covering its body. It usually lies under piles of rotting leaves during the day. The cottonmouth moccasin, often called a water moccasin, has a small head with dark skin and inhabits the banks of rivers. Florida also has two types of rattlesnake—the diamondback, with its thick body covered in a pattern of diamonds, and the gray-colored pygmy, which is so small you won't see it until it's too late. All are poisonous.

 **TRAVEL TIP**

You're unlikely to see a snake in the wild and snake attacks are even more rare, but if one should bite you, contact a ranger or a doctor immediately. It's a wise precaution to carry an inexpensive snakebite kit, available at most sporting goods and campground stores.

Florida also has 125 native species and 25 introduced species of reptiles and amphibians, none of which can be found anywhere else in the country. Encroaching development has reduced the reptile population considerably. However, in the protected areas where natural habitats remain, many native species still thrive.

The dolphin, often considered a fish, is actually a marine mammal just like a whale. Popular with people because of its high intelligence and friendliness displayed in captivity, it's Florida's most popular animal. Seeing them frolicking in the waves is a real delight.

### Alligators

Alligators, known to Floridians as "gators," are probably the best known of the state's animals. They live in wetlands and rivers; you'll see them on sunny mornings basking on logs or riverbanks. If you hear what sounds like thunder on an otherwise clear day, you may instead be hearing the bellow of a male alligator defending his territory. Alligators can grow to 12 feet. They primarily feast on turtles, fish, birds, crayfish, and crabs. Once overhunted for their hides and meat, alligators have made a strong comeback since the State of Florida passed a law protecting them in 1973. The law worked—by 1987, nearly a half million roamed the state.

Alligators usually aren't dangerous to humans. In fact, they usually back away when approached—but don't tempt fate. The few people attacked annually by alligators were either swimmers at dusk or small children playing unattended near a riverbank. You'll be surprised just how many alligators there are—they seem to be lying around all over the place, despite being nearly exterminated by uncontrolled hunting. Today, it's against the law to kill alligators without a license. And feeding one can get you two months in prison and a hefty fine. Why, you ask? Alligators lack the brainpower to distinguish between food and the feeder, so when fed by a person, they lose their natural fear of humans and associate them with food.

## ≡FAST FACT

The only truly dangerous alligator is a mother guarding her nest or tending her young. Even then, she'll give you plenty of warning, by showing her teeth and hissing, before attacking. After baby alligators hatch, their mother gently carries them to the water in her mouth.

Alligators roam all over Florida. They're believed to be over 150 million years old and belong to one of three groups of crocodilians in the world. Alligators have broad, rounded snouts. They're cold-blooded reptiles that inhabit freshwater swamps and marshes. Though they may appear lazy when sunning to increase their body heat and clumsy when walking, they're powerful swimmers. During mating season, you'll hear them bellow loudly, and males fight other males fiercely to defend their territory.

Often mistaken for crocodiles, alligators have tough black hides and webbed feet and nubs called scutes on their backs. Their bellies are soft and creamy yellow. One of their two sets of eyelids is transparent and can be closed so it can see underwater. Flaps cover its nostrils and small ears when it swims. Because alligators have a complex circulatory system with a four-chambered heart, they can hold their breath and stay submerged for up to forty-five minutes.

## Endangered Animals

While there are many endangered species, there are efforts to protect two important ones native to Florida—the West Indian manatee and the Florida panther. The gentle manatee, or sea cow, has long been a victim of civilization. Its numbers are dwindling despite efforts to save it. Manatees often feed trustingly at the water's surface close to boaters and fishermen where they have become victims of boat propeller blades and abandoned tackle.

The warm-blooded manatee, a distant cousin to the elephant, has been traced back to plant-eating mammals sixty million years ago. Weighing up to 1,000 pounds, they can grow to 15 feet long and live up to fifty years. They munch on aquatic plants for seven hours a day. They have flippers in front and a flat tail for propulsion in back. Manatees can stay submerged for about ten minutes before surfacing to breathe and must stay in water that's at least 65°. If they don't, they can get colds, and even worse, pneumonia. During the winter, they seek out warm springs or the warm-water discharge from power plants. Females are devoted mothers but bear their offspring only once every three to five years. Although Florida enacted the first law protecting manatees in 1893, it wasn't until 1978 that the Florida Manatee Sanctuary Act made the entire state a manatee refuge. Only about 1,000 survive today.

One of the world's most endangered animals, the Florida panther is near extinction, with some thirty-five to forty-five remaining in Big Cypress National Preserve and Everglades National Park, where they roam over as much as 150 to 200 square miles in a month. The graceful, agile, shy cat prowls mainly at night, usually alone, to reaffirm its territory and search for food. A healthy male feeds on about one deer or ten raccoons every ten days. A female while raising her offspring needs to eat a deer every three days to keep up her energy. They also hunt rabbits, wild hogs, cotton rats, birds, snakes, and armadillos. If a panther has more to eat at one time than it needs, it stores its prey covered with leaves for a later meal. Panthers avoid dogs, and no documented reports have been made of attacks on humans.

More like cougars, Florida panthers are tawny brown with white flecks on their shoulders and necks. A mature male normally weighs between 100 and 145 pounds and can grow to almost 7 feet long from nose to the tip of their long tail. Mating occurs every other year from November through March, and healthy females bear one to four spotted kittens, each weighing about one pound at birth. Kittens stay with the mother up to two years for food and protection from males, which may kill them. The normal life span of the panther is between ten and fifteen years.

## Water Birds

Everywhere you travel in Florida, you'll see water birds. They're conspicuous in the wetlands. Egrets, herons, and ibis, usually clad in white or gray feathers, wade in the shallow waters and stalk frogs, mice, and small fish. Turn-of-the-century plume-hunters nearly wiped out these beautiful birds, and during the last few decades, development has reduced them by 90 percent.

Nevertheless, you'll still see many in swamps, marshes, and mangroves. You'll also see the rarer roseate spoonbill in southern Florida's wetlands. Contrary to popular belief, tourism promoters imported flamingos into Florida from Mexico in the 1920s and 1930s.

Shore birds, such as the brown pelican, sea gulls, sandpipers, and terns, pack the beaches almost as thickly as the tourists. Ducks, geese, and many other migratory birds also make their winter homes in Florida.

## Fish

At least 200 species of natural freshwater fish, including largemouth black bass, bluegill, and catfish, swim in the rivers and streams of South Florida. Add to that fifty species of exotic fish and such saltwater denizens as barracuda, grouper, shark, tarpon, mullet, wahoo, and tuna and you have the makings of a fun-filled family fishing vacation. Plus, Florida is well known for its shellfish, such as clams, blue crab, stone crab, Florida conch, Florida lobster, oysters, scallops, and shrimp. Whether you're catching them or just eating them on the deck of a waterside restaurant, you'll find Florida a fisherman's paradise.

# CHAPTER 3

# Planning Your Vacation

PLANNING YOUR VACATION CAN often be as much fun as taking it. Selecting where you want to go and what you want to do as a family requires research into what's there, how to travel around, and how long it takes to see what you want to see. In addition, you'll need to take each family member's interests into consideration, so that everyone will enjoy themselves.

## Suggested Travel Itineraries in Coastal Florida

Once you've decided on Coastal Florida as your vacation destination, you'll need to figure out where you want to go. And that can be tough because there's so much to see and do. You've probably allowed a week to ten days for your vacation, and you'll need to leave some time to travel. So trying to see all of Coastal Florida on one trip is impractical. However, you can choose from one or more of the following itineraries that should help you see a particular region fairly well and at the same time allow for beach and relaxation time.

### Miami Solo

If you want to feel the pulse of modern Florida, visit Miami and its beaches. Many of the city's visitors think it's an airport joined to a strip of luxury hotels and a beach. A steady influx of Cubans and

South Americans have given Miami, Florida's second largest city, a distinctly Latin character. It enables you to get the feel of Florida and Latin America in one place. Here, you can eat black beans and rice while exploring the Art Deco District, or just catch a few rays.

Seafood, Cuban cooking, and Jewish deli specials all blend in a mélange of gastronomic taste delight where after you've had a Reuben sandwich with a kosher pickle, you can munch on a *churro*, dough fried in strips and sprinkled with sugar—a Cuban favorite.

Great cities have great museums, and Miami is no exception. Topping the list is Vizcaya, a restored fifty-room, art-filled Spanish mansion set amid 10 acres of formal gardens. There's also the Museum of Science, with its exhibits of birds of the Everglades, a living coral reef, and a planetarium. The Metro Dade Cultural Center, downtown, an impressive fine arts complex designed by Philip Johnson, resembles a Spanish fortress, and your kids will love the Miami Seaquarium, with its porpoises, seals, and rare tropical fish.

Much of Miami's flavor comes from its neighborhoods and suburbs—affluent Coral Gables, built in the early twentieth century, and Coconut Grove, a mix of billionaires and bohemians. But the liveliest one of them all is Little Havana, established by Cubans who fled Cuba following Castro's takeover. Lively Spanish conversation fills little cafés where locals sip strong *café Cubano* and eat *empanadas*.

And over the causeway from Miami lies Miami Beach, a resort made popular by sleek television shows. It's where the glitterati meet the glittering on sands backed by so many massive hotels and condominiums that you'll barely see the ocean until you're in it. Miami Beach is also a rainbow of neon art deco architectural wonder, filled with buildings so beautiful you may fail to notice the beautiful people sipping champagne at cafés out front.

### Out on the Florida Keys

South of Miami, the Florida Keys extend off the southern tip of Florida toward Key West like a string of jewels in a priceless necklace. When you're driving through them on the Overseas Highway, their silvery coral islets, golden bars of sand, and emerald mangrove trees create a dazzling scene. While the Upper Keys seem more Floridian, the lower ones seem more Caribbean. Each has a fascinating history. Here, you'll find yourself diving among schools of parrotfish, fishing off gleaming white ocean cruisers, and laughing and swimming with dolphins at the Dolphin Research Center on Grassy Key. And if you're lucky, you might see tiny endangered Key deer. And all along the Keys, you're sure to see flocks of herons, egrets, and brown pelicans wading along the shore.

## 🌂 RAINY DAY FUN

If you visit during the summer, you may experience a Keys-style rainstorm—pelting rain that lasts for just ninety seconds, followed by a burst of blinding sunlight. If the rain lasts longer, duck into one of several small museums in the Upper Keys, featuring exhibits on shipwrecks, natural history, and pirates.

Along the way through the Keys, stop at John Pennecamp Underwater State Park, containing the nation's only living coral reef, on Key Largo. Explore it by diving or snorkeling; if you don't want to get wet, take a glass-bottomed-boat tour. And while the rest of the Keys have individual personalities, none can match the wacky, artsy atmosphere of Key West.

Key West has had a fascinating history. It was settled by English, Bahamians, Cubans, New Englanders, and Southerners, each prospering in their own way. The island's residents have eked out a living by salvaging wrecked ships, making cigars, gathering sponges, and fishing for turtle and shrimp. In 1938 the Overseas Highway connected Key West to the mainland. Soon, writers such as Ernest Hemingway and Tennessee Williams discovered the island's alluring pace. Key West's pastel-hued clapboard houses, sprays of hibiscus and bougainvillea, year-round tropical climate, and crystal-clear waters make it a seductive spot.

Lying at the end of the Overseas Highway, 100 miles south of Miami, it's where Hemingway drank, fished, and wrote *A Farewell to Arms*; where international music star Jimmy Buffet first crooned "Margaritaville"; where Mel Fisher displays his cache of treasures from the sunken Spanish galleon *Atocha*; and where writers and artists come to work and dream. Rent a bike to see the sights, but only after you take the Conch Tour Train, a narrated ride through Old Town. Stand at the Southernmost Point in the continental United States, just 90 miles from Cuba. Beyond that you can go on a boat trip to the Dry Tortugas islands and Fort Jefferson, the largest nineteenth-century American coastal fort. And no trip to Key West would be complete without at least one sunset viewed from Mallory Square.

## Mother Nature's Tour

When you have had your fill of margaritas and fresh seafood, take the Overseas Highway north to Miami, then head west on the Tamiami (short for Tampa-Miami) Trail into Miccosukee Indian country. Farther on and you're in the heart of the Everglades, the legendary "River of Grass," the one-million-acre home to snakes, dolphins, alligators, raccoons, fish, and hundreds of different birds. Few experiences rival the exhilaration of an airboat ride across this mysterious swamp, and every boat captain has a spine-tingling backcountry tale to tell.

The Everglades Basin extends north from Cape Sable about 50 miles, and then continues east for another 30 miles. Everglades National Park takes up a portion of this territory. From the Royal Palm Interpretive Center you can walk the Anhinga Trail on an elevated walkway, from which you can see alligators, fish, and turtles. At the farthest extreme of the road leading into the park lies Flamingo, where you can walk through tropical hammocks and paddle through mangrove swamps. There are several clearly marked water tours for the adventurous. If you would rather just sit and watch the river flow, there are ninety-minute guided tours of the main waterways.

The Tamiami Trail skirts along the northern boundary of Everglades National Park. Starting in Miami, you can drive the Trail to the west coast and up toward Tampa, spending much of your trip in the backcountry. First, you'll cut through the northern Everglades, with its Seminole and Miccosukee villages. The western half of the Trail goes through Big Cypress National Preserve, which offers a variety of wildlife programs, including nature hikes, wildlife lectures, and canoe and boat trips into the preserve. Sunsets here are gorgeous, and you'll be able to enjoy it all to yourself since very few people venture into the swamp.

## ≡FAST FACT

Construction of the Tamiami Trail (Route 41), the overland route connecting Tampa to Miami, began in 1915. Taking thirteen years to construct and plagued by devastating heat, swamps, and mosquitoes, it became the major motorway through the Everglades, opening up the area to trade and tourism.

### The Circus, Inventions, and Shell Tour

Continue north on the Tamiami Trail to Sarasota, Florida's cultural mecca, where you'll be enthralled with the Ringling's incredible Museum of Art, a first-class ballet company, theater, opera, music, five-star shopping, and beautiful beaches.

A fashionable Gulf Coast resort, Sarasota lacks the hedonistic excesses of other west coast resorts. Instead, culture reigns here since John Ringling—part owner of the Ringling Brothers' "Greatest Show on Earth"—gave it three museums: Cà d'Zan, his palatial mansion; an art museum housing a magnificent collection of baroque art; and the Museum of the Circus, where you can see exhibits of memorabilia from many of Ringling's circus headliners.

Then take the kids to the Sarasota Jungle Garden to see an assortment of animal shows and exotic tropical flowers. Just west of Sarasota, Bird Key, Saint Armand's Key, Longboat Key, Lido Key, and Siesta Key offer sparkling white sand beaches.

JUST FOR PARENTS

Visit the Marie Selby Botanical Gardens near Sarasota Bay, with its beautiful displays of orchids, rare tropical flowers, and trees, plus collections of classic autos, including five antique cars owned by Ringling, and musical instruments and mechanical tune-makers that will set your feet tapping.

Farther down the coast lie Fort Myers and Thomas Edison's Winter Home. Here, you can see why people called Edison a genius inventor. Then it's off to Sanibel Island, off the coast of Fort Myers, for some spectacular shell collecting.

### The Cigar and Sponge Tour

More sedate than Miami Beach and Fort Lauderdale but less cultural than Sarasota, Tampa and Saint Petersburg, known affectionately as "Saint Pete," boast quiet beaches and beautiful harbors. Unlike many Florida cities that offer activities appealing primarily to tourists, these Gulf Coast communities will satisfy the desires of everyone in your family.

Tampa welcomes you with guided walks through historic Ybor City, Tampa's Latin Quarter, where Cubans created the famous Tampa cigar. Watch craftsmen make cigars in Ybor Square, the converted factory where Vicente Martinez Ybor launched the cigar industry in 1886. Fortunately, aside from this, the area has remained relatively unspoiled. Tour Henry Plant's Moorish Tampa Bay Hotel, the most fashionable resort hotel in 1889, now part of the University of Tampa. After exploring the city, hang out with gorillas and gazelles at Busch Gardens Tampa Bay, America's leading breeding zoo. Make a trip through the Serengeti Plain your first priority. You can watch more than 1,000 animals from the African continent roam the plain as you ride the Safari Monorail, then take a free tour of the Anheuser-Busch

Brewery. As evening approaches, stroll along Tampa's waterfront and watch banana boats from South and Central America unload at the docks.

After Tampa, Route 41 North beckons you to the magnificent Skyway, a sleek bridge that arches up and up into blue skies and white clouds, and then glides gracefully into Saint Petersburg. Million-dollar yachts bob in the harbor below. The Salvador Dali Museum houses the world's largest and most acclaimed collection of works by the mustachioed surrealist. At the Great Explorations Museum, your kids will love the science and creativity of the hands-on exhibits. But Saint Pete's main attraction is its beaches. And when you tire of the beach—if ever—visit the Sunken Gardens, with over 7,000 varieties of exotic flowers and plants, displayed in a walk-through aviary.

##  TRAVEL TIP

For a chance to see one of Coastal Florida's natural deep-water springs, travel 75 miles north of Tarpon Springs to Homosassa Springs. Take the boat that transports you along a tropical waterway for a glimpse of Floridian wildlife—an underwater observatory allows you to view both freshwater and saltwater fish together.

If you've wondered where sponges come from, head to Tarpon Springs, about 40 miles north of Saint Pete. Once a small Greek community whose members made their living from sponge fishing, today it's a picturesque town where the smell of Greek cooking and the sound of bouzouki music fill the air. Be sure to visit the Spongeorama, with its displays on the history of sponge diving and processing.

### The Miracle Strip

The hundred miles of shoreline from Panama City west to Pensacola is one of Florida's true family beach resort areas. You'll find everything to make your beach vacation enjoyable, including dazzling white sands. Not too far from the honky-tonk, you'll find Mother Nature's beaches at their finest. Head out to the barrier islands offshore to be enveloped in another world. Drive along the beautiful Panhandle coastline to see Panama City Beach's sugar-white sandy beaches or trek farther west to Pensacola and visit the National Museum of Naval Aviation and the Gulf Islands National Seashore.

The focus of activity for this Miracle Strip is Fort Walton Beach and its local beaches. Sure, you'll find airbrushed T-shirts and all sorts of beach doodads, but just a couple of miles out lie rolling stretches of uncrowded, quiet beach. When you get too sunburned from lying on the beach, visit the Indian Temple Mound Museum, showing the history of the area's first inhabitants through artifacts and a restored temple mound used by Native Americans.

Destin, "the World's Luckiest Fishing Village," lies 7 miles from Fort Walton Beach. Deep-sea fishing here is super and a year-round activity. Book passage on a deep-sea fishing charter, complete with tackle, bait, and ice, and enjoy the challenge of hooking the big ones for a day.

While beach aficionados pack the beaches between Fort Walton Beach and Panama City, Pensacola will lure you with its own chalk-white beaches and European charm. The town adds a splash of civility to this coast with its Spanish mission architecture and elegant Seville Square, encompassing Pensacola's historic district. In many ways, the Panhandle represents Old Florida, with its deep forests, clear springs, incredibly beautiful white sand beaches, and historic sites, and new Florida in the condo glitz of the Miracle Strip.

## History and the Beach

Jacksonville began as a winter resort for wealthy, sun-seeking New Englanders in 1878. Straddling the Saint Johns River, its beautiful neighborhoods filled with museums, manicured golf courses, outdoor cafés, elegant antique stores, and bookshops make it a perfect family destination.

## ☂ RAINY DAY FUN

The interactive Museum of Science and History is strictly for kids, with its many buttons to push and games to play in its Universe of Science Exhibit. There's also a planetarium and a Prehistoric Park, featuring dinosaurs skeletons and fossils (☎904-396-6674; *www.themosh.org*).

The Jacksonville Art Museum's contemporary art collection and the Cummer Gallery of Art, with its lavish gardens overlooking the Saint Johns River, will satisfy the art connoisseurs in your family. Its collection of Meissen porcelain is the largest in the country. Just a few minutes north of the city's commercial downtown, you can visit the wilds of an "African veldt" at Jacksonville's zoo, where a team of scientists ensure the survival of endangered species through breeding.

North of Jacksonville's beaches you can catch a car ferry across the Saint Johns River to Fort George Island, where you can wander around the majestically landscaped grounds of Kingsley Plantation, Florida's oldest, and examine the remains of the slave quarters as well as the big white plantation house. And if you have wondered what the Florida coast was like before dune buggies and fast food, visit Fernandina Beach on Amelia Island north of Jacksonville. In addition to an unspoiled shore, Fernandina has a small, pleasant downtown of renovated Victorian buildings.

## ≡FAST FACT

Ninety miles south of Jacksonville lies Daytona Beach, home of the Daytona International Speedway, site of NASCAR's Daytona 500, the Rolex 24-Hour, and other exciting auto races where cars take to the track at 150 miles per hour during Speed Weeks in February.

Heading south along Florida's beautiful shoreline, you'll drive past million-dollar mansions at Ponte Vedra Beach before arriving at historic Saint Augustine where Pedro Menéndez de Avilés of Spain arrived in 1565 to establish what became the oldest permanent European settlement in North America. Founded fifty-five years before the Pilgrims landed at Plymouth Rock, the city still has a Spanish flavor, and many parts have been tastefully preserved. Take the time to stroll through the narrow cobblestone streets and experience a part of Florida that's refreshingly different. You can tour Old Saint Augustine by tram, horse-drawn carriage, boat, or foot. Beyond the restored eighteenth-century Spanish colonial village, you can explore the Oldest House, Oldest Wooden Schoolhouse, Oldest Store, and Castillo de San Marcos, an eighteenth-century fortress built by Spanish settlers. Two former hotels, the Alcazar and the Ponce de León, both built in the 1880s, are now the Lightner Museum and Flagler College, respectively.

## Science and the Beach

The surfing in Cocoa Beach is said to be some of the best in Florida. Whether you intend to spend time here or are just driving down the coast, stop for the day to enjoy one of Florida's less cluttered beaches, where the sunbathers may actually be Floridians. The Kennedy Space Center, the area's primary attraction, is the site for all of NASA's blast-offs. The visitor center, Spaceport U.S.A., features IMAX movies, equipment demonstrations, and spacecraft exhibits. Two bus tours of the complex will acquaint you with all the behind-the-scenes goings-on for the space shuttle.

Merritt Island National Wildlife Refuge, with thousands of acres of unspoiled wilderness, surrounds the NASA complex. A haven for deer, small animals, alligators, and birds, exploring it will give you a chance to see Mother Nature at her best. Just north of Merritt Island is Canaveral National Seashore, 67,000 acres of undeveloped beach and dunes.

Go south of Cocoa Beach along the Indian River to San Sebastian, the site of *the* best surfing, and on to the beaches at Melbourne and Fort Pierce.

### Beach and City Combo

Many areas along Florida's 300 miles of east coast have been swallowed up by development. And no place is more developed than Fort Lauderdale, where waves of students have assaulted its beaches for decades during Spring Break. At other times, Fort Lauderdale Beach still has its younger moments, with bikini contests and country and western bars. But just a few miles away from the bronzed beach bodies, the wings of Mother Nature's most delicate and beautiful creatures flutter at Butterfly World.

To see the opposite of hedonistic pleasures, head north to suave and sophisticated Palm Beach, with its luxurious ocean yachts, palatial estates with separate entrances for "owners" and "servants," and Henry Flagler's exquisite Breakers Hotel. Here, you'll see none of the pickups that cruise the streets of Fort Lauderdale. Instead goldtoned Rolls Royces and sleek Jaguars provide the backdrop for this summery winter resort for the wealthy town-and-country set, freshly clad in whites for a game of croquet at the Breakers or a shopping trip to Worth Avenue, the pricey shopping area for fans of Gucci and Saks Fifth Avenue. Ogle prime real estate, bike or drive along South Ocean Boulevard where many a mansion resides, including the seaside retreat of the Kennedy clan. Palm tree–lined Las Olas Boulevard exudes wealth with Lalique crystal and Tiffany sterling available in stores fashioned from old brick and ironwork.

# Budgeting Your Trip

It's all well and good to entice you with exotic places to see in Coastal Florida, but to do so successfully without putting a strain on the family budget takes some planning. First and foremost, budget for your family's comfort level. If you can't afford to stay in accommodations in which everyone will be comfortable, then plan to stay fewer days, staying in hotels with amenities to your family's liking. Generally, you should plan on spending no less than $250 per day for a family of four for hotel, food, and rental car. That, of course, doesn't count the amount you'll need to spend on air or train fare, or gasoline if you're driving to Coastal Florida.

 **TRAVEL TIP**

Instead of eating three restaurant meals a day, picnic on the beach. State parks and recreation areas along the coast all have picnic areas. If you're flying down, stop at a discount store and pick up a Styrofoam cooler and a beverage thermos, plus some utensils and paper plates to use during your stay.

Depending on the location, good family resorts go for $150 to $250 per night. If you want to keep costs down, stay at hotels like Hampton or Comfort Inn where you'll also get a continental breakfast each morning.

### Carrying Your Money

The best way to carry your money is in travelers' checks. The most widely recognized are American Express and Visa. The advantage of using the better-known checks is that they can be cashed in more places—shops, restaurants, and gas stations. Get them in $20 denominations.

If you have a Visa, MasterCard, or American Express card, you really shouldn't leave home without it. Almost all stores, most restaurants, and many services will take some kind of credit card. In addition, hotels and car rental companies will ask for a card either to establish your creditworthiness or as security, or both.

## 📁 TRAVEL TIP

If your credit cards are stolen, contact the following to report your loss: for American Express, call ☎800-528-2121; for Visa, call ☎800-627-6811; for MasterCard, contact the bank that issued your card.

You can also use your Visa or MasterCard to withdraw cash at any bank displaying relevant stickers, or with the correct card and your Personal Identification Number (PIN), you can use an ATM machine. While you can't do this with an American Express card, you can use it and your PIN number to get travelers' checks from machines at most major airports. Using an ATM machine to get cash is safer, and at only about a dollar per transaction, it's also more economical.

## Keeping Your Family Safe in Coastal Florida

There are two kinds of problems that may affect your family while traveling in Coastal Florida: theft and drowning. For the first, make sure everyone keeps their valuables on them at all times. Don't leave bags unattended anywhere. If you're going to the beach, take just enough money for the day and don't flaunt expensive electronic devices like Game Boys, iPods, or portable DVD players. You're only asking for trouble. Use the hotel's safe or a safe in your room, if you have one, to lock up your valuables—cameras, extra money, and so on—when you're not using them. If driving, park your vehicle in a protected area and lock all valuables out of sight. And leave your expensive jewelry at home—purchase some fun jewelry at the beach. If you have a problem with theft, report it immediately to the local authorities.

Surrounded on three sides by water, Coastal Florida offers a myriad of water-based activities, thus drownings do occur now and then. They can be avoided as long as you respect the power of the water, heed appropriate surf warnings, and use good sense.

Unfortunately, young children rarely use common sense, so you need to always watch out for them near water. If you go boating in a canoe or motorboat, other than on an excursion sightseeing boat, make sure that everyone in your family wears a life jacket. With so much water available, the best protection for everyone is to know how to swim.

 **TRAVEL TIP**

Florida's tropical waters often contain dangerous creatures. In salt waters, you may confuse the fin of a dolphin with that of a shark. If you see a fin, head to shore calmly but quickly. In fresh waters, alligators have been known to drown swimmers or divers who venture into areas that are off limits. Heed warnings. They're there to protect you.

Wherever any member of your family swims, he or she should never do it alone. If the surf is high in either the Atlantic Ocean or the Gulf, keep your face toward the incoming waves to avoid unpleasant surprises. A good rule to follow is feet first, first time, even though Florida's coastal waters are often clear. Before you attempt surfing, take some lessons from an expert to learn the proper techniques and dangers. Heed signs or flags warning of dangerous currents and undertows. If you get caught in a rip current or any tow that makes you feel out of control, don't try to swim against it. Head across it, paralleling the shore. Make sure you and your children avoid using any type of floats, inner tubes, or rafts when playing in the surf. If you swim in or wade around in murky waters where shellfish may dwell, be sure to wear canvas or water shoes (sold as Hydro Sox) to protect your feet.

Bugs are a fact of life, especially if you travel to Coastal Florida in the summer. Bug season usually lasts from March until mid-November in the northern regions and all year in the southern ones. The mosquito should be Florida's official state insect. They follow the scent of carbon dioxide that humans give off and tend to be around warm, moist places. Only the female bites. Avoid them by staying clear of marshes and swamps—though this is almost impossible in South Florida. Be sure whatever insect repellent you use contains a high amount of DEET (N-diethylmeta toluamide) or permethrin.

# It's Time to Go

Now that you've planned your trip, it's time to enjoy it. But before you go, you need to pack. Luckily, not many places in Coastal Florida require formal attire. Try to pack as compactly as you can, taking only those things with you that you absolutely cannot do without. You can always buy anything you forget. The same or similar stores carrying the same brands exist in Florida as at home.

### Pack Light or Heavy?

For most trips to Coastal Florida, all you'll have to pack are some shorts, lightweight shirts or tops, cool cotton slacks, a couple of bathing suits and cover-ups, and something for any special event that might call for dressing up.

You can devote the rest of your luggage space to a couple of books and those essentials you can't do without—sunscreen (preferably not oils), high-quality sunglasses, and some insect repellent, especially if you're planning to travel in the summer or in swampy areas. If you're planning to spend a lot of time outdoors—where fire ants or stinging jellyfish might be a problem—take along a small container of a papain-type meat tenderizer. It won't keep them away, but it will ease the pain should they sting you.

## ≡FAST FACT

Papain is a protein-cleaving enzyme derived from papaya that cuts the protein chains in meat fiber, thus tenderizing it. It's combined with salt and sugar to produce the white powder sold under various brands as "meat tenderizer." South American Indians have used papaya juice for centuries to tenderize meat.

Also, take along an umbrella or light raincoat for those sudden showers that can pop up out of nowhere. If you visit the Panhandle or the northeast coast in winter, pack a warm jacket or coat. Even in the far south, you'll welcome a sweater on some winter days.

If you're a serious scuba diver, you'll probably want to bring your own gear, but it's certainly not essential. Underwater equipment of all sorts is available for rent wherever diving is popular. Many places also rent beach toys and tubes for floating down rivers. Fishing gear is also often available for rent, as are golf clubs.

##  TRAVEL TIP

Good soft, comfortable, lightweight shoes for sightseeing are a must. Despite its tropical gentleness, the terrain of Coastal Florida doesn't treat bare feet well except along the shore or beside a pool. Sturdy sandals will do. If you plan to do any hiking in the wetlands, wear canvas shoes that you don't mind wading in.

If you're a shell collector, take a plastic bag or two along for hauling your finds. For bird watching, binoculars are essential. And don't forget to bring along some sort of camera. With digital cameras coming down in price, you can easily purchase one for $100 to $150. They're so much more economical than regular 35mm cameras because you can use the media cards, on which you store your images, again and again. Since you probably won't be bringing along your computer, you can either buy several smaller-capacity media cards, say 128 or 256 megabytes, or take your media card into a photo outlet in a Wal-Mart or national chain drugstore to have your photos printed for about 25 to 30 cents each, or have a CD of the photos made. Do not bring along a large-volume media card, such as a 1 to 2 gigabyte card. If you have a problem with it, you'll lose *all* your pictures.

## Traveling with Little Ones

You'll find plenty of activities for children in Coastal Florida. But to make your vacation with your children problem-free, it pays to take a few precautions. Make sure you not only book your hotel reservations in advance, but have confirmed that the hotels you plan to stay in accept children. If you need a crib or extra cot, arrange for it ahead of time.

Most of Coastal Florida's hotels welcome children and usually don't charge for those under five. Many of the larger chain hotels often let children under sixteen or eighteen stay in the room free with their parents. Also, the hotel staffs are more likely to be used to noisy or slightly misbehaving children. These same hotels are also more likely to have swimming pools or game rooms to keep kids occupied. If you don't want your children to stay in the same room with you, ask about adjoining rooms.

If you're traveling by plane, try to reserve bulkhead seats where there's plenty of room, especially if you have younger children. Take along extras you may need, such as diapers and changes of clothing, plus snacks, toys, or small games to keep them occupied. And if you're traveling by car, take along plenty of water and juices to drink. Dehydration in the Florida heat, especially during the summer, can be a problem.

And don't forget a first-aid kit. Along with adhesive bandages, antiseptic cream, and something to stop itching, include any medicines your pediatrician might recommend to treat allergies, colds, diarrhea, or any chronic problems your children may have.

## ▐ TRAVEL TIP

If you're planning to spend time at the beach, go easy the first few days. A child's skin is usually more tender than an adult's, and severe sunburn can happen before you realize it. Bring along hats for everyone, plus a strong sunblock.

If you want to go out at night without your children, check to see if your hotel provides babysitters or if they can give you a list of approved ones.

Bring easily washed, stain-resistant clothes, and encourage your children to pack their own toys in a small bag—it makes them feel as if they're a part of the trip. Have a toy or two close at hand for long waits and take simple snacks, like a small box of raisins or crackers, for those moments when hunger strikes and food is miles away.

If you're spending your vacation traveling, rather than visiting one spot or engaging in one activity, break your trip into half-day segments, with travel time built in. Keep travel time on the road to a minimum of four or five hours each day. Also, involve your children in the planning of your family vacation to Coastal Florida. If they're as excited about the trip as you are, everyone will enjoy themselves. And try not to over-program a trip so that there's no chance for spontaneity.

Be flexible when traveling by car. Stop at souvenir shops or other places your kids might be interested in. Car travel also allows you to take more with you, such as a charcoal grill, ice chest, and box of picnic supplies. Stop frequently to let younger children run around and use up some of their energy. Also, keep some small toys, drawing paper and crayons, and games on hand. Encourage preteens to keep a record of their trip to make a scrapbook later.

When traveling by plane, avoid night flights. Your children will sleep on the plane, then won't be able to get to sleep for the night once you arrive. Try to schedule air flights during your little one's naptime. And stay away from peak travel between 7 and 9 A.M. and between 4 and 6 P.M. when business travelers may fill up the plane— they'll also be bothered more by an antsy child. If there's an extra seat, the airline will allow a younger child traveling free to sit in it. If you're going to be traveling with a child under one year old, let the airlines know. They sometimes will provide you with a special infant seat. Also, when the plane lands and takes off, make sure your baby is nursing or has a bottle, pacifier, or thumb in its mouth. This sucking will make the child swallow and clear stopped ears, the reason very young children cry on take-off. A small piece of hard candy will do the same for a small child. And remember, as a parent traveling with small children, you're allowed to board before the rest of the passengers.

 **JUST FOR PARENTS**

You're entitled to ask for a hot dog or hamburger instead of the airline's regular food when you make your reservation. Some, but not all, airlines have baby food aboard. While you should make sure to bring your own toys, ask about children's diversions. Some airlines may have coloring books or puzzles for your kids to play with in flight.

You'll find that practically all destinations in Coastal Florida have special events for children, except perhaps Palm Beach. These can be anything from children's movies at museums to puppet shows and magicians in city parks. You can find listings of these events, many of which are free, in Sunday editions of city newspapers or at a city's convention and visitors bureau. You may also find local events posted on bulletin boards in local supermarkets. Local or regional festivals, fairs, parades, or other special events add fun to a vacation and will capture your kids' imaginations.

### Alternative Phone Connections

If you're planning to use your cell phone in Florida, you'll most likely have to pay roaming charges. Check with your cell phone provider to make sure you can use your phone at the destinations you plan to visit in Coastal Florida. Or buy a rebuilt pay-as-go cell phone or look for promotions offering a free phone when you buy a set number of minutes. To use to call home or to communicate with whoever may be picking you up at the airport, this type of phone is fine—and very inexpensive.

# CHAPTER 4

# Getting There

NO MATTER WHERE YOU LIVE in the United States, it's easy to get to Coastal Florida. Not too long ago, families would pile into their car and drive twenty-four hours straight to their Florida coast destination from their homes up north—the husband and wife taking turns driving while the kids slept in the back seat. And while many still do that, the rise in gas prices has put a crimp in the savings using this method. Today, discount airlines often offer cheap fares, so if you're planning to vacation in Florida, this is probably the best way to go.

## Getting to Coastal Florida by Air

The fastest, most convenient way to travel to Coastal Florida is by air. At least eight major commercial airlines fly to Florida's coastal cities on regularly scheduled flights. Though these airline serve 100 cities in Florida, many of their flights fly into five major coastal airports—Fort Lauderdale, Jacksonville, Miami, Tampa, and West Palm Beach.

To keep down the cost of air travel, fly midweek. Prices can rise considerably if you fly over a weekend. Because competition in the Florida market is so keen, airlines like AirTran and JetBlue often have three-day "sales" when they offer super-discounted rates. The same roundtrip flight from Philadelphia to Jacksonville, for example, booked without benefit of the sale price may be over $200. By taking advantage of the sale, you could fly for half that. It also pays to book in advance. And booking your flight on the airline's Web site or on travel sales sites like Orbitz.com and Expedia.com can save you even more. At certain times of the year, some airlines offer special discounts, allowing you to travel for less. Roundtrip flights to Miami cost, including taxes, approximately $315 from New York, $279 from Chicago, $580 from LA, $593 from Dallas, on various airlines.

## ≡FAST FACT

The more flexible you are and the farther in advance you plan, the better the rate you'll find. The airlines set aside a limited number of seats on any plane for low excursion fares. These sell out quickly. When they expect a higher volume of passengers, airlines lower the number of reduced-fare seats and offer more of them when business is slow.

Excursion or discount fares come with restrictions. The more restrictive they are, the less they cost. In most cases, you must book your flight between seven and thirty days in advance, depending on the fare. And you must pay for your ticket at the time of booking. You may also have to stay at your destination for, say, no less than seven and no more than thirty days. Lastly, you can't change your plans without paying an extra fee, often between $50 and $100. So you can't decide at the last minute to get a few more days at the beach without paying more for the privilege.

Today, airlines often overbook flights to make sure the maximum number of passengers fills a plane and to compensate for no-shows. If everyone with a reservation does appear, there aren't going to be enough seats. So the airline will ask for volunteers who'll agree to give up their reservation in exchange for some sort of compensation and a seat on the next available flight. To protect yourself as best you can against getting bumped, arrive at the airport an hour ahead of the regular time, or two hours or more ahead for a domestic flight.

You'll most likely be given an electronic ticket or e-ticket by the airline, especially if you book your flight online. If the airline cancels your flight, you cannot exchange your e-ticket for a flight on another airline—only those holding paper tickets can do that. And very few people have paper tickets today, so you can see the potential problem.

## Luggage

The invention of lightweight wheeled luggage drastically changed how people travel with their bags. According to the Civil Aeronautics Board (CAB), you may take only one bag on the plane plus a small personal bag or purse. And, yes, the airplane manufacturers complied by designing overhead bins that can handle relatively large pieces. But that doesn't mean that you have to disregard the best perk of flying—letting someone else take care of your bag while you travel. When you fly, take only what you need and check your bags, except perhaps a small one for the plane with some emergency items like a toothbrush, toothpaste, a change of underwear, and some reading material. Carrying a bag that's too hard to lift into the overhead bin causes delays in loading and unloading the plane. If you plan to travel with a bike, golf clubs, or other sports equipment, be sure to check with your airline beforehand. Though it will have procedures for handling such baggage, you may have to pay a special charge for it.

If your luggage doesn't arrive in baggage claim after your flight or if it's damaged, report the problem immediately to the airline loss and damage desk. Some airlines require you do this within four hours after the arrival of your flight or they disclaim liability for missing or damaged luggage. After you receive a claim check for your lost or damaged luggage, hold onto it until you receive your bag. The airline is responsible for recovering lost luggage or must reimburse you for up to $750 for the loss. However, airlines today won't repair or replace a bag unless it's severely damaged, claiming that it's normal wear and tear.

## Booking Through a Carrier

If you're planning on booking a flight or a travel package through a specific airline, you may want to contact that airline directly, either through their 800 number or through their Web site:

TABLE 4-1

### DIRECTORY OF U.S. AIRLINES SERVING FLORIDA

| AIRLINE | TOLL-FREE NUMBER | WEB SITE |
|---|---|---|
| American Airlines | ☎800-433-7300 | ✐www.aa.com |
| Continental | ☎800-525-0280 | ✐www.continental.com |
| Delta | ☎800-525-1212 | ✐www.delta.com |
| JetBlue | ☎800-538-2583 | ✐www.jetblueairways.com |
| Northwest Airlines | ☎800-225-2525 | ✐www.nwa.com |
| United Airlines | ☎800-241-6522 | ✐www.united.com |
| US Airways | ☎800-428-4322 | ✐www.usairways.com |

## Booking Through the Web

Many airlines now offer special fares through their Web sites, which aren't available otherwise. These fares and promotions change frequently, so you need to check back regularly and be ready to book your flights when you find a good fare. When searching for flights and fares, be flexible. The more flexible you are, the better your chance of finding a really good fare.

Begin your search at one of the three all-purpose travel sites—Expedia.com, Travelocity.com, and Orbitz.com. Here, you not only can search for the lowest airfare, but for deals in hotels and car rentals. But they don't represent all airlines, so you may be missing out on a better deal. Also, they each charge a fee when you book a flight, hotel, or car rental. A site like Cheapflights.com scans various booking sites and gives you results from them. After this you can go directly to an airline's site to see if it can match the low fare you found elsewhere. By booking your flight directly with the airline, you'll save the booking charge. You'll find a comprehensive list of links for all U.S. airlines at *www.travelpage.com*. Be aware that in this day of more electronic, less human contact, some airlines actually charge a fee if you call their 800 number to book a flight.

## Booking Through a Travel Agency

It used to be that you could book an entire trip for free with a travel agent. Today, many charge a fee for this service because airlines and hotels have cut or eliminated the commissions the agents used to get. Nevertheless, the fee may be worth it for a travel agent to search out the best airfares, flights, hotel packages, and so on. Not only will you probably get good value for your dollar, but you'll save time, too. And that can be important if you live a time-crunched lifestyle. When you meet with the agent, know where you want to go in Coastal Florida and what you want to do there. Let the agent find the best airfare or package for you. And be honest about how much you want to spend. Don't waste their time fishing for information. The important thing to remember when using the services of a travel agent is to get referrals from friends about agents they've used. Otherwise, you're entrusting your vacation pleasures and dollars to a stranger.

## Packaged Trips

Travel packages, generally priced per person, offer you the best way to save money on the cost of travel to Florida. Some include only flights and hotel accommodations, while others may include car rentals or sightseeing options. Packages to South Florida's beach resorts offer the best value during the winter season from mid-December through mid-April. However, you may find off-season packages to be downright bargains.

 **TRAVEL TIP**

To know if you're getting a good deal on a package, call or check the airline's Web site for the cost of a roundtrip flight. Do the same for a hotel, tours, and so on. Don't forget roundtrip airport transfers, which can cost as much as $25 per person. If the total cost equals more than the package, then you've got a good deal.

Read the details of the tour package carefully. Package prices are usually for the lowest price at which it can be offered, but this price may be available during off-season only, during midweek, at the least expensive hotel, or in such limited numbers that it's sold out at once. Also, all prices are based on double occupancy and apply to the city of departure, which may or may not be your hometown.

## Airport Information

Of Florida's nineteen commercial airports, only two, Miami International and Tampa International, are coastal facilities.

### Miami Airport

Miami International Airport, the country's nineteenth busiest airport, lies 8 miles west of downtown. It's served by sixteen domestic carriers, including its chief carrier American Airlines, Continental Airlines, Delta Air Lines, Northwest Airlines, United Airlines, and US Airways, plus thirty-one international carriers. A monorail system links the terminals, and though you can walk between them, they're quite far apart. Taxis, vans, and limousine services are available from the airport from outside the baggage claim area. Metro-Bus (305-876-8494), Miami's city bus service, provides service to areas of Miami-Dade County from Level 1 of Concourse E. Or you can take Metro Mover, a light-rail train that provides transportation to various locations downtown. If you're flying into Miami but your final destination is in Palm Beach or Broward County, you can take the Tri-Rail Train, which runs along I-95. To get to the airport train station, you can take the free Metro-Bus shuttle if you have a valid Tri-Rail ticket. The airport also has Internet kiosks. (305-876-7000, *www.miami-airport .com*)

### Flying into Regional Airports

Relatively the same lines serve other large airports like Fort Lauderdale–Hollywood International, Palm Beach International, Jacksonville International, and Tampa International. Plus a number of airlines provide service into regional airports such as Daytona Beach, Fort Myers, Sarasota-Bradenton, Panama City–Bay County Municipal, and Pensacola, either directly from hubs like those in Atlanta, Georgia, or Charlotte, North Carolina, or from the major Florida airports. If you're flying to Key West, you'll have to change to a smaller plane run by one of the affiliates of the major lines, such as American Eagle or US Airways Express. If you're headed for the Everglades, you'll find it convenient to fly into Miami International Airport.

- **Fort Lauderdale:** ✆954-359-1200, *www.fll.net*
- **Jacksonville:** ✆904-741-2000, *www.jaxairports.org*
- **Tampa:** ✆813-870-8700, *www.tampaairport.com*
- **West Palm Beach:** ✆561-471-7420, *www.pbia.org*

# Driving to Coastal Florida

Driving your car used to be one of the most popular modes of travel to Florida until the drastic rise in gasoline prices. However, the more passengers, the more economical it will be—that is, unless you own a gas-guzzling SUV or van, in which case you lose that economic advantage. And while it's still the best way to explore Coastal Florida, the distance you'll have to drive will be a long one unless you live in an adjoining state.

From the northeastern and mid-Atlantic parts of the country, you can drive down I-95, America's consumer answer to the Daytona Speedway. Driving this superhighway for long distances can be stressful to say the least. So you might want to consider breaking up your trip and meandering down roads along the eastern seaboard from time to time. Good spots to enjoy the countryside and take a break from high-speed driving are at Richmond, Virginia, with a side trip to Williamsburg to see the historic sites or to visit Busch Gardens Williamsburg, or near Charleston, South Carolina, to visit that historic city.

If you're coming from the west, you'll most likely be taking I-10 through Houston and New Orleans, connecting with I-75 to go to the west coast or over to I-95 if you're headed to Jacksonville. If you're coming from the Midwest, you'll be coming into Florida on I-75 through Georgia.

## TRAVEL TIP

If traveling by car, bring the following along: your driver's license, car title, auto registration, insurance card, maps, flashlight with extra batteries, tire jack and pump, spare tire, emergency flasher, gallon gas can, tire pressure gauge, jumper cables, first-aid kit, extra car keys, sunglasses, extra water, and a white towel for signaling or wiping windows.

Consider joining a national automobile club like the American Automobile Association (AAA) to protect yourself in case of on-the-road breakdowns. These clubs offer insurance covering accidents, personal injury, arrest and bail bond, and lawyer's fees for defense of contested traffic cases. They also give you twenty-four-hour emergency service, including free towing to a garage within 3 miles. Plus, AAA provides a nationwide list of AAA-approved mechanics—unfortunately, not all mechanics are honest. And finally, they provide a travel- and vacation-planning service, including advice about which roads are best and maps. The cost for all this is $60 a year plus a $15 enrollment fee and includes spouse and family in your membership. (703-222-6000, *www.aaa.com*)

##  TRAVEL TIP

If you break down on the road, get your car off the highway, raise the hood as a signal that help is needed, and tie a white rag to the door handle or antenna. Don't leave the car unattended, and don't try to do major repairs on the road.

To reduce the amount of cash you need to carry on such a long trip, it's a good idea to apply for several gas cards from the major oil companies. All offer credit cards, which can be used nationwide to pay for gas, repairs, and most car parts at their respective service stations, where you can also pick up an application. It used to be that these cards allowed you to charge in two ways: some allow you to carry charges from month to month while others insist that you pay the full balance due at the end of each monthly period. But with the rise in gasoline prices, many companies have switched their gas cards over to regular MasterCard or Visa credit cards, allowing you to run up a tab on your trip and pay it off in either one payment or in installments with the addition of a 16 percent or higher monthly finance charge.

### Considerations for Your Car

Make sure your car is in top working condition before leaving home for Florida, paying special attention to your tires and brakes, including your spare. Get the car tuned up and be sure to check the lights, battery, radiator, transmission, brakes, engine, shock absorbers, tires, and horn. You may also want to have your car's timing adjusted to adapt to warm tropical weather. Instead of a bunch of road maps, you'll do better to purchase a Rand McNally *Vacation Guide and Road Atlas*, which not only shows the roads in the state but has an annotated attraction guide.

If your car breaks down, you may have serious problems. To save time and headaches, especially when driving a long distance, always carry spare parts—fan belt, spare tire, gas and oil filters, fuses, spark plugs, points, gaskets, distributor cap, and an extra gas cap—and learn how to install them in case of an emergency. Mechanics along the way will do their best to fix your car, but tales of car maintenance scams are legendary on the route to Florida.

Have your car serviced regularly when driving in Florida if you're on a long trip. The extra heat and humidity will put a strain on your car's engine and air-conditioning system. A little extra care will help to ensure a problem-free vacation.

It also pays to recognize when your car is telling you there's something wrong:

- **Your car has trouble starting:** You may have a vapor lock caused by Florida's hot weather. Place a cold, wet rag on the fuel line and pump.
- **Your car's engine misses after quick acceleration:** Clean the spark plugs.
- **There's a rattle in the rear:** Have the muffler or tailpipe tightened.
- **There's a rattle in the front:** Have a mechanic check for a bent fan blade or loose pulley.
- **There's a loud squealing noise when you turn the wheel:** Add power steering fluid.

Also, check for leaks by spreading paper on the ground under your car and look for the following:

- **Brown or black fluid** indicates an oil leak.
- **Pink fluid** near the wheel indicates a brake fluid leak.
- **Pink or reddish fluid** indicates an automatic transmission seal leak.
- **Greenish fluid** near the front of the car indicates a radiator leak.

## Considerations for Your Family

When traveling by car in Florida, especially with children, be sure to take along a supply of snacks and fresh water or juices. You may consider packing a lunch, or asking if your hotel restaurant can pack one for you, if you're planning on driving through mostly rural countryside. In addition to food, you should carry along some games or other activities for your children to keep them occupied on long distances. If you're driving a newer van, you may want to bring along some of your favorite CDs and DVDs and consider purchasing a portable DVD player if your vehicle doesn't already have one.

## Check Your Insurance

Before you leave, make sure all your insurance is up-to-date. Check with your health care provider to make sure you're covered in Florida. If not, you can get adequate coverage either from a travel agent's insurance plan or from specialist travel insurance companies such as Travelers (*www.travelers.com*) or TravelSafe (Toll-free 888-885-7233, *www.travelsafe.com*). If you are unable to use a phone or if the practitioner requires immediate payment, save all the forms to support a claim for subsequent reimbursement once you return home. Remember also that time limits may apply when making claims after the fact, so be prompt in contacting your insurer. Bring along the phone or fax number of your insurance agent to speed up your claim.

# ≡FAST FACT

Few insurance plans cover you against theft while traveling. While homeowner's or renter's insurance may compensate for this, it pays to check with your agent before you leave. Some policies cover you for up to $500 while traveling. Being covered, at a minimum, for liability and property damage, as well as theft, is a must.

The same applies to your car insurance if you're driving to or in Florida. Read over your policy to familiarize yourself with your coverage. Make sure your insurance card is in the glove compartment of your vehicle. Check with the American Automobile Association (AAA) or the Florida Department of Transportation for any Florida driving rules that are different from those at home. For instance, some states allow you to turn right after stopping at a red light if no traffic is coming, while others don't.

## Taking Your RV

Many families drive their recreational vehicles (RVs) to Florida. Though a recent study showed that you could save up to 70 percent on overall costs by taking your RV on vacation rather than flying, renting a car, and staying in hotels, it seems with adding in the extra costs like gasoline—RVs aren't known for their good gas mileage— and the cost of about $25 per night to stay in a campground that traveling by RV today isn't the bargain it once was. Of course, the total amount you spend will vary depending on the distance you travel, the size of your vehicle, and whether you own or rent the vehicle.

Renting an RV once you get to Florida is another option. If you don't enjoy driving, want to leave housekeeping chores behind you when you go on vacation, cannot stand to do any maintenance or simple handyman chores, and need lots of privacy, then an RV isn't for you. But if you don't mind doing all of the above, then renting an RV may be ideal.

You can rent a 31-foot Fleetwood Double-Sided RV for about $180 a day with a three-night minimum, plus 28 cents per mile over the 125 miles per day included in the daily rental. Costs can add up fast if you go over your allotted mileage. Considering that you could stay in a moderately priced hotel for $50 to $100 per night, this doesn't seem like such a good deal. Veteran RVers argue that you'll save money by cooking your meals in your RV. While that may be true part of the time, in reality, you'll want to go out to eat once in a while—after all, this is your vacation. They also contend that luxury campgrounds offer amenities like tennis courts and pools as part of the charge.

Most Florida hotels have pools and a good many have tennis courts, plus many other amenities.

Consider this: The cost for a family of four to fly to Miami ($300 per person) and rent an RV ($180 per day) would be approximately $3,000. Using low daily estimates, the same cost traveling by plane ($300 per person), renting a car ($35 per day), staying in a hotel ($100 per night), and eating out (about $85 per day) comes to $2,745—a savings of $255. Of course, the cost of either method doesn't include incidentals and admission charges to attractions, which can add up (e.g., nearly $150 to get into the Kennedy Space Center alone).

If you're still set on renting an RV, you need to reserve one at least a month in advance from any of the following dealers:

- **A & E Truck & Travel:** Panama City, ✆Toll-free 800-671-7839, *www.cruiseamerica.com/koa*
- **Adventure Touring RV Rentals:** Miami, ✆Toll-free 866-672-3572, *adventuretouring.com*
- **All Star Coaches:** Fort Lauderdale, ✆Toll-free 866-357-5025, *www.allstarcoaches.com*
- **Camp USA:** Pompano Beach, ✆Toll-free 800-971-8840, *www.rvmiami.com*
- **Florida RV Net:** Saint Petersburg, ✆727-631-7008, *www.Florida-RV.net*
- **M & M RV Rentals:** Fort Myers, ✆Toll-free 877-980-7368, *www.mandmrvrentals.com*
- **Recreation World:** Ormond Beach, ✆Toll-free 800-893-2552, *www.grwrv.com*
- **RV Rentals of Tampa Bay, Inc.:** Tampa, ✆Toll-free 800-671-7839, *www.cruiseamerica.com/koa*
- **RVs to Go:** Venice, ✆Toll-free 866-960-4678, *www.venicervrentals.com*
- **Silver Ghost Rentals:** Pensacola, ✆850-484-7585, *www.cruiseamerica.com/koa*
- **Thriftique Shoppe:** Jacksonville, ✆Toll-free 800-671-7839, *www.cruiseamerica.com/koa*

Since much of Florida's coastal terrain is flat, a well-equipped RV like a Fleetwood or Winnebago, complete with a portable toilet, propane stove and refrigerator, bed, and two 5-gallon water containers, will let you travel independently anywhere in Florida. It should also have oversized tires and heavy-duty shocks for better traction and to handle heavy loads if you plan on driving on rough back roads. To make getting around easier once you arrive at your destination if you're driving a larger RV, you can tow a small car behind it.

## Taking the Train

Amtrak runs three trains—the Palmetto, the Silver Meteor, and the Silver Star—from New York to Miami, with stops at Jacksonville, Orlando, Tampa, and Miami. You can travel for the regular coach fare of $133, and up to two of your kids, from two to fifteen years old, can go at half price with each adult. Since it's an overnight trip, you may want to reserve a roomette or a bedroom, accommodating two people, for an extra charge of $116 per room. The former includes only fold-down beds, with restrooms and showers nearby, while the latter includes a very compact private bathroom and shower. Larger bedrooms are sometimes available for families with small children. There's also a dining car, with a special kids' menu, where you can get dinner and breakfast for an extra charge. Traveling by train to Miami from Chicago isn't feasible, since the trip would take forty-five hours to complete at a cost of $458. From Houston via Chicago, it would take sixty-eight hours and cost $714. Here are some tips for traveling by train:

- When making reservations, check for special discounts that may apply.
- If you plan on reserving a roomette or bedroom, do so well in advance.
- Bring a light sweater and wear comfortable shoes.
- Check the hours of the dining car as soon as you board and plan your meals around them.

- Don't leave your luggage unguarded on the train.
- If traveling overnight in coach, secure your luggage to the baggage rack with a bicycle lock.
- Wear a money belt and keep your valuables in it when sleeping in coach cars.
- Bring earplugs along to help you get a good night's sleep.
- Bring along small games or coloring books for small children and a good book for yourself.

In most stations you can check your baggage—three pieces of luggage weighing a total of 150 pounds per person—through to your destination up to thirty minutes before departure and claim it within thirty minutes after arrival. On long-distance trains, you'll be allowed to carry on only enough baggage for essentials during the journey. Attendants on the train, or redcaps in most stations, will help you with your luggage for a tip.

If you're traveling to Florida from the northeastern United States for an extended period of time, you may want to consider taking your car on the Auto Train, operated by Amtrak from Lorton, Virginia, to Sanford, Florida, near Orlando. Trains depart every morning in either direction and take sixteen and a half hours to reach their destination. Vehicles are driven into special enclosed flatbed cars and carried piggyback style while you ride in regular coaches. But the trip is pricey—cars cost $364 and vans and SUVs cost $692 one-way, in addition to your per-person rail fare and the cost of sleeping accommodations should you want them (see page 68). However, dinner and continental breakfast are included. You can also rent a digEplayer, a portable device that allows you to watch movies or television shows or listen to music. (*www.amtrak.com*)

CHAPTER 5

# Staying and Eating

COASTAL FLORIDA OFFERS a variety of accommodations to suit every need from budget motels to posh upscale resorts and glistening high-rise condos. Chain motels line the main approach roads to cities and along beaches. Brand-name high-rise hotels predominate many sections of the coast and are sometimes the only accommodations in city centers. And if you plan to spend a week at the beach, there's nothing like an old-fashioned beach house on stilts where the salty air blows in off the sea.

## What Are Your Family's Needs?

Before booking a hotel in Coastal Florida, it's important to know what your family needs. While there are many chain hotels, which offer standardized accommodations and services you've come to know and trust, you also have a choice of a variety of upscale resorts. Florida hotels are generally spacious with room for up to four people in some double rooms. There's often no charge for children under eighteen sharing with their parents. You can also choose a suite with a kitchenette. And renting a condominium is an excellent solution if your family plans to stay for three to seven days, the minimum stay required. The best type of accommodations for your family may be a resort hotel, which in addition to accommodations offers game rooms, pools, tennis courts, health clubs, and several restaurants for dining.

### Are There Programs for Children?

Florida may be one of the few vacation getaway destinations that cater to the entire family and especially children. Children are welcome in restaurants, and many family-style eateries feature kids' portions. Many hotels along Florida's coasts offer free lodging for children sixteen and under staying with their parents in the same room.

 **TRAVEL TIP**

Along Florida's coasts, the greatest danger to young children is the sun. If your children are going to be exposed to the sunlight for any length of time, you should liberally douse them in high-protection sunblock and repeat after swimming. Both younger and teenage children should also wear hats and caps.

While most moderate and deluxe hotels and resorts cater to families, you won't find special kids' programs at too many places along the coast. Unlike the resorts found in the theme park wonderland surrounding Orlando, most coastal hotels offer basic to deluxe accommodations for families on vacations on which the kids will probably spend most of their time at the beach. Babysitting services are available at some of the larger resorts if you and your spouse want some time for yourselves. Many moderate hotels offer game rooms and playgrounds for children, and some also have kids' pools.

### Activities for Older Kids?

If you're traveling with teens, Coastal Florida offers a variety of activities to keep them busy. Activities suited to your active teens include hiking, kayaking, diving, snorkeling, and beachcombing.

Find out what they're interested in and let them be a part of the planning process. However, be careful not to let their activities dominate your trip. Try to achieve a good balance so everyone, including you, will have a good time.

# Keeping It Affordable

Accommodations will be your biggest expense while in Florida. It's as much when you stay as *where* you stay that governs how much you pay. High and low seasons vary depending on whether you're in the north or south, so planning carefully can save a lot. You can save money by visiting southern Florida from April to December when hotel prices drop by as much as half or by visiting the Panhandle and northeast coast where prices fall from October to May.

Check for local events that may inflate prices, such as Spring Break in Daytona Beach and Panama City Beach during March and April when thousands of vacationing college students descend upon the towns. Also be aware that during Speed Weeks, also in Daytona Beach, when hundreds of auto race fans pack the Daytona International Speedway in February, prices can triple what they are normally. And as real estate agents always say, "Location, location, location"—those hotels right near the beach or in a large city will naturally cost more. Since smart vacationers quickly snap up the least expensive or at least the most value-oriented accommodations along the more popular areas of the coast, it pays to reserve in advance.

Prices of hotels also vary by what they offer. Though motels and hotels offer the type of accommodations—regular double rooms with a bath, color television with cable, and phone—their operators may differ. Generally, individuals or husband-and-wife teams run motels, which are usually a bit less expensive—a room typically costs $50 or more per room per night. Nationwide chain hotels, on the other hand, typically cost $50 to $99. Most have swimming pools and free local phone calling. For $100 to $149, you can get a bigger room with a balcony and perhaps free Internet connections. Sometimes hotels in this category offer a gym or a tennis court, or perhaps have guest privileges at a nearby golf course. You can expect to spend $150 to $249 at a deluxe hotel or resort, for which you'll receive a spacious room, a restaurant for meals, and a few shops. Super deluxe resorts, with rooms costing $250 and above per night, offer a spectacular ocean view, in-room Jacuzzi, live entertainment, special activity programs, and a gourmet restaurant plus a café and several bars.

If you're on a tight budget, you can always stay at dependable budget-priced chain hotels, such as Econo Lodge and Red Carpet Inns. Hampton Inns, Comfort Inns, and Fairfield Inns fall into the moderate budget category at $80 to 100 per night and offer daily self-serve continental breakfast as well as a pool and maybe a playground for kids. Best Western, Howard Johnson's, and La Quinta are higher on the budgetary scale at $75 to 125. The rates at hotels a block or so from the beach are often lower than those fronting it.

 **TRAVEL TIP**

If you want an oceanfront room, be sure to ask for it specifically. A "waterfront" room can mean it faces a bay, inlet, or canal that may or may not be too pleasing. "Oceanview" means just that—you can see the ocean but don't face it.

Some hotels and motels offer efficiency units, which are rooms with cooking facilities ranging from a microwave oven and a sink with a compact refrigerator underneath squeezed into a corner to a fully equipped kitchen. These usually add $20 to $35 onto the basic room rate.

During off-peak periods many motels and hotels struggle to fill their rooms, and it's worth asking for a lower price. Staying in the same hotel room for three or more nights may also reduce the price.

Also, be on the lookout for discount coupons offered by tourist information offices or online.

# Picking the Right Vacation Scenario

How you choose to travel on your vacation with your family depends on the ages of your children. If you have kids six and under, you should consider staying at one hotel and exploring the area around it rather than traveling from one to another. The more you pack and unpack, the more agitated younger children get. Younger children are also affected more by the heat and humidity, so you'll need to give them time to acclimate. For this reason, it's probably best to travel in northern Florida during the summer and southern Florida during the winter.

### Bedrooms Versus Fully Equipped Suites

If you're traveling with younger children, it may be best to stay in a fully equipped suite. Similar to a small apartment, they offer your children a place that seems more like home. A standard hotel room can be limiting. Also, this type of accommodation, with its small kitchen, allows you to prepare snacks or food just for them. While some people may not consider cooking part of a vacation, it can get expensive to eat out for every meal with young children. Preparing a simple breakfast and picnic lunches will go a long way to keeping your little ones content.

 **TRAVEL TIP**

It's extremely important to make reservations—four to six months ahead of time if you're traveling over a holiday period—even if you're traveling in the off-peak season. Make sure you have a confirmation in writing from the hotel. If you book through a travel agency, be sure to ask for a copy of the confirmation they received.

### Beach House and Condo Rentals

If you don't like the controlled environment of a resort and are planning to stay in one place for a week or more, you may want to consider renting a beach house or condominium. You'll find the former in the Lower Keys and the latter along practically every major beach in the state. Luxury condos, offering one to three bedrooms, living room, dining area, kitchen, and one or more baths, are like staying in a home-away-from-home—except with maid service. Most have a three-night minimum stay requirement and offer weekly or monthly rates. Many are time-shares that are available for rent when their northern owners aren't there. On the other hand, beach houses—many on stilts—offer you a truly tropical way to enjoy Florida's shores. These are always rented by the week and often require you to bring along your own linens and such.

# A Taste of Coastal Florida

Feeding your family on vacation can be an expensive proposition. But in Coastal Florida, you needn't spend a lot to eat well. Good restaurants serving delicious food abound at coastal destinations. Diners and counter-service cafés, serving mounds of food for a few dollars, are everywhere. Each restaurant offers its own specialties, from gourmet to ethnic and downright southern. It may seem that trendier cuisines are taking over, but you'll find most Floridians like to eat good traditional down-home food and barbecued steak from over 20,000 ranches statewide.

Fish tops most menus, even those in the smallest mom-and-pop eateries. Whether you eat tuna or pompano from the ocean or catfish from a nearby river, you'll find it served boiled, grilled or charcoal-grilled, or fried. The Gulf of Mexico and the Atlantic Ocean yield fresh yellowfin tuna, pompano, grouper, swordfish, and mullet, among others. Shrimp, grilled or steamed, is a popular favorite. Plus, cooks in each coastal area serve up their own special dishes from its particular waters, such as smoked mullet on the west coast, oysters-on-the-half-shell from Apalachicola Bay in the Panhandle, and conch (pronounced "konk") chowder and fritters in the Keys. Some chefs in Miami's trendier restaurants combine local fish with an assortment of citrus fruits and juices.

## ≡FAST FACT

In many areas, during the winter you'll notice oranges, grapefruit, limes, and tangelos for sale at roadside stands. Varieties seem endless, with some fruit offering special qualities such as remarkable sweetness or no seeds. Pick up any locally grown citrus fruit and you'll immediately notice the difference between it and the ones you buy at your supermarket back home.

You'll find you get the freshest and cheapest fish at fish camps, rustic eateries located on the banks of a coastal river where your meal was swimming just a few hours before. Here, lunch or dinner will cost you no more than $8. And while fried catfish tops the menus at most fish camps, you'll find other selections as well.

Floridians love their shellfish, too. The tender claws of stone crabs, eaten dipped in butter, are just heaven during mid-October to mid-May. You'll find oysters served at "raw" bars along with regular and jumbo shrimp, dipped in spicy cocktail sauce. Spiny or Florida lobster is another favorite.

And right up there next to fish on the menus, you'll find alligator. Restaurants in the Everglades area have always served alligator tail in a variety of ways, including deep-fried. And, yes, it tastes like chicken. Now restaurants in other coastal resorts have added this Florida favorite to their menus.

### Southern Cooking

You'll find that good old-fashioned Southern home-style cooking and soul food also have their place in Florida cuisine, especially in diners and cafés in the northeast and the Panhandle. Southern fried chicken and fried fish both come with a choice of grits or hush puppies. And grits replaces potatoes with most breakfasts. Northern Florida cooks also add okra, collards, black-eyed peas, or fried eggplant to roast beef, with which you'll usually get cornbread to soak up the thick gravy poured all over everything. And because of their proximity to Louisiana, northern cooks use okra in gumbo as a way of using up leftovers. You'll find Cajun food, itself, usually served in more upscale trendy restaurants. Another Florida favorite is hearts of palm salad, based on the delicious heart of the sable palm tree.

## ≡FAST FACT

One traditional Southern dish is hush puppies, deep-fried balls of cornbread with tiny pieces of chopped onion. Hunters are believed to have tossed these treats to their dogs to keep them quiet while they prepared their supper following a hunt.

To top off any meal, most restaurants offer Key lime pie, a dessert with origins in the Florida Keys. Made from the small limes that grow there, it's similar to lemon meringue but with a tangier taste. You'll find the best in Key West.

### Ethnic Cuisine

The farther south you travel along Florida's coast, the more ethnic and exotic the food becomes.

Cuban food has become a staple of Miami cuisine. Simple Cuban dinners are often a better value than their equivalents back home. Most consist of pork, beef, or chicken—always fried with the skin on and spiced heavily—served with a combination of yellow or white rice, black beans, fried plantains (similar to bananas), and yucca. Thick seafood soups, like *sopa de mariscos* (shellfish soup), are also popular.

Don't be misled by trendier restaurants serving Cuban food. Often it's the same as you'll get in a place charging $4 to $6 for the same thing. Many Cuban cafés have street windows where you can buy a small cup of sweet and rich café Cubano, Cuban espresso, for less than a dollar. If you're feeling tired, this will definitely pick you up—it might even throw you around a bit, too. If you'd rather have something a little milder, try café con leche, Cuban coffee served with warm milk or cream.

Along the west coast, you'll find plenty of affordable, family-run Greek restaurants, serving specialties like moussaka and pastitsio and delicious Greek salads, originally brought to Florida by the sponge fishermen of Tarpon Springs. Minorcan food, found around Saint Augustine, offers a spicy stew of seafood and chicken mixed with vegetables and rice called pilau.

And if you're traveling in the Everglades area, try Indian fried bread and mashed cassava root.

# Coastal Florida's Top Ten Family Destinations

While you'll find many picturesque places to explore along Florida's coast, there are some that offer your family a more diverse, fun-filled vacation. Choose your destination based on your personal interests and those of your family.

### Tampa

Tampa, third most populous city in Florida, boasts the second largest attraction in the state, Busch Gardens, a safari-like park filled with exotic species like gazelles and gorillas. Or take a walk through historic Ybor City, Tampa's Latin Quarter, where Cubans created the famous Tampa cigar. Here, the traditions and atmosphere of a Spanish neighborhood have been meticulously preserved.

Taking the sleek Skyway across the Tampa Bay will take you into the clouds and then gracefully back down to Saint Petersburg,

Florida's million-dollar city. Tops on the list is a visit to see the collection of magnificent works by Salvador Dali. Your kids will have a ball in the Great Explorations Museum. Then it's on to the panoramic beaches of Saint Petersburg Beach, Clearwater Beach, Belleair Beach, Indian Rocks Beach, Redington Shores, and Treasure Island.

A little farther north, the city of Tarpon Springs, steeped in Greek customs and folklore, is another Old World delight.

### Cocoa Beach

Using Cocoa Beach, along Florida's Space Coast, as a vacation base allows you to visit the Kennedy Space Center, plus explore the beach towns down the coast, including Florida's sailfish capital, Stuart. This area offers an array of vacation possibilities. But the primary reason most families come to Cocoa Beach is to visit Spaceport U.S.A. and Merritt Island National Wildlife Refuge, both part of the Kennedy Space Center. Cape Canaveral, a triangular spit midway down the coast, identified on early thirteenth-century maps, is today the site of NASA's gateway to outer space.

The pounding Atlantic also provides surfers with thrills and spills from Cocoa Beach south through Melbourne, Sebastian, Vero Beach, and Fort Pierce. A series of barrier islands extend the entire length of this part of Florida's coastline, making up the east bank of the Indian River where you can water-ski, windsurf, and fish to your heart's content. You can also become acquainted with jai alai, the Basque handball game in which the ball reaches speeds of 150 miles per hour at frontons in Fort Pierce and Melbourne. The influence of the Gulf Stream a few miles offshore gives deep-water sports anglers a chance at sailfish, dolphin, amberjack, wahoo, and king and Spanish mackerel, from spring until fall.

### Panama City

Panama City lies at the center of Coastal Florida's main family seaside resort area. Even during the peak summer season, you can find a remote, undeveloped beach on an isolated barrier island just a short boat ride away from popular resort areas. But if you have active kids, Panama City Beach offers a fun-filled world of amusement parks, go-cart racetracks, miniature golf courses, water parks, and a zoo—that is, if you can pry them away from the sparkling sugary white sand beach. And as a break from the sun, you can take scenic drives along the shore toward the wide mouth of the Apalachicola River and inland to Apalachicola National Forest. The waters around the resorts contain a wide assortment of game fish to test your skills. Or you can just sit in a low-rise beach chair and let the warm blue-green Gulf waters wash over you.

### Sarasota

On the barrier island beaches off Sarasota, center stage is reserved for the evening sunset, which daily showers the shoreline of the Gulf of Mexico with shades of glowing reds and oranges and golds. The blue-green Gulf waters and wide sand beaches are an irresistible lure to vacationers.

Numerous tours are conducted on pirate-style ketches, sailing sloops, and pleasant double-decker cruisers. The region's pure white Gulf coast sands are ideally suited to early morning walks along shell-covered beaches and afternoon fitness treks in the warm glow of the setting sun. Barrier islands on the lower west coast crosscut the Gulf Stream current, resulting in a tidal wash that produces some of the world's finest shell-collecting sites.

Cultural activities are concentrated in the Sarasota area. The Ringling Museum complex draws thousands of visitors annually. Willed to the State of Florida by circus king John Ringling, the complex includes an art museum, a circus museum, a theater, and the palatial home of John and Mable Ringling. Fort Myers carries an air of casual sophistication, featuring posh shopping and dining facilities. And just offshore, the picture-book islands of Sanibel and Captiva have become a major destination for shell collectors. More opulence is evident farther south in the sleek tropical community of Naples.

## Everglades

The mighty Everglades, where airboats skim across the grassy plains, have a primordial beauty all their own. Wildlife runs freely here, and nature hikes offer glimpses of lazy alligators, skittish wild deer, colorful water birds, and possibly even a Florida panther or an American bald eagle—just some of the animals that call this wild region home. One of the world's natural wonders, the Florida Everglades sprawls over 5,000 square miles of wilderness. It has been called the wildest, shallowest, strangest river in the world. From its rich soil comes most of the nation's winter crop of vegetables and a generous supply of sugar cane.

Here, in this vast wet wilderness, several hundred Seminole Indians took refuge as a last chance to remain in Florida during the Seminole Wars. This fragile ecosystem, unlike any other in North America, teeters on the edge of destruction at the hands of humans.

## Florida Keys and Key West

The Florida Keys, a string of coral islands boasting the best underwater diving reefs in the continental United States, have lured underwater adventurers, artists, and musicians for over a hundred years to their subtropic paradise. You can sail aboard a sleek yacht or catamaran or windsurf across the emerald green waters of the Gulf of Mexico. The Overseas Highway, with the Atlantic Ocean on one side and the Gulf of Mexico on the other, links the 113-mile chain by way of forty-two bridges. Each key has its own personality, history, and local traditions. Key Largo, the largest, is home to John Pennekamp Coral Reef State Park, the first underwater preserve in the country. Fishermen have dubbed Islamorada "the Sports Fishing Capital" of Florida. Long Key offers nature trails through tropical hammocks, and across the magnificent Seven Mile Bridge lie the Lower Keys, a paradise of colorful water birds; Big Pine Key is also a refuge for tiny Key deer. Finally, there's Key West, the most famous of the Keys, with its gingerbread mansions and kitschy lifestyle.

## Jacksonville

As a travel destination, the Jacksonville area offers a diverse mixture of historic and natural attractions. Here, you'll find a land of many contrasts and moods. In the center of it all lies Jacksonville and the Jacksonville Beaches, bustling resort cities with a myriad of cultural events, recreational highlights, and landmarks from other eras. To the south is Saint Augustine, first New World outpost and oldest permanent city within the United States, and to the north lies Amelia Island, site of luxurious sports resorts boasting three of the nation's most challenging and beautiful golf courses, plus old-time Fernandina Beach, with its restored nineteenth-century houses. You may walk in the footsteps of conquistadors and pirates, pilot your own houseboat, or canoe in settings little altered by time or people. Four centuries of history have been carefully preserved and brought to life in a timeless setting of wind-sculpted dunes and broad Atlantic beaches that still await your footprints.

From Juan Ponce de León's first step onto the shore near Saint Augustine to conflicts over who held the territory to the emergence of a new nation, the Jacksonville area overflows with history. Before 1900, Henry Flagler recognized the area's potential as a place of leisure. He focused the country's attention upon it, and upon Florida, by building the first of his string of plush resorts that eventually would stretch the length of the state's east coast and change Florida forever.

The hard-packed sands of Daytona Beach have lured car drivers from the beginning of the development of the automobile. Both speed and cars exceeded the capabilities of the beaches and Daytona International Speedway became the natural offspring.

## Pensacola

From the vast expanse of sugar-white panhandle beaches lining the barrier islands of Gulf Island National Seashore to the broad Choctowhatchee Bay, the area around Pensacola revels in its claim as Florida's best-kept secret. And this least-discovered region provides you with the opportunity to experience perhaps the widest variety of Coastal Florida's spectacular outdoor offerings in an atmosphere of gracious Old South hospitality. Here, you can canoe down a clear, spring-fed river beneath a canopy of oaks, play a round or two on an inviting array of golf courses, venture into the blue-green Gulf of Mexico on a deep-sea fishing charter, or just stretch out under the sun on the shimmering white sand. The region's most powerful lure lies within the 100-mile stretch of quartz-sand beaches, which winds its way from Florida's western tip through Fort Walton Beach where breezes off the Gulf of Mexico send sloops skimming during annual regattas.

### Fort Lauderdale

The Fort Lauderdale area offers sparkling resorts along the Atlantic Ocean, including Hollywood, Pompano Beach, and Boca Raton, with the best in nightlife, beaches, shopping, and tropical cuisine; the Palm Beaches—from Boca Raton to Jupiter—offer a somewhat slower pace. Visit the island of Palm Beach, walk down elegant Worth Avenue or drive the full length of the island to glimpse homes of the very rich. Stroll the miles and miles of public beaches or go shopping for a day—if you can afford it. The Intracoastal Waterway here is a playground for boaters, skiers, and fishermen. Offshore waters beckon the angler with marlin, amberjack, tuna, king mackerel, barracuda, dolphin, bonito, and the most popular catch of all, sailfish. Charter fleets sail out of Hollywood, Fort Lauderdale, Pompano Beach, Boca Raton, Boynton Beach, Palm and West Palm Beach, Riviera Beach, and Jupiter. If you're a golfer, you'll find more courses in this area than anywhere else in Florida.

### Miami and Miami Beach

The rich, the famous, and the talented all have found a special spot in the sun along the palm-fringed beaches of South Florida—and you will, too. From golden beaches with slender palms swaying in the salt breezes to nightclubs, racing, and the opera, Miami and neighboring Miami Beach pulse with a Latin rhythm that's hard to beat. This cosmopolitan duo, with its museums, theaters, nightclubs, attractions, shops, and restaurants, is perhaps the most universally recognized of all Florida resorts. Stay in fabulous resort hotels, eat in many of Florida's best restaurants, place bets on dogs, horses, and jai alai, and do it all under year-round sunshine.

Miami Beach, wrapped in rainbow neon, its art deco buildings all aglow in pastel hues, is a backdrop for the beautiful people. Bronzed beauties sip champagne by the seashore as muscle men stroll the beach showing off their bodies. This is South Beach, famous for its association with the diet of the same name, now becoming an artsy district rivaling New York's SoHo. Everything in this area reflects a passion for beauty.

# CHAPTER 6

# *Family Activities in Coastal Florida*

WHEN YOUR FAMILY ENGAGES in activities they're interested in, your vacation is all the more enjoyable. While some people enjoy just soaking up the sun and sipping cool drinks, Coastal Florida offers so much more than that. And if you don't take advantage of at least some of the unique vacation activities that Coastal Florida affords, you'll be missing out on opportunities that you may not find elsewhere. There's so much to do that your biggest problem will be finding the time to do it all.

## Considerations when Planning Your Activities

Today, it's just as important to consider what you'll be doing on vacation as it is how to get there reasonably. The length of your vacation, as well as the time of year and whether you'll need to rent equipment, all affect your budget. Some activities are only available at certain times of the year or even on certain days of the week. And how long you stay will determine just how much you can do.

### Making a Budget

With so much information available on the Internet, it's a lot easier to plan a budget for your vacation activities. Some places along the coast of Florida aren't cheap. Activities such as golf and fishing can get expensive, while others, like lying on a beach, cost nothing. But it's important to budget for one or two memorable activities, like sailing on a schooner or parasailing over a white sand beach.

### Gear You Can Bring or Rent

You'll find just about any type of gear you'll need for sale or rent in Coastal Florida. While you may be the kind of sports person who feels more comfortable playing with your own equipment, such as golf clubs, tennis rackets, or scuba gear, you may not want the hassle and worry of lugging it with you on a long trip. After all, unless you plan a golfing vacation in which you play a round of golf daily, it's better to rent a set of clubs for the one or two rounds you'll play on a more leisurely family vacation.

## On the Water

Throughout Coastal Florida, you'll discover a number of ways to have fun on the water. Perhaps you'd like to sail out on the sea on a sleek sailboat, or skim across it on a sailboard, or race the waves in a WaveRunner, or ride the surf on a surfboard. Or maybe you'd prefer paddling a canoe on a tropical lagoon or down a river overhung by cypress branches hung with Spanish moss. As if all this isn't enough, you can also go water-skiing and Jet-Skiing on the Intracoastal Waterway.

 **TRAVEL TIP**

If you like to "hang ten," then you'd better head for Florida's Atlantic coast. The surf is high enough from Saint Augustine south to Daytona Beach to get some good wave action. The best place to surf is San Sebastian where you can also take surfing lessons.

Hobie Cats are also a fun way to get on the water when the wind kicks up. And Jet-Skiing or water-skiing offers an exhilarating alternative. You'll find concessionaires offering rentals at most of the major beaches in Coastal Florida.

Surfing requires high-energy shorelines with good wave action. Some of the best include the North Jetty and Pier at Jacksonville Beach; Mantanzas Inlet at Saint Augustine Beach; Ponce de León Inlet; Playalinda Beach; Cocoa Beach; Indialantic at Melbourne Beach; Sebastian Inlet at Stuart, and Jupiter Inlet on the Atlantic; Siesta Beach at Sarasota; Lido and Longboat Keys; Saint Andrews State Recreation Area; Panama City Beach; Fort Walton Beach; and Gulf Beach at Pensacola on the Gulf side. You'll find that shorter and broader boards are better suited for Florida surf with less energetic currents than in California.

### Parasailing

Perhaps you'd like the exhilarating feeling of parasailing. Nothing beats being towed high in a parachute behind a powerful motorboat—an activity that may be extreme, but nevertheless is safe. At beaches like Daytona or Fort Lauderdale, all you need do is wait your turn. A ten-minute ride costs about $30—and don't forget to bring along lots of nerve.

### Sailing and Boating

What better way to see the Gulf or Atlantic coastline than to spend a day sailing aboard a luxurious sailboat or an old-time schooner, looking down into the clear blue-green sea at dolphins, sea turtles, and manatees. Luxury day sails often include open bar, lunch, and snacks, as well as fishing and snorkeling equipment, depending on the location. If you're an experienced sailor, you'll want to rent a boat for a few hours and sail down the Indian River between Titusville and Stuart. You can purchase navigational charts of the Intracoastal Waterway from local marine supply shops.

 TRAVEL TIP

It's important to take safety precautions when boating. Wear your life jacket, sunscreen, and a hat at all times, never operate a boat under the influence of alcohol, carry signaling gear and a fire extinguisher, and be aware of sharp fishing hooks if you go angling.

## Canoeing and Kayaking

The art and skill of Florida canoeing is as old as its Indian culture. Native Americans carved canoes from huge cypress logs not only to travel on inland rivers and coastal areas but also for exploring throughout Florida Bay and the Keys. The Florida Department of Natural Resources promotes this outdoor sport with a Florida Canoe Trail System that currently includes thirty-six designated rivers or sections of rivers for 1,300 miles. The State of Florida requires every occupant of a canoe or kayak to wear a life jacket. You can obtain a map and description of each canoe trail, plus a Canoe Liveries and Outfitters Directory, Canoe Information Resources Guide with safety tips and regulations, and listing of organizations that offer canoeing activities, from the Division of Recreation and Parks (Toll-free 877-822-5208, *www.dep.state.fl.us/parks*).

You'll discover the best sea kayaking along the Gulf coast where the waters remain relatively calm. Numerous inlets and coves offer plenty of places to explore. If you've never gone kayaking before, Coastal Florida offers excellent places to do so. For $70 per person, you can take a basic kayaking course that will teach you entry and exit skills, basic strokes, and rescues, all done in a kayak in the water. If you already know how to kayak, you can rent one at over sixty rental centers for $20 per half day, $30 per full day. Many kayak outfitters also offer one- to five-hour guided kayak tours through Coastal Florida's waterways.

# Fishing

You'll have a tough time choosing between saltwater and freshwater fishing in Coastal Florida. The state's 2,276 miles of tidal coastline along the Intracoastal Waterway provide clusters of mangroves where you can drop a line for snapper, sheepshead, sand perch, and grunts. The influent of the Gulf Stream a few miles offshore gives you a chance to hook blue and white marlin, dolphinfish, black-fin tuna, barracuda, amberjack, wahoo, king and Spanish mackerel, and the most popular of all, sailfish, from spring until fall. Tarpon and king mackerel stay close to shore following the shrimp boats. And big game fish gather around offshore oilrigs and artificial reefs.

## ≡FAST FACT

Fishermen can catch fish throughout the year since Florida has no closed season. But freshwater anglers over 16 must purchase a license for $16.50 from any tackle shop, county courthouse, or fishing camp, or online. A three-day saltwater license costs only $6.50. (✆Toll-free 888-347-4356, ✍www.myfwc.com/license)

No one species of saltwater fish brings on more acute attacks of fishing fever than the tarpon, silver king of Florida game fish. The tarpon leap from mid-May until August. In fact, most fishermen go after them to experience their balletic leaps from the water as they struggle to get away, then toss them back when the battle is over. All the major Florida ports have excellent fleets of sleek charter boats carrying as many as six anglers and making half- and full-day fishing trips. You'll pay $200 and up for a six-hour run. Though some provide snacks and drinks, you most likely will have to bring your own. Some of Coastal Florida's great fishing areas include:

**Alligator Alley:** The canal paralleling Route 84 between Naples and Fort Lauderdale has loads of bluegills and bass.

**Boca Grande Pass:** Famous for tarpon from March through October, but best in June.

**De Soto Canyon:** Also known as Billfish Alley, this offshore depression near Pensacola parallels the coast for 100 miles and is known for its abundance of tuna, sailfish, white and blue marlin, and swordfish.

**Destin:** Has the state's largest fishing fleet of 100 charters and party boats going after grouper, pompano, king mackerel, and sailfish.

**Ten Thousand Islands:** A mangrove wilderness of coves and creeks stretching 60 miles along the Gulf Coast below Marco Island, noted for its snook.

**The Florida Keys:** Islamorada, Marathon, and Key West are the three main centers for bonefish and tarpon.

Rivers emptying into the waters of the Gulf and the Atlantic offer excellent freshwater fishing. Bridges and piers also offer good vantage points for hooking trout, snook, redfish, and sheepshead. Along many of these, you'll find fishing camps where you can rent a boat and buy bait and tackle. You can catch bluegills, shellcrackers, stumprockers, and crappie using cane poles baited with worms, crickets, or minnows, as well as light spinning tackle or a fly rod baited with flies. Coastal Florida also has generous bag limits for freshwater fish.

# Under the Water

Florida's southern coastline offers some of the best snorkeling and scuba diving locations in the country. The clear, warm waters off the Florida Keys barely conceal brilliant coral, tropical fish, and exotic marine plants and animals. At John Pennekamp State Park, you can swim among magnificent coral gardens and schools of brightly colored fish, as well as see guns and anchors from shipwrecked fifteenth-century Spanish galleons. Yet, it's only been in recent years that the popularity of these sports has caught on in Coastal Florida. Today, you'll find numerous dive shops where you can rent snorkel or diving gear.

Your trip to Coastal Florida won't be complete without a view of its underwater world in which live a great variety of multicolored marine animals and plants. In the clear warm waters of the Atlantic and the Gulf, you'll see schools of porgy, grunt, spadefish, squid, sea urchins, sea fans, sea whips, serpulid plume worms, gorgania, sponges, jellyfish, moray eels, and, in the more tropical waters, beautiful angelfish, parrot fish, and butterfly fish. In addition, you'll discover varied coral formations, reefs, fossils, treasure sites, and shipwrecks to explore off the Florida Keys. The following diving fees are typical at Coastal Florida resorts:

| DIVES | TYPICAL DIVING FEES |
|---|---|
| One-tank night dive | $70 |
| Two-tank day dive | $70, including two tanks, weights and belt, divemaster, small snack, and beverages |
| EQUIPMENT RENTAL (PER DAY) | |
| Wet suit | $10–$15 |
| Regulator and gauges | $10–$15 |
| Tank with fill | $7 |
| Nitrox cylinder | $13 |
| Dive light | $5 |
| Buoyancy compensator | $10–$15 |
| Mask/snorkel/fins | $5–$12 |
| Dive computer | $15 |
| Complete gear package | $25–$50 |
| LESSONS | |
| Discover Scuba course | $100–$175 |
| PADI Open Water Scuba Certification course | $450 (four days) |
| Advanced Open Water Scuba Certification | $250 |

If you're a novice snorkeler, you can begin with a guidebook and equipment. You can take a two-stop snorkeling tour for about $45 per person at some southern Florida beaches. Unfortunately, scuba diving is more complicated. Though some of the equipment is the same as in snorkeling, scuba diving involves breathing through a regulator tank of pure compressed air.

 **TRAVEL TIP**

If you want to learn to scuba-dive, be sure to look for instructors sanctioned by the Professional Association of Dive Instructors (PADI) or the National Association of Underwater Instructors (NAUI). To sign up for courses, contact the Professional Scuba Association International, headquartered in Ocala (✆352-861-7724, ✐www.mrscuba.com).

Before you go to Coastal Florida, check to see if your local YMCA or YWCA offers a scuba course. You can also take a certification course once you're in Florida, although you'll have to allow at least four days for this. A four-hour Discover Scuba course will cost you $100 to $175. You cannot get certified with this course, however. A full PADI Open Water Scuba Certification course will run you $450. And an Advanced Open Water Scuba Certification course is $250.

## On the Links

The lush scenery and ideal weather at most of Coastal Florida's hundreds of golf courses make it hard to concentrate on your game. Florida has more courses than any other state. Here, golf is a year-round sport, with many exciting and challenging courses laid out by top-name designers. You'll find superb golf available in or near all of Coastal Florida's primary resort destinations. Each has its own personality, often with seashore vistas or tropical woodland borders. Some even have wetlands with live alligators.

## Available Courses

Florida has over 1,000 golf courses to choose from, and over 800 of those lie on or near the coast. The coast of southwest Florida offers the most courses at 239, with the coast of southeast Florida a close second at 233—and new ones are being built every day. The following table shows some of Coastal Florida's top golf resorts:

## A Selection of Top Coastal Florida Golf Resorts

**Bluewater Bay**
Niceville
✆800-874-2128
✐*http://bwbresort.com*
Greens fees: $39–$72
Number of 18-hole courses: 1

**Marriott Bay Point**
Panama City
✆850-235-6950
✐*www.baypointgolf.com*
Greens fees: $45–$95
Number of 18-hole courses: 2

**PGA National Resort & Spa**
✆800-633-9150
✐*www.pgaresort.com*
Greens fees: $198–$319 daily
Number of 18-hole courses: 5

**Westin Innisbrook Golf Resort**
Tampa
✆800-473-8402
✐*www.innisbrookgolfresort.com*
Greens fees: $100–$210
Number of 18-hole courses: 4

### Greens Fees and Club Rentals

Greens fees, including cart rental, vary from as little as $39 in the off season at some courses to over $210 in peak season at some of the championship ones that host PGA tournaments. Most courses offer clubs for rent for about $40 to $60.

# Outdoor Activities

Coastal Florida offers many possibilities for outdoor recreation. But in contrast to the forests of the north and west, here you'll be exploring tropical woodland hammocks and grassy wet prairies where you'll discover unusual species of birds and animals. And though some say a beach is a beach, Coastal Florida's beaches vary from sparkling white to sandy brown, and many are as wild as Mother Nature intended them to be, just waiting to be explored.

### Horseback Riding

The only coastal location where you can feel the wind blowing through your hair as you ride through the surf on horseback is Amelia Island. However, you'll find 450 miles of designated equestrian trails in Florida. Most of these run through areas like Apalachicola National Forest in the Panhandle, and Big Cypress Preserve, north of Everglades National Park. Though shorter trails do exist in state parks, you may not find anywhere close by to rent horses. For information on horseback riding in Florida, including a list of liveries and trail maps, contact the Sunshine State Horse Council (813-651-5953, *www.sshc.org*).

### Hiking

Florida has 1,600 miles of hiking trails, 500 miles of nature trails, and more than 400 miles of multiuse trails for walking, jogging, and bicycling, many of which are along or near the coast. Most are shorter trails to an observation point or through a particular ecosystem in state parks and preserves, botanical gardens, and national wildlife refuges. Florida's more than eighty different natural communities present more botanical diversity than any other states on the East Coast. Bahia Honda, Florida's southernmost park covering 276 acres, has palm-fringed beaches fronting both the Atlantic Ocean and the Gulf of Mexico. You'll find that winter, when the temperature moderates and the insects are either gone or less bothersome, is the best season to go hiking, especially in the south.

You'd best bring along your own hiking equipment. Though you can take short hikes with a good pair of casual walking shoes, you'll find those trails not on elevated wooden boardwalks are often wet and soggy, so a pair of sturdy hiking boots may be preferable. You'll definitely need them on longer hikes.

If hiking in the spring, summer, or fall, you can wear a short-sleeved shirt, shorts, and canvas shoes. However, if you're planning to hike on rougher trails in the backcountry or in the Everglades where you may go through patches of sawgrass, saw palmetto, or briars, be sure to wear a long-sleeved cotton shirt and long pants. A lightweight wide-brimmed hat is a good idea anytime. Casual shoes will do for shorter trails, but you'll need light-duty hiking boots for longer ones—don't wear sandals if you're walking on anything but a boardwalk in the parks. And though Coastal Florida is usually sunny, sudden storms can pop up, so take along a lightweight windbreaker with a hood that you'll find in discount stores. And if you're hiking in the Panhandle during winter, make sure to bring along a fleece shirt, sweater, and perhaps a windproof jacket. On a longer hike, pack an extra change of dry clothes to prevent hypothermia.

Sunblock is mandatory, as is plenty of insect repellent like Deep Woods' Off! or Cutter. Be sure to spray it not only on your skin but also on your clothes. Or use a lotion like Avon's Skin-So-Soft. And be sure to carry at least four quarts of water with you for an all-day hike.

Florida experiences some powerful thunderstorms. Should you be caught in one on the trail, don't cross marshes or streams and get out from under trees. On the barrier islands, stay away from the beach and open boats. Seek shelter immediately. If you go on an overnight hike during hurricane season, take along a portable radio for weather updates.

### Bird Watching

Birds love Coastal Florida and birders do, too. Some sort of species is either coming or going all the time. In parks, preserves, woodlands, and sanctuaries, you'll see spectacular displays of migrant birds, arriving in September and October and leaving in April and May. Diehard bird watchers descend on Florida's coasts in mid-May to see some of the nearly 450 species of birds. Of these, 25 percent are water birds.

If you've never gone bird watching, you're in for a treat. Go out very early—6 A.M. isn't too early. Wear soft shoes and proceed slowly and quietly. Bring along a good pair of binoculars, a bird handbook, and a notepad and paper to record what you've seen. For information on locations, organized birding walks, and bird watching in Coastal Florida, contact the Florida Audubon Society (305-371-6399, *www .audubonofflorida.org*).

### Bicycling

Florida has almost 1,900 miles of bicycle trails. You can pedal easy-riding routes along backcountry roads, through towns and villages, and along some beaches. While some locations have bicycle trails paralleling their roads and streets, such as on Sanibel Island, other routes follow old railroad right-of-ways. You'll find that the best time to go bicycling falls between Labor Day and Thanksgiving when there are fewer tourists.

## Cultural Activities

Today, Coastal Florida is more than sun, sand, and sea. Within the last several decades, some of Florida's larger coastal cities—Miami, Sarasota, Tampa, and Jacksonville—have developed into cultural centers with a full schedule of events. Besides sophisticated museums and galleries, you'll also find state-of-the-art performing-arts centers where you can experience the best in opera, dance, and theater.

Miami boasts seven theatrical companies, offering everything from Shakespeare to Broadway, with contemporary and African-

American in between. And even though the city seems to move to the beat of salsa these days, you'll find five dance companies, from the world-class Miami City Ballet and Ballet Theater of Miami to the contemporary Momentum Dance Company to the Ballet Flamenco La Rosa. Plus, the city has a symphony and a philharmonic orchestra and the Greater Miami Opera. Six museums also offer you the chance to view a world of art, from old master paintings to traditional to contemporary to Cuban.

## ≡ FAST FACT

With the wide assortment of ethnic groups living in Florida comes a choice of cultural festivals. The Epiphany Festival, held in Tarpon Springs each January, draws over a quarter of a million people. A half million attend the Festival of the States in Saint Petersburg, and thousands attend the Highland Games each April in Dunedin.

For its size, Sarasota offers a variety of cultural experiences. Five theatrical companies keep the curtain up in season at a number of theaters, including the Van Wezel Performing Arts Hall, offering pop and jazz concerts as well as children's programs and dance performances. Sarasota also has its own ballet company, an opera company, symphony orchestra, and symphonic band. But John Ringling made sure the best of Sarasota exists at the John and Mable Ringling Museum of Art complex, the city's top attraction.

The ever-growing City of Tampa doesn't take a back seat to any one. With a first-class opera and orchestra, it also has two theatrical companies and three performing-arts venues, including the Tampa Bay Performing Arts Center, Ruth Eckerd Hall, and the Mahaffey Theater.

Jacksonville, Florida's largest city, offers a cultural calendar to match. Drawing some of the top names in the arts, it boasts three theatrical companies, including the Alhambra Dinner Theater, which join the Jacksonville Symphony with its impressive docket of fifty concerts per year. Two top art museums—the Cummer Gallery of Art and the Jacksonville Art Museum—boast collections of traditional, pre-Columbian, Asian, and contemporary art, while the Museum of Science and History will keep your kids happy with its hands-on exhibits.

## City Tours and Sightseeing

While you'll probably rent a car and sightsee on your own, you can also take Grayline Bus Tours in Tampa, Miami, and Fort Lauderdale. Tours run one-and-a-half to five hours and cost $15 to $25 per person. For instance, in the Tampa area, you can take the longer city tours of Tampa or Saint Petersburg/Clearwater or the shorter Ghost Tour of Saint Petersburg.

In Saint Augustine, you have a choice of three ways to see the Old Town: sightseeing trains, open-air trolley tours, or carriage tours. The first two offer stop-off privileges at major attractions, as well as a narrated lecture en route. The third is a little more personal, taking your family on a horse-and-buggy ride through Old Town.

Key West likewise has its own version of these tours—the Old Town Trolley and Conch Trains. Each wends its way through Key West's neighborhoods as guides point out interesting historical sights. Miami also offers you "the Magic City Tour" by Old Town Trolley, a great way to get to know its neighborhoods.

Other cities, like Jacksonville, offer river cruises. These are a great way to enjoy the city from a different angle. As you glide under Jacksonville's bridges, mirrored office buildings gleam in the sun. A variation on this is the water taxi tour of Fort Lauderdale. Water taxis go anywhere within the Intracoastal Waterway, enabling you to see incredible mansions and other sights. You can hop off and on as you go, enjoying the watery view as you travel.

## Shopping

Coastal Florida isn't all T-shirt and beach souvenir shops. You'll find sophisticated shopping in the larger cities like Miami, Tampa, and Jacksonville. Farther south and along the central west coast, you'll discover a myriad of shops selling every kind of shell imaginable, as well as items made from them.

The diversity of goods for sale will astound you. While a $10 T-shirt from Daytona Beach may satisfy some, others will want to spend several thousand dollars on fine jewelry in shops along Worth Avenue in Palm Beach. And though you may not feel the need to be so extravagant, you'll want to pick up something that reminds you of Coastal Florida—a poster, a collectible, a painting or sculpture.

# R&R

If you just need some rest and relaxation, then Coastal Florida is the place for you. Simply being there and adjusting to the slower pace of life may be enough to calm your frazzled nerves. But if you want to really relax, you'll need to spend some time lying under a palm tree on a quiet beach or letting all your muscles relax in one of South Florida's new spas.

### Beaches

If you're a beach lover, you'll love Coastal Florida, especially the beaches around Saint Petersburg on the west coast and Fort Walton Beach in the Panhandle. The state abounds with fine beaches spread out along its miles of Atlantic and Gulf coastlines.

The white powder beaches of the Gulf attract thousands of people each year. Though resorts line many of them, there are some like Captiva Island that offer not only quiet seclusion but also spectacular shell collecting. Unexplored coves and quiet lagoons dot the shoreline, but you may have to search for them as development is growing at a frenetic pace.

Rainy season begins in late May and lasts until October, and between June and October, tropical storms and hurricanes occasionally hit Florida's beaches. Though you can enjoy Florida's beaches along the Gulf all year, except in the Panhandle where the temperature gets too cool to swim, the temperature of the Atlantic Ocean drops the farther north you are, and it can get quite choppy and dangerous at times.

## ≡FAST FACT

While the beaches along the Gulf of Mexico are soft and white, those along the Atlantic Ocean are more tan in color. Unlike the Gulf beaches, those along the eastern shoreline have strong lateral currents and undertows, so heeding warnings and beach flags is essential.

Though all Florida beaches are public, getting to them may be another matter. Beach access is often limited by luxury hotels that make it seem as if the beach is all theirs. If you can get to the waterline on the beach, you can swim there. If you want privacy, there are plenty of secluded beaches on barrier islands up and down Florida's coasts.

But all of Coastal Florida's beaches offer something different. The following list will help you find the best for your interests:

**Bird watching:** Shell Key off Saint Petersburg Beach
**Horseback riding:** Amelia Island, north of Jacksonville
**Kids:** Siesta Public Beach in Sarasota
**Sharks Teeth:** Venice Beach, below Sarasota
**Shelling:** Sanibel Island, off the coast of Fort Myers
**Snorkeling:** Dry Tortugas, off Key West
**Surfing:** Sebastian Inlet State Park, south of Melbourne Beach
**Tropical sands:** Bahia Honda State Park in the Lower Florida Keys

### Spas

Interest in fitness is on the rise around the world, and Coastal Florida is no exception. Ever since the 1880s when the rich discovered Florida's mineral springs, visitors have been flocking to them. Most are inland, but newer European spas operate at resorts closer to shore. Some of the top spas in Coastal Florida include:

- **Avanyu Spa at Cheeca Lodge & Spa:** Islamorada, Florida Keys. If you spend too much time in the sun, try the Soothing Sunburn Facial or Body Treatment, designed to cool your skin and replace needed moisture. (✆Toll-free 800-327-2888, ✐*www.cheeca.com*)
- **Eden Roc Renaissance Resort and Spa:** Miami Beach. This legendary spa offers chakra-clearing Reiki treatment and a Lavender Waves Aromatherapy Massage. (✆Toll-free 800-327-8337, ✐*www.edenrocresort.com*)
- **PGA National Resort & Spa:** Palm Beach Gardens. A spa famous for its Waters of the World mineral pools. (✆800-633-9150, ✐*www.pgaresort.com*)
- **Stillwater Spa, Hyatt Regency Coconut Point Resort:** Bonita Springs. Experience Watsu Freedom, a transcendent eighty-minute Japanese stretching massage given in a pool of warm water. (✆239-444-1234, ✐*www.spahyatt.com*)
- **Sanibel Harbour Resort & Spa:** Fort Myers. Receive a holistic, total-body experience with the Betar (Bio Energetic Transduction Aided Resonance) Sound Bed, a geodesic-domed platform that surrounds you with soothing music and aromas. (✆Toll-free 800-767-7777, ✐*www .sanibel-resort.com*)
- **The Doral Golf Resort and Spa:** Miami. A "your-wish-is-our-command" spa to lose yourself in for a day or more. (✆Toll-free 800-71-DORAL, ✐*www.doralresort.com*)
- **The Pier House Resort and Caribbean Spa:** Key West. This spa offers the Caribbean Coma, a soothing treatment to neutralize the effects of all-night partying. (✆Toll-free 800-327-8340, ✐*www.pierhouse.com*)
- **The Ritz-Carlton Spa:** Naples. Between a rose garden and the Gulf, this spa specializes in a Meranthus Ocean

Synergy Progression, a mineral-rich skin treatment, plus a Spa Concierge. (☎239-514-6100, ✎*www.ritzcarlton.com*)

- **The Don CeSar Beach Resort and Spa:** Saint Pete Beach. The spa specializes in thalassotherapy treatments, using products of the sea. (☎Toll-free 800-282-1116, ✎*www .doncesar.com*)

Today, the word "spa" conjures up a wide range of health and beauty options offered by ultradeluxe resorts, including facials and massages, body wraps with herbs and mineral salts, yoga, tai chi, reflexology sessions, as well as beauty treatments like hair styling, nail care, sauna, and daily personalized exercise sessions.

 **JUST FOR PARENTS**

A good way to find the spa that matches your interests is to look in *The Spa Finder*, an international guide published by Frank van Putten. The guide, in book and Web form, offers comprehensive listings of day and stay spas. (☎Toll-free 800-255-7727, ✎*www.spafinder.com*)

Unfortunately, spas are becoming almost as prolific as golf courses in southeast Florida, each one boasting that it offers the best in therapies. And while they may soothe Mom and Pop for a few hours, their effects are relatively short-lived—and they do little for kids on a family vacation.

# CHAPTER 7

# Miami

MIAMI IS, BY FAR, Florida's most exciting city, though not as kid-friendly as some other Coastal Florida destinations. It's a stunning and beautiful place, set beside the blue waters of Biscayne Bay, its roads lined by lush tropical foliage, its buildings washed by intense sunlight, its air filled with the scent of jasmine. At the same time, it's a city with a contemporary beat—albeit a salsa one—and a key gateway for U.S.–Latin American trade. Ultramodern skyscrapers designed by I. M. Pei and Philip Johnson stand proudly alongside Florentine Renaissance and art deco buildings. This once sleepy southern town is now a busy international commerce center.

## Getting to Know Miami

Sprawling across 2,054 square miles, Miami is a huge and cosmopolitan metropolis. Greater Miami is composed of twenty-seven municipalities within Metropolitan Dade County.

In 1890, it was a swampy outpost where 1,000 mosquito-tormented settlers barely survived from hurricane to hurricane. To reach it, they had to go by boat around a trading post and a couple of coconut plantations or on foot along the beach from the north. The arrival of Henry Flagler's railroad in 1896 connected Miami with the rest of the country, resulting in a real estate boom in the 1920s that saw entire communities appear overnight.

In 1959, thousands of Cubans fleeing Fidel Castro's communist regime began arriving. Over the years, they changed Miami's demographics until the city was not only half Hispanic but more like a South American capital than a city in the United States. The 1960s and 1970s brought decline, followed by the Liberty City racial riot of 1980, which severely damaged the city's tourist industry.

## ≡FAST FACT

Television's *Miami Vice*, an offbeat cop show less about crime than designer clothes and tropical landscapes, had much to do with Miami's renewal. The show filled viewers' minds with images of Miami that, in reality, didn't quite exist. While Miami actually had a horrendous crime rate, the show forced it to improve this and its visual image to uphold visitors' perceptions.

Today, Miami enjoys a surge of optimism and affluence, thanks in part to the Hispanic immigration of the last several decades. Predominantly Spanish-speaking downtown businesses have turned Miami's beat around and given the city a new image.

## Getting Around Miami

Designed for driving, Miami is laid out on a grid with four quadrants—northeast, northwest, southeast, and southwest—all of which meet at Miami Avenue and Flagler Street. The first separates east from west, while the second separates north from south. Avenues run north-south, and streets run east-west. Traffic can be heavy at times, but Miami's expressways will get you from one area to another quickly. Drive only on the streets and avenues to get to your local destination, since traffic often clogs them, especially during rush hours from 7 to 9 A.M. and 4 to 6 P.M.

The Metrorail, a futuristic train that glides over a 21-mile elevated track, runs trains every seven to fifteen minutes from 5:30 A.M. to midnight between downtown Miami north to Hialeah and south along Interstate 95 to Dadeland, including stops at Vizcaya, Coconut Grove, and Coral Gables. A single journey costs $1.50 for adults, 75 cents for kids. Avoid it during rush hours. On weekends it stops at 6:30 P.M.

The free Metromover, an automated driverless monorail system employing rubber-tired cars, circles downtown Miami on twin elevated concrete loops and several branches during the day. Trains operate weekdays every ninety seconds from 6:30 A.M. to midnight. On weekends they operate from 8:30 A.M. Transfers to Metromover from Metrorail are free, but those from Metromover to Metrorail cost 75 cents. (305-638-6700)

Taxis are plentiful but expensive. One will stop if you wave it down, but it's more common to call one from Metro Taxi (305-888-8888) or Miami-Dade Yellow Cab (305-633-0503 or 305-444-4444).

### Best Time to Go

The best months for sun and warmth in Miami are November, April, and May. Between December and March, average daytime temperatures range from 60° to 80°. It often rains in January, however, and cold fronts occasionally arrive, bringing with them chilly days and near-freezing nights. Summer can be extremely hot, with rain every afternoon.

### Cautions and Safety Concerns

Though some sections are still extremely dangerous, Miami has cleaned itself up considerably. The city still has its share of crime, violence, and drug trafficking, but it's not as bad as Hollywood movies and television shows make it seem. Nevertheless, it pays to take precautions. Be aware of your valuables at all times and don't walk side streets at night.

# Family-Oriented Resorts and Hotels

You'll find mostly chain hotels in downtown Miami. And while Coral Gables may be appealing, it's expensive, and the stylish high-rise hotels of Coconut Grove are even more so.

### InterContinental Miami

Reservations: ☏Toll-free 877-314-2424

✍*www.icmiamihotel.com*

A 639-room luxury hotel located next to the Bayside Marketplace and Bayfront Park, offering contemporary ambiance, an outdoor pool, lounge, health and fitness center, restaurants, and children's rates.

### River Park Hotel and Suites

Reservations: ☏305-374-5100

This 135-suite hotel, located next to the Miami River, has small kitchens in each suite, a restaurant, fitness center with whirlpool, pool, valet parking, and special rates for kids.

### Holiday Inn Marina Park Port of Miami

Reservations: ☏Toll-free 800-356-3584

✍*www.holidayinn.com*

A 200-room hotel with an unbeatable location across from the Bayside Marketplace, with tropically furnished rooms, restaurant, bar, room service, car rental, complimentary morning newspaper, free parking, fitness center, and child care.

### Days Inn Civic Center

Reservations: ☏305-324-0200,

✍*www.daysinn.com*

This central downtown hotel has 210 comfortable rooms, each with small kitchen and balcony with riverfront water view, plus a restaurant and bar, room service, car rental, complimentary morning newspaper, parking garage, fitness center, complimentary breakfast, pool, and children's rates.

# Things to Do

Start your exploration of Miami downtown. Flagler Street cuts through downtown Miami. Taxis and Cuban street vendors vie for territory, creating the loudest, busiest strip in the city. Begin your exploration at its eastern end by visiting the Metro-Dade Cultural Center, a post-modern Mediterranean-style piazza designed by noted architect Philip Johnson. Three buildings—the Historical Museum of Florida, the Miami Art Museum, and the Main Public Library—all face the plaza.

 **TRAVEL TIP**

There are now two awesome ways to see Miami—by taking a sixty-minute air tour in a single-engine airplane for $135 per person (kids same price) with Miami Flightseeing (✑www.miamiflightseeing.com) or by going up in the new Miami Skylift, a helium balloon that will take up to thirty passengers 400 feet into the air (☎305-444-0422, ✑www.miamiskylift.com).

The Historical Museum of Southern Florida offers two floors of exhibits showcasing South Florida history, from the artifacts and photographs of the Seminoles to the early white settlers and the city's maritime history and antique maps. You can even sit in an old trolley, wearing a period costume, or relax in a rocking chair on the front porch of a "Cracker" home. Admission is $5 per adult, $2 per child (305-375-1492). Next door to the history museum stands the Miami Art Museum, with an ever-growing permanent collection of twentieth-century art (305-375-3000). Admission is $5.00 per adult, $2.50 per child, with Sundays free. (Both open Tuesday through Friday 10 A.M.–5 P.M., weekends noon–5 P.M.)

## For the Kids

Downtown Miami lacks attractions for younger children. The closest to downtown is the Children's Museum on Watson Island. To see others, you have to drive south to the Monkey Jungle, Parrot Jungle, Metro Zoo, and the Gold Coast Railroad Museum.

The Miami Children's Museum encourages younger children to learn, imagine, and create while playing together. The contemporary facility includes 56,500 square feet of space with twelve galleries, offering hundreds of interactive exhibits, including a two-story sand castle that kids can climb through, a safety zone where they can see what it's like to be a policeman and fireman, a television studio where they can become a news anchor or camera operator, a walk-though piggy bank where they learn how to save, and lots more. There's also a 900-gallon marine tank and a rock-climbing wall. (Open daily from 10 A.M.–6 P.M., 305-373-5437, *www.miamichildrensmuseum.org*)

# RAINY DAY FUN

When an afternoon shower hits, take the kids roller skating. Miami kids love to roller-skate at Hialeah Roller Rink (☎305-887-9812) and Tropical Roller Skating Center (☎305-667-1149). If it gets too hot for them, take them ice skating at the Polar Palace (☎305-634-3333).

At the Monkey Jungle, covered walkways will keep you "caged" as you walk through a steamy hammock where up to 400 primates representing thirty species, including baboons, gibbons, spider monkeys, orangutans, and lemurs, wander and swing from trees. You can see South American monkeys in their own Amazonian rain forest. Monkey shows start at 10 A.M. and run every forty-five minutes. Admission is $8.75. (Open daily 9:30 A.M.–5:00 P.M., 305-235-1611, *www .monkeyjungle.com*)

Parrot Jungle Island, one of Miami's oldest and most popular tourist attractions, has more than 1,100 exotic birds—parrots, parakeets, cockatoos, and macaws of rainbow plumage squawking loudly as they fly through a giant aviary, eat from your hand, ride bicycles, and pose for photographs. To get the birds' attention, your kids will need seeds, which you can buy from gumball machines. While you're there, you can also watch baby birds in training. Parrot Jungle has a natural hammock of subtropical flowering trees and plants where you can stroll among ferns, orchids, bald cypress trees, and massive live oaks. Also, be sure to see the cactus garden and Flamingo Lake, with its seventy-five Caribbean flamingos. Admission is $27.95 per adult, $22.95 per child. (Open daily 10 A.M.–6 P.M., 305-400-7000)

The best place for kids to view wildlife is the Metro Zoo, a 290-acre zoological park where animals roam free on islands designed to resemble their natural habitats and surrounded by moats. Since its opening in 1981, Metro Zoo has grown into one of the largest zoos in the country. Besides its unique open compounds, it features a replica of a Malayan village where your children can observe animals close up from viewing "caves." In its Wings of Asia exhibit, over 300 exotic birds from Southeast Asia fly, chirp, and hop about a spacious rain forest beneath a protective net. But its snow-white Bengal tigers and cuddly koala bears are its prize displays. The zoo also features 3 miles of walkways, a monorail with four stations, a lakefront restaurant, observation deck, and an amphitheater where you can see a wildlife show daily at noon, 2, and 4:30 P.M. You can also feed pelicans at 10:30 A.M. and 4:30 P.M. for $1, the cost of a cup of fish. Admission is $11.50 for adults and $6.75 for children 12 and under. (Open daily 9:30 A.M.–5:30 P.M., 305-251-0400, *www.miamimetrozoo.com*)

Next door stands the Gold Coast Railroad Museum, one of the premier railroad museums in Florida and one of the best of its type in the country. Rows of historic trains stand waiting for you to climb aboard for a closer look, including the ornate Ferdinand Magellan car, built for President Franklin Roosevelt, and the Florida East Coast Railway locomotive #153, which pulled the rescue train out of Marathon, Florida, after the 1935 hurricane. You can also ride for twenty minutes in the cab of a diesel locomotive for $11 per person, or you can ride in an air-conditioned coach around the grounds for

$5.50. You can even take your toddlers for a ride on the Edwin Link Children's Railroad for $2.25 per person at 1 and 3 P.M. All rides are held on weekends only. Admission is $5. (Open daily 10 A.M.–4 P.M., 305-253-0063)

The Museum of Science and Space Transit Planetarium in Coconut Grove is another science playland for kids, with more than 150 hands-on sound, gravity, and electricity exhibits. A wildlife center houses native Florida snakes, turtles and tortoises, birds of prey, and large wading birds. And its planetarium, where your kids can "walk on Mars," presents multimedia astronomy and laser shows. Admission is $19.95 per adult, $12.95 per child. (Open daily 10 A.M.–6 P.M., 305-854-2222)

## Little Havana

The first Cubans to come to Miami settled a few miles west of downtown in a predominantly Jewish neighborhood called Riverside. As more and more arrived, and the area's Jewish residents moved to the suburbs, and Riverside became Little Havana, a 3.5-square-mile area of Cuban *loncherias* (lunch counters), *fruterias* (fruit stands), *zapaterias* (shoe stores), art galleries, flower shops, and flamenco bars. Here, corner *bodegas* offer exotic delicacies while music shops blare mambo, merengue, salsa, and tango rhythms into the streets. Though it's still one of the most interesting Miami neighborhoods, it's less Cuban now than it used to be since immigrants from other Latin American countries began settling here.

Between December 1965 and June 1972, over a quarter of a million Cubans left the island taken over by Fidel Castro. Their impact on the city over the last four decades is apparent everywhere you look because, unlike most Hispanic immigrants to the United States, Miami's first Cubans were the affluent elite of their society. Today, their offspring have established themselves in positions of power in the city.

There aren't many attractions for you to see in Little Havana. Visiting it is more about soaking up the atmosphere. In fact, you need only stroll along the neighborhood's main drag, Southwest Eighth Street—

or as it's known locally, Calle Ocho—to feel the pulse of Latin life as people pause at streetside counters to down a quick cup of café Cubano. As you walk, you'll smell the aromas of cigars being rolled and bread being baked, you'll see statues of Catholic saints staring blankly ahead from the windows of religious shops, and you'll hear a cacophony of salsa mixed with mambo mixed with merengue that is almost enough to drive you crazy.

## ≡FAST FACT

Florida has also been a place of refuge for Cuba's activists, who came to the United States to campaign and raise funds. The first was José Martí, who in the 1890s solicited cigar workers in Tampa for money to buy illegal weapons. And there is Fidel Castro himself, who came to Florida in the early 1950s to gather support for his revolutionist movement.

You'll discover that Calle Ocho is one long, noisy thoroughfare, adorned with sparkling neon lights and Spanish-style street lamps. The best way to take it all in is to drive down it once, pick out the sections you find the most interesting, then park your car and stroll. Although Miami's Anglo and Hispanic cultures coexist elsewhere in the city, in Little Havana you're immersed in Latin culture. And while Spanish is the language of choice, most restaurants and shops have bilingual personnel.

About the only attraction worth visiting is the free Museum of Cuban Arts and Culture, which houses a permanent collection of 200 or so paintings reflecting the main historical trends in Cuban art. (Open Tuesday through Friday, 10 A.M.–3 P.M.)

To see a slice of Latin life, stop at Antonio Maceo Park on Calle Ocho at Fourteenth Avenue. Here, elderly Cuban men clad in *guayaberas*, or loose-fitting pleated shirts worn outside the pants, gather daily to play chess and dominoes.

## 🧳 TRAVEL TIP

Learn about Miami's Hispanic heritage and folklore on a tour with Miami-Cuba USA and Hispanic Florida Tours aboard the Azucar ("Sugar") Trolley as it jams with Cuban and salsa rhythms. (📞305-491-5884, ✍www.miamicubausa.com)

### Festivals and Seasonal Events

And there is always a festival of art, music, and culture going on, from Carnaval Miami to Coconut Grove's Arts Festival. Each offers a chance to sample traditional foods, see unique art, and hear exotic music.

**Carnaval Miami:** As the nation's largest Hispanic celebration and world's largest block party, this festival attracts over one million people each year for its nine days of festivities, including a parade, fireworks display, plenty of dancing, and top Latin entertainment. (📞305-644-8888, ✍*www.carnaval-miami.com*)

**Coconut Grove Art Festival:** Held in mid-February, it's Florida's largest art show. (📞305-447-0401)

# Exploring

The best way to see Greater Miami is by car. Though you'll find the points of interest spread out, Miami has an extensive system of highways and expressways that makes them easy to reach.

Immediately south of Little Havana lie the broad boulevards of wealthy Coral Gables, and south of downtown Miami lies trendy Coconut Grove.

## Coral Gables

Coral Gables, the dream-come-true city of poet George Merrick, is Miami's prestigious planned community. Elegant gates to his city still stand in testament to Merrick's grand scheme to build "a place where castles in Spain are made real."

He cleared citrus groves, laid streets and sidewalks, and built Mediterranean-style buildings, calling it his "Miami Riviera." In his extensive promotions, he boasted that "those who visited Coral Gables would find endless golden sunlight and bronzed people." He laid out 12 square miles of broad boulevards and leafy streets lined with elegant Spanish and Italian homes and commercial structures.

Merrick differed from his fellow real estate developers in that, instead of building fast and cheap to make a quick fortune, he designed his community to last. He was more of an artist and creator than a developer, and was in love with Mediterranean Europe. To achieve his goal, he enlisted the expertise of architect Phineas Paist and artist Denman Fink, Merrick's uncle, to plan the plazas, fountains, and carefully aged stucco-fronted buildings that made up his Mediterranean town. The city is a labyrinth of winding streets that's often difficult to navigate.

## ≡FAST FACT

As soon as workers paved the first streets and completed the first buildings, Coral Gables land started selling overnight. In five years beginning in 1921, Merrick took in $150 million, a third of which he used to fund the biggest promotional campaign ever known. And though Coral Gables developed quickly, the Florida real estate boom ended just as fast as it began, and Merrick went bust.

Merrick planned eight grand entrances to his city, so visitors would know it was someplace special. He completed only four by the time he went bankrupt. Entering Coral Cables through the Douglas Entrance on Northwest Twenty-second Street, Merrick's most ambitious, you'll travel along a two-block commercial strip known as the Miracle Mile, the centerpiece of his dream city's business district. Nearby along Coral Way stands the Coral Gables House, Merrick's childhood home. In 1899, when George was twelve, his family arrived here from New England to operate a 160-acre fruit and vegetable farm, which became so successful that his parents replaced the farm's original frame house with an elegant coral-rock home with gabled windows in 1907. It was this house, in which he lived until 1916, that inspired Merrick to create the name of his new city. You must take the forty-five-minute guided tour to see it. Admission is $5 per adult, $1 per child. (Open Sunday and Wednesday 1–4 P.M., 305-460-5361, *www.coralgables.com*)

Once you're in "the Gables," as locals call it, you'll spot the stately spire of the Biltmore Hotel on Anastasia Avenue, Merrick's crowning achievement. He promoted it as "the last word in the evolution of civilization." Everything about the place was pretentious, from its 25-foot-high fresco-coated walls to its vaulted ceilings, imported marble and tile, immense fireplaces, and custom-made carpets. To mark its opening in January 1926, Merrick chartered special trains to bring in his guests. They dined on pheasant and trout and had the run of the casino. During their stay, they could play polo, go fox hunting, or swim in the country's biggest pool under the watchful eye of Johnny Weissmuller, the hotel's first swimming instructor and later Olympic champion and the first to play Tarzan on the big screen. Today, it once again stands as a pinnacle of high society as a superdeluxe resort boasting the largest swimming pool in the country. (Toll-free 800-727-1926, *www.biltmorehotel.com*)

The Venetian Pool was another of Merrick's inspired ideas. In 1924, with the help of Paist and Denman, he took a limestone quarry pit and created a sprawling lagoon retreat, favored by celebrities such as Esther Williams and William Jennings Bryan. Bordered by a Mediterranean villa, surrounded by palm trees, it was originally called the Venetian Casino. Coral caves, vine-covered loggias, shady porticos, Venetian lampposts, and cascading waterfalls that spill into a free-form lagoon, with coral caves and a palm island, add beauty. (Open weekdays in summer 11:00 a.m.–5:30 P.M., weekends 10:00 A.M.–4:30 P.M., closed Mondays in winter, 305-460-5357, *www.venetianpool.com*)

 **JUST FOR PARENTS**

The Fairchild Tropical Botanical Garden, established in 1938, features 83 acres of rare tropical plants and trees, eleven lakes, a tropical fruit pavilion, and a conservatory with an extensive collection of unusual tropical flora. Take the narrated tram ride around the grounds, departing on the hour from 10 A.M. until 4 P.M., to learn more about them. Admission is $20, $1 extra for the tram. (Open daily 9:30 A.M.– 4:30 P.M., ☎305-667-1651, *www.fairchildgardens.org*)

One place you may want to visit while exploring the Gables is the Lowe Art Museum, which houses a collection of 8,000 pieces of Renaissance and baroque art, including works by Goya and El Greco, Greco-Roman antiquities, Latin American art, American paintings, and Native American baskets and textiles. Admission is $7 for adults, $5 for children. (Open Tuesday, Wednesday, Friday, and Saturday 10 A.M.–5 P.M., Thursday noon–7 P.M., and Sunday noon–5 P.M., 305-284-3535, *www.lowemuseum.org*)

## Coconut Grove

Coconut Grove, known as the Greenwich Village of South Florida, was the area's first winter resort, catering to wealthy winter residents in the late nineteenth century. The Grove, as locals call it, offers a blend of bohemian and chic. Hippies, seeking a laid-back lifestyle in a warm climate, thronged here in the 1960s, followed in the 1990s by jet setters, intellectuals, and Yuppies. And though posh estates exist next to modest frame houses, the Grove has become more upscale and sophisticated, with art galleries and sidewalk cafés where the literati hang out along Main Highway. Stroll along its red-bricked pavement or take an evening rickshaw ride, a truly Grove experience.

Brickell Avenue, Miami's version of New York's Wall Street, was *the* address in 1910s Miami. Grand homes of the rich lined Millionaire's Row, as residents affectionately called it back then. The money remained. Today, the largest group of international banks in the country stretches for half a mile, the sheer-sided glass walls softened only by the sculpture-filled piazzas, fountains, and palm trees. Miami, cashing in on political instability in South and Central America by offering a secure home for Latin American money, became a corporate banking center in the late 1970s.

## ≡FAST FACT

With all of the Grove's new, if not necessarily clean, money came a batch of new ultramodern condominiums a few blocks beyond. These million-dollar, pastel-colored towers include the Atlantis, the most striking building in Miami, whose style is referred to tongue-in-cheek as "beach-blanket Bauhaus." A giant square hole through its middle, revealing a palm tree, a Jacuzzi, and a red-painted spiral staircase, is its focal point.

Coconut Grove's prime attraction is Vizcaya Museum and Gardens, the palatial estate of International Harvester magnate James Deering, perched on the shore of Biscayne Bay. In 1914, he spent nearly $22 million recreating a sixteenth-century Italian villa between Miami and Coconut Grove. It took 1,000 workers—one-tenth of the population of Miami at the time—two years to complete this gargantuan task. Unfortunately, Deering and his designer, Paul Chalfin, had more money than good taste. Deering's eclectic art collection, plus the his idea that the villa should appear to have been inhabited for 400 years, resulted in a mix of baroque, Renaissance, rococo, and neoclassical fixtures and furnishings. It houses a magnificent collection of European antiques, oriental carpets, precious china, and artworks spanning eighteen centuries that will impress you, even if you're not an art lover. Thirty acres of formal gardens with fountains, pools, and statuary, with a Great Stone Barge anchored in front, surround the seventy-room Venetian palazzo. It's a good idea to take one of the guided tours of thirty-four of the rooms and halls, which leave frequently from the entrance loggia, after which you can roam around on your own. It helps to purchase a guidebook for $2 at the ticket booth. Admission is $12 for adults, $5 for children. (Open daily 9:30 A.M.–4:30 P.M., 305-250-9133, *www.vizcayamuseum.org*)

James Deering's half-brother, Charles, himself a wealthy industrialist and amateur botanist, became so enchanted by South Florida's natural beauty that he purchased the town of Cutler, south of Coconut Grove. He demolished all its buildings, except one, to make way for his Charles Deering Estate at Cutler, completed in 1923 and today encompassing a 420-acre park. Deering kept the wooden Richmond Cottage Inn, Cutler's only hotel, to live in while he built the Stone Mansion, with its interior decorated with checkerboard-tile floors, spacious halls, and immense chandeliers. The park, in which the mansion resides, contains pine woods, mangrove forests, and tropical hardwood hammocks. You can take a free one-hour walking tour of the buildings at either 10:30 A.M. or 2:30 P.M. Admission is $7 per adult, $5 per child. (Open daily 10 A.M.–5 P.M., 305-235-1668, *www.deeringestate.org*)

## 📋 TRAVEL TIP

A more exciting way to see the Deering Estate is on a three-hour guided canoe tour, departing at 8:30 A.M. for $25 per adult and $15 per child, which navigates the mangrove-fringed inlets. If you're in town during a full moon, you may want to take a special nighttime canoe trip for $35 per person.

### Extra Special

Supposedly, it took Latvian-born Edward Leedskalnin twenty-eight years to carve his Coral Castle from 1,000 tons of coral using homemade tools. Located in Homestead along the South Dixie Highway, 31 miles south of Miami, the castle is an engineering marvel. It even has a nine-ton gate that swings open easily at the slightest touch, plus solar-heated bathtubs, and a coral "telescope" aimed at the North Star. Leedskalnin built his masterpiece as a tribute to his fiancée, Agnes Scuffs, who had jilted him decades earlier, just hours before their wedding. Take the thirty-minute audio tour to hear all about it. Admission is $9.75. (Open daily Sunday through Thursday 8 A.M.–6 P.M. and to 9 P.M. Friday and Saturday, 305-248-6345, *www.coralcastle.com*)

# By Day

Miami is a major city, and as such, you'll find daytime activities limited to sightseeing, either on land or water. Of course, with it being located on Biscayne Bay, fishing is also an option. And if you're a golfer, you may end up playing continuous rounds at its excellent courses.

### On the Water

To get a comprehensive view of Miami's skyline, you really need to see it from Biscayne Bay. Several companies operate cruises from the marina adjacent to Bayside Marketplace. Captain Jimmy's Fiesta Cruises offers daily sightseeing cruises aboard his 52-foot catamaran (305-371-3033, *www.fiestacruises.com*), and Island Queen Cruises, Inc. offers daily one-and-a-half-hour Millionaire's Row sightseeing boat tours (305-379-5119, *www.islandqueencruises.com*).

The *Heritage of Miami*, a tall ship modeled after an early twentieth-century coastal schooner that traveled between Florida, the Bahamas, and Cuba, also offers cruises around Biscayne Bay. These two-hour cruises, offered several times a day, provide excellent views of Vizcaya, Key Biscayne, and the city skyline (305-442-9697).

With 354 square miles of protected waters, over fifty marinas, and thousands of registered boats, Miami is a boater's wonderland. If you know how to sail, you can rent a 19- to 127-foot sailboat by the hour or for the day from Easy Sailing in the Dinner Key Marina in Coconut Grove (305-858-4001). The marina also offers motorboat and sailing lessons and deep-sea fishing charters.

Miami's waters abound with pompano, dolphinfish, grouper, yellow-fin tuna, and swordfish. To hook one for yourself, sign on to a half- or full-day fishing charter from Bayside Cruises (305-888-3002) or Chuck Smith Charters at Bayside Marketplace (305-378-2332).

## On the Links and on the Courts

Miami has over thirty-five public golf courses where you can test your golfing skills. Greens fees range from about $60 to $90, including cart, plus you can rent clubs for about $45. Some of the best include:

- **Crooked Creek:** Miami, 305-274-8308
- **Golf Club of Miami:** North Miami, 305-821-0111
- **Kendale Lakes:** Miami, 305-279-3130
- **Miami Shores Country Club:** Miami Shores, 305-795-2366
- **Palmetto Golf Course:** Kendall, South Dade County, 305-238-2922
- **The Miami Lakes Golf Club:** Miami Lakes, 305-821-1150

Many Miamians love to play tennis, so you'll find many public centers for racket play. All charge nonresidents a fee. Choose to play at any of the following:

- **Coral Gables Tennis Center:** Coral Gables, 305-460-5360
- **Flamingo Park Capital Bank Tennis Center:** Miami, 305-673-7761
- **Metro-Dade at the International Tennis Center:** Key Biscayne, 305-361-8633

- **Morningside Park:** Miami, ☎305-754-1242
- **Salvadore Park Tennis Center:** Coral Gables, ☎305-460-5333

## Spa Time

Miami has some spectacular European-style spas. You'll find most in deluxe hotels. Take a few hours for yourself and relax while your spouse takes the kids to have some fun. Choosing from any of the following will assure you a first-class—albeit expensive—spa session:

- **Boutique Spa at the Ritz-Carlton Coconut Grove:** Ritz-Carlton Hotel, Coconut Grove, ☎305-644-4684, *www.ritzcarlton.com*
- **Spa Internazionale:** Fisher Island Hotel & Resort, Fisher Island, ☎305-535-6030, *www.fisherisland.com*
- **Spa at Mandarin Oriental:** Mandarin Oriental Hotel, Downtown Miami, ☎305-913-8288, *www.mandarinoriental.com/miami*
- **Willow Stream Spa:** Fairmont Hotel Turnberry Isle, Aventura, ☎305-932-6200, *www.fairmont.com/turnberryisle*

## Shopping

Greater Miami has more than a dozen major shopping malls, plus miles of commercial streets lined with shopping centers and storefronts. You'll find plenty of major department stores, with most malls having at least three.

But if department store prices give you sticker shock, perhaps you'd rather discover bargains in more than thirty factory outlets and discount fashion stores in the Miami Fashion District, located along Fifth Avenue from Twenty-fifth to Twenty-ninth streets. The Miami Free Zone, an international wholesale trade center with products from seventy-five countries, lies five minutes west of Miami International Airport (305-591-4300).

Bayside Marketplace, a huge lively indoor/outdoor complex of shops and restaurants on the waterfront, is as much a shopping as an entertainment experience. The peach-colored shopping mall is a great place to people-watch while being entertained by strolling musicians, magicians, and jugglers. (305-577-3344)

## 📰 TRAVEL TIP

If you're a bargain hunter, you can spend an entire day or more browsing the more than 1,300 vendors at the Opalocka/Hialeah Flea Market, South Florida's largest flea market. Should you get hungry, you can choose between thirteen different restaurants. (Open daily 5 A.M.–7 P.M., ☎305-688-0500)

Every Saturday, vendors of the Coconut Grove Farmers Market set up booths, offering honey, seafood, homegrown tropical fruits and vegetables, macrobiotic foods, plants, and ethnic foods from the Caribbean, the Middle East, and Southeast Asia, in a vacant lot on Margaret Street, west of Southwest Thirty-second Avenue. You'll also find jewelry, crafts, candles, and handmade clothing.

# Dining Out and Nightlife

There are thousands of restaurants in Greater Miami ranging from expensive gourmet to inexpensive sidewalk cafés. Considering the influence of Hispanic culture, it's no wonder that socializing centers around eating out, especially long, late dinners. It's wise to make reservations, especially at spots popular with locals. You'll find concentrations of the best eateries in Little Havana and Coconut Grove.

If you love Cuban cuisine, you'll find plenty of choices at family-owned restaurants throughout Little Havana. For lunch, try a hot-pressed Cuban sandwich—honey-baked ham, pork, Gruyère cheese, pickles, and butter on crispy Cuban bread—and for dinner, *moros y cristianos* (black beans and rice), *masas de puerco* (fried pork), *arroz con pollo* (chicken and rice), and *paella* (seafood with seasoned rice). For dessert, choose flan (creamy custard with a caramelized crust), mango ice cream, or a *churro* (a long spiral of deep-fried sweet dough) accompanied by a café Cubano. Here are a few restaurants to get you started:

**Captain's Tavern:** Ultrafresh seafood, including fresh clams, oysters, and native fish, served with generous portions of salad. Look for the fish of the day posted on the blackboard. (9621 South Dixie Highway, ✆305-666-5979)

**La Tasca:** This Cuban-Spanish restaurant in Little Havana serves hearty servings of roast chicken, pork, and fish stews, accompanied by mounds of rice with black bean sauce. There's also a good Spanish wine list. (2741 West Flagler Street, ✆305-642-3762)

**Malaga:** This Little Havana courtyard restaurant serves some of Miami's best Cuban cuisine at quaint wooden tables grouped around a mass of trees and vines. Pot roast simmered in sausages, spicy fried veal and pork, and a great paella are the specialties. (740 Southwest Eighth Street, ✆305-858-4224)

**S & S Diner:** A Miami institution just north of downtown features down-home Southern cooking, plus all the regular dinner entrées—meat loaf, chopped steak and onions, roast pork, and roast turkey. (1757 Northeast Second Avenue, ✆305-373-4291)

**Shorty's Bar-B-Q:** A family favorite that can't be beat for barbecued ribs, chicken, and fresh corn on the cob, served at long tables; there's also a kids' menu. (9200 South Dixie Highway, ✆305-665-5732)

Miami nightlife begins around 9 P.M. and continues until dawn. Rhythm-and-blues bands provide entertainment at one of the city's best bars, Tobacco Road, which began as a speakeasy and supposedly has a secret closet where the owner stashed illegal liquor (305-374-1198).

The Gusman Center for the Performing Arts hosts top names in classical and contemporary music and dance from October to June. This former vaudeville theater, designed to resemble a Moorish palace, has towers, turrets, ornately decorated columns, and a crescent moon shining from a star-studded ceiling (305-372-0925).

 **TRAVEL TIP**

During the busy winter season, Miami's calendar fills with cultural events, gallery exhibits, concerts, lectures, and dance and theater performances. The *Miami Herald* publishes information on the performing arts every Friday in its Weekend section. You can also find information in *Miami Today* and the *New Times*, both free weekly newspapers, as well as in the Greater Miami Calendar of Events (☎305-375-4634).

Miami also offers opportunities to see professional theater at the Coconut Grove Playhouse (305-442-4000). There's also the Miami City Ballet (305-532-4880), the New World Symphony (305-673-3331), and the Greater Miami Opera (305-854-7890).

And Bayside Marketplace offers reggae, jazz, and rhythm-and-blues bands on the waterfront stage most evenings. Or if you feel like laughing, check out the Improv Comedy Club and Restaurant (954-342-2898). Calle Ocho's Cuban restaurants come alive after dark as flamenco dancers, attired in red satin and lace, swirl and pound their feet onstage in age-old Spanish dances.

# CHAPTER 8

# Miami Beach

OFTEN CALLED THE AMERICAN RIVIERA, Miami Beach, a string of seventeen natural and artificial islands, is a landscape of hotels, palm trees, golf courses, and tennis courts where you can rub elbows with models and movie stars. Immortalized in the 1950s when Hollywood starlets would sun themselves on the beaches of luxury hotels, it has gained new life with the restoration of 1930s art deco buildings along South Beach and 1950s hotels on Central Beach, as well as being the setting for numerous television shows and movies. Rising like a phoenix, it has once again become a playground for the famous and the beautiful.

## Getting to Know Miami Beach

Miami Beach lies on a narrow 12-mile-long stretch of barrier islands nestled between the Atlantic Ocean and Biscayne Bay, 3 miles from Miami. Originally a mangrove wilderness, it's now a famous resort that has had more facelifts than most movie stars.

Today, Miami Beach is divided into three distinct areas, each catering to a different type of tourist. Along South Beach, at the extreme southern end, rows of restyled art deco buildings, containing avant-garde art galleries and progressive clubs, have become the chic gathering places for artists, writers, and other creative types. Hollywood starlets headed north to Central Miami Beach in the 1950s, creating Miami Beach's glamorous image that still lives on today. Farther on, North Miami Beach splits into several distinct communities favored by European package tourists.

## Getting Around Miami Beach

Six causeways cross Biscayne Bay between Miami and Miami Beach. Each offers striking views of the city, especially at night when the illuminated downtown buildings twinkle over the bay's dark waters. The gleaming Venetian Causeway crosses six islands—San Marino Island, Dilido Island, Biscayne Island, San Marco Island, Belle Isle, and Rivo Alto Island, each covered with plush residential areas. The northern causeways, each with a different sumptuous view, are Julia Tuttle, North Bay, Sunny Isles, and Lehman. And to the south, the Rickenbacker Causeway leads to the smaller, less developed Virginia Key and larger Key Biscayne.

 **TRAVEL TIP**

Parking can be expensive in South Beach, so the city sells a $25 parking pass good at its six garages and all parking meters—$1 per hour (in quarters) at meters and $1 an hour with a maximum of 24 hours in garages—plus on the South Beach Local Shuttle, which makes stops every ten minutes from 7:45 A.M. to 1:00 A.M. on a loop around South Beach. (✆305-673-7275).

Over nineteen of the sixty-three Miami–Dade County Metrobus routes run between Miami Beach and downtown Miami, as well as the Metrozoo and the Seaquarium. You'll pay $1.25 each way for an adult and 60 cents per child ages 6 to 12, plus 25 cents for transfers. Buses operate from 4:30 A.M. to 2:13 A.M. (305-770-3131)

### Best Time to Go

With its subtropical climate, where the temperature hovers between 70° and 80° most of the time, Miami Beach is good to visit all year long, except perhaps in mid-summer when the temperatures on some days can reach 90°. And with those higher temperatures come afternoon showers to cool things off.

### Cautions and Safety Concerns

The biggest precaution you need to take in Miami Beach is over-exposure to the sun. You're in the tropics here, so wearing sunblock any time you go out in the sun, even for a walk, is absolutely necessary. You should only spend twenty minutes in the sun the first day, thirty the next, fifty the next, and an hour the next. Besides wearing a shirt and hat, protect your lips with a lip balm. Unfortunately, most people don't budget enough time into their vacation to build up their sun exposure and get severely burned in the process.

## ≡FAST FACT

How much time you spend in the sun determines the color of your tan, but location is also important. You'll seriously burn while over open salt water when boating or fishing. Reflected rays burn you even if you're deeply tanned. You'll also burn faster sunbathing on a white beach by the ocean.

Though crime due to drugs has been on the upswing more in Miami than Miami Beach, it's still a good idea to stick to the main streets and be aware of your valuables at all times.

# Family-Oriented Resorts and Hotels

High-rise hotels and condominiums line Miami Beach's central shore. And though many have been made over in recent years, they still aren't what they used to be. However, prices remain high, except during the summer, when temperatures soar. Prices of refurbished art deco hotels remain constant all year due to their popularity.

### Cardozo Hotel

Reservations: ☎Toll-free 800-872-6500

The first art deco hotel to be brought back to life and one of the chicest, with its high gloss and modern decor, U-shaped design that offers the most ocean views of any on the strip, and rooms decorated in deco blue and shiny lacquer furniture, plus a lobby bar/café.

### Days Inn Oceanside

Reservations: ☎Toll-free 800-356-3017

Located on Collins Avenue, this ten-story hotel offers the best ocean views at moderate prices. It features a pink-and-silver lobby and guest rooms that sparkle, plus an Olympic swimming pool and restaurant.

### Fontainebleau Hilton Resort & Towers

Reservations: ☎Toll-free 800-548-8886

The queen of Miami Beach hotels once again holds court along Ocean Drive. It has 1,206 rooms in three curving, fourteen-story buildings surrounding connecting pools with rushing water, hidden rocky caves, and palm tree islands. The hotel features an opulent lobby with floor-to-ceiling windows, marble staircases, and huge crystal chandeliers, plus thirteen restaurants, four bars, and rooms furnished in French provincial style. Excellent service demands high prices.

### Traymore Hotel

Reservations: ☎Toll-free 800-445-1512

Located in Central Miami Beach along Collins Avenue, this eight-story, restored deco-style hotel features a cream-colored facade with rows of pink ledges, shiny terrazzo floors, and vast Greek columns in its lobby; Formica furnishings and pastel decor in its modern rooms;

and a clay-tiled loggia surrounding a Mediterranean-style swimming pool and bar.

### Apartment and Condo Rentals

If you're planning to stay in Miami Beach for longer than a few days, you may want to consider renting an apartment or condominium with full kitchen from either Florida Sunbreak (Toll-free 800-786-2732) or Miami Habitat (Toll-free 800-385-4644).

# Things to Do

For a glimpse into Miami Beach life in the 1930s, stroll the streets of the Art Deco District, eighty square blocks, bordered by the Atlantic Ocean, Lenox Court, and Sixth and Twenty-third streets, overflowing with more than 800 historic buildings. As the most concentrated historic district in the United States, it brings to life the nostalgic era of the 1930s and 1940s. Originally, these buildings glowed a gleaming white, but the updates done to them have used a palette of cake-icing pastels more influenced by *Miami Vice* than the 1930s. Today, this area of chic hotels and breezy alfresco cafés has become known as South Beach, or as the locals fondly call it, SoBe. Here, you can sip an espresso or eat a frozen yogurt while watching the passing parade of sexy models and musclemen while the sea breeze carries calypso and reggae melodies from Lummus Park across Ocean Drive.

 **TRAVEL TIP**

Take the $20-per-adult, ninety-minute guided walking tour through the Art Deco District, sponsored by the Miami Design and Preservation League, departing at 10:30 A.M. on Wednesdays, Fridays, Saturdays, and Sundays and 6:30 P.M. on Thursdays, from the Art Deco Welcome Center at Ocean Drive and Tenth Street. Or take the self-guided audio tour for $15 per adult, $10 per child. (☎305-672-2014)

Miami Beach architects first began to employ Streamline Moderne design features in their designs in 1930s. Their new style, Tropical Art Deco, featured streamlined curves, porthole windows, balconies stretched to look like luxury liner sundecks, and ship's funnels on rooftops to make the buildings resemble the ocean liners people wanted to travel on but couldn't afford. Window "eyebrows" shaded rooms from the sun, and neon lights brightened up the night. They also used Florida motifs—herons, pelicans, blooming flowers, and blazing sunsets—to decorate the facades and porches, and incorporated abstracted patterns from Aztec, Mayan, Babylonian, and Egyptian designs. Their buildings became a symbol of progress for a resort emerging from the Great Depression.

To best absorb Miami Beach's deco atmosphere, stroll south along Ocean Drive for fourteen blocks beginning at the Hotel Cardozo at Thirteenth Street where the art deco revitalization movement itself began. Named after 1930s Supreme Court Justice Benjamin Cardozo, the hotel features symmetrical cantilevers and strokes of cream paint, emphasizing its streamlined shape. Hollywood featured it in the 1959 film *A Hole in the Head*, starring Frank Sinatra.

##  TRAVEL TIP

Take a stroll along the beach side of Ocean Drive after dark. This gives you a clear view of the art deco hotels' neon illuminations, casting shimmering lines and circles of bright blues, pinks, and greens around the contours of the buildings, away from the crowded cafés.

In the middle of the next block, the Carlyle Hotel, built in 1941, has a pink and peach succession of curves, vertical columns, and eyebrowed windows to keep out the sun. And across the street in Lummus Park, a grassy area that separates the beach from Ocean Drive, stands the classic deco-inspired boat-shaped Beach Patrol Station, with its vintage oversized date and temperature sign. Two blocks down, you'll see what look like flying saucers at the Clevelander Hotel.

In addition to the deco buildings, you'll see Mediterranean-style buildings scattered throughout the district. These feature archways, bell towers, balconies, rough stucco walls, and red clay–tile roofs. The majestic Amsterdam Palace is modeled after the Alcazar de Colón, the home of Christopher Columbus's son in the Dominican Republic. Nearby, an ornamental lighthouse sits atop the Waldorf Towers.

##  RAINY DAY FUN

If it's a rainy day, you might stop into the streamlined Bass Museum of Art, which contains a limited collection of old master paintings, objets d'art, sculptures, and period furniture, plus temporary exhibits of contemporary European and American art. Admission is $8 for adults, $6 for children. (Open Tuesday through Saturday 10 A.M.–5 P.M., Sunday 11 A.M.–5 P.M., (☎305-673-7530, ✎www.bassmuseum.org)

Three blocks farther along, you'll come to the 1936 Beacon Hotel, with parapets climbing its facade and thin racing stripes wrapping around its sides. The four-story, powder-blue-and-white 1937 Park Central Hotel is a geometric wonder with dramatic vertical columns, fluted eaves, and octagonal windows. For a look at what South Beach life was like in the 1930s, climb the wrought-iron stairway to the mezzanine level to see a display of old black-and-white photographs.

Swing over two blocks to Washington Avenue to see one of Miami Beach's grandest art deco buildings, the 1928 Main Post Office, crowned by a marble and stained-glass lantern. As you enter, note the streams of sunlight filtering through the glass, reflecting on murals and bronze grillwork that sweep around a rotunda.

Movie producers also love Española Way, a small street completed in 1925 as a Spanish-styled artist colony, which lies between

Washington and Drexel avenues. Here, vintage clothing shops, alfresco cafés, and artists' studios and galleries fill the peach-colored Mediterranean buildings, with their colorful striped canopies, arched windows, and narrow overhanging wrought-iron balconies, all framed by palm trees and gas lamps. Unfortunately, the artists' colony idea went bust, but Cuban bandleader Desi Arnaz is supposed to have started the rumba craze here.

In the 1950s, Hollywood celebrities stayed in the glitzy hotels along Central Miami Beach, north of Twenty-third Street. Here, the trendy scene of South Beach's Ocean Drive gives way to Collins Avenue as it follows a 5-mile route through the area. International jet setters came for the luxurious accommodations and exclusive bars, restaurants, and lounges where celebrities cavorted with other celebrities, as the rest of America watched them enviously on newsreels in movie theaters.

The Fontainebleau and its neighbor hotel, the Eden Roc, began a new style of architecture called Miami Modernism, MiMo for short. Frank Sinatra, a Fontainebleau regular, started a scrambled-egg fight in the coffee shop and also shot scenes for the 1960s movie *Tony Rome* here. Drop in for a look around the curving lobby, overhung by weighty chandeliers, and venture through the tree-coated grounds to the swimming pool, complete with rock grottoes and waterfalls to match.

##  TRAVEL TIP

For a truly bizarre nighttime experience, stand on Collins Avenue around Forty-second Street and behold the ten-story, 13,000-square-foot trompe l'oeil mural of the Fontainebleau Hilton, painted by Richard Hass. Unveiled in 1986, it creates the illusion of a great hole in the wall exposing the hotel directly behind.

Miami Beach blossoms with tropical flowers throughout the year. Nowhere is that more apparent than at the Miami Beach Botanical

Garden Center and Conservatory, just west of the Miami Beach Convention Center. It's a showcase for rare orchids in a tropical cloud forest setting, plus one of the largest collections of bromeliads in the country along with many species of ferns, anthuriums, a manicured Japanese garden, over a dozen varieties of subtropical palms, and exotic plants from central and northern South America. (305-673-7256, *www.miamibeachbotanicalgarden.org*)

## For the Kids

Other than the beach, there aren't many attractions for kids in Miami Beach. About the only major one is the 35-acre Miami Seaquarium, on the Rickenbacker Causeway on Virginia Key. Here, your little ones can look at killer whales and other local marine and bird life in a 235,000-gallon aquarium. Spend three to four hours watching the sharks being fed, getting hugs from performing sea lions, feeding tide pool creatures, and watching dolphins perform clever tricks. Admission is $13.95 per person. (Open daily 9:30 A.M.–6:30 P.M., 305-361-5705, *www.miamiseaquarium.com*)

## Festivals and Seasonal Events

Thanks to Miami Beach's cultural diversity, you'll find some sort of festival going on at just about any time of year. The following are the three biggest:

**Art Deco Weekend:** One of the top events of the year, this street fair, held in January and featuring eighty-five events along Ocean Drive, focuses on art deco architecture and collectibles, with food and dealer booths and live entertainment. (✆305-672-2014, ✐*www.mdpl.org*)

**The Miami Beach Festival of the Arts:** Held in mid-February at Ocean Terrace, this cultural event showcases the artwork of 150 artists from across the nation, with paintings, sculpture, glass, ceramics, jewelry, and photographs in a juried exhibition.

**Annual Taste of the Beach:** Some of the finest restaurants in Miami offer an array of food and wine tasting along Lincoln

Road, accompanied by sidewalk fashion shows, comedy acts, and musical performances. You can also attend chef demonstrations and lectures. (✆305-672- 1270)

# Exploring

While most of the action in Miami Beach occurs in the South Beach and Central Beach areas, you may want to venture south to the quieter isles of Virginia Key and Key Biscayne.

To get to Key Biscayne you'll have to take the Rickenbacker Causeway, which begins south of downtown Miami and soars high above the turquoise water of Biscayne Bay. But first you must cross Virginia Key, a tiny island smothered in immense Australian pines and quiet beaches. Here, Planet Ocean and the Miami Seaquarium will entertain both you and your kids (see the preceding "For the Kids" section).

Farther on, you'll arrive at the larger isle of Key Biscayne, a lush flatland dotted with bushy sea grape trees and willowy pines. Ponce de León dubbed it the Cape of Florida when he ran across it in 1513. Charming strip shopping centers, golf fairways, and manicured low-rise condominiums line Crandon Boulevard, the Key's main road, which cuts 2 miles through the length of the island without a single fast-food restaurant or high-rise. An excellent cycling path runs its entire length.

At the end of Crandon Boulevard on the island's tip in the 406-acre Bill Baggs Cape Florida State Park stands the Cape Florida Lighthouse. You can take a ranger-led tour Thursdays through Mondays at 10:00 A.M. and 1:00 P.M. to climb the 109 steps in the lighthouse and see the keeper's home. Afterward, go for a swim on the beach lining the Atlantic side of the park. You can see several stilt houses, built decades ago by fishermen to escape paying taxes, clustered together offshore. Admission to the park is $5 per car. (Open daily 8 A.M.– sunset, 305-361-5811)

## ≡FAST FACT

Cape Florida Light, built in 1825 and the state's oldest remaining lighthouse, rises 95 feet from the dunes and looks out over the Atlantic. It survived a Seminole Indian attack in 1836 as well as an onslaught by Confederate sympathizers to disrupt Union shipping during the Civil War.

# By Day

There's a lot to do during the day in Miami Beach. Just let your interests be your guide. You can do nothing but lounge by the sea, taking in the salt air, or you can play an active game of volleyball, stroll Ocean Drive, or even go diving to see marine life on artificial reefs offshore.

### On the Beach

Miami Beach's 12 miles of firm, crushed-coral-rock sands are excellent for sunbathing and swimming. While most of the beaches have lifeguards on duty daily during the winter and summer, those at Surfside and Bal Harbour do not.

At the northern end of Miami Beach, near Bal Harbour, is Haulover Beach Park, a mile and a half of tropical vegetation with panoramic views not marred by high-rise condominiums. The beach got its name in the early twentieth century when residents "hauled" their boats over surrounding swamps to reach the ocean. It's probably the most beautiful beach here, with hilly sand dunes of chestnut-colored sand and thick grassy areas. This is a great place for you and your kids to toss a line out over the jetty and fish while enjoying a panoramic view of Miami Beach. There's also inexpensive all-day parking. (305-947-3525)

The stretch of beach between Twenty-fifth and Eighty-seventh streets is what made Miami Beach *the* resort of the 1950s. Though still the focus of vacationers here, it now has competition from South Beach and other resorts along Florida's coast. At the upper end between Seventy-second and Seventy-fourth streets, you'll find palmetto chickees—huts similar to those built by the Seminoles—for shade. A single row of palms and lush sea grapes border the shell-encrusted beach, which stretches for 150 feet out to the ocean. Again, you'll enjoy the rainbow panorama of deco South Beach. Beaches south to Twenty-fifth Street all have lifeguards and water sports rentals. Or you can rent water sports equipment from Aquasports Unlimited on Collins Avenue at Forty-eighth Street (305-458-3133, *www.playtimewatersport.com*).

The beach in front of Lummus Park, from Sixth to Fourteenth streets across from the art deco hotels, has fine white sand spreading out twice as far to the ocean as the upper beaches. But unlike them, neon umbrellas and refreshment stands dot the sands. And if they don't suit you, there are always the sidewalk cafés across Ocean Drive. This is an active beach where you can fly a kite, go bicycling, listen to music playing all day, have the kids play in the playground, or go windsurfing. You can rent sailboards from Penrod's (305-538-2604). A sandbar extends fifty yards out, making for excellent ocean swimming.

 **TRAVEL TIP**

Late in the afternoon on Thursdays and Saturdays, you may want to amble over to South Pointe Park, a 17-acre grassy area with meandering sidewalks. Sit on a bench and watch the cruise ships depart on voyages to the Caribbean from the Port of Miami through Government Cut. It's a dramatic sight.

Today, South Beach is *the* place to see and be seen on the sands in Miami Beach. In fact, more people jam onto this one block of southern beach than in all the others combined. Definitely catering to a younger, hipper crowd, it offers a sports bar, volleyball competitions, and loud music throughout the day. Walk the boardwalk down to the ocean. Here, strong winds and currents churn up waves, making it the only place to surf in Miami Beach, though most beachgoers tend to do more bodysurfing and boogie-boarding than surfing.

Families spend weekends at Crandon Park Beach on Key Biscayne. This wide swath of golden sand bordered by clusters of palm trees and a grassy meadow stretches for 3 miles down to a knee-deep sand bar that extends nearly 300 yards out, making it an excellent swimming beach for families with young children. Watch for dolphins and manatees offshore. The park has full amenities, including bicycle trails, concession stands, changing rooms with showers, and lifeguards. And though it's filled with the sounds of kids laughing and sizzling barbecues on weekends, it's all but deserted at other times. Admission is $2 per car. (Open daily 8 A.M.–sunset, 305-361-5421)

## On the Water

Miami Beach offers all sorts of water sports. You can rent a cigarette boat and pretend you're Sonny Rocket as he speeds across Biscayne Bay or just go for a ride in one. Or you can get soaked in the surf on a Jet Ski as it bounces over the waves. You can rent Jet Skis at American Watersport Clubs, Inc. (305-538-7549, *www.jetskiz.com*).

For the best windsurfing and kite-sailing in Miami Beach, head to Hobie Beach, a ribbon of fluffy sand along the south side of the Rickenbacker Causeway on Key Biscayne. It gets its name from the Hobie Cats that whiz up and down in front of the beach. Windsurfers also glide by on heady gusts of wind. When the Florida sun gets too hot, you can duck under broad Australian pines and enjoy the view of downtown Miami. It's always crowded, so get there early. Sailboat, sailboard, Jet Ski, and windsurfing rentals are all available.

## 💼 TRAVEL TIP

With so much water around Miami Beach, both ocean and bay, boating is a big-time sport. If you've handled a motor or sailboat before, you can rent one from Club Nautico South Beach (☎305-361-9217) or Beach Boat Rentals (☎305-534-4307) and cruise around Biscayne Bay.

You'll find several piers and sea walls on the Biscayne Bay side of Miami Beach from which you can hook snook, red snapper, yellowtail, and jack. The farther out you go in the ocean, the better the chance of catching yellowfin, grouper, and dolphinfish. Why not make it a family outing and pay $35 per person to fish aboard a 70-foot party boat for four hours from the Reward Fishing Fleet (305-372-9470, *www.fishingmiami.com*) or Sissy Baby Sport Fishing (305-531-4223, *www.sissybaby.com*).

Surf and offshore saltwater fishing is available year-round in Miami Beach. Both the MacArthur and Rickenbacker causeways have catwalks for fishing, and there's a fishing pier at Haulover Beach Park. Newport Beach Pier, at Sunny Isles on the northern end of Collins Avenue, is a great place to fish for bluefish, mackerel, and jacks. Built in 1936 and destroyed by hurricanes three times and rebuilt, it's a favorite spot for pelicans (305-949-1300).

### Under the Water

Snorkeling and scuba diving haven't always been done on Miami Beach. Because the natural reef lies farther south, the city fathers decided to create artificial reefs by sinking tugboats, freighters, and Army tanks, creating a unique diving opportunity. Wrecks, starting in only 45 feet of water, and corals and sponges at only 30 feet harbor a variety of tropical fish and crustaceans.

You can also go on a four-hour snorkeling excursion to John Pennekamp Marine Sanctuary off Key Largo for $65 per person, including all gear, with South Beach Divers (305-531-6110, *www.southbeachdivers.com*). Children under 15 must be accompanied by an adult. You can dive the artificial reefs in a two-tank dive for $75, including tanks and weights. If you need scuba equipment, you can rent it for $100.

You can also snorkel or dive over the wreck of the *Half Moon*, a steel two-masted schooner that sank in about 1930, for $59, all equipment included, with Tarpoon Lagoon Dive Center. (305-532-1445, *www.tarpoondivecenter.com*)

## On the Links and on the Courts

Though you'll find many golf courses in Greater Miami, there are just three 18-hole public courses in Miami Beach. Greens fees range from about $50 to $185, depending on the time of day and the season.

**The Links at Key Biscayne:** The spectacular views of Biscayne Bay may distract you from your concentration as you try to navigate the fairways that weave through mangrove swamps in what's known as one of the best courses in the Miami area. (✆305-361-9129)

**Miami Beach Golf Club:** Designed by Robert von Hagge and Bruce Devlin, this public golf course includes a driving range, a pro shop, and a clubhouse. Since caddies aren't available and walking the course isn't permitted, golf carts are included in the greens fees. Rental clubs are available. (✆305-532-3350, ✍*www.miamibeachgolfclub.com*)

**Normandy Shores Golf Club:** A challenging eighteen-hole golf course, featuring water hazards on twelve holes, plus a pro shop, a snack bar, a driving range, and putting green. You can also take instructions from a PGA professional. (✆305-868-6502, ✍*www.pcmgolf.com/normandyshores.html*)

While most of the larger resorts along Central Miami Beach have tennis courts, you can also play at the Flamingo Park Tennis Center on Twelfth Street (305-673-7761).

## Spa Time

When you vacation with the beautiful people, you may want to pamper yourself. Most of the major resort hotels in Miami Beach have some sort of spa. But you can also go to any of the following for spa treatments:

- **Crescent Resort and Spa on South Beach:** ☎305-531-9954, ✍*www.crescentsuites.com*
- **Energy Fitness Center Spa Studio:** ☎305-695-4200, ✍*www.energyfitnesscenter.com*
- **Le Spa Lancôme:** ☎305-674-6744, ✍*www.lespamiami.com*
- **Sanctuary Salon and Spa:** ☎305-674-5455

## Shopping

Miami Beach's oldest shopping center, the Lincoln Road Mall on Lincoln Road, between Alton Road and Washington Avenue, offers stores along a plant-bordered, eight-block, pedestrian-only, open-air mall decorated with water fountains, flowers, and greenery. Specialty shops feature jewelry, furs, art, and clothing. Competition from other air-conditioned supermalls has hurt it, but you can still find some interesting shops and art galleries to explore.

## ═FAST FACT

Carl Fisher carved the Lincoln Road Mall out of mangrove swamps in 1913 as part of his long-range plan of development. Known as "the Fifth Avenue of the South," it sported such high-priced fashion and jewelry stores that even into the 1950s, many considered it to be the swankiest shopping district outside of New York City.

A few blocks west in the mall near Lenox Avenue, you'll discover the Lincoln Road Arts District. Here among a number of art galleries are the studios and showrooms of the South Florida Art Center, Inc., stretching for three blocks along the mall. Eighty or so Miami artists work here, focusing on contemporary works in all media, though you may discover some impressionist and exotic Caribbean paintings and sculptures. (305-674-8278)

For designer goods, head to the Bal Harbour Shops on Collins Avenue at Ninety-seventh Street. Well-groomed shoppers meander through the two levels of eighty luxurious shops set amid tall palms, tropical foliage, waterfalls, and over 100 flowering orange trees, searching for Gucci, Cartier, and Fendi apparel and accessories. (305-866-0311)

Kids have fun at Sugar 'n Spice in Surfside, a discount clothing store jammed with children's fashions and accessories. (305-865-5265)

Washington Avenue in the Art Deco District is the place to find vintage clothing and furniture. Bohemian and ultrahip boutiques fill the lower floors of restored deco buildings. Flashbacks, for example, sells twentieth-century collectibles, including flower power mirrors, Beatles paraphernalia, and other items from the '60s and '70s. (305-674-1143)

If you know someone who loves a good cigar, stop into the South Beach Cigar Factory along Collins Avenue and select a hand-rolled Cuban cigar. (305-604-9694)

# Dining Out and Nightlife

Dining in Miami Beach can run the gamut from cheap burger joints along the beach to fabulous gourmet dining rooms in some of the glitzy resorts of Central Beach. For real atmosphere, the restaurants and cafés running for twenty blocks along the ocean in the Art Deco District will help you relive the fabulous 1930s and 1940s. Here is a selection of some of the best:

**Joe's Stone Crab:** You absolutely must visit this South Beach institution for its succulent Florida stone crabs dipped in mustard sauce and served with extra-large homemade fries, followed by the best Key lime pie in the country. Closed May to October. Get there early or you'll have to wait. (227 Biscayne Street, 305-673-0365)

**Lulu's:** If you like Southern cooking, you'll enjoy this down-home restaurant that serves standbys like chicken-fried steak, meat loaf, and fried catfish in a decor of old hubcaps and gas station signs on the first floor and a dining room dedicated to Elvis Presley on the second. (1053 Washington Avenue, ✆305-532-6147)

**Mermaid Beach Bar:** Thick, juicy hamburgers and addicting fries and pizza are the specialty of this beachside bistro. There's an indoor section, but the best spot is outside where you can dine barefoot at plastic tables right over the sand. Swimsuit-clad servers double as bartenders. (4525 Collins Avenue at the Eden Roc hotel)

**News Café:** Join the bohemian crowd at the small outdoor wooden tables and wrought-iron chairs of this South Beach landmark and watch the people as you sip your cappuccino or latte. (800 Ocean Drive, ✆305-538-6397)

**Wolfe Cohen's Rascal House:** This local landmark in the Jewish community has waitresses in white pinafores serving heaping plates of corned beef, chicken in the pot, kreplaches, and stuffed cabbage in a bustling atmosphere. (17190 Collins Avenue, Sunny Isles, ✆305-947-4581)

##  JUST FOR PARENTS

If you've got a sweet tooth, head for CoCo's Sidewalk Café in the Bal Harbour Shops for calorie-laden desserts like "death by chocolate," an ultra-indulgent concoction of four chocolates, served in this American-style eatery with terra cotta floors and wicker furnishings. It's expensive, but worth it. (9700 Collins Avenue, ✆305-864-2626)

For the hottest nighttime action, head straight to Washington Avenue in the Art Deco District. Avant-garde clubs and breezy sidewalk cafés cater to the artsy set. Most of the action here is late-night, with many establishments staying open until 5 A.M. The trend is toward alfresco jazz as well as the more unusual clubs like The Strand with its wavy glass-block bar where you can relax and soak up South Beach chicness (305-532-2340). Live bands play rock-and-roll at the New York–style Washington Square (305-534-1403). The Island Club is a subdued corner bar with a restored warehouse atmosphere with live reggae and jazz (305-538-1213). An after-dinner crowd shows up at Crawdaddy's to hear weekend jazz played on a waterfront board-walk (305-673-1708).

Miami's premier Latin cabaret, Club Tropigala in the Fontaine-bleau Hilton, is a facsimile of a lavish Brazilian samba club. The 650-seat pink-and-purple showcase hosts extravagant Las Vegas–style revues (305-672-7469).

## ▐▌ TRAVEL TIP

If you need to check your e-mail, stop into Kafka's Cybernet Kafe, a funky café on Washington Avenue, where you can browse not only the Internet but also thousands of new and used books while having a cup of coffee and a sandwich. High-speed Internet connections are available. (Open daily 10 A.M.–11 P.M., ☎305-673-9669)

If you prefer to attend road shows of top Broadway musicals and musical concerts by international and national orchestras, you'll find them at the 2,705-seat Jackie Gleason Theater of the Performing Arts, with its sleek, rounded facade fronted by pop artist Roy Lichten-stein's expressive mermaid sculpture. For four years, Jackie Gleason broadcast his national television series from this Miami Beach the-ater (305-673-7300, *www.gleasontheater.com*). The Miami City Ballet performs modern jazz and ballet from September through March at the restored 465-seat Art Deco Colony Theater, built in 1934 by Para-mount Studios (305-532-7713, 305-674-1026). But if you'd rather listen to the soft strains of acoustic guitar in a romantic garden, head over to the Fairmont on Collins Avenue (305-531-0050).

# CHAPTER 9

# Fort Lauderdale

FORT LAUDERDALE, ALONG FLORIDA'S GOLD COAST, is best known for the wild beach parties once held during Spring Break, but those days are long gone as the resort "Where the Fun Never Sets" is now more of a family place. It's least known for its Spanish-style mansions that hug the banks of canals jutting into the Intracoastal Waterway, giving the city the nickname "Venice of America." But it still attracts sun worshipers who come to get bronzed, reel in some big fish, and play golf and tennis.

## Getting to Know Fort Lauderdale

Fort Lauderdale received its name from a Second Seminole War fort built on the banks of the New River in 1838. The fort, one of three, got its name from Major William Lauderdale, who led a detachment of soldiers into the area to fight the Seminoles. The building of a primitive road and ferry crossing on the river brought Ohioan Frank Stranahan to Fort Lauderdale in 1897, and three years later he established a successful trading post. It was only after Henry Flagler extended his Florida East Coast Railway that the village grew enough to become incorporated in 1911. The 1920s saw spectacular growth as well as new canals, created from the mangrove swamps.

After the town took action in the 1980s, college students moved northward to Daytona Beach for their partying, leaving a mix of wealthy retirees and affluent yuppies, both desperate to play down the beach party image.

## ≡FAST FACT

Intercollegiate swimming contests beginning in the 1930s and the 1960 teen-oriented movie *Where the Boys Are* instantly made Fort Lauderdale the country's number-one Spring Break destination. Things got so bad by the late 1970s that the city decided to fight back by enacting strict ordinances to restrict drinking and wild behavior around the beach.

## Getting Around Fort Lauderdale

Since most of Fort Lauderdale area's sights are far apart, it's essential to have a car. Fort Lauderdale's beach strip runs for 6 miles between Oakland Park Boulevard to the north and Las Olas Boulevard to the south, but you may want to venture northward. Free cobalt blue trolleys tool around the Riverwalk Arts and Entertainment District every ten minutes on Fridays from 5 to 11 P.M. and Saturdays from noon to 11 P.M. (954-463-6574).

##  TRAVEL TIP

Fort Lauderdale's local bus network offers twice-hourly service along Los Olas Boulevard between downtown and Fort Lauderdale Beach until 9 P.M. daily. You can buy a weekly bus pass for about $5 at most beachside hotels. (✆954-357-8400)

But the best way to see the city's beautiful residential neighborhoods is by taking a bright yellow Water Taxi of Fort Lauderdale from any dock. They offer an inexpensive scenic way to go anywhere within the city's 7-mile network of waterways. Single rides cost $4 per person; an all-day ticket will cost you $11 and after 7 P.M. costs only $5.

Bicycling also affords an easy way to see the sights. The best places to ride in the Fort Lauderdale area are along the wide paved roads on the west side of the city. You can rent bicycles for about $5 per hour, $10–$12 per day, or $36 per week from any of the following:

- **Downtown Bicycles:** ☎Toll-free 866-813-7368
- **Florida Bicycle:** ☎954-763-6974
- **International Bike Shop:** ☎954-764-8800

### Best Time to Go

Because of its close proximity to the Gulf Stream, the Fort Lauderdale area enjoys a subtropical climate noted for its year-round breezes and moderate temperatures ranging from 75° to 85°. Though the peak season is January to April, summer draws more of a family crowd.

### Cautions and Safety Concerns

Fort Lauderdale is a safe place to take your family. The city has done much to clean things up. As with other beach resorts, about your only concern should be for the strong Florida sun. Be sure to use a strong enough sunblock whenever you're out in it.

# Family-Oriented Resorts and Hotels

In Fort Lauderdale, you'll find mostly high-rise hotels belonging to major chains. Since a local ordinance bans construction between Route A1A and the beach, you won't find any oceanfront hotels.

**Doubletree Guest Suites Galleria:** Reservations: ✆Toll-free 866-613-9330

This conveniently located fourteen-story, 229-suite hotel has concierge service, restaurant, fitness center, and pool, and offers special rates for children.

**Lago Mar Hotel Resort and Club:** Reservations: ✆Toll-free 800-524-6627, ✍*www.lagomar.com*

With 204 rooms and suites, two swimming pools, tennis courts, a putting green, two restaurants and a lounge, plus rooms with white furniture and accents of rose and forest green, this resort lets you relax in a contemporary setting.

**Hyatt Regency Sixty-Six Resort & Spa:** Reservations: ✆Toll-free 800-327-3796, ✍*www.pier66.com*

This 388-room marina hotel, topped off with a rooftop revolving lounge, dominates the city skyline from its 22 landscaped acres. Spacious accommodations offer subdued tropical color schemes; small lanais overlooking the Intracoastal Waterway, the city, and ocean; several restaurants, tennis courts, swimming pool, Jacuzzi, spa and health club; and children's rates.

# Things to Do

Fort Lauderdale's beauty goes well beyond its shoreline. You'll quickly discover majestic estates, hardwood hammocks, and a maze of waterways, all creating a laid-back tropical feeling.

Though the city is only a little over a century old, you'll still find plenty of historical interest. The oldest section of town lies along the banks of the New River. Begin your exploration along the Riverwalk, a meandering footpath that travels along the river. Here, you'll come upon manicured gardens and parks with gazebos. One of these, Esplanade Park, features a science exhibit complete with giant kaleidoscopes, a rain gauge and sextant, and plaques honoring the world's famous mathematicians and scientists (954-561-7362).

Frank Stranahan, a successful trader in otter pelts, egret plumes, and alligator hides, opened a general store in 1901. The pine building, the county's oldest, with its high ceilings, narrow windows, and wide verandas, is a fine example of the Florida frontier style. Later, Stranahan converted it into a residence for his bride, Ivy. He added bay windows, electric wiring, and modern plumbing. The two-story cottage overlooking Los Olas Boulevard has been restored and furnished to 1910, and the guided tour tells his story. Stranahan, financially devastated by the late-1920s Florida real estate crash, later drowned himself in the Intracoastal Waterway. Admission is $5 for adults, $2 for children. (Open Wednesday through Saturday 10 A.M.–3 P.M., Sunday 1–3 P.M., 954-524-4736)

As you travel west along the Riverwalk, you'll come to the Old Fort Lauderdale Village and Museum, operated by the Fort Lauderdale Historical Society. The museum, housed in the 1905 River Inn built by contractor Edwin T. King, a pioneer in hollow cinderblock construction, stands where Flagler's East Coast Railway crossed the New River. It contains a scale model of the old fort, clothing of the Seminole and early Fort Lauderdale settlers, as well as old dolls and toys. The village consists of several historic structures, including the King-Cromartie House, built by King of local pine with joists of ship's timbers for himself and his wife in 1907. It was originally a bungalow; King added a second story and the city's first indoor bathroom in 1911. Behind the house stands a replica of Fort Lauderdale's first one-room school from 1899. Stranahan's wife was the first teacher. Guided tours of the museum and village are $8 per adult, $3 per child. (Open Tuesday through Saturday 10 A.M.–5 P.M., Sunday 12–5 P.M., 954-463-4431, *www.oldfortlauderdale.org*)

The Museum of Art on Las Olas Boulevard, displaying Florida's best art collection, features exceptional pre-Columbian, Mesoamerican, North American, South Seas, and West African art, as well as lots of local Tequesta Indian objects. You'll also enjoy its collection of Dutch and Flemish art. It's especially known for its paintings from the CoBrA Movement, which began in 1948 with a group of artists from Copenhagen, Brussels, and Amsterdam, and features bright expressionistic canvases combining playful innocence with deep emotional power. The Museum also houses works by Henri Matisse,

Andy Warhol, Salvador Dali, Pablo Picasso, and Henry Moore. You can take a guided tour at noon and 6:30 P.M. on Tuesdays, at noon Wednesdays through Fridays, and at 2 P.M. on weekends. Admission is $6 per adult, $3 per child. (Open daily 11 A.M.–7 P.M., Thursday until 9 P.M., 954-525-5500, *www.moafl.org*)

Chicago muralist and art collector Frederick Clay Bartlett built the Bonnet House, one of the few remaining oceanfront estates in southern Florida, in 1921. Situated on 35 jungle-like acres, the house and studio reflect Bartlett's personality. He designed not only the house but also the plantation-like surroundings, including a small lake dotted with white swans bordered by a forest where Brazilian squirrel monkeys play in the trees along the Atlantic Ocean. Bartlett had an eccentric passion for art and architecture, as well as for collecting ornamental animals, dozens of which fill almost all of the thirty rooms. The Shell Room, with its inlaid shells and an impressive collection of paired specimens, alone is worth seeing. Be sure not to miss his studio, containing many of his original paintings. You can tour the beautifully preserved two-story house and walk the nature trails from May through November. Admission is $15 per adult, $11 per child. (Open Tuesday through Saturday 10 A.M.–4 P.M., Sunday noon–4 P.M., 954-563-5393, *www.bonnethouse.org*)

 TRAVEL TIP

Take a nighttime lantern-led, 60- to 90-minute ghostly tour of Fort Lauderdale's most haunted places through the city's historic district along the New River. It's $15 per adult, $10 per child with either the Fort Lauderdale Ghost Tour (☎954-290-9328) or Ghosts, Mysteries & Legends of Old Fort Lauderdale (☎954-523-1501).

Even if you're not a swimmer, you'll enjoy the exhibits at the International Swimming Hall of Fame Museum and Aquatic Complex. Medals, trophies, and Olympic memorabilia from swimmers and divers from 100 countries fill 10,000 square feet of exhibit space on two levels. Computerized exhibits let you pretend you're an Olympic diver, swimmer, or judge. You'll also see turn-of-the-century woolen bathing costumes, sweatshirts that once belonged to Olympic champions Mark Spitz and Cynthia Potter, and swim-related artworks by such noted artists as Leroy Nieman and Norman Rockwell. Be sure to browse the room of nations, where you can learn about any swimmer or diver who has won an Olympic metal. Admission is $8. (Open Monday through Saturday 10 A.M.–5 P.M., Sunday 11 A.M.–4 P.M.), 954-462-6536; *www.ishof.org*)

If you love gardens, you'll love the 60-acre Flamingo Gardens and Wray Botanical Collection, founded by Floyd L. Wray and his wife, Jane, who began them as a display of citrus plants and a laboratory to discover new varieties. Walk through the 25,000-square-foot Everglades "free-flight" aviary, featuring five ecosystems and housing one of the largest collections of wading birds in America. Then visit the Bird of Prey Center, with its rare Florida birds in their naturalistic habitat, and the Tropical Plant House, full of orchids and other exotic plants. Flamingos feed amid tropical foliage and waterfalls on Flamingo Island, plus there are natural habitats for river otters and bobcats and a lagoon with alligators. You can take a twenty-five-minute narrated tram ride through the tropical rainforest, native hammock, wetland areas, and citrus groves to see the largest collection of towering champion trees in the region. Admission is $15 for adults, $8 for children. (Open June through September, Tuesday through Sunday 9:30 A.M.–5:00 P.M., 954-473-2955, *www.flamingogardens.org*)

### For the Kids

The rainbow-colored combinations and geometric patterns of more than 100 types of butterflies create a world of wonder at Butterfly World, the largest park of its kind on the planet. It began as the hobby of Ronald Boender, who collected butterflies while growing up on his family farm in Illinois. Opened in 1988 as the first U.S. center for butterflies, it has since become the most complete facility of its kind, dedicated totally to the preservation of butterflies and their habitat. Nearly 2,000 specimens, many raised from larvae, live out their short lives around the nectar-producing plants inside several aviaries. Some survive twice as long as their normal lifespan in the wild.

#  RAINY DAY FUN

Spend a rainy afternoon in the Museum of Discovery & Science and 3-D IMAX Theater exploring hundreds of hands-on exhibits highlighting technological and ecological themes, with masses of pushbuttons and working models. Your kids can bend a ray of light, hang out with bats, or pet a green iguana. (Open Monday through Saturday 10 A.M.– 5 P.M., Sunday noon–6 P.M., ☎954-467-6637, ✐www.mods.org.)

You can stroll along flower-lined pathways inside a giant aviary where clouds of butterflies fly, feed, and bask in Florida's sunshine. In the tropical rain forest, thousands of exotic butterflies glide through waterfalls and lush dense foliage. Between the aviary and the tropical rain forest, butterflies drink nectar from fragrant flower-filled hanging baskets. You'll also see the different stages of a butterfly's development in the Museum and Insectarium, with its amazing collection of mounted butterflies, moths, spiders, wasps, and exotic beetles. Admission is $18.95 per adult, $13.95 per child. (Open Monday to Saturday 9 A.M.–5 P.M., Sunday 1–5 P.M., 954-977-4400, *www .butterflyworld.com*)

The founders of the Children's Museum of Boca Raton at Singing Pines named it for the sound made by pine trees blowing in the breeze. The house itself, said to be the oldest unaltered wood-frame building in the city, is a Florida "Cracker" cottage constructed of Dade County pine floors and timber found on the beach. Inside kids can explore a corner store, a KidsCents bank, post office, fossils, plus pioneer Florida memorabilia, including a kitchen equipped with an old wood stove, a vintage Singer sewing machine, and an old-fashioned telephone. (561-368-6875, *www.cmboca.org*)

The Gumbo-Limbo Environmental Education Center, also in Boca Raton, protects the area's West Indian hardwood hammocks. The free educational facility features an ocean research center, biology lab, and naturalist exhibits that allow kids to touch the skin of a snake or the pelts of small animals. Four saltwater aquariums showcase brilliant fish, stingrays, crabs, shrimp, and other ocean wonders. One tank allows them to pet a live conch, sea urchin, or horseshoe crab. From here, a wide boardwalk leads to an observation tower where you can take in a panorama of the 67-acre park and beach. Be on the lookout for ospreys, brown pelicans, and manatees swimming in the warm waters. Admission is $3 per person. (Open Monday through Saturday 9 A.M.–4 P.M., Sunday noon–4 P.M., 561-338-1473)

Intended to teach kids about sea turtles, the Loggerhead Marinelife Center of Juno Beach features a turtle hatchery as well as displays on their life cycles. Kids can see a giant leatherback sea turtle, plus other local wildlife, as they take a virtual walking tour on the ocean floor. This is one of several places along Florida's coast where your kids can go on a "turtle walk" along a nearby beach in June and July to watch turtles come ashore to lay their eggs after dark. Admission free. (Open Tuesday through Saturday 10 A.M.–4 P.M., Sunday noon–3 P.M., 561-627-8280, *www.marinelife.org*)

Over 900 animals from sixty-three species, including lions, rhinos, elephants, zebras, and giraffes, roam the 500-acre Lion Country Safari in West Palm Beach while humans, caged in their automobiles with windows rolled up for security, tour the park for nearly an hour on paved roads. Rental vehicles are available. When it opened in 1967, it was the first "cageless" zoo in the country. Though it's far from the Serengeti Plain in Africa, the park gives kids an opportunity to get close to exotic animals. There's also the walk-through Safari World, with a petting zoo, aviaries, and reptile exhibits. Admission is $20.95 per adult, $16.95 per child under 9. (Open daily 9:30 A.M.–4:30 P.M., 561-793-1084, *www.lioncountrysafari.com*)

### Extra Special

A feeling of peace and serenity will overtake you as you enter the Morikami Museum and Japanese Gardens, 10 miles northwest of Boca Raton. The centerpiece of this 200-acre pine forest preserve is the museum, devoted to Japanese folk arts and the history of the Japanese Yamoto Colony, an early twentieth-century settlement whose members came to Florida to grow tea and rice and farm silkworms, but ended up selling pineapples until a blight killed off the crop in 1908. The museum also houses a Shinto shrine, plus displays on Japanese baths and tea ceremonies and hands-on exhibits of obi tying, origami, and musical instruments. You can also stroll through a 2-acre garden, laid out in Japanese style with a koi pond and a bonsai garden in the rear. On Wednesday afternoon there's a guided garden tour. (Open Tuesday through Sunday noon–5 P.M., 561-495-0233, *www.morikami.org*)

### Festivals and Seasonal Events

Area festivals include fun events like the Lauderdale Sandblast, held on the Fourth of July, when thousands of sun worshipers competitively create elaborate sand sculptures on the beach, or the Las Olas Art Fair in September, when 250 national artists exhibit their works in an outdoor street fair. (954-472-3755)

# Exploring

If you have a car, your own or a rented one, drive north on Highway A1A from Fort Lauderdale to explore the beach communities of Boca Raton, Deerfield Beach, and Palm Beach.

Here, you can see how the other half lives as you take in the luxurious homes of the rich and famous.

### Boca Raton

Boca Raton, one of the fastest-growing communities along Florida's southeast coast, attracts large numbers of retirees and golfers. The name, meaning "mouth of the rat," may have originated with Spanish pirates, who feared this inlet for its jagged rocks.

Boca Raton's Mediterranean architecture goes back to Addison Mizner, who designed the mansions of Palm Beach's wealthy through the 1920s. Mizner arrived in Boca Raton in 1925 at the peak of Florida's real estate boom, and in partnership with his brother, Wilson, bought 1,600 acres of farmland and began selling plots of a future community. The Mizner brothers envisioned a luxury hotel, gondola-filled canals, and a cathedral dedicated to their mother. Unfortunately, the land boom ended before they barely began to build their exclusive community, and they returned to Palm Beach embarrassed.

But the few buildings the Mizners did complete left their mark on Boca Raton. Their million-dollar Cloister Inn, a pink palace of marble columns, sculptured fountains, and carefully aged wood ("distressed" by their workmen's hobnail boots), is now the Boca Raton Hotel and Club. You can take a guided tour, run by the Boca Raton Historical Society between December and April, for $4. (561-395-8655)

### Palm Beach

Palm Beach has been synonymous with unlimited wealth and luxury for over a century. It got its name from its palms, which first came ashore in 1878 when the *Providencia*, a Spanish ship bound from Trinidad to Cádiz, ran aground, spilling its cargo of coconuts. The island's few residents planted the coconuts, giving birth to Palm Beach.

When Henry Morrison Flagler, John D. Rockefeller's partner in Standard Oil, saw this palm-tree-lined island in 1893, he decided that Palm Beach would make the perfect winter escape for America's rich and famous. He extended his East Coast Railroad south from Saint Augustine, and on February 11, 1894 opened the world's largest wooden resort, the immense Italianate Royal Poinciana Hotel, with 1,150 rooms and a staff of 1,400. There were more workers than the population of any town on the coast, so Flagler built West Palm Beach, on the mainland side of Lake Worth, to house them. They pampered the likes of Rockefellers, Astors, Carnegies, Morgans, and Vanderbilts on Palm Beach Island, transporting them around the island in rickshaw-like vehicles and catering to their every whim.

## 💼 TRAVEL TIP

You can watch a chukker or two as polo, the "sport of kings," gets underway on Sunday afternoons from January to mid-April at the Palm Beach Polo & Country Club on the mainland in West Palm Beach (☎561-793-1400), or at the Royal Palm Polo Sports Club in Boca Raton (☎561-994-1876).

Based on the success of his first hotel, Flagler built a second, the Palm Beach Inn, on the beach of the Royal Poinciana. Soon guests began requesting rooms "over by the breakers." So when Flagler doubled the hotel's size, he renamed it The Breakers. But during the expansion in 1903, fire destroyed it. In February 1904, it reopened with rooms starting at $4 per night, including three meals. In March 1925, fire again destroyed the hotel. Rebuilt on a grander scale in 1926, its exterior resembled the Villa Medici in Rome, with twin Belvedere towers with graceful arches and a fountain in the central courtyard like one in Florence's Boboli Gardens. Seventy-five Italian artisans completed the magnificent ceiling paintings of the 200-foot-long main lobby and first-floor public rooms, each graced by tapestries and ornate vaulted ceilings. Today, The Breakers is an award-winning luxury oceanfront resort on the National Register of Historic Places. Its Alcazar Lounge, where you can catch a free guided tour at 3 P.M. on Wednesdays, has a case of photos and memorabilia from the hotel's past that are worth studying.

Flagler built his own home next to the Royal Poinciana on the shores of Lake Worth (the Intracoastal Waterway) in 1902. The architectural firm of Carrére & Hastings, who had also worked on the Ponce de León Hotel for Flagler in Saint Augustine, designed the immense fifty-five-room marble mansion, originally called Whitehall. White Doric columns grace the facade of the most ostentatious home on the island. The 71-year-old Flagler, who was thirty-seven years older than his bride, spent $4 million satisfying the opulent tastes of his third wife, Mary Lily Kenan. Her portrait graces the music room, where she's wearing a wedding gift from her husband, a half-million-dollar hip-length strand of pearls. She's noted in the Guinness Book of Records as a woman who in a twelve-year period never wore the same dress twice. You can see some of her gowns displayed in her upstairs dressing rooms.

Whitehall's huge foyer, with seven kinds of rare marble, suggests the atrium of a Roman villa, covered by a baroque ceiling like those of Louis XIV's Versailles. Flagler decorated the guest bedrooms to represent epochs in world history while his own resembled Versailles. He took from the great buildings of Europe an Italian library, a French salon, a Swiss billiard room, a hallway modeled on Saint Peter's in Rome, and a Louis XV ballroom—all overflowing with rich ornamentation.

Now a museum, Whitehall contains not only Flagler furnishings and memorabilia but also collections of porcelain, paintings, silver, and clothing of the period. There's so much to see that you should take one of the continuous forty-five-minute free guided tours from the entrance hall to learn more of the details about Flagler and the house. And don't forget to tour the Rambler, the railcar that Flagler himself used, parked in the rear yard. Built in 1886, its elegant interior, with papered ceiling, inlaid wood, and tulip chandeliers, has been completely restored. Admission $3. (Open Tuesday through Saturday 10 A.M.–5 P.M., Sunday noon–5 P.M., 561-655-2833)

## ≡FAST FACT

Palm Beach is the headquarters of the United States Croquet Association, as well as sixteen croquet clubs. Association staff members give private croquet lessons throughout the year and from October through May run a weekly three-day croquet school (☎561-627-3999).

After touring Whitehall, you should take a few hours to explore Palm Beach. A good way to get acquainted with its posh neighborhoods is to pedal out to see them on the bike trail. You can rent a bicycle from the Palm Beach Bicycle Trail Shop at 223 Sunrise Boulevard, and they will direct you to the trail (561-659-4583).

Besides Flagler, the man who most influenced the look of Palm Beach was flamboyant architect Addison Mizner. By the time he was 46, he had established himself as a "society architect," designing fabulous homes for New York's wealthy and powerful. When his friend Paris Singer, the heir to the Singer sewing machine fortune, invited him to Palm Beach in 1918 for a vacation, Mizner headed south in search of new opportunities. His arrival heralded the age of the posh winter residence, for he knew how to design them as status symbols that also took advantage of Florida's climate.

Inspired by the medieval buildings he'd seen around the Mediterranean, Mizner, financed by Singer, built the Everglades Club along Worth Avenue. The Club, the first public building in Florida built in the Mediterranean Revival style, rapidly became the island's most prestigious social address. Singer had thought about building a "convalescent club" for the rich with the winter blahs, staffed with doctors and dance directors. Singer gave Mizner free rein to design living spaces next to patios, cloisters, and loggias, letting the air and sunshine flow through the interiors.

##  RAINY DAY FUN

The most jai alai frontons, or large indoor stadiums, in the country exist in South Florida. Watching the world's fastest ball game at Palm Beach Jai Alai in West Palm Beach from September through July is a great way to spend a few hours on a rainy day. (℡561-844-2444)

Striving for a medieval, lived-in appearance, Mizner used untrained workman to lay roof tiles crookedly, sprayed condensed milk onto walls to create an impression of centuries-old grime, and fired shotgun pellets into wood to imitate worm holes. After he built a house for Eva Stotesbury, the queen of Palm Beach society, wealthy patrons began checking out of their suites in Flagler's hotels for million-dollar cottages of their own. By the mid-1920s, Mizner had created the Palm Beach Style, designing homes in the old-world style for the newly rich.

# By Day

Whether you like lying in the sun soaking up rays, angling for some big game fish, taking a swing around a tropical golf course, or touring historic sites, you'll find plenty to keep your family occupied in the Fort Lauderdale area.

## On the Beach

Fort Lauderdale boasts 23 miles of balmy beaches. Route A1A remains one of the most developed strips on the Gold Coast. Most of Fort Lauderdale Beach lies in full view, not blocked by condominiums as are other stretches of Florida's coast. The least-crowded area is South Beach Park, a surfing favorite, located in front of the major hotels south of South Route A1A. Red Reef Park, a mile farther, is far better for sunbathing and swimming.

The narrow 12,000-foot-long white sand beach at 244-acre John U. Lloyd Beach State Recreation Area offers the gentlest surf for swimming, making it ideal if you've got younger children along. Stroll to the tip for a panoramic view of the oceanfront to the south. You can walk the self-guided nature trail through a subtropical coastal hammock, where you'll spot water birds and perhaps a manatee or two in Whiskey Creek, in about forty-five minutes. If you'd rather spend some time fishing, you'll find the jetty at the north end of the park the perfect place (954-923-2833).

The mile-long strand of Deerfield Beach is one of the few places on the Gold Coast where you can collect seashells. The sand is soft and deep and studded with boulders at the low-water mark, and the southern part is more serene.

You can only reach 55-acre Deerfield Island Park by the free ferry from the dock at the Riverview Restaurant in Deerfield Beach, and then only on Wednesday and Saturday mornings. During the 1930s, noted mobster Al Capone, along with his fellow gangsters, frequented the casino in the Riverview Restaurant. He almost purchased Deerfield Park Island, but his arrest for tax evasion stopped his bid, leaving the island to Mother Nature. Allow two hours to walk the two trails—one, a 1,500-foot raised boardwalk, leads through 8 acres of red, white, and black mangroves; the other leads toward the Intracoastal Waterway and a rocky overlook. On the way, keep an eye out for gray fox, raccoons, and armadillos. (954-428-3463)

### On the Water

Fort Lauderdale is a boater's paradise. You can explore the Intracoastal Waterway, which extends the length of the Gold Coast, by sailboat or motorboat—Sunfish rent for $20 per hour or $70 per day and ski boats seating eight for $49 per hour or $269 per day, skis and tow rope included. The following rent sail and motorboats in Fort Lauderdale:

- **American Boat Rental:** ☎954-761-8845
- **Bill's Sunrise Boat Rental:** ☎954-763-8882
- **Club Nautico:** ☎954-779-3866
- **Everglades Holiday Park:** ☎954-434-8111
- **Sawgrass Recreation Marina:** ☎954-389-0202

Or perhaps you'd rather enjoy the sights, cold drink in hand, from the deck of the *Jungle Queen*, a 538-passenger riverboat that meanders through downtown and Port Everglades and stops at the Seminole Indian Village for a look at native trees and birds. Departing at 10 A.M. and 2 P.M. from the Bahia Mar Yacht Center for a three-hour sightseeing cruise, it costs $14.50 per adult, $10.50 per child. For a fun way to spend an evening, take their 7 P.M. nightly all-you-can-eat barbecue-and-shrimp dinner cruise with variety show for $32.95 per person (954-462-5596, *www.junglequeen.com*). Or cruise under full sail on a 63-foot schooner with Wind Dancer Charters on either a daytime sightseeing or sunset cruise (954-895-5408, *www.wind dancercharters.com*).

 **JUST FOR PARENTS**

After sipping a cup of rich espresso and sharing a piece of heavenly Chambord mousse torte, take a romantic thirty-minute gondola tour in an imported Venetian gondola from Stork's Café and Bakery along Las Olas Boulevard. You can do this from November to June, Wednesdays through Sundays from 5 to 11 P.M. for $50 per couple. (✆954-561-7650, ✉*www.gondolaservizio.com*)

If you like to surf or windsurf, you'll find all the equipment you need at any of the following places:

- **BC Surf & Sport:** Fort Lauderdale, ✆954-564-0202
- **Fun Boards:** in Delray Beach, ✆561-272-3036
- **Island Water Sports:** Fort Lauderdale, ✆954-491-6229
- **Singer Island Sailboard Rental:** Riviera Beach, ✆561-848-2628
- **Windsurfing Madness:** Fort Lauderdale, ✆954-525-9463

Watersports Unlimited (954-467-1316) and Aloha Watersports (954-462-7245), located on the beach at the Marriott Harbor Beach Hotel in Fort Lauderdale, rent WaveRunners, which are like two-person Jet Skis, only more stable. Both also offer parasailing.

With the Gulf Stream less than 2 miles offshore, you have an opportunity to catch marlin, wahoo, pompano, kingfish, shark, dolphin, and sailfish. Deep-sea fishing is one of the most popular sports on the Gold Coast, and there seems to be no end of charter outfits in the area. Among them are Action Sportfishing (954-423-8700, *www .actionsportfishing.com*) and All-Inclusive Sportfishing (954-761-1066).

But if you're on a budget or just don't want to bob around at sea for six hours, you can pay the nominal fee to fish off Anglin's Fishing Pier (954-491-9403), where you can rent equipment, buy bait, and fish to your heart's content.

## Under the Water

The clear waters and abundant marine life along the Gold Coast create great conditions for diving sunken wrecks and artificial reefs. Just one mile off Fort Lauderdale Beach in 97 feet of clear water lies the *Mercedes I*, a 197-foot German freighter that's become a hot spot for coral, barracuda, angelfish, sea turtles, and the scuba divers who love photographing them. Plus, there are dozens of other wrecks you can dive along the Gold Coast, with names like Wreck of the Rebel, Ancient Mariner, and Houseboat Wreck. The artificial reef varies in depth from 15 feet to 100 feet, making it good for either snorkelers or divers. Average visibility is 40 to 60 feet.

One of the best dive shops in Fort Lauderdale is Pro Dive (954-776-3413, *www.prodiveusa.com*), which offers daily reef and wreck dives as well as basic, open-water, and advanced certification classes and snorkeling. Similar services are available from Lauderdale Diver (Toll-free 800-654-2073) and Undersea Sports (Toll-free 800-842-9798).

If you don't dive, you can take a two-hour glass-bottom boat and snorkeling tour from the Bahia Yacht Basin with Pro Dive aboard their 60-foot glass-bottom boat. The tour leaves at 10 A.M. daily and costs $22 for adult riders, $29 for adult snorkelers, $14 for child riders, and $20 for child snorklers.

## On the Links and on the Courts

Fort Lauderdale is one of the Southeast's major golf centers, with more than fifty courses on lush greens interspersed with lakes and tree-shaded hammocks. Some of the best include:

- **American Golfers Club:** Fort Lauderdale, ☎954-564-8760
- **Bonaventure Country Club:** Fort Lauderdale, ☎954-389-2100

- **Grand Palms Golf Country Club:** Pembroke Pines, ☎954-437-3334
- **Sabal Palms Golf Course:** ☎954-731-2600

If you'd rather play tennis, public courts in the beach area include lighted ones at Holiday Park and George English Park (954-761-2621). Courts and instruction are available through the City of Fort Lauderdale Parks and Recreation Department (954-761-5346) or you can play at any of the following:

- **George English Park:** Fort Lauderdale, ☎954-566-0622
- **Holiday Park:** Fort Lauderdale, ☎954-761-5378
- **West Lake Park:** Hollywood, ☎954-926-2410
- **Memorial Park:** Boca Raton, ☎561-393-7978

## Spa Time

Several superdeluxe resorts offer full European-style spas, with a complete menu of spa services to relax and rejuvenate you.

- **Elizabeth Arden Red Door Spa:** ☎954-564-5787
- **Marriott's Harbor Beach Resort & Spa:** ☎Toll-free 800-222-6543
- **The Atlantic:** ☎954-567-8020
- **The Breakers:** ☎Toll-free 888-273-2537

## Shopping

Despite all the shopping malls along the Gold Coast, the best place to shop in Fort Lauderdale is along Las Olas Boulevard, where you'll find mostly one-of-a-kind boutiques, fashioned from old brick and ironwork, selling Lalique crystal and Tiffany sterling. Sawgrass Mills, an enormous mall, has over 200 brand-name and designer outlets, specialty shops, and restaurants.

**TRAVEL TIP**

If you'd like to purchase some Seminole Indian crafts to take home, visit the Seminole Reservation in west Fort Lauderdale or the Anhinga Indian Museum and Art Gallery (☎954-581-0416), which carries a large stock of fringed clothing, turquoise and silver jewelry, woven rugs, and beaded dolls in traditional Seminole patchwork designs.

A trip to Palm Beach wouldn't be complete without a stop on Worth Avenue, Florida's answer to California's Rodeo Drive and a mecca for fans of Gucci, Louis Vuitton, Van Cleef & Arpels, and Chanel. Rolls Royces, Mercedes, and Jaguars cruise by world-famous designer stores, high-class art galleries, and gourmet restaurants. You'll also find small shops hidden at the end of side streets, called *vias*, off Worth Avenue. These vias have the picturesqueness of Old Spain, with their light stucco walls in pastel tints topped with tile roofs, and weathered cypress woodwork.

High-class clothing and accessories, some of it discarded after only one use, turns up in Palm Beach's thrift stores, although the prices are above those you'd normally find in thrift stores back home. Browse The Church Mouse, Goodwill Embassy Boutique, or Thrift Store Inc., and have your wallet handy.

If you love flea markets, head for South Florida's largest, the indoor-outdoor Swap Shop. The 87-acre, seven-day-a-week market with more than 2,000 dealers has live circus shows, a giant carousel, and loads of secondhand treasures, plus a thirteen-screen drive-in theater. (954-791-7927)

## Dining Out and Nightlife

With limited outlets filling the gap between gourmet restaurants and fast-food franchises, Fort Lauderdale isn't the best place for your family to eat well and inexpensively. However, the following are known not only for their good food but also for their relatively moderate prices:

**15th Street Fisheries:** A local waterfront favorite with excellent views and two levels of dining where wait staff serve blackened tuna, grouper, dolphin, and snapper, as well as steaks, in a nautical atmosphere of shrimp nets and floral prints. (1900 Southeast Fifteenth Street, Fort Lauderdale, ☎954-763-2777)

**Ernie's Bar B Que and Lounge:** Ernie's dynamite sauce packs them in to eat a choice of chicken or pork barbecue and ribs, accompanied by corn on the cob, cole slaw, and gallons of iced tea. (1843 South Federal Highway, Fort Lauderdale, ☎954-523-8636).

**Shirttail Charlie's Restaurant:** This multilevel restaurant features an alfresco dockside luncheon of seafood salad, grilled fish, or kebabs of steak, chicken, shrimp, or fish, and at night serves scampi, conch, steaks, and alligator in the upstairs dining room overlooking the river. (400 Southwest Third Avenue, Fort Lauderdale, ☎954-463-3474)

**The Southport Raw Bar:** Located behind the Southport Mall along the Intracoastal Waterway, this casual eatery specializes in spicy conch chowder, thick sandwiches, and fried shrimp. (1536 Cordova Road, Fort Lauderdale, ☎954-525-2526)

You'll find the best live music away from the beach. Rock bands appear most nights at half a dozen clubs along the Intracoastal Waterway, drawing lofty yachts that vie for prime dock space.

Mombasa Bay, with its tropical atmosphere, is the place to relax Florida-style. Reggae bands play nightly except for blues night on Tuesday (954-565-7441). A first-class house band gets the over-thirty crowd at September's rocking from Thursday through Saturday (954-563-4331), while DJs at Roxy's play a mix of current Top-Forty hits and oldies on two dance floors with a wall of thirty televisions (954-565-3555). The Musician's Exchange presents jazz, reggae, rhythm-and-blues, and rock-and-roll concerts in a comfortable lounge environment (954-764-1912).

**JUST FOR PARENTS**

Find a sitter for the kids and take your spouse out for a romantic dinner at Burt and Jack's (☎954-522-5225), followed by a Royal Horse-Drawn Carriage ride from the Intracoastal Waterway to the Broward Performing Arts Center, beginning at 7 P.M. nightly (☎954-971-9820).

Parker Playhouse hosts road companies of Broadway shows with top-name actors (954-764-0700), and the Broward Center for the Performing Arts offers an impressive lineup of Broadway plays, regional opera, and drama (954-462-0222). If you're in the mood to laugh, check out the Comic Strip, where well-known comedians come from as far away as New York and Los Angeles (954-565-8887).

CHAPTER 10

# Cocoa Beach

SOUTH OF DAYTONA lies Florida's Space Coast, home of the NASA Kennedy Space Center, Spaceport U.S.A., and the U.S. Astronaut Hall of Fame. But before rockets shot off into space, the 72-mile area was home to exceptional wildlife, from sea turtle nests on Melbourne Beach to alligators and bald eagles on Merritt Island. While the main draw is the Space Center, the coastal towns of Titusville, Cocoa, Cocoa Beach, Melbourne, and Melbourne Beach offer a more laid-back family vacation than some of Florida's glitzier coastal resorts.

## Getting to Know Cocoa Beach

Though the Suruque Indians lived along the inland waterway and on the islands from what's now Titusville to Fort Pierce, along Florida's central east coast, not much else happened there until the late nineteenth century when southern farmers immigrated to the area to plant citrus trees and raise cattle. Most of the coastal towns grew slowly as distribution ports for produce and fresh fish until the late 1940s when postwar families began to vacation near the area's beaches. It wasn't until the 1960s and the creation of NASA's Space Center that Cocoa Beach began to blossom. Today, over nine million people visit the Space Center annually, injecting millions of dollars into the local economy.

# Getting Around Cocoa Beach

Public transit is nonexistent in Cocoa Beach, so it's necessary that you rent a car. To get around Cocoa Beach, you can rent a bike from the Ron Jon Surf Shop for $5 an hour or $30 a week. (Toll-free 888-757-8737, *www.ronjons.com*)

### Best Time to Go

Winter, spring, and fall are the best times to visit the Space Coast, when tens of thousands of migratory birds fill the skies and when mosquitoes are nowhere in sight. Daily highs range from 71° to 82°. The summer months, however, are stormy, hot, muggy, and buggy, though it only reaches 90°.

### Cautions and Safety Concerns

If you plan to swim off the beaches along this section of Florida's coastline, you'll need to stay on your guard because the currents can get rough, and you have to watch out for stinging jellyfish and Portuguese man-of-wars. During the summer, violent lightning thunderstorms can suddenly hit. If you find yourself caught in one, get out of the water immediately and wait out the storm under a shelter. If you travel the Space Coast in summer, be sure to bring ample insect repellent.

# Family-Oriented Resorts and Hotels

Cocoa Beach makes a good base for exploring the Space Coast. Most of the family accommodations are chain hotels and resorts near the ocean, with the better ones located in Cocoa Beach itself. However, the city of Cocoa, on the other side of the Banana River from the beach, is closer to the Kennedy Space Center if you just want to visit that.

### Doubletree Cocoa Beach Oceanfront

Reservations: ✆321-783-9222

This Doubletree resort offers luxurious rooms with refrigerators, coffeemakers, microwaves, hair dryers, irons and ironing boards, and free high-speed Internet access, plus a restaurant and lounge with ocean views.

### Holiday Inn Cocoa Beach Oceanfront Resort

Reservations: ✆Toll-free 888-465-4329

✐*www.holidayinn.com*

A 501-room beach resort with suites with kitchenettes, special family suites with a separate room for kids, two restaurants, several bars, Olympic-size pool and kids' pool, Jacuzzi, tennis court, and shuffleboard.

### Beach Island Resort

Reservations: ✆321-784-5720

✐*www.beachislandresort.com*

A family resort located on Cocoa Beach, featuring one and two-bedroom suites with full kitchens, plus a beachfront pool, hot tub, and gas barbecue grills.

### Best Western Oceanfront Resort

Reservations: ✆Toll-free 800-962-0028

✐*www.5500northcorp.com*

The closest oceanfront resort to the Kennedy Space Center, this hotel offers 180 courtyard and balconied tower rooms and suites with kitchenettes overlooking the Atlantic Ocean, plus two restaurants, outdoor heated pool and sundeck, fitness center, bar, and laundry.

### House and Condo Rentals

If you'd rather have your family stay in a condominium or a vacation home, contact the Space Coast Association of Realtors (321-452-9490) to find a realtor in the location you wish to stay in.

# Things to Do

The city of Cocoa and the town of Cocoa Beach are the main focal points of the Space Coast. You can take a guided tour through the cobblestone sidewalks of Olde Cocoa Village, a restoration of the historic downtown, into a neighborhood of tree-lined streets filled with unique specialty shops, sidewalk cafés, and art galleries (321-433-0362).

If you're interested in Florida history, the Brevard Museum of History and Natural Science in Cocoa will take you back in time through exhibits and dioramas depicting life from the prehistoric era to the Space Age. Fossils, Indian tools and pottery, and Victorian furniture help bring each era to life. The museum also displays an extensive shell collection. Your little ones will enjoy the museum's Discovery Room, with lots of objects they can touch. After you finish your visit inside, you can walk the nature trails over the museum's 22 acres. Admission is $4 per adult, $4.50 per child. (Open Tuesday through Friday 10 A.M.–5 P.M., Saturday 10 A.M.–4 P.M., Sunday noon–4 P.M., 321-632-1830, *www.brevardmuseum.org*)

## RAINY DAY FUN

If a sudden rain shower disrupts your beach time, head to the BCCP Astronaut Memorial Planetarium and Observatory on the Brevard Community College Campus in Cocoa. It offers the largest telescope in Florida to give you a bird's-eye view of the heavens, as well as space memorabilia and multimedia programs. Admission is $4–$14 (321-631-7889, *www.brevardcc.edu/planet*).

For the baseball fans in your brood, Cocoa Beach and Vero Beach each hosts a major league baseball team for spring training—see the Houston Astros at Cocoa Beach and the Los Angeles Dodgers at Vero Beach during March. Two minor league teams, the Vero Beach Dodgers and Daytona Beach Astros, play exhibition games in August.

If you're interested in buried treasure, visit the McClarty State Museum, the site of an old Spanish salvage camp at the south edge of the Sebastian Inlet State Recreation Area. In 1715 a fleet of twelve Spanish ships with heavy cargoes of gold, silver, and jewels from Mexico and Peru wrecked in a violent storm. Though 1,000 passengers drowned, the 1,500 who survived set up camps on shore to salvage some of the treasure. Today, Mel Fisher, who has salvaged Spanish galleons off the Florida Keys, has salvage rights to the underwater treasures. You'll see exhibits about Spanish trade, other area shipwrecks, and the history of the local Indians. Admission is $1. (Open daily 10:00 A.M.–4:30 P.M., 772-589-2147)

## Nature Activities

The Indian River, also known as the Mosquito Lagoon for obvious reasons in the summer, is a 160-mile-long mixture of fresh water and salt water that runs down the coast between the barrier islands and the mainland from Titusville to Sewall's Point at the end of Hutchinson Island. It's the most diverse estuary in the country, with more than 4,000 species of animals, including 700 species of fish and 310 kinds of birds. Driving the Indian River Lagoon Scenic Highway, following U.S. Route 1 and A1A down the coast from Titusville to Wabasso, will introduce you to a variety of coastal ecosystems. Teeming with marine life and dotted with hundreds of island wildfowl habitats, it varies in width from 5 miles near Merritt Island National Wildlife Refuge and the John F. Kennedy Space Center to one-tenth of a mile at Vero Beach.

## 📰 TRAVEL TIP

Spend a day at the Lone Cabbage Fish Camp on the Saint Johns River, riding a fifteen-passenger airboat for thirty minutes to see alligators, tropical birds, and tall cypress trees. Afterward, fish for catfish and bass, then eat raw oysters, frog's legs, or alligator tails in the family dining room. Boat ride is $18 for adults, $10 for children. (☎321-632-4199)

Here, you'll find a wealth of opportunities to explore Mother Nature's handiwork. You can hike 25 miles of unspoiled beach in Canaveral National Seashore and 22 miles of trails through slash pine and cypress forests. You can also choose between biking on land or fishing, water-skiing, sailing, boating, and board sailing on water. You'll find the best diving and snorkeling at Vero Beach and Jupiter Inlet.

### For the Kids

When your kids get all spaced out, take them to the unusual Brevard Zoo, where you'll stroll along shaded boardwalks and see over 550 animals in a tropical setting. You can rent a kayak, ride a train, or feed a lorikeet or a giraffe. Admission is $9.95 per adult, $6.95 per child. (Open 9:30 A.M.–4:15 P.M., 321-254-9453, *www.brevardzoo.org*)

 **TRAVEL TIP**

For some real earthbound thrills, take the kids to the Andretti Thrill Park, with its go-cart race tracks and kiddy karts for the little ones, miniature golf, bumper cars, laser tag, and an electronic arcade. A three-hour pass is $27.95 and a four-hour is $31.95. (321-956-6707, *www.andrettithrillpark.com*)

Visit the American Police Hall of Fame and Museum, honoring U.S. police officers killed in the line of duty. There are over 10,000 objects on display, plus an indoor gun range and police helicopter rides. Admission is $12 per adult, $8 per child. (Open 10 A.M.–6 P.M., 321-264-0911, *www.aphf.org*)

### Festivals and Seasonal Events

While you'll find lots of smaller community events along the Space Coast, the following are some of the major ones that you shouldn't miss if you're in the area when they're scheduled:

**Grant Seafood Festival:** If you like seafood, plan on attending this festival held in Grant, a small community south of Melbourne, during the third weekend in February. (✑*www.grant seafoodfestival.com*)

**Tico Warbird Air Show:** This annual event is a must-see if you're in Titusville in mid-March. (✆321-268-1941)

# Exploring

You'll find lots to explore beyond Cocoa and Cocoa Beach. Small beach towns along the Space Coast offer a respite from the hustle and bustle of some of Florida's more touristy resorts. And within the sight of the launch pads is a natural world of native wildlife and plants that exemplifies much of Florida's environment.

### Merritt Island National Wildlife Refuge

While standing in the shadow of the giant gantries of the Kennedy Space Center, you can watch a 4-foot-tall great blue heron devour his fish dinner at the Merritt Island National Wildlife Refuge, south of Titusville.

Established in 1963, this 140,000-acre preserve on the grounds of the Kennedy Space Center offers a variety of both drive-through and walk-through habitats, where indigenous wildlife thrives. NASA chose this 220-square-mile portion of Merritt Island because it would enable them to launch rockets over water instead of land, thus decreasing danger to nearby communities.

## ⫤FAST FACT

While you have no doubt witnessed a space shuttle blasting skyward in a cloud of smoke and fire on television, what you probably don't know is that on the grounds of the Kennedy Space Center there are more endangered species of wildlife than at any other refuge in the country, including 65 species of amphibians, 117 of fish, 25 of mammals, and 310 of birds.

The best time to observe the birds in the preserve's shallow marches and among the dunes is early morning and late afternoon. Plan to take the forty-minute ride along Black Point Wildlife Drive, a dusty road that snakes through watery marsh and pine flatwoods where you'll discover plenty of waterfowl and wading birds to photograph. Before you leave, stop at the entrance to pick up the free leaflet that describes specific stops along the route, including one from which you can observe several nests of bald eagles, and another by the mudflats where kingfishers, gulls, and terns swoop in for a meal. Several species of migratory waterfowl retreat here during the coldest months of the year, making this one of Florida's prime bird-watching areas.

Or you can hike the Oak Hammock Trail, a thirty-minute walk through a hardwood hammock, or the short self-guiding Turtle Mound Trail leading to the top of a 50-foot-high Surruque Indian oyster shell mound, from which you'll get a panoramic view of the Indian River and the NASA launch pads.

##  TRAVEL TIP

Don't miss the unique sculpture, created in 1971 by Tampa sculptor Lewis Vandercar, on the southern tip of Merritt Island. A 100-foot-long dragon, constructed of twenty tons of concrete and steel, overlooks the Indian and Banana rivers. Vandercar added four hatchlings in 1982. Legend says a dragon once rose out of the river to chase away enemies attacking island Indians.

Be sure to stop at the Refuge's Visitor Information Center for maps, brochures, and wildlife books. Admission is free. (The refuge is open daily 8 A.M.–two hours before sunset while the visitor center is open Monday through Friday 8:00 A.M.–4:30 P.M., Saturday and Sunday 9:00 A.M.–5:00 P.M., closed Sundays in April–October, 321-861-0667, *www".fws.gov/merrittisland*)

## Titusville and Melbourne

The main focus of downtown Titusville is its National Historic District. Along the main street you can walk past turn-of-the-century buildings that are now home to a historical museum, floral and antique shops, and cafés.

 **JUST FOR PARENTS**

Take in an exciting jai alai match at the Melbourne Jai-Alai Fronton from January to March and October to December, or the huge Fort Pierce Jai Alai Fronton from March to September. The fast-action sport of jai alai was originally played by Basque peasants in the Pyrenees Mountains of Spain.

Much like Titusville, downtown Melbourne, on the banks of Crane Creek, has charming turn-of-the-century buildings that now contain restaurants, art galleries, boutiques, antique shops, and book, jewelry, and craft stores. Both towns offer places to just sit on a bench and watch the boats in the harbor.

## Fort Pierce

Though named for an 1838 palmetto-log fort built by U.S. Army troops to defend the area against the Seminole Indians that once stood here, Fort Pierce didn't become an official town until 1901. Not only is it famous as a citrus distribution center, it also has great beaches.

Take a break from lying in the Florida sun to visit the Saint Lucie County Historical Museum, which features coins and other artifacts from a 1715 shipwreck of a Spanish treasure fleet sailing from Havana, plus military artifacts from the Seminole Wars and exhibits on growing pineapples and raising cattle. There's also a excellent collection of 1,500 glass-plate negatives taken in the area by photographer Harry Hill between 1890 and 1920, a full-size Seminole chickee (a palm-thatched, open-sided hut) and a re-creation of the turn-of-the-century Chubbs General Store. Outside, you can wander into the Gardner House, a restored "Cracker" cottage from 1907, with its tall ceilings and many windows to allow the steamy Florida air to flow through it. Admission is $4 per adult, $1.50 per child. (Open Tuesday through Saturday 10 A.M.–4 P.M., Sunday noon–4 P.M., 772-468-1795)

Nearby on North Hutchinson Island is the UDT-Seal Museum, with exhibits and artifacts relating to the Navy Underwater Demolition Teams (UDTs) who trained on Fort Pierce beaches during World War II. The Navy created the Sea Air Land (SEAL) units, a modern equivalent, during the 1960s. Admission is $5 per adult, $2 per child. (Open Monday through Saturday 10 A.M.–4 P.M., Sunday noon–4 P.M., 772-595-5845, *www.navysealmuseum.com*)

Hutchinson Island runs from Fort Pierce to the area across the Saint Lucie and Indian rivers from the town of Stuart, 72 miles below Cocoa. Here, you'll find two historical sites to explore. Gilbert's Bar House of Refuge, 5 miles east of Stuart and the oldest house in the area, is a restored three-story frame house built by the U.S. Coast Guard in 1875—one of five erected along Florida's east coast. You'll learn about the refuge's rooms, furnished with Victoriana as they were when shipwreck survivors stayed there, by taking the free guided tour every day except Saturday. The boathouse exhibits early lifesaving equipment and a reconstructed 1875 surf-boat constructed with nails and clinkers, or wooden screws. Admission is $4 per adult, $2 per child. (Open Monday through Saturday 10 A.M.–4 P.M., Sunday 1–4 P.M., 772-225-1875)

The Elliott Museum nearby displays the works of Sterling Elliott, who invented the first address-stamping machine and knot-tying machinery in the 1870s and the steering system used in automobiles before the advent of power steering. Assembled by Elliott Jr., the museum contains collections of early toys, classic cars, motorcycles, bicycles, and antique photographic equipment, as well as period rooms with needlepointed objects and tools, and an old-time apothecary shop. Admission is $3. (Open daily 1–5 P.M., 772-225-1961, *www .elliottmuseumfl.org*)

## 🧳 TRAVEL TIP

If you're interested in bonsai, be sure to stop by the Heathcote Botanical Gardens, a beautiful display of exotic flowers, tropical trees, and brightly colored foliage, featuring a Japanese bonsai collection, located just off Indian River Drive in Fort Pierce. Admission is $4 for adults, $2 for children. (Open Tuesday through Saturday 9 A.M.–5 P.M., ☎407-464-4672, ✎www.heathcotebotanicalgardens.org)

Twenty-five miles south of the Elliott Museum at the junction of the wild Loxahatchee River and the Jupiter Inlet stands the Jupiter Inlet Lighthouse, not far from the town of Jupiter. Built between 1854 and 1860, the 105-foot conical brick lighthouse is one of the oldest still operating on the Atlantic Seaboard. The lighthouse keeper's cottage contains a small museum. Admission is $6. (Open Saturday through Wednesday 10 A.M.–4 P.M., 561-747-6639)

### Extra Special

The NASA Kennedy Space Center is the main attraction along the Space Coast and a fascinating and educational place to spend the day with your family. Arrive at the Space Center early to avoid the crowds, or visit on weekends and during May and September when there are fewer people. Buy your all-inclusive tickets from the ticket pavilion as soon as you arrive.

The first U.S. satellite rose from the launch pad at the U.S. Air Force Base on Cape Canaveral in 1958. Alan Shepard and Gus Grissom became the first and second Americans to fly into space, both on suborbital flights, in 1961. Less than a decade later, in 1969, Apollo 11 lifted off from the Kennedy Space Center on Merritt Island, between the mainland and Cape Canaveral, for the first manned landing on the moon. In 1981, the first space shuttle flight rose from Pad A. Today, the Kennedy Space Center remains the heart of the American space program and the area's biggest family tourist attraction.

As with Central Florida's theme parks, crowds pack the Space Center daily. Two narrated bus tours, departing every fifteen minutes from the visitor center, give you a behind-the-scenes look at operations. You'll get to know about this mammoth 220-square-mile complex during the two-hour narrated "Red Bus" tour, which departs regularly. After first crossing the "crawlerway," the tracks on which the massive six-million-pound crawler/transporters carry the space shuttles to their launch pad, your double-decker bus will stop at the unmanned rocket launch sites, the mission control building, then proceed to the fifty-two-story Vehicle Assembly Building where technicians assemble the shuttles and fit them with their payloads. Though you can't go in, you may be able to peek in the door if it's open to see the interior of one of world's largest structures. It's so high that NASA had to install special air conditioning to prevent clouds from forming inside. Afterward, you'll ride out to Launch Complex 39 and Pad A and B, where NASA prepares and launches the space shuttles. If you're lucky, a shuttle may be awaiting launch. And you can even photograph your family standing around a Saturn V rocket. The Flight Crew Training Building, where you can experience a simulation of the Apollo 11 launch and see an actual lunar module, is probably the tour's most interesting stop.

##  TRAVEL TIP

To witness a launch of the space shuttle, phone the Kennedy Space Center between 8 A.M. and 4 P.M. to reserve a free pass (☏321-449-4444). However, you can see one from a beach vantage point anywhere within a 40-mile radius of the Space Center. Call for launch schedule. (☏Toll-free 877-893-6272)

The "Blue Tour" shows you the Cape Canaveral Air Force Station, as well as the sites where America's first astronauts rocketed into space in the Mercury and Gemini space capsules. You'll also stop at the Air Force Space Museum to see its collection of space memorabilia and missiles.

You'll began and end your tours at the Visitor Center, Spaceport U.S.A. Here, your kids can climb aboard the Ambassador, a 68-ton replica of a space shuttle orbiter, to receive an astronaut point of view. Then you'll stroll through Satellites and You, an exhibit showing how satellites affect your daily life, using interactive videos and animatronics. For a look at artistic interpretations of space travel, browse the Gallery of Space Flight, which chronicles the history of human space exploration with full-size models of the lunar rover and the Viking Mars Lander, followed by a look into the Galaxy Art Center, which contains the NASA Art Gallery, displaying 250 paintings commissioned by NASA, and two movie theaters, one an IMAX. Spaceport U.S.A. also contains a collection of Mercury, Saturn, and Gemini rockets, as well as models of rocket engines and the lunar module, lunar rover, space suits, the Viking craft used on Mars, and a reproduction of the flight deck of a space shuttle, plus the recovered capsules of a number of manned flights.

Outside, your little ones will enjoy playing among Saturn and Juno rockets, a lunar module, and an Apollo launch tower in the Rocket Garden. Just beyond, the Astronauts Memorial honors the courage and spirit of the U.S. astronauts who have given their lives while exploring space.

The Astronaut Hall of Fame stands next to the Kennedy Space Center entrance on the NASA Parkway. Here, you can get to know the accomplishments of America's first team of seven astronauts through videotapes, photographs, and professional mementos, plus feel the pull of four Gs in the G-Force Simulator and take a virtual walk on the moon. Admission is $38 per adult, $28 per child for all of the above. (Open daily 9 A.M.–7 P.M., 321-449-4444, *www.kennedyspacecenter.com*)

West of Spaceport U.S.A. on the mainland in Titusville stands the Valiant Warbird Museum, featuring displays of 350 vintage American warplanes, such as a C-47 used in the D-day invasion and the Flying Tigers that flew with the Chinese Air Force to stop the Japanese invasion of the mainland. Admission is $9 per adult, $5 per child. (Open daily 10 A.M.–6 P.M., 321-268-1941, *www.vacwarbirds.org*)

 **TRAVEL TIP**

Allow time to see at least one of these films. In the Visitor Center's IMAX theater, you'll join shuttle astronauts in flight in *The Dream Is Alive*. In *Blue Planet*, crews of five space shuttle missions show you the environmental effects of man and nature from 300 miles up.

# By Day

You'll find plenty to do to make your days fly by along the Space Coast. The beaches here offer great sunbathing and good swimming, and with so many waterways, you'll want to take a cruise of some kind every day. And several golf courses offer challenging rounds to break up your beach time.

### On the Beach

Just a few miles south of the Kennedy Space Center and east across the Hubert Humphrey Bridge and Merritt Island Causeway lies Cocoa Beach, a resort town with hundreds of small motels, fast-food outlets, and souvenir and T-shirt shops—and some of the largest waves in Florida. Needless to say, surfers love it. If you want to try surfing, you can rent a board from Ron Jon Surf Shop for about $8 a day (Toll-free 888-757-8737, *www.ronjons.com*). You can also take lessons if you're a beginner. From the end of Cocoa Beach Pier, a historic landmark that reaches 840 feet out over the Atlantic, you'll get a great view of the beach with its crowds of sun worshipers. It's also a great place to hang out your fishing line.

If you're a beach lover, you can spend a day on the less crowded Playalinda or Apollo beach, both within the Canaveral National Seashore. The 57,000-acre coastal preserve, near the Kennedy Space

Center, has 25 miles of beach and dunes and is the largest undeveloped and protected area of Florida's Atlantic coast. You can reach Apollo Beach on the north end and the Playalinda Beach on the south end by driving, but the wild central area, Klondike Beach, can be reached only by walking. Both have parking areas with crosswalks leading to the beach over the dunes. These are natural beaches, without hot dog stands and bathhouses. Only Apollo Beach, within the 676-acre Apollo State Park, has running water, so you'll have to bring food and drink with you. But if you're seeking sand, sun, and solitude, you'll find plenty here. The park closes from late spring through August so that sea turtles can come ashore at night to nest.

##  TRAVEL TIP

Take your kids on a Turtle Walk to watch sea turtles lay their eggs at high tide, from May to August. Females use their hind flippers to dig a hole and deposit up to 300 white Ping-Pong-ball-size eggs. The eggs hatch within sixty days. Approximately one in 10,000 survives. Walks usually last from 9:00 P.M. to midnight. Contact the Brevard Turtle Preservation Society for a (required) reservation (℡321-676-1701).

Farther south lies Sebastian Inlet State Recreation Area, halfway between Melbourne and Vero Beach. Less than a mile wide, this 643-acre park is, without a doubt, the best place to surf along Florida's east coast. Surfers of all levels enjoy riding the roaring 6-foot waves that pound the north-side beach, especially in April. If you don't know how to surf, you can take lessons from the pros. The park, with its lagoons, coastal hammocks, and mangrove swamps, is also a habitat for about 200 species of birds. While you're there, search the beach for pieces of eight from Spanish wrecks washed ashore by storms. Admission is $2 per car. (Open daily 8 A.M.–sunset, 772-984-4852)

## On the Boat

You can take a number of different types of cruises from ports along the Space Coast for $20–$25 per person. The following selection offers you plenty of variety:

**Florida Dolphin Watch:** With only six passengers per boat, you get up close to wild dolphins and even get to feed them on this two-hour tour. (☎772-466-4660, *www.floridadolphinwatch.com*)

**Grasshopper Airboat Ecotours:** An informative hour-and-a-half airboat tour along the Saint Johns River. (☎321-631-2990, *www.airboatecotours.com*)

**Indian River Cruises:** Sail aboard a 47-foot catamaran, departing three times daily from the waterfront park in Olde Cocoa Village. (☎321-223-6825)

**Island Boat Lines:** A variety of cruises from two to six hours to search for wildlife and manatees. (☎321-302-0544, *www.islandboatlines.com*)

**Little Dixie River Queen:** A forty-nine-passenger tour boat that takes daily ecology tours from Sebastian State Recreation Area. (☎Toll-free 888-755-6161)

**Schooner Sails:** Sail aboard the tall ship *Wanderer* out of Port Canaveral on a sightseeing day or sunset trip. (☎321-783-5274, *www.schoonersails.com*)

**Space Coast Nature Tours:** Cruise along the Intracoastal Waterway and up rivers in search of wildlife near the Kennedy Space Center. (☎321-267-4551, *www.space-coast.com*)

If you're a bit more adventurous, you can join a two-to-three-hour kayaking tour of mangrove forests and islands with Adventure Kayak of Cocoa Beach for $25 per adult and $15 per child under 16; paddling lessons included. (321-480-8632, *www.advkayak.com*)

The Space Coast offers plenty of opportunities to fish. The shallow brackish water and dense grass of the upper reaches of the Indian River provide ideal fishing for mullet and redfish. You can also go clamming, crabbing, and shrimping. Within the Merritt Island

Wildlife Refuge, you'll find great fly fishing for 6- to 12-pound "gator" trout in the shallow grass flats of the broad Banana River, but to fish here you must purchase a license at the Refuge's Visitor's Center. There's also good surf fishing for whiting, pompano, and scrappy bluefish along beaches facing the Atlantic Ocean. You might also spend a day aboard a deep-sea charter if you want to reel in some mackerel, sailfish, marlin, wahoo, or tuna. Make arrangements with Obsession Fishing Charters (321-453-3474, *www.fishobsession.com*) of Cape Canaveral or Gettin' There II Sportfishing Charters (321-631-5055, *www.gettinthere.com*) of Cocoa.

## Under the Water

The best place to snorkel along the Space Coast is Bathtub Reef Park, where an offshore reef near the southern tip of Hutchinson Island forms a bathtub-calm shallow area that's perfect for snorkeling. You can rent equipment from Oceansports World in Cocoa Beach (321-783-4088, *www.oceansports.com*). Though the diving isn't the best, you can rent equipment from Cocoa Beach Scuba Odyssey, also in Cocoa Beach (321-537-9751).

## On the Links and on the Courts

While rockets dominate the Space Coast, you can get in a round or two between seeing the sights. The following courses have multiple tees, enabling you to play challenging golf no matter what your skill level.

**Baytree National Golf Links:** This semi-private eighteen-hole course, designed by Gary Player, is in Melbourne. (321-259-9060, *www.baytree.com*)

**Cocoa Beach Country Club:** This twenty-seven hole, semi-private championship golf course has a pro shop, a driving range, and a clubhouse with lighted tennis courts and an outdoor pool with children's pool. (321-868-3351)

**The Habitat at Valkaria:** The third Brevard County course is a championship eighteen-holer, designed by Charles Ankrom and located south of Melbourne, nestled in a coastal estuary environment with mounded fairways. Greens fee and services are the same as the preceding Brevard courses. (✆321-952-4588)

**The Savannahs on Merritt Island:** Situated next to a natural savannah, this is another of Breward County's eighteen-hole courses that golfers share with exotic water birds. Greens fee and services are the same as at Spessard Holland. (✆321-952-4588)

**Spessard Holland at Melbourne Beach:** Designed by Arnold Palmer Enterprises, this extremely popular executive eighteen-hole course—one of three Brevard County courses—offers an oasis of golfing pleasure between the Atlantic Ocean and the Indian River. The constant ocean breeze presents a challenge for most golfers. Greens fee is $17. (✆321-952-4588)

## Shopping

It's fun to browse through the craft and clothing shops of Cocoa and Cocoa Beach. And be sure to stop by the Ron Jon Surf Shop, a Cocoa Beach landmark since 1963 and a destination in itself. This mind-boggling store, stocked with T-shirts, swimsuits, beach bikes, surfboards, boogie boards, Jet Skis, water-skis, and scuba-diving gear—everything you need to make your beach vacation complete—calls itself the world's largest surf shop and is open twenty-four hours (Toll-free 888-757-8737, *www.ronjons.com*). The Dinosaur Store in Cocoa Beach offers the largest selection of fossils in the country, including pieces of amber and amber jewelry, meteorites, and minerals (321-783-7300). If you want to bring home some Indian River oranges, you can get then from Harvey's Indian River Groves (321-636-6072).

East New Haven Avenue is a quaint Melbourne neighborhood of antique stores and art galleries. But the best reason to visit it is City News Books (407-725-0330), a shop full of racks of regional publications, travel guides, and maps.

If your family begins to suffer from mall withdrawal, take them to the Merritt Square Mall, with ninety-five stores to suit every need (321-452-3272, *www.merrittsquaremall.com*). Bargain hunters beware!

The Super Flea and Farmer's Market in Melbourne, an indoor and outdoor market with over 300 dealers in 900 booths and eight food stalls has bargains by the carload (321-242-9124, *www.superfleamar ket.com*).

# Dining Out and Nightlife

Enjoy French, Italian, or Caribbean dishes at a variety of ocean or riverside restaurants in all price ranges along the Space Coast. Freshly caught seafood tops most menus. Be sure to sample the local favorite, rock shrimp.

**Bernard's Surf:** A landmark in Cocoa Beach for over sixty years, this restaurant and raw bar offers the freshest crab, lobster, and fish, plus a variety of steak and ribs—and Cajun-fried alligator tail. (2 South Atlantic Avenue, Cocoa Beach, ✆321-783-2401)

**Dixie Crossroads:** If your family likes to eat, take them to this large family-style restaurant, serving all kinds of seafood dishes in plentiful helpings, as well as a variety of shellfish served in one dozen, two dozen, or all-you-can-eat portions—all accompanied by overflowing glasses of sweet iced tea. (1475 Garden Street, Titusville, ✆321-268-5000)

**Herbie K's Diner:** A contemporary, all-American diner serving burgers, fries, shakes, malts, and sandwiches in stylized 1950s decor, complete with tabletop jukeboxes. (2080 North Atlantic Boulevard, Cocoa Beach, ✆321-783-6740)

**Kountry Kitchen:** Home-style food like chicken and dumplings and spareribs, and especially its famous Southern-style breakfasts, served in a large friendly dining room. (1115 North Courtenay Parkway, Merritt Island, ✆321-459-3457)

**Nannie Lee's Strawberry Mansion:** Dine on pastas, veal, chicken, and steak in the rooms of a pink Victorian house with stained glass and floral wallpaper. (1218 East New Haven Avenue, Melbourne, ✆321-724-8078)

**JUST FOR PARENTS**

One of the newest entertainment facilities on the Space Coast is the Melbourne Greyhound Park, where many of the top racing kennels send their stars to the post. You can watch the action from the Winner's Club dining room. (☎772-259-9800)

Generally, nighttime entertainment has a youthful bent in Cocoa Beach. At Desperadoes you can munch on Mexican appetizers washed down with ice-cold margaritas while you listen to live soloists (321-784-3363). Or you can join in on the fun outside at Coconuts on the Beach (321-784-1422).

If you like to dance, head for the flashing neon flamingo sign of the Tropicana, an entertainment complex featuring a bar with a huge TV, a big mirrored dance floor, and a pool room (321-799-3800). The spacious dance floor at Brassy's Take II fills with a sizable crowd after 10 P.M.( 321-784-1277). If all you want to do is relax after a day in the sun and surf, nestle into the bookshelf-lined interior of Dino's Jazz Piano Bar (321-784-5470). All are in Cocoa Beach.

# CHAPTER 11

# *Jacksonville*

IN THE JACKSONVILLE AREA, history and legends are so intermingled it's difficult to tell where one stops and the other begins. In Jacksonville, skyscrapers signal the progress of the twenty-first century while standing watch over French and Spanish fortresses of the sixteenth and seventeenth centuries that protected the country's earliest settlements. And a short way down the coast, Saint Augustine, the oldest city in the nation, offers a look at those early times. Later, this area's beach resorts were the first to draw winter visitors to the Sunshine State.

## Getting to Know Jacksonville

Situated on the banks of the Saint Johns River, Jacksonville is the state's largest city and the commercial hub of northeast Florida. The peaceful Timucua Indians were the area's first inhabitants. But it wasn't until 1822 that settlers founded Jacksonville on the banks of the Saint Johns River.

During the Civil War, the city acted as the main Confederate port for timber, cotton, and citrus fruit from the surrounding area. Union soldiers occupied it four times, destroying the port. It took until 1883 when the railroads connected it to other parts of the state for it to recover. It was then that the wealthy made it the vacation capital of the United States, serving as the gateway to warm spring health spas, steamboat cruises on the Saint Johns River, hunting and fishing at sports resorts, and magnificent Victorian hotels at broad, sandy beaches.

During the late nineteenth century, Standard Oil tycoon Henry Flagler spent his second honeymoon on a steamboat trip up the Saint Johns River. He fell in love with Florida and saw the potential to make a fortune through development. He became obsessed with his dream, financing a coastal railroad and resort hotel chain from Jacksonville to Key West.

Skyscrapers now soar above the Saint Johns River. Universities, museums, and art galleries give Jacksonville a sophisticated aura that reflects its wealth. But unlike the wealthier resort towns farther south, it doesn't flaunt it but welcomes the average family to its sites.

# Getting Around the Jacksonville Area

Because of Jacksonville's sheer size—at 841 square miles, the second largest city in the country—you'll find driving a car the ideal way to get around. However, in Saint Augustine you have the option of traveling aboard the Saint Augustine Sightseeing Trains. These are a series of open-air trains that pick up passengers over a 7-mile narrated tour route, allowing them to stop off to see more than twenty attractions and reboard a later train. The trains run every fifteen minutes between 8 A.M. and 5 P.M. and charge one price of $18 per adult, $5 per child for a three-day ticket (904-829-6545). You can also catch a local bus to the beach in Daytona, then catch the A1A Beachside Trolley Monday through Saturday, noon–7 P.M., to get to different sites along it (386-761-7700, *www.votran.org*).

### Best Time to Go

The Jacksonville area lies fully in the temperate zone, with winter highs only in the mid-60s and lows in the mid-40s. Summers, with highs in the pleasant mid-80s, are the best time to visit. However, stay away from Daytona Beach during March and April when half a million college students arrive for Spring Break.

## Cautions and Safety Concerns

As with any seaside resort, be mindful of your valuables. Carry only what you need to the beach and when walking in crowded tourist areas. And be sure to take along plenty of sunscreen.

# Family-Oriented Resorts and Hotels

You'll find mostly middle-market chain hotels in and around Jacksonville, offering the usual amenities, so the cost of staying here is moderate. There are some deluxe resorts up and down the coast, but for the most part, hotels here cater to families.

### Amelia Island Plantation

Reservations: ☎904-261-6161

Located at the southern end of Amelia Island, this deluxe family resort offers sprawling grounds with one-, two-, and three-bedroom beachfront villas, a health club, boating and fishing facilities, nature and jogging trails, horseback and bike paths, kids' programs, plus forty-five holes of excellent golf and twenty-five tennis courts.

### Perry's Ocean Edge Hotel

Reservations: ☎386-255-0581

This 206-room oceanfront hotel in Daytona Beach features regular or enclosed-garden rooms, plus garden efficiency or full suites, two outdoor and one indoor/outdoor pool, and whirlpool.

### Sea Turtle Inn

Reservations: ☎Toll-free 800-874-6000

A beachfront resort in Jacksonville Beach, featuring oceanfront suites with refrigerator and free wireless Internet, plus a restaurant and a pool with cabana bar.

### House and Condo Rentals

Condominiums line the ocean boulevards from Fernandina Beach to Daytona. Contact any of the following for rental information:

- **All South Realty, Inc.:** Jacksonville Beach, ☎904-241-4141
- **Ponte Vedra Beach Realty:** Ponte Vedra Beach, ☎Toll-free 888-575-0077
- **Suncastle Properties, Inc.:** Ponte Vedra Beach, ☎Toll-free 800-386-5585

# Things to Do

Jacksonville's crowning glory is two fine museums—the Cummer Museum of Art and the Jacksonville Art Museum.

The Cummer Museum of Art and Gardens has occupied the building since 1961. In it, you'll discover a furnished room from the 1907 Cummer house, plus an eclectic collection occupying eleven galleries, including a relief of Ramses II from 1280 B.C., a fine collection of eighteenth-century Meissen porcelain tableware, and ivory and jade netsuke. Outside, you can walk through the formal gardens of the original Cummer mansion. Admission is $6 per adult, $1 per child (open Tuesday through Saturday 10 A.M.–5 P.M., weekends noon–5 P.M., ☎904-356-6857). The Jacksonville Art Museum, also free, has collections of Chinese and Korean porcelain and pre-Columbian artifacts (open Tuesday, Wednesday, and Friday 10 A.M.–4 P.M., Thursdays to 10 P.M., weekends 1–5 P.M., 904-398-8336).

For a bit of history, visit the 119-acre Fort Caroline National Monument, commemorating the site of an attempt by the French to settle in Florida. Here, you'll see a reproduction of the original triangular earthworks-and-palisade fort, built 4 miles from the mouth of the Saint Johns River by a party of 300 French Huguenots in July 1564. Unfortunately, they fought among themselves after having narrowly escaped starvation. As they were about to abandon their fort, Jean Ribault arrived in August 1565 with reinforcements. Spanish admiral Pedro Menéndez de Avilés thought that Ribault's forces were going to attack San Augustín. So he marched on Fort Caroline while a storm kept the French ships occupied, killing over 140 French Protestants and taking the fort on September 20. Two weeks later, Menéndez killed half of Ribault's shipwrecked men. Two and a half years later, after Fort Caroline had become Fort San Mateo, French troops mounted a counterattack, burning the fort and executing the Spanish soldiers. Though the museum displays Indian and European artifacts of the period, you'll find the real attraction is the fort. Admission is free. (Open daily 9 A.M.–5 P.M., 904-641-7155)

 ## JUST FOR PARENTS

Spend an afternoon at the dog track watching greyhounds race to the finish line at the Jacksonville Kennel Club from May to September and at the Orange Park Kennel Club from September to May—both in Jacksonville. (✆904-646-0001)

On Fort George Island, now a part of the City of Jacksonville, you'll find the 14-acre Kingsley Plantation Historic Site, containing what historians believe to be Florida's oldest plantation house and part of the 46,000-acre Timucuan Ecological and Historic Preserve run by the National Park Service. At the end of an oyster-shell road lined with moss-hung oaks and palmettos stands an early-nineteenth-century frame plantation house and the adjoining Juan McQueen House from 1791, on the riverbank. When Scotsman Zephaniah Kingsley acquired the island in 1817, he built the main house, with its nine rooms, because he didn't think the original house, deeded to McQueen by the Spanish, was appropriate for an early-nineteenth-century businessman growing cotton and trading slaves. From 1813 to 1839, Kingsley became wealthy from the labors of his 200 slaves. His wife, Anna Jai, a black woman from Madagascar who spoke three languages, took care of the house. A later owner of the house turned it into a Victorian resort. Learn about the plantation's fascinating history on daily ranger-led tours of the house and grounds. Admission is free. (Open daily 9 A.M.–5 P.M., 904-251-3537)

### For the Kids

You'll find plenty to keep your little ones from getting bored in Jacksonville. Begin with a visit to the Jacksonville Zoo, where they can wander the grounds observing over 2,000 animals ranging from ostriches and wildebeest to kangaroos, parrots, white rhino, and giraffes. Opened in 1914, it has become famous for its breeding programs. Instead of fences, the 89-acre zoo separates its animals from visitors with moats, allowing your kids to get a closer view. You'll walk on a boardwalk stretching over The African Veldt, an 11-acre recreation of an African savannah, and see grazing wildebeest and lions roaming the "plains" of Mahali Pa Simba, the lion exhibit.

 **TRAVEL TIP**

For real excitement, your kids will thank you for taking them to Adventure Landing in Jacksonville Beach, an entertainment park with go-carts, laser tag, a mega-arcade, and miniature golf. And in summer, they can splash in the Shipwreck Island Water Park. (Open daily, ☏904-246-4386, ✉www.adventurelanding.com)

The highlight of the zoo is the Okavango Village Petting Zoo, where they can get friendly with miniature horses, pygmy goats, dwarf zebu, and Sardinian pygmy donkeys. They'll go ape at Chimpanorma, and alligators lurk in the wetland habitat. At 11:30 A.M. on weekdays and at noon and 2:30 P.M. on weekends and holidays, they can watch the keepers bathe the elephants in "Elephant Encounter," then take a ride on one. Another show, "Animals and Us," presented three times daily on weekends, highlights the habitats and food of native animals. Admission is $9.50 per adult, $6.50 per child. (Open daily 9 A.M.–5 P.M., 904-757-4463, *www.jaxzoo.org*)

Even more exciting is a trip to the Saint Augustine Alligator Farm, the state's oldest attraction, operating since 1893. Time your visit to coincide with the twice-daily alligator show. You'll see a handler drag an alligator around by its tail while it bellows loudly, arches its back, and opens its mouth in anger. But when he sits on the animal's back and sticks his fingers between the gator's teeth, your kid's heart will stop for a moment. Admission is $17.95 per adult, $9.95 per child. (Open daily 9 A.M.–5 P.M., 386-824-3337, *www.alligatorfarm.com*)

Kids can swim with a dolphin for twenty minutes at Marineland's Dolphin Conservation Center for $120. Opened as Marine Studios in 1938 as the world's first underwater motion picture studio, its dolphin shows have thrilled visitors for decades. Toll-free 888-279-9194, *www.marineland.net*)

### Festivals and Seasonal Events

There are a variety of local events, including food and art festivals that you may find interesting, but the following are three of the top ones:

**Speed Weeks:** For two weeks in February, crowds gather at Daytona International Speedway for the action-packed twenty-four-hour Rolex 24 at Daytona and other races leading up to the Daytona 500. Tickets go for $25 and up and sell out in advance. (✆386-253-7223, *www.daytonainternationalspeedway.com*)

**Isle of Eight Flags Shrimp Festival:** Fishermen welcome you aboard their crafts in early May, with food, folk music, and mock pirates. (✆Toll-free 866-426-3542, *www.shrimpfestival.com*)

**Birthplace of Speed Celebration:** This three-day event over Thanksgiving weekend on Ormond Beach commemorates the first auto races in 1903 with antique car races today. (✆386-677-3454)

# Exploring

Begin your exploration of Florida's northern coast by following the Buccaneer Trail, a 125-mile oceanside highway that starts where the first French and Spanish explorers first walked in Florida at Fernandina Beach and continues to Saint Augustine. Buccaneers like Sir Francis Drake, Edward Teach (alias Blackbeard), and Jean Lafitte pillaged the Indians and exploited each other. But as you drive past peaceful islands, inlets, and forts, it's hard to imagine the turbulence of those early years. And while history comes alive in Saint Augustine, vast aquatic preserves, coastal wildlife sanctuaries, salt marshes, the state's oldest live oak forest, and nine beach parks stretch along the Atlantic.

## Fernandina Beach and Amelia Island

Amelia Island, 13 miles long by 2 miles wide, has only one town, Fernandina Beach, named by the Spanish for King Ferdinand VII of Spain in 1811. Great sand dunes fringed with sea oats frame sweeping Atlantic beaches. Birds live in its salt marshes and ancient live oaks draped in Spanish moss hang over streets lined with Victorian mansions.

It's the only place in the United States to have been under the rule of eight flags. To learn about this, you must visit 1,086-acre Fort Clinch State Park, located at the northeastern tip of the island. French explorer Jean Ribault arrived first in May 1562, calling the island Isle of Mai (Isle of May). Rene de Laudonnier took over for Ribault in 1564 and built Fort Caroline. Three years later, Spaniards captured the fort, followed by the British in 1735, renaming it in honor of Princess Amelia, King George II's daughter. In 1812, the "Patriots of Amelia Island" flew their flag, and in 1817, the Green Cross of the Florida Republic appeared. That same year, privateer Luis Aury flew the flag of the Republic of Mexico.

After Florida became a part of the United States, the U.S. Army built Fort Clinch as one of a chain of U.S. masonry forts along the Atlantic Coast. And though its ramparts with their mounted cannon are impressive, it never saw action. Construction on the pentagonal fort began in 1847, but the Confederate troops seized it in 1861 and in 1862 abandoned it to Union troops, who used it as prison for the remainder of the Civil War. Visit the museum to learn about the fort's history, then take a guided tour of the bastions, restored barracks, infirmary, bakery, and blacksmith's shop. Or take the candlelit tour on summer weekends. Admission $2 per person. (Open daily 9 A.M.–5 P.M., 904-277-7233)

 ## JUST FOR PARENTS

Midway between Jacksonville and Ormond Beach lies Washington Oaks State Gardens, a 390-acre park on the grounds of the former Belle Vista Plantation, site of one of Florida's first orange groves. The original plantation house now acts as a horticultural center, featuring rose, camellia, and tropical gardens set amid reflecting pools. Admission is $2 per car. (Open daily 8 A.M.–sunset, ☏904-445-3161)

After visiting the fort, you can take a two-hour guided tour at 3 P.M. of Fernandina Beach's fifty-block historic district, with its restored nineteenth-century Victorian buildings. One of these, the Palace Saloon, is Florida's oldest tavern. You should also take the forty-five-minute tour at 11 A.M. or 2 P.M. of the Museum of History, housed in the former jail. Admission is $1. (Open Monday through Friday 11 A.M.–3 P.M.)

### Ormond Beach

Ormond Beach, north of Daytona, used to be sugar plantation country. Just north of town stands Bulow Plantation Ruins Historic Site. Looking more like a movie set than the ruins of an old plantation, the crumbling remains of an eighteenth-century sugar mill stand eerily in the thick subtropical growth. A visit to the visitor center will help you understand plantation life and the use of slave labor to produce sugar cane, rice, and cotton. Eventually, the Seminole Indians burned it in retaliation for being displaced by white settlers. Admission is free. (Open daily 8 A.M.–5 P.M., 386-517-2084)

Not much changed until the 1880s, when Henry Flagler bought and enlarged the Ormond Hotel to house tourists from his railroad.

Legend says that in 1918 John D. Rockefeller, upset with his treatment at the Ormond, bought his own three-story winter home across the street, which he called "The Casements." Admission is free. (Open Monday through Friday 10:00 A.M.–2:30 P.M., 386-676-3216)

## Daytona Beach

When you think of Daytona Beach, you probably think of college students whooping it up at all-night beer parties, but it was car enthusiasts such as Henry Ford, Louis Chevrolet, and Ransom Olds who came here during the early twentieth century to race their prototype vehicles on the straight, hard-packed beach. Those were daring days when someone broke the land speed record regularly. In 1935, Malcolm Campbell sped along at 276 miles per hour in his Bluebird with its V-12 engine.

Daytona Beach, named for Mathias Day, an 1870s immigrant from Ohio, began to blossom after Flagler's hotel in Ormond Beach became a success. The wide sand beaches became an ideal place for wealthy entrepreneurs to test the speed and maneuverability of their new motor vehicles. In 1903, the Florida East Coast Automobile Association formed to promote beach racing. And for the next three decades, drivers from all over the world came to Daytona Beach to set world racecar records.

By 1936, William Henry Getty (Bill) France began racing his father's Model-T and by 1938 organized and promoted racing events on Daytona's 3-mile course. The American Automobile Association sanctioned the races, offering $5,000 in prizes, attracting many of the country's top drivers. But World War II temporarily halted racing at Daytona.

As soon as the war ended, racing resumed. A large crowd watched the first successful stock-car race in 1947. Later that year France and a group of leading drivers formed the National Association for Stock Car Auto Racing (NASCAR). He petitioned the State of Florida in 1955 to build a racetrack. Daytona International Speedway, with 150,000-person capacity, two-and-a-half-mile oval track, and a twisting infield road course, today plays host to some of the world's premier motor racing events.

It used to be that the only way to experience a Speedway race was to buy a ticket. Now you can spend several hours at Daytona U.S.A., a 60,000-square-foot interactive motor sports theme park at Daytona Speedway. You can play TV announcer and call the race, drive a stock car on the track using a computer simulator, interview top drivers using interactive DVD technology, and lots more. Then you can view *NASCAR 3D: The Imax Experience* and *Daytona 500 Movie* on a four-story IMAX screen. Admission is $21.50 per adult, $15.50 per child. For an additional $8.50 you can take a thirty-minute behind-the-scenes tram tour around the track, into the pit road, and through the garage. (386-947-6800, *www.daytonausa.com*)

 **TRAVEL TIP**

If you want a real thrill, you can experience Daytona Speedway's banked curves at 160 miles per hour with the Richard Petty Driving Experience. For $134 per person, you can ride shotgun in a real stock car for three laps. (✆Toll-free 800-237-3889)

Daytona's Museum of Arts and Sciences is a must-see. Displaying an eclectic collection—such as a skeleton of a 13-foot-tall, 130,000-year-old giant ground sloth, American furniture and paintings from 1700 to 1910, and an exhibit spanning 200 years of Cuban culture from 1759 to 1959, including paintings donated by former Cuban dictator Batista—it also features a planetarium and outdoor nature trails. Admission is $2. (Open Tuesday through Friday 9 A.M.–4 P.M., weekends 9 A.M.–5 P.M., 386-255-0285, *www.moas.org*)

After all that culture, I'm sure your kids will agree it's time for some fun. Stroll the Boardwalk and be spooked at Baron Fun Frite's Castle, have fun at the Forest Amusement Park, and get a spectacular view of the beach from the Space Needle and Sky Ride.

Ten miles south of Daytona stands the restored Ponce de León Inlet Lighthouse, built in 1883. Climb the 203 spiral steps for an exhilarating view of the Atlantic and the inlet. Stop into the museum in the restored keeper's cottages to view a video presentation on the area's history, as well as exhibits on the keeping of the light and the shipwrecks that have occurred on this part of the coast. (Open daily 10 A.M.–5 P.M., 386-761-1821)

### Extra Special

Once you see it, you'll agree that Saint Augustine, America's oldest city, is the most interesting place in Florida because the guides make its history come alive through stories of the town's original families.

Although Spanish explorer Juan Ponce de León probably landed here for fresh drinking water in 1513, it wasn't until September 8, 1565 that Spanish religious zealot Pedro Menéndez de Avilés brought a colony ashore. He named his settlement San Augustín because he arrived on the saint's feast day. With three sides flanked by rivers and the fourth protected by a fort, it was an ideal military location. Unfortunately, the first nine wooden forts suffered severe damage in attacks.

 **TRAVEL TIP**

For a truly unique way to see Saint Augustine, sign up for one of the Ghostly Experience tours. To get up close, take the walking tour for $12 through cemeteries and haunted houses. Or ride along old city streets to the haunted lighthouse for $22. And for a nautical ghost tour, sail aboard the schooner *Freedom* for $35. (✆Toll-free 888-461-1009, ✍*www.ghosttoursofstaugustine.com*)

In the late seventeenth century, the king of Spain invested today's equivalent of $30 million to build Castillo de San Marcos, a massive fort constructed of coquina stone, a natural aggregate of seashells embedded in limestone, to protect the Spaniards from buccaneers like Sir Francis Drake. Begun in 1672 and completed in 1756, its walls are 14 feet thick at the bottom, tapering to 7 at the top. Even when Sir Francis Drake burned Saint Augustine in 1586, the town's residents remained safe inside the fortress. The British renamed it Fort Saint Mark and used it as a base for attacks on Georgia and South Carolina during the Revolutionary War. During the Civil War, the Confederate Army used it as a prison. Take one of the free guided tours given five times daily beginning at 10 A.M. Admission is $6. (Open daily 8:45 A.M.–5:15 P.M., 904-829-6506)

Before the Civil War, Saint Augustine acted as a shipping center for the sugar plantations. Then, in the 1880s, Henry Flagler established resort hotels here and ran his railway south. Today, the Old Town, running along Saint George Street and south of the Plaza de la Constitución, acts as a living history museum. Before exploring Old Town, see the film *The Dream of Empire* in the Museum Theater at the Visitor Center.

Saint Augustine's restored Spanish Quarter, a group of mostly reconstructed eighteenth-century Spanish buildings, offers a look into its past. The González-Alvarez House, the town's oldest house, is a good place to start your tour. Begun in 1723 and extensively remodeled over the centuries, this simple building was once a one-story coquina stone house. Later owners added a second story of wood. You'll be impressed by its tabby floors, hand-hewn cedar beams, and huge hearth. As you walk through it, you'll notice that the furnishings change from the first and second Spanish period to the British period. A blacksmith demonstrates his skills and an eighteenth-century weaver and spinner hers. Also included is the Manucy Museum, with exhibits tracing the city's history, and the Museum of Florida's Military, depicting the history of Florida's soldiers through military uniforms and memorabilia. Admission to all is $8 per adult, $4 per child. (Open daily 9 A.M.–5 P.M., 904-824-2872, *www.oldesthouse .org*)

Also in the restored Spanish Quarter is the Oldest Wooden Schoolhouse, with its original red cedar and cypress clapboard siding and tabby floors from 1778, built to be a residence but later used as a school. The oldest wooden building surviving in town, it has been restored as a school but also includes a Spanish-style kitchen. Admission is $3 per adult, $2 per child. (Open daily 9 A.M.–5 P.M., 904-829-6545)

You'll learn a lot about life in a Spanish colony at the Old Saint Augustine Village, a complex of nine reconstructed homes and workshops, featuring costumed volunteers going about their daily chores. Go early to avoid the summer crowds. Admission is $7 per adult, $5 per child. (Open daily 9 A.M.–5 P.M., 904-823-9722, *www.old-staugvillage.com*)

The Doctor Peck House, also on Saint George Street and named for a Connecticut doctor who moved his family here in 1837, is among the oldest in the city, having been originally built for the Spanish royal treasurer before 1764. In true Spanish style, the house contains an interior arcaded courtyard into which livestock could be driven in case of attack. Admission is $4.50 per adult, $2.50 per child. (Open Monday through Friday 12:30–4:00 P.M., Saturday 10:30 A.M.–4:00 P.M., 904-829-5064)

##  RAINY DAY FUN

If you need to seek cover from a sudden shower, step into the Potter's Wax Museum to see more than 170 wax representations of notable figures from history, television, sports, and politics. Admission is $9 per adult, $6 per child. (Open daily 9 A.M.–9 P.M., *www.potterswax.com*)

But not all structures in Saint Augustine's Old Town are of Spanish origin. Some have been restored to show the Victorian Era. The Oldest Store Museum is a re-creation of a turn-of-the-century general store chock-full of more than 100,000 items, including Gibson Girl corsets, high wheeled bicycles, and animal-powered treadmills, many of which came from the original warehouse. Admission is $3. (Open Monday through Saturday 9 A.M.–5 P.M., Sunday 10 A.M.–5 P.M., 904-829-9729)

Henry Flagler built the Hotel Ponce de León in 1888, the first of its kind in Florida. He sent architects to Spain to study Spanish and Moorish architecture so they could design this Spanish-Moorish-style masterpiece. It features a central dome and corner towers, Tiffany glass, and murals depicting the history of Saint Augustine. It's now the home of Flagler College. (904-819-6400)

Franklin W. Smith, a Boston architect, designed and built a rival hotel across the street. Later he sold it to Flagler, who rechristened it the Alcazar. Today it houses the Lightner Museum, a collection of nineteenth-century decorative arts, including a large collection of American cut glass, a Tiffany room, an Oriental room, cloisonné, fine china and porcelains, and a Victorian village re-creation. Louis Comfort Tiffany designed the interior. The Alcazar hosted up to 25,000 guests from 1889 to 1896. It closed in 1931; Chicago publisher Otto C. Lightner purchased it in 1946 to house his collections. The music room, containing instruments dating from 1870 to 1920, is one of the most interesting. Staff members play period tunes on many of them in informal daily concerts. Admission is $8 per adult, $2 per child. (Open daily 9 A.M.–5 P.M., 904-824-2874, *www.lightnermuseum.org*)

 **TRAVEL TIP**

Though you should see Old Town on foot, you can tour it in open-air trolleys with Saint Augustine Historical Tours; they allow you to park free for the day at their office (☎904-829-3800). Colee's Sightseeing Carriage Tours show you the city by horse and buggy (☎904-829-2818). Or you can rent a bike from Buddy Larsen's (☎904-824-2402).

Just beyond the Lightner Museum stands Zorayda Castle, built by Smith in 1883. This brightly colored Moorish-style home, which inspired Flagler, is a copy of a wing of the thirteenth-century Alhambra in Spain, but just one-tenth its size. A wealthy Egyptian consul purchased it 1913 to store his collection of carpets and treasures, including a bizarre 2,300-year-old sacred cat rug and a magnificent gaming table inlaid with sandalwood and mother-of-pearl. Admission is $3.50. (Open daily 9:30 A.M.–5:00 P.M., 904-824-3097)

# By Day

The Jacksonville area offers a variety of family fun activities from swimming to boating, fishing, kite flying, surfing, golf, and tennis.

### On the Beach

Jacksonville Beach, 12 miles east of downtown Jacksonville, lies in the heart of nearly 35 miles of broad, open beaches. Because of its location, it tends to be more crowded on weekends than Atlantic and Neptune beaches north of it. You'll find the beach itself to be the main attraction, but you may prefer to watch people along the Boardwalk or fish from the pier. You can rent rods and reels and buy bait here. Good swimming and lifeguards make these perfect family beaches. If you want to get some exercise, you can pedal on the beach with a bike from the American Bicycle Company in Jacksonville Beach (904-246-4433).

To see what Florida looked like before the dawn of the Condo Age, visit Little Talbot Island State Park, located on a 2,500-acre barrier island north of the mouth of the Saint George River. Here, wild sea oats and flowering morning glories hold a series of wild dunes in place against the ravages of the sea. You can take long walks along the 5 miles of beach, accessible by two dune crossovers or along the 4-mile Island Hiking Trail, passing through a hammock of holly, magnolia, and live oak trees before ending by high sand dunes at the beach. Admission is $4 per car. (Open daily 8 A.M.–sunset, 904-251-2320)

Amelia Island Beach, at the island's southern tip, is unquestionably the most perfect beach on Florida's east coast. Its 5 miles of dark, fine, packed sands are uncrowded and often covered with shells. An almost perfect backdrop of multiple dunes covered in waving sea oats makes for excellent horseback riding, biking, and hiking, plus there's good surfing and scuba diving. Climb up to the observation deck for a fine view of Fort George Inlet. You can rent horses by the hour from Sea Horse Stable (904-261-4878) or bicycles from Fernandina Beach Schwinn Cyclery (904-277-3227).

Anastasia State Recreation area, near Saint Augustine, is one of Florida's most popular oceanside parks. Its 1,722 acres of hard-packed beaches, dunes, salt marsh, and coastal hammock covers the site where the Spaniards quarried coquina rock to build Castillo de San Marcos. Besides excellent swimming, you'll find a myriad of shore birds feeding in the tidal marshes. For a quieter time, explore the shores of the Salt Run Lagoon. Admission is $2 per car. (Open daily 8 A.M.–sunset)

## ≡FAST FACT

Unlike other Florida beaches, at Daytona you can drive at 10 miles per hour along the 23 miles of 500-foot-wide, hard-packed beach all day for $3. Just be sure to park on the beach perpendicularly to the ocean, and stick to the marked "lanes." And be wary of high tides.

Except for the crazy time during Spring Break and March Bike Week motorcycle races at the Daytona racetrack, Daytona Beach is a typical family seaside resort where you can just relax in a sand chair, letting the waves wash over you while your kids fly kites and swim in the surf. Actually, only 4 miles of this beach lie within the city limits. To the north it's called Ormond Beach and to the south Daytona Beach Shores. You can rent bicycles at Ormond Schwinn in Ormond Beach (904-677-2425) or at Volusia Schwinn South in South Daytona (904-756-0008) for a ride along the Intracoastal Waterway on John Anderson Drive.

### On the Water

With so many miles of beaches, surfing and windsurfing have become popular around Jacksonville. To find out the latest sailing and surfing conditions, call the Aqua East Hotline (904-246-9744).

You can rent surfboards, boogie boards, sailboards, and wetsuits from several shops along the coast, including:

- **Aqua East Surf Shop:** Neptune Beach, ☎904-246-2550
- **Blue Sky Surf Shop:** Saint Augustine, ☎904-824-2734
- **Surf Station:** Saint Augustine, ☎904-471-9463
- **Daytona Beach Surf Shops:** Daytona Beach, ☎904-253-3366
- **Sandy Point Sailboards:** Holly Hill, ☎904-255-4977

If you love to fish for trophy-size largemouth bass, you'll find plenty in the Saint Johns River. This same area produces bluegills, speckled perch, and shell crackers from January to April. Should you prefer to go for saltwater game fish, especially during spring and summer, you'll find sailfish, dolphinfish, amberjack, and bonito abundant. During the spring and fall, king mackerel and tarpon follow the shrimp boats closer to shore near Saint Augustine. You can get onboard a half-day or full-day fishing charter from the following outfitters:

- **Conch House Marina:** Anastasia Island, ☎904-824-4347
- **Sea Love Charters:** Saint Augustine, ☎904-824-3328
- **Sea Love Marina:** Ponce Inlet, ☎904-767-3406
- **Tradewinds:** Fernandina Beach, ☎904-261-9486
- **King Neptune Deep-Sea Fishing:** Mayport, ☎904-246-0104

In the Jacksonville area you'll fine four canoeing routes, along the Saint Mary's and Santa Fe rivers and Pellicer and Bulow creeks. You can rent canoes at Daytona Recreational Sales and Rentals in Ormond Beach (904-672-5631). Club Nautico in Saint Augustine (904-825-4848) provides motor boat rentals. If you prefer to go sailing, you can rent a boat from Marina Port Orange in Port Orange, south of Daytona Beach (904-767-6408).

## On the Links and on the Courts

In the last decade, amateurs and professionals alike have discovered a treasure trove of golfing opportunities in the Jacksonville area. Some courses rank among the most beautiful and challenging in the country. Greens fees range from $50 to $295. Here are several to choose from:

- **Amelia Island Plantation:** Three 18-hole courses by top designers. ☎904-261-6161
- **Daytona Beach and Country Club:** Daytona Beach, ☎904-258-3119
- **Jacksonville Beach Golf Club:** Jacksonville Beach, ☎904-247-6184
- **Pine Lakes Golf Club:** Jacksonville ☎904-757-0318
- **Queen's Harbor Yacht and Country Club:** Jacksonville, ☎904-220-2118
- **Tournament Players Club at Sawgrass:** Ponte Vedra Beach, ☎904-273-3230
- **Windsor Parke Golf Club:** Jacksonville, ☎904-223-4971

And if you're in Saint Augustine, be sure to visit the World Golf Hall of Fame to discover little-known facts about golf's best players. In addition to the exhibits, the price of admission includes a viewing of a film in the IMAX theater. Admission is $15 per adult, $10 per child. (Open Monday through Saturday 10 A.M.–6 P.M., Sunday noon–6 P.M., Toll-free 800-948-4653, *www.wghof.org*)

You can play tennis almost all year in the Jacksonville area. There are a number of public courts, including twenty-two lighted ones, from which to choose:

- **Boone Park:** Jacksonville, ☎904-384-8687
- **Cypress Courts:** Daytona Beach, ☎904-258-9198
- **Hendricks Avenue Courts:** Jacksonville, ☎904-399-1761
- **Huguenot Park:** Jacksonville Beach, ☎904-249-9407
- **Ormond Beach Tennis Center:** Ormond Beach, ☎904-677-0311

## Shopping

Home to dozens of well-known retail shops like Banana Republic and the Sharper Image, the two-story Jacksonville Landing offers a pleasant shopping experience along the Saint Johns River. The Avondale District is known locally as "Antique Alley." Here you can browse for several hours for that piece you're missing from your collection. Down the road from the Avondale shops is Saint Johns Landing, a smaller version of Jacksonville Landing. There's also the Regency Square Mall. (904-725-1220)

Daytona Beach Outlet Mall has forty outlet stores selling clothing and such for half off department store prices (904-756-8700). And, of course, there are loads of seashore souvenirs at the beach.

# Dining Out and Nightlife

While there are a variety of restaurants to choose from in the Jacksonville area, most are moderate places in keeping with its laid-back family atmosphere. Some, like those here, are Jacksonville landmarks.

**Crawdaddy's:** Built to look like an abandoned warehouse, with eclectically decorated rooms on different levels, this unique eatery serves Cajun dishes made with alligator, chicken, and seafood. (1643 Prudential Drive, Jacksonville, ✆904-396-3546)

**Crab Pot Restaurant:** A Jacksonville Beach landmark, with a spacious interior where you'll dine on all sorts of fresh seafood, including peel-'em-yourself shrimp, steamed blue crabs, and conch fritters. (12 North Oceanfront Drive, Jacksonville Beach, ✆904-241-4188)

**Chiang's Mongolian Bar-B-Q:** Large portions characterize this large Asian buffet of pork, beef, chicken, and vegetables, or you can order à la carte. (1504 North Third Street, Jacksonville Beach, ✆904-241-3075)

**The Homestead:** For deep Southern home-style cooking featuring seafood and chicken dishes, this local favorite can't be beat. (1712 Beach Boulevard, Jacksonville Beach, ✆904-249-5240)

**The Marina Restaurant:** If you're hankering for large portions of fresh lobster and shrimp, served in a simple nautical atmosphere accompanied by various side dishes, this is the place. (101 Centre Street, Fernandina Beach, ☎904-261-5310)

## ═FAST FACT

The spectacular Friendship Fountain, spraying 17,000 gallons of water per minute 120 feet into the air, stands in front of the Museum of Science and History. Lit with colored lights at night, it acts as a focal point for Jacksonville's Riverwalk, a cement promenade along the south bank of the Saint Johns River.

If you're looking to dance, head to the Warehouse (904-249-2050) or Bukkets Baha (904-246-7701), both in Jacksonville Beach, or Pappa's (904-641-0321) or the Bombay Bicycle Club (904-737-9555), both in Jacksonville, for some cold beer and Top-Forty tunes played by a DJ. For music of the '50s and '60s, 57 Heaven, also in Jacksonville, is popular with the baby boomer set.

If you're looking for good theater, you'll find several venues in Jacksonville. The Alhambra Dinner Theater offers a buffet dinner followed by a Broadway musical (904-641-1212). The River City Playhouse puts on adult's and children's plays (904-388-8830). And the Sunday afternoon concerts in Metropolitan Park by the Jacksonville Symphony Orchestra are sure to please (Toll-free 877-662-6731).

# CHAPTER 12

# The Florida Keys

THE FLORIDA KEYS, a 100-mile-long chain of forty-eight islets off the southern tip of Florida, are the only tropical islands within the contiguous United States. Under the azure blue to jade green waters of the Atlantic Ocean, Florida Bay, and the Gulf of Mexico that surround them exists a wonderland of living coral, a reef alive with varied marine life. Exotic birds drift on the warm currents over hardwood trees in dense hammocks. The Keys offer a unique destination where your family can enjoy wonders of nature unlike any others in the country.

## Getting to Know the Florida Keys

Though the Keys are an extension of the Florida peninsula, they're a world apart. They can be divided into three groups—the Upper Keys, the Middle Keys, and the Lower Keys. Each island group has its own unique history, culture, and activities.

First discovered by Spanish explorers in the sixteenth century, the Keys have been home to pirates, smugglers, salvagers, shipwreck survivors, and now retirees and urbanites from Miami seeking the paradise of their dreams. Novels, films, and folklore have portrayed the Keys as a place of sultry romance and intrigue. In fact, nature dominates them.

# ≡FAST FACT

Key is a spelling variation of the word "cay," a small island or bank composed of coral fragments. Although the Florida Keys are the largest, others exist along Florida's southern coasts. Some of them, the highest being only 18 feet above sea level, have been formed from red mangrove thickets while others are the product of limestone and ancient coral.

The 127-mile Overseas Highway connecting the Keys began as the Overseas Railroad, the brainchild of Henry Flagler. Reporters nicknamed it "Flagler's Folly." Constructed by thousands of men, more than 700 of whom died during the project, the railroad, begun in 1906 and finished in 1912, became "the eighth wonder of the world," according to newspaper accounts. In the first year alone, 130 workers drowned in a hurricane. And in 1909, another hurricane washed away 40 miles of track and embankment. The track bed ran over viaducts of imported German cement, still standing today. On January 22, 1912, the *Extension Special* departed Miami with Flagler riding in his own luxurious railcar, the Rambler, and with four passenger cars filled with reporters and dignitaries. Key West welcomed Flagler's train with open arms. His dream had come to fruition, but two dozen years later, a horrific Labor Day hurricane swept the railroad into the sea.

In 1938, workers completed the Overseas Highway, also known as Route 1, laying it out over the rail route and utilizing Flagler's bridges. With the roadway only 22 feet wide, bridge crossings were hair-raising experiences and stuck drawbridges caused endless traffic jams, so travelers partied along the roadside to pass the time. Many of the bridges have since been replaced, including a new Seven Mile Bridge, constructed at a cost of $45 million, which opened in the early 1980s. The old bridges have since become long fishing piers.

The Upper Keys—Key Largo through Long Key—are nearest to the great Florida Reef. Beautiful corals captivate divers as well as passengers of the glass-bottom boats. Bird lovers seek out many rare winged birds. From backcountry guide fishing to the thrilling hunt for deep-sea big game, the fishing is great year-round near Islamorada.

Islamorada, which means "purple isles," was so named by Spanish explorers because of the way the beaches, covered with purple janthina (sea snail) shells found there in the spring, looked at a distance. It is the centerpiece of a 20-mile strip of islands including Plantation Key, Windley Key, and Upper and Lower Matecumbe Keys, collectively known as Islamorada. The Calusa Indians enslaved or killed shipwrecked sailors here. Today, fishing is king, and tales of catches of giant tarpon and marlin are common.

## ≡FAST FACT

Many Keys natives can trace their ancestry to the island of Eleuthera in the Bahamas where a colony of English and Bermudian refugees, known as the Eleuthera Adventurers, sought religious freedom. These early farmers planted groves of Key limes, tamarind, and breadfruit.

The town of Marathon sits in the center of the Middle Keys—Long Key to Seven Mile Bridge. The Marathon of yesterday was on the route of ocean lanes sailed by pirates Jean Lafitte, Henry Morgan, and Edward Teach, the notorious Blackbeard. On these same ocean lanes today sail thousands of sportsmen-vacationers who enjoy fishing, scuba diving, and snorkeling.

The Lower Keys, which comprise forty-eight various size islands, begin at Mile Marker 40 below the Seven Mile Bridge and continue to Mile Marker 5. They're different from the rest of the Keys—different in their geological makeup, different in their plants and animals, and different in their pace. Mostly, they have a foundation of fossilized coral, interspersed with limestone granules called *oolite*. On some, pine trees flourish, while on others tropical hardwood trees festooned with bromeliads and orchids thrive in the tropical climate. Generally, life is slower here, more laid-back, more Caribbean.

# Getting Around the Florida Keys

The Overseas Highway acts as the spine of the Keys. Beginning with MM127 just south of Homestead and ending with MM0 in Key West, you can see the railroad's original green-and-white mile markers, still in use today, as you drive down the highway. Besides driving, the only way to get around is by boat.

### Best Time to Go

Florida's Keys boast the only tropical climate in the United States—where you can count on near-perfect weather with sunny skies and ocean breezes all year long. Temperatures range from winter highs in the 70s to over 90° in summer. And though humidity increases during the summer season, the constant sea breezes make it bearable.

### Cautions and Safety Concerns

Generally, the Keys are safe. However, you'll need to make sure to wear sufficient sunscreen and, in the summer, insect repellent if you walk any of the trails through the tropical hammocks, which are pockets of woodland on ground only a few feet above surrounding wetlands.

# Family-Oriented Resorts and Hotels

You'll find hotels, motels, apartments, villas, efficiencies, and condominiums, even botels with docking at the door. The variety is so great that you're sure to find accommodations to fit your budget. If you prefer the active environment of a large resort, you'll find them on Key Largo and Vaca Key, but if you prefer the peace and quiet away from the crowds, there are plenty of small motels with efficiency units to choose from in the Lower Keys.

### Holiday Isle Resorts and Marina

Reservations: ✆Toll-free 800-327-7070

✍www.holidayisle.com

A five-story, 176-room hotel with a three-story neighboring building on Islamorada offering oceanfront rooms, suites, efficiencies, and apartments with kitchens and wraparound balconies in a complex of pools, bars, restaurants, and shops fronting a beach.

### Marina del Mar Resort

Reservations: ✆Toll-free 800-451-3483

✍www.marinadelmarkeylargo.com

A complete resort on Key Largo with seventy-six regular rooms and suites with kitchens, each with a whirlpool bathtub, plus a restaurant, pool, tennis courts, fitness center, nightclub, boat rentals, glass-bottom boat tours, and dive and fishing charters.

### Sheraton Key Largo Beach Resort

Reservations: ✆888-627-8545

✍www.keylargoresort.com

A 200-room resort nestled on twelve-and-a-half acres of lush hardwood forest along the Gulf of Mexico near John Pennekamp State Park, two pools, private beach, water sports, and lighted tennis courts.

### Sombrero Resort and Lighthouse Marina

Reservations: ✆Toll-free 800-433-8660

✍www.sombreroresort.com

This airy, tropical waterfront family resort in Marathon offers both garden and waterfront accommodations, including suites with kitchens, plus a great pool, alfresco restaurant and lounge, tennis courts with pro shop, sauna, and marina.

### House and Condo Rental Options

If you'd rather have one place as your base while exploring the Keys, Big Pine Vacation Rentals may be just the ticket. You can rent a vacation home on a canal away from the Overseas Highway with a boat dock and fishing opportunities, but you must stay at least three nights. (305-872-9863)

 **TRAVEL TIP**

To have the feel of a real nautical vacation, consider staying in a double-decker houseboat in the Faro Blanco Marina Resort in Marathon. Each houseboat is luxuriously furnished and comes with French doors that offer a splendid harbor view. (✆Toll-free 800-759-3276, ✑www.spottswood.com)

## Things to Do

You'll find lots to do in the Florida Keys, most of which has to do with the sea in one way or another. Go swimming or look for rare bottles on a remote beach or search for a Pink Queen Conch.

### For the Kids

Your children can have an experience of a lifetime swimming with the dolphins at Dolphins Plus on Key Largo where researchers study the therapeutic relationship of dolphins to disabled and handicapped people (305-451-1993). A similar facility, the Dolphin Research Center on Grassy Key near Marathon, was once the site of Flipper's Sea School where Hollywood filmmakers shot Flipper's original movie in the 1950s. You can play and swim with the dolphins for twenty minutes for a tax-deductible contribution of $65 with a reservation. You can take a tour of the center from Wednesday through Sunday at 9:30 and 11 A.M. and 1 and 3 P.M. for a donation of $5 (305-289-0002).

## ≡FAST FACT

Scientists at the Dolphin Research Center have been studying dolphins' use in cancer patient therapy and in teaching disadvantaged children. The center also provides much needed R&R for dolphins that have become overworked from long years of performance in marine parks. Believe it or not, they actually suffer from stomach ulcers from too much stress, just like humans.

The Florida Keys Children's Museum, located in the Crane Point Hammock in Marathon, offers exhibits on a tropical lagoon, a marine touch tank, a Native American chickee (hut built of palm fronds), and a historic sailing vessel. (305-743-9100)

### Key Largo

Key Largo is the first of the Keys you'll reach as you drive the Overseas Highway, heading south from Florida City. Spanish explorers called it *Cayo Largo*, Long Island. The largest of the Keys, it gained fame as the setting of the movie *Key Largo*, starring Humphrey Bogart and Lauren Bacall, a film about a crime and a hurricane on the Key. Director John Huston chose Key Largo as the film's title for no other reason than it suggested some place tropical and exotic. And though he shot a few scenes on the island, he shot most of the film in Hollywood. The businesspeople of the town of Rock Harbor, Key Largo's main town, decided to change its name to Key Largo in 1952 to cash in on the notoriety from the film. But the focus here is diving, since the only living coral reef within the U.S. limits lies due east.

**JUST FOR PARENTS**

If you remember the steamy film *African Queen*, in which Katherine Hepburn and Humphrey Bogart found romance while battling the jungle, then you'll enjoy taking a ride on the original boat used in the movie from the Holiday Inn Marina at Mile Marker 100 in Key Largo.

To get a peek at what life was like back during the farming days of the Keys, stop at the village of Tavernier at Mile Marker 92 and wander its streets. Here and there among the dense foliage you'll see old wooden houses with big shutters to protect their occupants from hurricanes.

### Islamorada

You can take two 3-hour boat trips from Indian Fill Key at Mile Marker 78 to both Indian Key State Historic Site and Lignumvitae Key State Botanical Site, respectively. Boats depart at 8:30 A.M. for Indian Key and at 1:30 P.M. for Lignumvitae Key for a cost of $6 per person. You must make reservations (305-664-4815). The first tour presents the tragic tale of the once-prosperous seat of Dade County. It got to be so from the profitable salvaging of goods of reef-wrecked ships by Captain Jacob Housman, a wealthy salvager from New York. He stole one of his father's ships and sailed to Key West, looking for a piece of the lucrative salvaging trade. Not welcomed there, he purchased Indian Key in 1831 and made $30,000 the first year salvaging wrecked ships. He outfitted the 11-acre island with warehouses, a store, and a hotel and persuaded the Florida state legislature to designate it as the county seat. Unfortunately, Housman achieved his fortune through less than honest means. It seemed he used an old smuggler's trick: He'd tie a lantern around the neck of a donkey and lead him along the shore, luring unsuspecting ships onto the reefs. Eventually, he lost his salvaging license and sold the island to Dr. Henry Perrine, a botanist and physician, who cultivated tropical plants for their medicinal uses. But in 1840, Seminole Indians destroyed it and killed Perrine. Today, you can still see the wild tamarind, mango, and Mexican sisal planted by Perrine and get a feel for what life would have been like on ranger-led walks down reconstructed village streets.

The second trip takes you to the Lignumvitae Key State Botanical Site where you can learn about the forming of the Key islands. On its 332 acres stands a virgin tropical forest, which should give you some idea of what the islands looked like before humans arrived. Ranger-led walks will introduce you to unique species of plants and trees found in the Keys. One in particular, the lignum vitae, for which the Key is named, is supposedly one of the trees in the Garden of Eden, believed to be the "tree of life." Your kids will enjoy watching the giant golden orb spiders who regularly weave their webs across the pathways. After your nature walk, you can visit the former house of William J. Matheson, built in 1919, which will show you how the first island settlers lived in the early days of settlement on the Keys. Even though the house blew away during the 1935 hurricane, workers found it and brought it back.

## ≡FAST FACT

On Labor Day, 1935, the worst hurricane in Keys' history drowned 423 people when a 17-foot tidal wave swept over their evacuation train on Upper Matecumbe Key and nearly wiped out the town of Islamorada. The barometer dropped to 26.35, the lowest ever recorded in the Western Hemisphere, and the recorded wind speed reached 200 miles per hour. A monument at Mile Marker 81.5 honors them.

The Theatre of the Sea, one of the world's oldest outdoor marine parks, is the main attraction on Windley Key at Mile Marker 84.5. Though not as sophisticated as some of the newer parks like Sea World, this one allows you to touch sea lions and swim with dolphins (with a reservation). You'll also be given a raincoat to wear as you ride in a "bottomless" boat while porpoises jump before you. Admission is $11. (Open daily 9:30 A.M.–4:00 P.M., 305-644-2431)

### Marathon

The area around Marathon stretches from Conch Key at Mile Marker 65 to the Seven Mile Bridge at Mile Marker 47. Besides the busy town of Marathon on Vaca Key, you'll find sights to see on many smaller islands. The first dramatic view you'll get of the area will be from the top of Long Key Bridge. It's here that the Atlantic Ocean meets the Gulf of Mexico, and it's also here that you'll feel the thrill of literally riding over the azure blue and blue-green sea. The second longest bridge in the Keys, it provides pull-off areas for your enjoyment of this spectacular scene.

 **RAINY DAY FUN**

When a shower hits, take the kids bowling at Stull Bowling Lanes behind the Marathon Cinema, where, if the rain continues, you can take in a movie (☎305-743-0288). Or you can bowl a few games at the Fish Bowl at Mile Marker 83.2 in Islamorada (☎305-664-9357).

In the center of the town of Marathon at Mile Marker 50 is Crane Point Hammock, headquarters of the Florida Keys Land and Sea Trust. This steamy 63-acre bayside preserve also contains tropical hardwood and mangrove forests, plus a historic conch-style house and archaeological sites. You'll also find the comprehensive Museum of Natural History of the Florida Keys within the Hammock. Here, some exhibits tell the story of pirate life on the Keys, while others display Indian and shipwreck artifacts and re-create a coral reef. Admission is $3.50 per person. (Open daily, except Tuesday, 10:30 A.M.–6:30 P.M., Friday until 8:00 P.M., 305-743-3900)

## Lower Keys

Big Pine Key is the largest island in this group, second only to Key Largo in the Upper Keys. Here, you'll find shopping centers and wildlife refuges coexisting side by side. Progress seems to have been controlled here, even though there are small developments. Here, you'll experience the Keys the way they used to be in the 1940s and 1950s.

The most impressive sight is Seven Mile Bridge, which spans the sea between Marathon and Sunshine Key. This bridge replaced the original, much narrower one in 1982. Locals now refer to the former one, which Henry Flagler built in 1912, as "the longest fishing pier in the world." From the lower peninsula of Bahia Honda Key, now a state park, you can see the structure of Flagler's original railroad bridge, a masterpiece of engineering at the time.

The 7,962-acre National Key Deer Refuge shelters tiny white-tailed Key deer, which only grow about 2 feet high, and great white herons. The best time to see the deer is in the early morning or late in the day. If you haven't visited the Everglades, you'll have a chance to see an alligator at Blue Hole, a freshwater rock quarry pond and the only one like it in the Keys. Usually, he lies just off shore waiting for prey but sometimes suns himself on the path. (305-872-2239)

One of the most bizarre sights in the Keys is the 35-foot-tall Perky Bat Tower at Mile Marker 17. No, it's not full of perky bats. Rather the contrary. It seems real estate speculator Richter C. Perky built it of local pine in 1929 to house insect-eating bats to help control the mosquitoes that plagued Sugarloaf Key. Perky, inspired by a get-rich-quick book, *Bats, Mosquitoes, and Dollars*, sent away for the expensive bat bait that he was assured would lure an army of bats to his tower. No bats ever appeared and the mosquitoes continued to plague the island. So Perky lost everything. Nevertheless, the bat tower still stands as a monument to ingenuity and greed.

## Extra Special

The John Pennekamp Coral Reef State Park at Mile Marker 102.5 is the first underwater park in the country. Consisting of a living coral reef, it covers 2,289 acres of land and 52,722 acres offshore.

Stop at the excellent Visitor Center (open daily 8 A.M.–5 P.M.) to see a giant reconstruction of a living piece of the reef housed in a circular underwater aquarium and touch tank, as well as other exhibits on hardwood hammocks and mangrove swamps. Afterward, climb the observation tower to get a panoramic view, then take the two-and-a-half hour tour on the glass-bottom boat *Discovery* for $12 at 9 A.M., noon, and 3 P.M. to see the actual reef. Follow this with a picnic and a swim, or fishing among the mangrove trees for trout, snook, or sheepshead, or canoeing the park's mangrove-lined inner waterways. For an extra-special treat, set sail on a sunset glass-bottom boat cruise with underwater lights.

However, the best way to see the reef is underwater. If possible, take the snorkeling tour for $20 per person, departing at 9 A.M., noon, and 3 P.M. If you're a certified diver, you can go on a guided scuba-dive for $30 per person at 10 A.M. and 1 P.M. You'll need to make a reservation for any of these and the glass-bottom boat tours, except perhaps in summer. Admission is $2 per car. (Open daily 8 A.M.–sunset, Toll-free 800-432-2871)

 **TRAVEL TIP**

If you're a certified diver, you can sample an aquanaut's life by staying at Jules Undersea Lodge, in the Key Largo Undersea Park, the only underwater hotel in the world. The hotel lies within a lagoon 30 feet below the surface at Mile Marker 103.5. When you want to explore outside the hotel, you can connect to the lodge's oxygen-supply system for unlimited air. (☏305-451-2353)

Diving is the best method for seeing many of the 650 species of tropical fish, orange sponges, purple sea fans, blue-eyed squid, coral shrimp, and spiny lobsters. Otherwise, snorkeling is the only other way to get close to the reef. Visibility is best in summer. Whichever you choose to do, you'll need an experienced guide, as the reef lies 5 miles offshore. This is a must-do experience for the whole family, no matter how you do it.

### Festivals and Seasonal Events

Marathon hosts four fishing tournaments annually. Top names in pro sport fishing participate in early May for tarpon, late May for dolphinfish, early October for bonefish, and early November for sailfish.

- **Nautical Flea Market:** This annual Nautical Flea Market, held in February in Islamorada, offers boats, clothes, antiques, and electronics. (✆305-453-3802, ✍*www .nauticalfleamarket.org*)
- **Marathon Seafood Festival:** This food festival showcasing delights from the sea is held in March in Marathon. (✆Toll-free 800-262-7284)
- **Florida Keys Island Festival:** Islamorada celebrates life on the Keys with food and entertainment. (✆Toll-free 800-322-5397)
- **Big Pine Winterfest:** Come to a holiday fair Keys-style, held in December on Big Pine Key. (✆Toll-free 800-372-3722)

# By Day

Though the Keys don't have large beaches, they do have several fine parks and recreation areas for swimming. Most daytime activities center on the water, either under or on it. Snorkeling and diving the coral reefs is the leading activity, but the waters off Islamorada provide excellent opportunities for sport fishing.

### On the Beach

If you want to take time out for a swim, head to Long Key State Recreation Area, an 849-acre park on Long Key, in the middle of the Florida Keys. With a shoreline punctuated by mangrove lagoons, shallow flats, and narrow beaches with gentle surf, this long and narrow park also features excellent salt and freshwater fishing, picnicking, boating, swimming, diving, and boardwalk nature trails that lead you through a tropical hammock to an observation tower and to the beach where you can wade or snorkel out onto the flats. The most intimate way to enjoy this area is to rent a canoe and follow the marked canoe trail through the tidal lagoons, with nothing more than the wading shore birds to keep you company.

Many consider the palm-fringed beaches fronting both the Atlantic Ocean and the Gulf of Mexico at the 276-acre Bahia Honda State Recreation Area, Florida's southernmost park, to be the best swimming beaches in the Keys. The park's northeast section circles a blue and green lagoon. Here, remnants of the undeveloped Keys remain. Rare birds like the roseate spoonbill fly through satinwood and silver palms while dwarf morning glories provide color along the nature trail that meanders along the shoreline and through a hammock. Plan to stop for a picnic and a swim, or perhaps to fish in the bay or the ocean. Birding is especially good here, with sightings of great white herons, roseate spoonbills, crowned pigeons, and giant ospreys, whose nests top telephone poles along the highway. You can also rent windsurfing equipment at the marina in the southern part of the park. (Open daily 8 A.M.–sunset, 305-872-2353)

##  TRAVEL TIP

When bridges have catwalks, fishing is only permitted from the catwalks. Many of the old bridges now serve as long fishing piers. To catch big tarpon and the elusive bonefish, found only in the warm waters of the Keys, you'll need to hire a backcountry guide.

### On the Boat

In the Keys, the best points of departure for deep-sea fishing are Key Largo, Tavernier, Islamorada, Duck Key, Key Colony Beach, and Marathon. If you're an experienced angler, you'll delight in going after bonefish, a fish found nowhere else in North America and an elusive scrapper that anglers actually stalk. Even if you're not experienced, go out and try your hand at catching some world-class fish. Charters provide all tackle and bait, and special fly-fishing guides will help you if you're not a seasoned angler.

The waters of the Keys teem with tuna, marlin, wahoo, grouper, dolphinfish, and sailfish. All boats come with state-of-the-art fishing equipment. For a unique fishing trip, try fishing at night for swordfish. Other charters specialize in fishing for tarpon and shark in shallower waters. Here is a selection of charter companies:

- **Bounty Hunter:** Marathon, ☏305-743-2446
- **Charters Unlimited:** Key Largo, ☏305-451-9289
- **Choice Backcountry Charters:** Islamorada, ☏305-664-2972
- **Two Conchs Charters:** Marathon, ☏305-743-6253
- **Vagabond Charters:** Key Largo, ☏305-310-1962
- **Yellowfin Charters:** Islamorada, ☏305-664-5333

If you can get a group of six or more together, you can hire a party boat from:

- **Gulf Lady:** Islamorada, ☏305-664-2628
- **Marathon Lady:** Marathon, ☏305-743-5580
- **Sailor's Choice:** Key Largo, ☏305-451-1802

## Under the Water

Divers and snorkelers find an underwater array of colorful fish darting among forty species of corals along the reef that parallels the Keys. Besides the reefs at the John Pennekamp Coral Reef State Park and the adjacent Key Largo Coral Reef National Marine Sanctuary off Key Largo, there are the Crocker and Alligator Reefs, just off Islamorada, both with almost vertical walls containing cracks and crevices that provide homes for crabs and shrimp that attract larger predators.

## ≡FAST FACT

The largest wreck in Key waters is the 510-foot U.S.S. *Spiegel Grove*, which lies within the Key Largo National Marine Sanctuary. Other wrecks include the 287-foot freighter *Eagle* off Islamorada, the 188-foot *Thunderbolt* off Marathon, and the 210-foot *Adolphus Busch, Sr.* off the Lower Keys. All are within easy depth ranges and now host incredible resident populations of marine life.

One of the most interesting sites in the Islamorada area is the San Pedro Underwater Archaeological Preserve, south of Indian Key. A hurricane drove the *San Pedro*, a 287-ton Spanish galleon that set sail from Havana in July 1733, onto the reefs. Today, it lies just 18 feet below the surface and is accessible as a scuba-dive or aboard a glass-bottom boat. You'll see the original anchors, concrete canon replicas, ballast, and bricks. If you dive to the site, you can follow an underwater nature trail to observe a variety of fish, corals, and conchs.

Around Marathon, you'll find the best snorkeling and diving in the dramatic coral canyons of Sombrero Reef, which provides homes to thousands of colorful tropical fish. There's also Molasses Reef and the underwater caves of French Reef.

##  TRAVEL TIP

If you're visiting the Keys in July and like to snorkel or dive, you should be sure not to miss Big Pine Key's Underwater Music Festival, where you can tap your fins to musical tunes generated from underwater speakers. (✆305-872-2411)

If you like to snorkel, one of the best spots is the Looe Key National Marine Sanctuary (toll-free 800-942-5397), southeast of Big

Pine Key. You'll see spectacular brain coral, tangles of staghorn and elkhorn coral, tall coral pillars, and purple seafans just below the clear water's surface, as well as several wrecked ships, including the British frigate H.M.S. *Looe* which sank in 1744. Some of the better dive shops along the Keys include the following:

- **American Diving Headquarters:** Key Largo, ✆Toll-free 800-322-3483
- **Captain Slate's Atlantis Dive Center:** Key Largo, ✆305-451-3020
- **Looe Key Dive Center:** Ramrod Key, ✆Toll-free 800-942-5397
- **The Diving Site:** Marathon, ✆Toll-free 800-634-3935
- **Tilden's Pro Dive:** Marathon, ✆305-743-5422

## On the Links and on the Courts

Several of the Keys' resorts have golf courses, but mostly you'll find par-three resort courses rather than regular ones. The eighteen-hole championship course at the Sombrero Country Club is probably the best in the Keys (800-433-8660, *www.sombreroresort.com*). For a fun round, try the Key Colony Beach Golf Course, a nine-hole par-three resort course in the Key Colony Beach development on Key Largo. There are no tee times, but clubs are available for rental (305-289-1533).

You won't find much tennis on the Keys, except for a court here or there at a resort. The Islamorada Tennis Club at Mile Marker 76.85 has four clay and two hard courts available day and night, plus a pro shop (305-664-5340).

## Shopping

Being close to the mainland, Key Largo has a full complement of shopping centers, as well as the usual seaside T-shirt and souvenir shops. For handmade pottery, head to the Village Pottery on Islamorada, or if you're a fisherman, you'll love browsing through

H. T. Chittum & Co. General Mercantile, also on Islamorada. For locally designed and made T-shirts, stop in at Handprints of the Keys in Marathon, where you can watch them being made and afterward buy some at discounted prices.

# Dining Out and Nightlife

You'll find a wide assortment of dining possibilities. Most serve native seafood cooked in many ways, but there are also small Cuban restaurants serving traditional dishes: picadillo, ground meat and saffron rice, black beans, fried plantains, and crispy Cuban bread.

> **Brian's in Paradise:** With a twelve-page menu, this restaurant has something for everyone, but the best is the Marathon Meal, a sampling of local favorites, including conch chowder, conch fritters, fried shrimp, and Key lime pie. (Mile Marker 52, Marathon, ✆305-743-3183)
>
> **Castaway:** Go where the locals go and you're sure to find good food, and this restaurant, serving steamed-in-beer shrimp with seconds on the house, accompanied by homemade honey buns, is no exception. (Mile Marker 48, Marathon, ✆305-743-6247)
>
> **Coral Grill:** A great family restaurant, featuring a sumptuous buffet upstairs or a menu of traditionally prepared Keys seafood downstairs. (Mile Marker 83.5, Islamorada, ✆305-664-4803)
>
> **Dip 'N Deli:** This restaurant's name says it all. Salads, twenty-two types of sandwiches, soups, and ice cream treats, including old-fashioned ice cream sodas and milkshakes, will please the little ones—and Mom and Pop, too. (Mile Marker 31, Big Pine Key, ✆305-872-3030)
>
> **Monte's Restaurant and Fish Market:** This basic family place, with plastic tablecloths, serves up some of the best local specialties, including conch chowder, conch salad, conch fritters, shrimp in beer, and stone crabs. (Mile Marker 23, Summerland Key, ✆305-745-3731)

**Mrs. Mac's Kitchen:** A small down-home eatery, serving steaks and the best chili on the Keys accompanied by homemade pita bread. A fun family place. (Mile Marker 99.4, Key Largo, ☎305-451-3722)

**The Green Turtle Inn:** A busy place, serving not only traditional seafood, but also conch and turtle chowders, as well as turtle and alligator steak, accompanied by homemade bread. (Mile Marker 81.5, Islamorada, ☎305-664-9031)

Most visitors to the Upper Keys go diving by day, then like to party at night. You'll find typical watering holes along with clubs like Coconuts (305-451-4107) on Key Largo, with a variety of nightly entertainment and a deck to enjoy the sunset, drink in hand. Supposedly, the Caribbean Club (305-451-9970) was the setting for several parts of the movie *Key Largo*. It, too, has a deck for watching the sunset.

 ## JUST FOR PARENTS

Get a sitter for the kids so the two of you can escape to a romantic seafood dinner while watching the sunset at Snook's Bayside Club on Key Largo overlooking Florida Bay. Go early enough for the sunset celebration at the Tiki Bar. (Mile Marker 99.9, ☎305-451-3847)

Most of the nighttime action on Islamorada centers around the Holiday Isles Resort, but if you prefer more laid-back music, try the Harbor Bar (305-664-9888) for live rock music and raw bar or the Cabaña Bar (305-664-4338) on the bay side, where you can listen to reggae while watching the sunset.

Nightlife in Marathon seems to be centered around the lounges of the several resorts. If you want to mingle with the locals, try the Hurricane (305-743-5755) or the Quay (305-289-1810), both of which provide music and dancing on weekends.

For good pizza and more than seventy kinds of beer, try the No Name Pub on Big Pine Key (305-872-9115) which sometimes has a band.

# CHAPTER 13

# *Key West*

KEY WEST IS AMERICA'S SOUTHERNMOST CITY—
where the land meets the sea. Long an artist's haven, it has attracted
some of the top names in writing and the arts. It's rich in old-world
charm, steeped in the lore of island people, and endowed with an
exciting history of rum runners, pirate ships, and Civil War intrigue.
Although Key West is a hip place with sidewalk cafés, museums, and
historic old homes, it's also a center for fishing and shrimping. Key
West is truly a city of contrasts of old and new.

## Getting to Know Key West

Closer to Cuba than to the U.S. mainland, Key West has a history that
stretches back to the Calusa Indians, Spanish conquistadors, and
Caribbean pirates. Spanish explorers called it *cayo hueso*, meaning
"bone key," because of the piles of human bones found here by early
visitors. Eighteenth-century English buccaneers called it Key West.

When Florida gained statehood in 1822, the U.S. Navy established
a base there. Commodore David Porter and his famous West Indies
Squadron chased the buccaneers who had long controlled the area,
opening the way for the growth of a new industry—shipwreck salvaging. This became the island's main industry, bringing in millions
of dollars, making Key West the wealthiest city in the United States
by 1850.

But after the U.S. Navy built lighthouses along the reef to warn ships, Key West's salvaging industry went bust. However, the city continued to prosper as Greeks began sponge diving and Cubans, who emigrated from their homeland just 90 miles away, began making cigars. A blight on the sponges drove the Greeks to Tarpon Springs. After disastrous fires nearly destroyed the city, including the cigar district, in 1859 and 1866, most of the cigar-makers relocated to Tampa.

By the late nineteenth century, the number of residents had grown to 18,000—a mix of people from all over the world, many of whom had washed onshore after their ships had run aground on the reefs. Many were Englishmen coming from the Bahamas or Florida after the American victory in the Revolutionary War. There were also seafaring settlers from New England, Virginia, the Carolinas, Louisiana, and Cubans fleeing from the revolution in Cuba.

In 1912, the Overseas Extension of the Florida East Coast Railroad reached Key West via a series of bridges, traversing 70 miles over water and 25 miles on land.

By the 1930s, the island and the city were in dire straits. With the cigar and sponge industries gone, residents had nothing to fall back on. Those who insisted on staying had to live on coconuts and fish. They declared bankruptcy in July 1934 and sought assistance from Roosevelt's New Deal. Under that plan, workers got the city ready for tourism, but the next year, the devastating Labor Day hurricane wiped out the railroad that connected the city to the mainland, so tourists couldn't get there. Construction on the Overseas Highway began soon after. With it came Julius Stone, who helped bring tourism to Key West.

World War II brought a much-needed injection of dollars through a build-up of naval forces. And in the postwar era, spying operations on communist Cuba helped bolster the economy until large numbers of tourists began arriving in the early 1980s.

Today, a large number of hotels and guest houses service the needs of tourists, many of whom return again and again. Its residents with their relatively tolerant attitudes seem to live in another world adrift in the sea, giving the whole place an individual spirit. As in the rest of the Keys, the locals call themselves "Conchs," because of all the conch meat eaten by their ancestors.

Yet, Key West is far from the dropout paradise it was twenty-five years ago. Restoration and revitalization have made the island into a twenty-first-century tourist mecca.

# Getting Around Key West

Since the town of Key West is only 2 miles wide and 4 miles long, getting around is easy. You can take either the ninety-minute Conch Tour Train (305-294-5161, *www.conchtourtrain.com*), which allows you to get on and off at nine stops along the way, or the Old Town Trolley Tour (305-296-6688, *www.historictours.com*), which for $25 per person takes you on a tour through the neighborhoods as friendly guides point out over 100 sights while telling tales of pirates, rum-runners, and famous ancestors drawn to a city. Or you can rent bikes from the Bicycle Center (305-294-4556) or Key West Bicycle Rentals (305-296-3344) and make it a family affair. And, of course, a town of this size is also small enough to walk.

### Best Time to Go

Since Key West lies in the tropics, there's not much difference in its climate throughout the year. As with other tropical destinations, the rainy season occurs in summer, making the air more humid, although there are sea breezes to cool things off. Year-round temperatures hover between 80° and 90°.

### Cautions and Safety Concerns

Being such a small place, Key West is generally safe. About your only concern should be how long you stay out in the sun and whether you're wearing enough sunscreen.

# Family-Oriented Resorts and Hotels

You have a choice of a variety of accommodations in Key West, from luxurious waterfront resorts to gingerbread-style guesthouses to traditional motels. Prices range from moderate to superdeluxe, though all cost less in summer.

### Banyan Resort

Reservations: ☎Toll-free 800-225-0639

✐*www.banyanresort.com*

This 58-unit condominium resort offers studios and one- and two-bedroom apartments, each with full kitchen, living and dining areas, and often multiple baths.

### Sunrise Suites Resort

Reservations: ☎Toll-free 888-723-5200

✐*www.sunrisekeywest.com*

Here are 46 condos, each with two bedrooms, two baths, and a full kitchen, a living room, and balcony.

### The Inn at Key West

Reservations: ☎Toll-free 800-330-5541

✐*www.innatkeywest.com*

A 105-room hotel, featuring rooms with king or queen beds, courtyard café, pool, hot tub, and the island's largest poolside bar.

### Wyndam Casa Marina Resort

Reservations: ☎Toll-free 800-626-0777

✐*www.casamarinakeywest.com*

A large 322-room luxury resort, built in the 1920s, with two pools, restaurants, tennis courts, health club, and water sports.

## House and Condo Rental Options

If you'd rather not stay in a traditional hotel, you can rent a fully furnished vacation home or condo from one of the following:

- **1800 Atlantic Condominiums:** ☎Toll-free 800-433-2819, *✐www.1800atlantic.com*
- **At Home in Key West, Inc.:** ☎Toll-free 888-459-9378, *✐www.athomekeywest.com*
- **Florida Keys Vacation Rentals, Inc.:** ☎Toll-free 800-598-7727, *✐www.rentalsfloridakeys.com*
- **Old Island Realty Vacation Rentals:** ☎Toll-free 800-621-9405, *✐www.keywestvacations.com*

## Things to Do

Key West overflows with interesting sights and things to do for the whole family—all within roughly a square mile of Old Town. Though in season it may seem like you're seeing more tourists than residents, it's only because they tend to congregate around Mallory Square and Duval Street, the main thoroughfare. While you can comfortably see all of Old Town in a day, you should allow at least two, slowing down to enjoy the atmosphere. Pick up a self-guided walking tour map from the Key West Welcome Center at 3840 North Roosevelt Boulevard (305-296-4444).

Once a seedy strip, mile-long Duval Street has been transformed into a manicured tourist center of beachwear shops and boutiques. At its northern end, you'll see examples of late nineteenth-century "conch houses." Many now sport colorful paint jobs, having been transformed into six-figure winter vacation homes.

## ≡FAST FACT

Conch houses are a blend of Victorian and tropical architecture, built on coral slabs and finished off with gingerbread decoration. Originally built by ship's carpenters using wood from salvaged ships and dovetail joints to withstand hurricanes, many were left unpainted. Each has thick-louvered shutters and roof vents for better ventilation, plus a cistern underneath to collect rain water.

Several of these houses are worth a closer look. Of all of them, only two actually came from the Bahamas, then were assembled in Key West. These Bahama Houses each feature mahogany window sashes, broad verandas, and beaded siding. Ship's carpenters fitted many of these houses together with wooden pegs.

One of the best examples of peg construction is the three-story Audubon House. The revitalization movement in Key West got its start with its renovation, the first of the elegant Victorian houses to be restored. Though the house has Audubon's name, he never owned it or lived there, but only painted the trees in its yard. It belonged to a wrecker, Captain John H. Geiger, and his wife, who took in orphans from shipwrecks. Today, it houses a collection of works by Audubon. Admission is $10 per adult, $5 per child. (305-294-2116, *www.audubonhouse.com*)

## ═FAST FACT

John James Audubon spent several weeks in Key West in 1832 looking for birds to include in his *Birds of America* portfolio. What most people don't know is that he loved shooting birds as much as drawing them, and if he didn't bag at least a hundred, he considered it a bad day.

Key West was the home of inspiration for not only Audubon, but many other artists and writers, including the town's most notable celebrity, Ernest Hemingway. The first had a passion for preservation and the second a zest for living. And it's that combination that gives Key West its unique personality. It's no wonder that the island became a favored vacation retreat of many American presidents and European royalty.

About the only place that doesn't encourage you to spend your money on Duval Street, except for its modest $5 admission (only $1 for kids), is the Wrecker's Museum. Here, you can learn about the salvaging industry from the island's early days. The museum resides in Key West's oldest conch house, built in 1829, which once belonged to Captain Watlington, a wrecker who lived there in the 1830s. Its nine rooms contain period antiques, sea artifacts, ship models, and wrecker's documents. Be sure to notice the scale model conch-style dollhouse with a mural of early Key West in the dining room. (Open daily 10 A.M.–4 P.M., 305-294-9502)

To learn more about the Cuban community in Key West, stop in at the San Carlos Institute, otherwise known as "La Casa Cuba," several blocks up the street. The original institute, established in 1871 with a $100,000 grant from the Cuban government, became the center of Cuban exile life. Exiled Cubans brought soil from Cuba's six provinces and spread it on the grounds, and also brought the cornerstone from the tomb of José Martí, the legendary campaigner for Cuban independence. After the break-off of diplomatic ties with Cuba in 1961, the building became a movie theater, among other things. Today, after a million-dollar restoration, it once again presents opera in its auditorium, as well as exhibits detailing Cuban life in Key West. (305-294-3887)

 **TRAVEL TIP**

Don't forget to have your picture taken next to the large buoy that says "Ninety miles to Cuba" at the southernmost point of the United States, located at the end of Whitehead Street. Go early before the crowds of camera-toting tourists arrive.

During the early nineteenth century, the auction houses lining Mallory Square acted as distribution centers for salvaged goods. Today, the square is the touristy heart of Key West, lined with souvenir, T-shirt, and ice cream shops. Take some time to explore Key West's Historic District, with its 3,100 structures covering 190 blocks. The architecture of these buildings tells the entire history of the island from the early nineteenth century to the present. A fine example is the 1838 Dr. Joseph Y. Porter House on Carolina Street, with its double verandas and Bahamian and Yankee influence.

With its history of salvaging, it's no wonder that the Keys have become known for buried treasure ever since Mel Fisher discovered the *Santa Margarita* and the *Nuestra Señora de Atocha*, two seventeenth-century Spanish galleons that sank during a hurricane in 1622, 40 miles southeast of Key West. You can see some of the $20 million in bounty Fisher brought up from the deep—jewel-studded crosses, bejeweled daggers, vases, cannon, gold bars, and more than 4,000 gleaming silver coins—in Mel Fisher's Maritime Museum, housed in an old naval storehouse on Greene Street. Admission is $11 per adult, $6 per child. (Open daily 9:30 A.M.–5:00 P.M., 305-294-2633)

This same naval storehouse was originally part of the Truman Annex, formerly part of the original U.S. Naval Base. You can still see some of the buildings from the base, such as the Romanesque Revival Customs House, established in 1822 to control piracy in Key West, now the home of the Key West Museum of Art and History after a nine-year, $9 million renovation. Admission is $10 per adult, $5 per child (open Monday through Friday 10 A.M.–3 P.M., weekends 9 A.M.–5 P.M., 305-295-6616). Using the free walking guide, follow the markers and explore the Annex for yourself. In 1986, a developer from Maine bought the 103-acre Annex at auction and has built upscale condominiums, houses, and a hotel.

## ≡FAST FACT

President Harry S. Truman spent nine vacations covering 175 days in the Little White House, built in 1890 on the waterfront as the first officer's quarters of the naval base. Later, it became the home of the base commandant. Tours are available. (☎305-294-9911, ✆www .trumanwhitehouse.com).

The Curry House, once the home of William Curry, Florida's first millionaire, and now a luxurious bed and breakfast, shows the wealthier side of life in Key West with its solid mahogany paneling and Tiffany glass windows. Admission is $5. (Open 10 A.M.–5 P.M.)

Surrounding the Key West Lighthouse are the narrow streets of the Bahama Village, a restored area of former cigar factories that's been turned into a neighborhood of restaurants, bars, and shops.

The biggest tourist draw in Key West has to be the Ernest Hemingway Home and Museum. However, tours of the house contain more fiction than fact. Even though Hemingway owned the house for thirty years, he lived there for only a third of that time with his wife Pauline. Hemingway bought the house in 1931 for $8,000, which he received as a gift from Pauline's uncle. He took the rundown home of a nineteenth-century merchant and turned it into a luxurious retreat complete with servants and a swimming pool. Imagine Hemingway at his typewriter creating some of his most notable works, including the short story "The Snows of Kilimanjaro" and the novel *For Whom the Bell Tolls*. After divorcing Pauline in 1940, he packed up his belongings and moved to Cuba with his new wife, journalist Martha Gellhorn. You'll need to take the half-hour guided tour to see the inside of the house, but you can wander through the garden on your own. Admission is $11 per adult, $6 per child. (Open daily 9 A.M.–5 P.M., 305-294-1136, *www.hemingwayhome.com*)

 **TRAVEL TIP**

Pick up a copy of the *Key West Reader: The Best of Key West's Writers 1830–1990* at the Key West Island Bookstore on Fleming Street for some examples of excellent writing from Ernest Hemingway, Wallace Stevens, Gore Vidal, and other writers who have lived on the island. (☎305-294-2904)

The East Martello Gallery and Museum, housed in an 1862 fortress that was built to protect the city's southern flank, is one of two Civil War lookout posts. You'll find an art gallery here, along with extensive exhibits on local history that include memorabilia from the island's sponge and cigar industries and from movies shot in Key West, including Sidney Pollack's *Havana*. The spiral staircase and vaulted ceilings of the fort's tower, plus the view from the top of it, make this a worthwhile visit. Admission $6 for adults, $3 for children. (Open daily 10 A.M.–5 P.M., 305-296-3913)

The trapezoidal Fort Zachary Taylor is Key West's other Civil War post. Built in 1845 to defend what was then Florida's largest city, it has walls varying from 5 to 8 feet thick. Union forces controlled it throughout the Civil War. Today, it's a state historic site containing the largest collection of Civil War cannon in the country. (Open daily, 305-292-6713, *www.fortzacharytaylor.org*)

##  JUST FOR PARENTS

As the only frost-free city in the continental United States, Key West gardens display tropical plants that grow outdoors nowhere else in North America but Mexico. One of the best is the Peggy Mills Garden. To see a tropical garden within the walls of an old fort, visit Martello Towers. Or take the Orchid Tour with the Orchid Lady to see three gardens (✆Toll-free 800-747-2718).

Though not your usual tourist attraction, be sure to visit the Key West Cemetery to see some of the unique tombstones. Because the island lies on a limestone bed, people have to be buried above ground in stone caskets, many of which have curious messages on them. A grieving widow put "At Least I Know Where He's Sleeping Tonight" on her husband's tomb. Or the ultimate I-told-you-so found on another: "I Told You I Was Sick." The most poignant, however, is the memorial to all those who died on the U.S.S. *Maine*, the battleship that the Spanish sunk in Havana Harbor in 1898, sparking the Spanish-American War.

### For the Kids

You kids will love visiting the Key West Aquarium, built in 1934 as the first attraction in the Keys, where they can see marine life that lives in local waters—squirrel and porcupine fish and smaller sharks peer out from inside the tanks. For a great show, stop by at 11 A.M., 1, 3, and 4:30 P.M., when they feed the fish. Admission is $5. (Open daily 10 A.M.–7 P.M., 305-293-7229, *www.keywestaquarium .com*)

If you want to tire your kids out, take them to the 86-foot-tall Key West Lighthouse Museum. Built in 1848, it functioned as an active lighthouse for 121 years. After climbing the eighty-eight steps to the observation platform and looking out over the island and ocean, they should be ready for a nap. And you probably will be, also. (Open daily, 305-294-0012)

What kid doesn't like to play pirate? At the Pirate Soul Museum, they'll get a chance to live like a pirate through interactive displays that unravel the mysteries of twelve famous pirates. They'll walk in a pirate's shoes through the streets of Port Royal, Jamaica, by traversing the alleyways within the museum containing pirate artifacts, including the only authentic pirate chest belonging to Captain Thomas Tew. Admission is $15 per adult, $8.50 per child ten and under. (305-292-1113, *www.piratessoul.com*)

##  TRAVEL TIP

Your kids will be thrilled to walk through the Butterfly and Nature Conservatory where colorful butterflies and birds flutter about. It's not only a great experience for them but an educational one as well. Admission $10 per adult, $7.50 per child. (✆305-296-2988, ✐*www .keywestbutterfly.com*)

## Festivals and Seasonal Events

Give the residents of Key West an excuse to celebrate, and they'll hold a festival. There always seems to be something going on here. In addition to annual events, you'll find an art show, a house tour, or a food festival going on just about any time you visit.

**Old Island Days:** From mid-January through May, the whole town celebrates the Bahamian heritage of the Keys with Bahamas Village night, sidewalk art shows, a flower show, local foods, theater performances, a conch-shell-blowing contest, house and garden tours, and more. (✆305-294-9501, ✐*www.oirf.org*)

**Civil War Heritage Festival:** Re-enactors set up camp at Fort Zachary Taylor State Park and participate in skirmishes and a mock sea battle in February. (✆305-295-3033, ✐*www*
*.fortzacharytaylor.org*)

**Hemingway Days:** Held during the week around July 21, the anniversary of Hemingway's birth, this festival not only features a serious writer's workshop, short story competition, and conference, but a not-so-serious Hemingway Lookalike Contest, arm-wrestling competition, and a mock "running of the bulls." (✆305-294-2587, ✐*www.hemingwaydays.net*)

**Fantasy Fest:** Hosted by the "Conch Republic" and culminating on Halloween, this wild Caribbean-style carnival features ten days of street fairs, costume balls, mask-making workshops, and costume competitions topped off by a wild Saturday night parade of floats and costumed dancers. (✆305-296-1817, ✐*www*
*.fantasyfest.net*)

**Pirates in Paradise Festival:** A November tradition in Key West, this festival features pirate-style escapades with Tall Ship Sea Battles, the Seaport Pirate Fest, children's activities, and art exhibits. (✆Toll-free 877-895-2848, *www.piratesinparadise.com*)

**Offshore Power Boat Race:** In early to mid-November high-performance boats, drivers, and crews from around the world descend on Key West to determine the world offshore champion in four racing classes. (✆305-296-8963)

# Exploring

Take a thirty-minute seaplane flight with Seaplanes of Key West (Toll-free 800-950-2359, *www.seaplanesofkeywest.com*) for $189 or $325 per person (half-day and full-day, respectively) to Dry Tortugas National Park. You'll view spectacular Fort Jefferson, built in the mid-1840s on Garden Key in the Dry Tortugas, 65 miles west of Key West in the Gulf of Mexico, as a protection for the coast.

Nicknamed "Gibraltar of the Gulf," Fort Jefferson was the largest nineteenth-century coastal fort in the country. Though never finished, it served as a prison, with such notable inmates as the "Lincoln Conspirators," four men convicted in the conspiracy to assassinate President Abraham Lincoln. But the lack of fresh water, intense heat, outbreaks of yellow fever, and hurricanes forced the U.S. Army to close it in 1874. After following the marked trail through the fort, you can swim or go snorkeling. The plane trip alone is worth it for the breathtaking views of the coral reefs and shipwrecks in the clear shallow waters (open daily 8 A.M.–dusk, 305-242-7700). The National Park Service also operates the *Yankee Freedom II*, a 100-foot high-speed catamaran, to Fort Jefferson, including breakfast and lunch, as well as swimming and snorkeling for $139 for adults and $94 for children (Toll-free 800-634-0939, *www.yankeefreedom.com*).

# By Day

During the daytime, you'll find fun and sun activities galore, including swimming, boating, parasailing, sailing, snorkeling, and diving, plus sports like golf and tennis. For such a small island, Key West has plenty to do for the whole family.

## On the Beach

Key West has two beaches where you can take a dip in the clear coastal waters. Higg's County Beach offers the best facilities for families, with a playground, tennis courts, Hobie Cat and windsurfing equipment rentals, and concession stands with picnic areas. You can also go parasailing here with Key West Water Tours for $40 per person (305-294-6790) and rent small sailboats here. The city-owned Smathers Beach, near the airport, offers many of the same amenities, including parasailing with Sunset Watersports for $29 per person (305-296-2554), but the swimming area has rocks on the bottom and isn't very good for little ones.

### On the Boat

To see the coral reef out in the Atlantic, take the 80-foot glass-bottom boat *Discovery* from Key West Historic Seaport at 11:30 A.M., 2:30 P.M., and sunset (an hour earlier in winter) for $38 per person (Toll-free 800-262-0099, *www.discoveryunderseatours.com*). Both also offer sunset cruises. To set sail on a catamaran for either a snorkel tour or a champagne sunset cruise for $37 per adult, with kids at half price, contact Sebago Key West (Toll-free 800-507-9955, *www.keywestsebago.com*), or to see dolphins in their natural habitat, take a cruise with Sunny Days Catamarans for $35 per adult and $20 per child (Toll-free 800-236-7937, *www.sunnydayskeywest .com*).

 **TRAVEL TIP**

Experience the thrill of an old-time sailing ship aboard the *Western Union*, the last wooden schooner built in Key West. Learn about the history of Key West while under full sail. You can even join in and help raise and lower the sails. You can sign up for either a day sail, a sunset sail, or a stargazer sail where you'll learn about navigating by the constellations. Parents pay $40 or $59 while kids pay $25 for the day or sunset sails and $45 for the nighttime sail. (☎305-292-1766)

If you'd rather pilot your own boat, you can rent a variety of craft from Boat Rentals of Key West (305-294-2628, *www.boatrental sofkeywest.com*).

Key West has dozens of fishing charter companies that will take you out to the Atlantic or for several days on the Tortuga Banks to look for marlin, tarpon, and wahoo. Choose from any of the following:

- **C Hawk Charters:** ☎305-294-0412, ✐*www.chawkkeywest .com*
- **Charter Boats Linda D:** ☎Toll-free 800-299-9798, ✐*www .charterboatlindad.com*
- **Hog's Breath:** ☎305-294-9311, ✐*www.hogsbreath.com*
- **Mean Green Charters:** ☎305-304-1922, ✐*www .meangreenfishing.com*
- **Odyssea Light Tackle Fishing:** ☎305-797-5060, ✐*www .odysseafishing.com*

## Under the Water

Key West offers excellent diving opportunities, especially on the Marquesas, a group of atolls 20 nautical miles west of Key West with large coral heads beached in shallow water. Treasure hunters found the Spanish ships *Santa Margarita* and the *Atocha* here. Who knows? Perhaps you'll find some buried treasure. But more likely you'll discover the majesty of the spur and groove coral formations decorating Sambo Reef. Here are a few dive shops:

- **Dive Key West:** ☎305-296-3823
- **Reef Raiders Dive Shop:** ☎305-294-3635
- **Subtropic Dive Center:** ☎305-296-9914

## On the Links and on the Courts

You can try out your golf skills at the Key West Resort Golf Course, an eighteen-hole championship layout designed by Rees Jones on Stock Island, featuring mangrove islands and a rare-bird sanctuary by a lake behind the tenth hole. Greens fees are $150 in winter, $85 in summer and at twilight. Juniors can play for $47. Club rentals available for $40. (305-294-5232)

If you like to play tennis, you'll find six unlighted courts at Astro Park across from Higgs County Beach. Bayview Park has five lighted courts and a pro shop if you like to play when it's cooler in the evenings.

### Shopping

You can get some of the best aloe products anywhere, watch cigars rolled by hand at the Key West Cigar Factory (305-294-3470), see brightly colored hand-printed fabrics made right before your eyes at Key West Hand Print Fabrics (305-294-9535), and find original Key West artwork or gifts from around the world.

If you're an art lover, you'll be astounded at the marvelous finds in the numerous Key West galleries.

 **TRAVEL TIP**

If you want to take back a little of Key West's magic, stop in at the Key West Art Center on Front Street, located in a historic old grocery. This local artist cooperative offers drawings and paintings of seascapes and street scenes, as well as unique sculpture.

As on many of the Caribbean islands, shopping on Key West offers lots of choices when you just have to get out of the sun. Besides trendy boutiques, you can see hand-painted fabrics made into chic resort apparel or exotic shells made into jewelry. There's even a perfume factory where you can sample and buy tropical fragrances. Be sure to visit Key West's famous Conch Market where you can buy colorful shells and sea curios.

## Dining Out and Nightlife

Intimate restaurants with island decor feature traditional Key West cuisine—fresh-caught fish, roast pork with yellow rice and black beans, lobster, snapper, stone crabs, grouper—all topped off with a big slice of

Key lime pie. And don't forget to try a Cuban sandwich for lunch, and get "conched out" on conch, whether in chowder, salad, or fritters.

- **Abbondanza Italian Restaurant:** Generous portions of reasonably priced Italian cuisine, served in a bright family atmosphere. (1208 Simonton Street, ☎305-292-1199)
- **Conch Republic Seafood Company:** Dine alfresco on succulent seafood, prepared Caribbean style, in a former sponge-inspection warehouse on the wharf, overlooking the Key West Historic Seaport. (631 Greene Street, ☎305-294-4403, ✐*www.conchrepublicseafood.com*)
- **Kelly's Caribbean Bar, Grill and Brewery:** This microbrewery, housed in the former offices of Pan American Airways, serves up a varied menu, accompanied by its own beers. (301 Whitehead Street, ☎305-293-8484)
- **Lobo's Mixed Grill:** One of the best lunch eateries in Key West and one of the best family values, serving conch chili and thirty different types of wraps, each a unique culinary creation. (5 Key Lime Square, ☎305-296-5303)
- **Mangoes Restaurant:** This restaurant serves a blend of Caribbean and Mediterranean food, plus brick-oven pizzas, in five different dining areas—in dining rooms upstairs and down, on a balcony overlooking the action on Duval Street, in a tropical garden, and on an outdoor patio. (700 Duval Street, ☎305-292-4606)
- **Pepe's Café:** The town's oldest restaurant and its funkiest, dating from 1909, serving three meals a day, including gourmet coffees, great burgers, pork chops, and steaks. (806 Caroline Street, ☎305-294-7192)

Unlike the rest of the Keys, Key West hops at night due to its rather bohemian atmosphere. The festivities begin with the nightly sunset celebration at Mallory Square. Though it began as a spontaneous celebration and an excuse to drink beer and smoke pot in public back in hippie days, today it's a choreographed tourist affair, but fun, nonetheless. Singers, dancers, jugglers, and magicians in colorful costumes are all part of the scene.

##  JUST FOR PARENTS

Step onto the 43-foot yacht *Dreamchaser* for a gourmet dinner for two to six of lobster tail or steak prepared by your own private chef. You'll receive a welcome rum punch or cold beer and conch fritter and shrimp appetizers, and strawberry shortcake for dessert, for $82 per person as you sail into the sunset. (☎305-292-8667)

Sample some culture by attending a play, concert, or dance performance at the Tennessee Williams Fine Arts Center from November to May. You can also tour this modern Bauhaus-inspired theater during the off season (305-296-1520, *www.tennesseewilliamstheatre .com*). There's also the Waterfront Playhouse (305-294-5015) and the Red Barn Theater, which stages new plays by local playwrights (305-296-9911).

Bars of every description make up the bulk of Key West nightlife. Most stand along the upper end of Duval Street and offer a gregarious mix of locals and tourists dancing to live rock or country music. One of the most popular among tourists is Sloppy Joe's on Duval Street, normally packed to the walls. Hemingway drank here in the 1930s. And, of course, there's the Margaritaville Café, owned by Florida singer and songwriter Jimmy Buffet.

# CHAPTER 14

# The Everglades

THE EVERGLADES, STRETCHING 100 MILES south from Lake Okeechobee, has one of the most unusual ecosystems in the world. The lifeblood of "the Glades," as the locals call the area, is water. Not only do its plants and animals need it to survive, but it's also what gives the Glades their unique character. Over 400 species of birds, twenty-six types of snakes, and forty species of four-legged animals call the Glades home. A family vacation here is not only a fun adventure but educational as well.

## Getting to Know the Everglades

At the southern tip of the Florida peninsula lies Everglades National Park, a small portion of this vast wilderness, plus a part of the Ten Thousand Islands and much of Florida Bay, which has been set aside as a preserve. It contains over 1.4 million acres of land and water with an average elevation of only 5 feet above sea level. Plus it harbors fourteen endangered species, including the American crocodile, manatee, Florida panther, Everglades mink, peregrine falcon, short-tailed hawk, and three kinds of sea turtles—hawksbill, green, and loggerhead.

Fresh water from the north flows slowly and gently through the Glades in a shallow river, known as the Shark Valley Slough, 50 miles wide and only 6 inches deep, that empties into Florida Bay on the Gulf Coast.

The Everglades rests on a foundation of solid limestone bedrock, which geologists estimate to be over 100,000 years old. A substance much like peat called *marl* accumulates in pockets in the limestone bed. Over time, this builds to a thickness that can support trees, which grow into hammocks. In some areas of the Glades, clusters of hardwood trees, including mahogany, form dense hammocks ranging in size from a few feet to hundreds of acres. Here palms, live oaks, pond apple, and woody vines grown in profusion. On these trees in the dim light of the hammocks grow orchids, ferns, and vines. The Park has a total of 1,000 species of plants, including 120 species of trees.

## ═FAST FACT

Sawgrass, often referred to as Everglades river grass, gets its name from the its saw-tooth-edged blades. It can grow as high as 10 feet in dense stands that cover acres of the Glades. Many forms of wildlife use sawgrass as a source of food and nesting sites for a variety of birds and animals.

As the river nears the ocean and fresh water mixes with salt water, the marshy grasses (muhly grass, Everglades beardgrass, arrowhead, and sawgrass), hammocks, and pine woods give way to dense thickets of mangroves, important for the food and shelter they offer both land and sea life. The level of the river changes with the seasons. Spring rains turn into torrential downpours and thunderstorms during the summer, dumping up from 60 to 100 inches of water on the Glades. But during winter, the water slows to a trickle, leaving only puddles.

## ≡FAST FACT

The origin of the name "Everglades" is obscure. The Calusa Indians originally called it *pa-hay-okee*, or "grassy water." According to legend, early maps designated the area as the "River Glades." On later maps the name became "Ever Glades" and finally, the term "Everglades" appeared on a map in 1823.

The Calusa Indians roamed the Everglades before Columbus discovered America. And it was into this area that the remnants of the proud Seminole Indian tribes retreated before the advance of white settlers. A few Miccosukee Indians still live within the vast wilderness of the Glades outside the Park. The Glades originally encompassed all the marshland south of Lake Okeechobee. Until 1915, only explorers, hunters, and local Native Americans knew these wild sawgrass marshes and dense hammocks. The following year, the Florida Federation of Women's Clubs acquired the Royal Palm Hammock and turned it over to the State of Florida, which then established Royal Palm State Park as a wildlife sanctuary. Ernest F. Coe, known as "the Father of the Everglades," began a campaign to create an Everglades National Park in the 1920s. Civilian conservation workers, under the WPA program, built shelters and trails between 1934 and 1935. But it took another twelve years until President Harry S Truman signed a bill setting aside 2,000 square miles of the Glades as Everglades National Park, dedicated on December 6, 1947. During that same year, Marjory Stoneman Douglas published her book *The Everglades: River of Grass*, which created a public awareness of the fragility of the Glades. But the Park covers only 12 percent of the Everglades.

To further draw attention to the plight of the Glades, the United Nations designated the Park a Biosphere Reserve, and in 1979 it designated it a World Heritage Site. Both put Everglades National Park under further protection against encroachment by developers.

It's here in this protected environment that you become aware of the vital links that hold the Glades together—the alligators that dig for water with their tails, the tree hammocks that provide sanctuary to animals during the wet season—and the importance of the cycle of wet and dry seasons. The alligators have become known as "the keepers of the Glades." During the dry season, they dig "gator holes," which provide temporary homes for other wildlife until the rains return. Wispy willows surround these gator holes. Tree islands or hammocks dot the endless sawgrass expanse. Though only a few feet above sea level, they're fertile enough to support various types of trees. In the slightly higher areas, pinewoods prevail.

But the biggest danger to the Glades is development. As Florida's population grows, the demand for fresh water and land for farming, roads, and housing is causing damage to this fragile ecosystem. Over 1,500 miles of canals have been built to divert fresh water away from the Glades, and the poison from agricultural chemicals from farmlands around Lake Okeechobee is making its way into the Glades.

# Getting Around the Everglades

You can reach the main entrance of Everglades National Park by departing from U.S. Highway 1 at Florida City and traveling 9 miles along State Road 27. From the Park entrance, a road providing interesting vistas leads 38 miles to Flamingo on Florida Bay. Side roads from it lead to the Royal Palm Visitor Center, the Pa-hay-okee Overlook, and the Mahogany Hammock and Mangrove self-guiding trails. A primitive auto trail allows you to drive through the highlands of the park. However, the trail may be closed during spring and summer months due to flooding from seasonal rains. Be sure to check at the Main Visitor Center for current information on driving conditions before venturing out. You cannot travel from one part of the park to another, except by the canoe trail.

# 🧳 TRAVEL TIP

To view wildlife successfully, ride slowly during early morning hours with your lights on. If you spot a bird or animal, pull well off to the side of the road and turn off your engine. When viewing wildlife from your car during the summer, do *not* roll down your windows and walk along paved or wooden walkways because of the mosquitoes.

You can also hike or bicycle along the loop road at the Shark Valley Visitor Center. You must park your car near the visitor center's entrance as vehicles aren't permitted on the loop road. Admission to the Park is $5 per car at the Flamingo and Shark Valley Entrances, is valid for a week, and can be used at either place. Entrance by boat or canoe from Everglades City is free.

Though there's no public transportation within the Park, you can take one of the Shark Valley Tram Tours, a 15-mile loop departing four times a day in summer and every hour on the hour in winter from the Shark Valley Visitor Center. It's better to take the in-park tram tours.

For information about all five of the visitor centers in Everglades National Park, visit ✑*www.nps.gov/ever.*

## Best Time to Go

The best time to visit the Everglades is from December to April, during the dry winter season, when average daily temperatures hover between 70° and 80°, dipping to the mid-50s at night. Though summer highs rarely exceed the mid-90s, near-daily rain showers increase the humidity, making it seem warmer and encouraging the growth of mosquitoes. May through October is also hurricane season, and with the recent increase in storms, late summer and early fall can be a risky time to visit.

 **TRAVEL TIP**

The Everglades National Park is huge—over 1.5 million acres. From your car, it will look dead and empty, but you need to take a closer look. Don't do like many visitors and only go to walk along the Anhinga Trail to see alligators. Plan on spending at least a day exploring the Park's many trails, and be sure to participate in interpretative walks whenever possible.

### Cautions and Safety Concerns

You cannot bring your dog or cat into Everglades National Park unless you have it on a leash and under control at all times. Pets, other than guide dogs, aren't allowed in the visitor centers or along self-guiding trails.

It's extremely important to watch out for poisonous snakes along any of the trails. Also, during the summer months, it's imperative that you use lots of non-aerosol insect repellent, wear no fragrances, wear protective clothing (a long-sleeved shirt and pants), avoid grassy areas and shady places, and close doors quickly. Since there's very little shade in the Glades, it's also important to wear protective sunscreen. Walking can be tricky if you venture off the trails, so watch your step and watch out for holes. Sharks and barracudas lurk beneath the saltwater areas.

## FAST FACT

Snakes are not always easy to spot. Of the various species of snakes found in the Glades, only four are poisonous—the eastern diamondback, eastern coral snake, dusty pygmy rattlesnake, and, the worst of all, the cottonmouth moccasin. You'll also see Florida king, green, and peninsula ribbon snakes. If you see a snake, give it plenty of room and never pick it up.

If you decide to explore by boat or canoe, be sure to carry a compass and map, which you can obtain at the visitor centers. Also, carry ample provisions in hard containers, including at least a gallon of water per person per day. And be sure to leave a detailed plan of your trip and how long you expect to be gone with a park ranger.

# Family-Oriented Resorts and Hotels

Though you can easily stay in Miami or Naples and drive to the Glades, there's nothing like staying in them or nearby. The following resorts and hotels offer comfortable spots for your family to stay while exploring the beautiful surroundings.

### Captains Table Inn
Reservations: ☎239-695-4211
Located on the edge of Everglades National Park, this hotel offers many different types of accommodations as well as a good seafood restaurant.

### Flamingo Lodge, Marina, and Outpost Resort
Reservations: ☎305-253-2241
A 120-room family resort located at Flamingo at the southern tip of Everglades National Park, the Flamingo offers motel-style rooms and housekeeping cottages, plus a swimming pool and dining room that are closed May 1 through October 31.

### River Wilderness Waterfront Villas
Reservations: ☎239-695-4499
With the splendor of the Glades outside your door, your family can stay in one of fourteen apartments with all the amenities, plus a pool.

# Things to Do

Begin your exploration of the Everglades at the Ernest C. Coe Visitor Center of Everglades National Park, located at the junction of U.S.

Route 1 and West Palm Drive in Florida City, where you can view a fifteen-minute orientation film, as well as exhibits on the history of the Everglades and life within the park (open daily 9 A.M.–5 P.M., 305-242-7700).

 **TRAVEL TIP**

Be sure to bring drinks and snacks along with you when touring the Everglades parks, as they're sparsely available. The only restaurant in the National Park is at Flamingo, and that's only open during the winter. Water is an absolute necessity, especially during the hot summer season.

Each of the satellite visitor centers—at Royal Palm, Flamingo, Gulf Coast, and Shark Valley—offer displays about life in that region. For instance, the Gulf Coast Visitor Center (open daily 9:00 A.M.–4:30 P.M., 239-695-3311) will show you typical shore and marine life while the Flamingo Visitor Center (open daily 8:30 A.M.–5:00 P.M., 239-695-2945) has exhibits depicting the plants and wildlife of that area. Park Service naturalists offer guided walks, talks, and demonstrations throughout the year at all but Flamingo, where they're offered only in winter.

Self-guiding trails from the Royal Palm Visitor Center (open daily 8:00 A.M.-4:15 P.M.) will allow you to get a closer view of the vegetation and wildlife. Unlike the other visitor centers, rangers lead walks and give talks all year.

Because the half-mile Anhinga Trail offers the best views of wildlife in the Glades, it's also the most crowded. The trail gets its name from the anhinga, a black-bodied bird, which, after diving for fish, spreads its wings to dry on the tree branches. Alligators sun themselves on trail banks, swish through marsh grasses, and occasionally one may even cross your path. But mostly you'll see raccoons, turtles, and marsh rabbits.

## 📼 TRAVEL TIP

Never get closer than 15 feet to an alligator. If it opens its mouth or hisses, back off. They're capable of running up to 30 miles per hour. Alligators tend to keep very still and lurk in freshwater ponds. If you come across a female with a baby on her back, watch them from a safe distance since mothers are extremely protective of their young.

Go early to beat the crowds, then head to the nearby half-mile Gumbo-Limbo Trail, which leads through a jungle-like hardwood hammock with 160 species of plants.

About 6 miles from the park's main entrance lies the half-mile Pineland Trail, which meanders through an area of slash pine forest, featuring over 200 varieties of plants, including 30 found nowhere else in the world. The endangered Florida panther makes its home here. You'll find dry ground, and see patches of the limestone rock that lies under South Florida. Farther down the road, you'll spot bald cypress trees hung with gray moss standing in the tall sawgrass. Because of conditions in the Glades, they remain dwarfed.

Six miles beyond the Pinelands, you'll arrive at the Pa-hay-okee Overlook trailhead. After a short walk along the boardwalk, you can climb the observation tower, which offers an excellent bird-watching perch, for a magnificent panoramic view of the sawgrass prairie dotted with hardwood hammocks and dwarf cypress trees.

## FAST FACT

Bald cypress trees lose their leaves at the beginning of the dry season and take on a spindly "bald" or wintry look, then grow bright green needles at the beginning of the wet season. Wood storks like to nest in their gray branches draped with moss.

The half-mile Mahogany Hammock Trail comes up about 7 miles beyond the overlook. In the cool, damp environment of this dark, jungle-like hardwood hammock, massive mahogany trees shelter Liguus tree snails as golden orb spiders weave their webs. Be sure to listen for the hoot of the barred owl.

Beyond the Mahogany Hammock, the road heads toward the sea. Soon you'll begin to see mangrove trees, a sign that the fresh water of the Glades is beginning to mix with the salt water of Florida Bay. For a closer view of the mangroves and to see life in an estuary environment, follow the half-mile West Lake Trail, winding through mangrove and buttonwood trees along the edge of the lake where shrimp, spiny lobsters, and stone crabs seek protection from the sea. If you're visiting during the winter months, stop at Mzarek Pond, where roseate spoonbills come to feed with other exotic water birds.

Driving on, you'll soon arrive at the Flamingo Visitor Center, which stands on the site of a former fishing village. Since the village remained isolated, accessible only by boat, illegal activities, such as making moonshine and poaching water birds for their colorful plumage, went on for years. Nothing remains of it today, as it has been replaced by the visitor center, a marina, and concessions. The village didn't have a name until the U.S. Post Office chose Flamingo because of the abundant roseate spoonbills, pink-plumed birds that the residents mistook for flamingos.

## ☂ RAINY DAY FUN

When a shower hits, visit the Museum of the Everglades in Everglades City. Housed in a former laundry dating to the early twentieth century, it offers exhibits of artifacts and photographs showing the 2,000-year history of human habitation of the Glades. Admission is $2. (Open Tuesday through Saturday, 10 A.M.–4 P.M., ☎239-695-0008)

Among the nearly 300 varieties of birds you may see in the park are bald eagles, limpkins, egrets, and roseate spoonbills. The only wild crocodiles in the country can be found in the park and on a few of the Florida Keys. Alligators, black bears, panthers, wildcats, otters, raccoons, and white-tailed deer still inhabit this area.

Depending on the season, you can also go bicycling, oystering, crabbing, and, of course, birding, which is best in mid-winter.

If you'd rather ride in comfort, take the two-hour tram ride, which departs hourly from the Shark Valley Visitor Center (open daily 9:15 A.M.–5:15 P.M., 305-221-8776), along the 15-mile loop road to a 25-foot-high observation tower for a dramatic panoramic view of the Everglades. Along the way, the tram stops for bird and alligator sightings, as a park ranger points out geological formations and native vegetation, and offers information on the park's water system. Tram service isn't available during periods of high water from mid-September through mid-November (305-221-8455). During the summer, the Park Service offers four tram tours at 9:30 and 11 A.M. and 1 and 3 P.M. Since wildlife is most active in the early morning hours, you should take the first tour of the day.

## Miccosukee Cultural Center

Besides the natural wonders of the Glades, you can also visit the Miccosukee Cultural Center, a touristy re-creation located west of the Shark Valley Visitor Center on Route 41, where you'll learn about how these people lived in the Glades during the nineteenth century. Even though they're descendants of several hundred Seminoles who hid in the Everglades after being driven out of Central Florida by arriving white settlers, the Miccosukee weren't recognized by the U.S. government as a tribe until 1962. They lived on hammocks in open-sided chickees, constructed from cypress wood with cabbage palm roofs, and hunted and traded by canoe. You can either go on a guided tour or see the museum, chickees, women cooking, and men carving logs into canoes on your own. Afterward, you can take a ride on a propeller-driven airboat with Miccosukee Airboat Rides to an old Indian camp, followed by lunch of traditional pumpkin bread and fried catfish at the Miccosukee Restaurant across the road. Admission is $5 per person. (Open daily 9 A.M.-5 P.M., 305-223-8388)

 **TRAVEL TIP**

The smallest and most photographed U.S. Post Office building—only 8 by 9 feet—stands in Ochopee on Route 41. You can't miss it. It will be the building flying the American flag with all the tour buses parked outside. Send some postcards to the folks back home from here.

### For the Kids

Take the kids swimming in an artesian water pool in a natural depression inside a hammock at Chekika State Recreation Area, 15 miles from Homestead. This 640-acre park offers much of the same landscapes as Everglades National Park. Your little ones will enjoy walking along the boardwalk looking for sleeping alligators.

 **TRAVEL TIP**

Pick up a newspaper listing kids' activities at both the Ernest C. Coe Visitor Center in Everglades National Park and at the Oasis Visitor Center in Big Swamp Preserve. Planning ahead will help you make the best use of your time and keep your children interested.

Make sure to have your kids register for the Junior Ranger Program at both Everglades National Park and Big Cypress Preserve. After completing at least three activities in each park, they'll receive a Junior Ranger Badge for that park. And if they complete all the activities listed in the Junior Ranger Booklet, they'll receive a Junior Ranger Patch.

### Festivals and Special Events

Since the focus of the Glades is on nature, there aren't many events. The following are the most popular:

- **Everglades Seafood Festival:** An annual festival with entertainment, music, arts and crafts, and food held the first weekend in February (✆239-695-3941).
- **Clyde and Nikki Butcher's Labor Day Weekend Gala and Swamp Walk:** Held every year at the Big Cypress Gallery (52388 Tamiami Trail, Ochopee, ✆239-695-2428).

# Exploring

Perhaps more than any other place in Coastal Florida, the Everglades has a wealth of locations fit for exploring.

### Chokoloskee Island

To get a sense of history of the Glades, visit Chokoloskee Island. The first white men to settle here in the late nineteenth century hunted animals for their hides and fur, and birds for their plumes. Soon families joined them, and they made a living by farming, fishing, and hunting. In 1906, Ted Smallwood opened a trading post to provide goods and mail to the new settlers. When the store closed in 1982, many of the original goods and furnishings remained. Today, you can get a feeling of what it was like to be an early pioneer in the Glades by visiting the Smallwood Store and Museum. (Open daily 10 A.M.–5 P.M., December 26 to May 1 and 11 A.M.–5 P.M. Friday through Tuesday, May 2 to December 23, 239-695-2989)

Afterward, take one of the park-sanctioned boat trips, departing from the dock on Chokoloskee every half-hour from 9:30 A.M. to 4:30 P.M., for about $10 per person. You can get information on these cruises, offered from November to March only, as well as ranger-led canoe trips, departing at 10 A.M. on Saturdays during the dry season, from the dockside visitor center.

### Big Cypress National Preserve

To protect the fresh water supply crucial to the survival of Everglades National Park, the U.S. Congress created Big Cypress National Preserve, a 729,000-acre area, in 1974. By traversing either U.S. Route 41, locally known as the Tamiami Trail, or Interstate 75, lovingly referred to as Alligator Alley—both of which cross the preserve—as well as State Route 29, you'll be able to explore this vast wet wilderness. The word "Big" in the preserve's name refers more to its size than to the size of the cypress trees that grow there. Part of the overall Everglades, it consists of similar natural features—hardwood hammocks, marshes, mangrove forests, pine islands, and wet prairies. And like those in the park, you'll see orchids and bromeliads perching on the cypress and hardwood trees. Egrets and herons wade in the shallow waters under cypress festooned with Spanish moss while wood storks, wild turkeys, and bald eagles fly overhead and panthers stalk deer and mink in the soggy forests.

## ≡FAST FACT

Airboats are flat-bottomed boats powered by a large airplane propeller attached to an aircraft engine and housed in a large metal cage to protect passengers. The boat's flat bottom allows it to navigate easily through shallow swamps. The driver sits high on a platform to improve visibility so he can spot floating obstacles and animals in the path of the boat.

You'll find Preserve Headquarters at the Oasis Visitor Center, west of Ochopee or 55 miles east of Naples, on U.S. 41 (open daily 8:30 A.M.–4:30 P.M., 941-695-4111). You can enjoy the preserve's seemingly limitless horizons by taking an airboat ride, which is forbidden within the confines of the National Park. Fishing is also excellent here.

### Fakahatchee Strand Preserve State Park

Another area of swamp set aside by the State of Florida is the Fakahatchee Strand Preserve State Park, also on Route 41. As the main drainage slough of the Big Cypress Swamp, it contains a tall, dense forest of bald cypress and royal palm trees, festooned with sweet-smelling orchids. You can walk the boardwalk through the forest, or on weekends from November to February you can take part in a narrated "wet" walk through the swamp given by park rangers. You can also drive along an 11-mile gravel road to see some other areas of the park. (Open daily 8 A.M.–sunset, 239-695-4593)

### Corkscrew Swamp Sanctuary

As the best of all the National Audubon Society sanctuaries, the 11,000-acre Corkscrew Swamp is popular with bird watchers and photographers. Nearly 200 species of birds, including nesting wood storks, as well as hundreds of alligators inhabit the area. Walk the 3-mile boardwalk trail through the country's oldest bald-cypress forest and tropical fern jungle with its many fragrant orchids. Naturalists conduct early swamp walks once a month in winter from 7 to 10 A.M. for $11 per person, plus two-hour twice-monthly sunset walks at various starting times, and twice-monthly night walks from 7 to 9 P.M., each for $18 per person. Admission is $6.50 for adults, $3.00 for kids 6 to 18, and free for those under 6. (Open daily 7:00 A.M.–5:30 P.M., October 1–April 10 and 7:00 A.M.–7:30 P.M., April 11–September 30, 239-348-9151)

# By Day

You'll get your first glimpse of the Glades by driving the 38 miles from park headquarters at the eastern entrance to the Visitor Center at Flamingo. But you'll view little from your car window, except sawgrass as far as your eyes can see.

To fully experience the Glades, you'll need to walk through the park's 60 miles of boardwalks and trails. Trails range from easy walks of less than a quarter-mile to more strenuous ones 14 miles long. As you walk along them, you'll observe cypress and mahogany trees, orchids and lilies, deer, otters, snakes, and alligators, and flocks of snowy egrets. Park naturalists give hikes, talks, canoe trips, tram tours, and demonstrations throughout the year. You can choose from sunrise bird walks, paddles out into Florida Bay, a cross-country "slough slog," and a moonlight tram tour. You'll find schedules for all these activities at the park's visitor centers.

Since much of the Everglades is water, boating opportunities, including 65 miles of marked canoe trails, rivers, Whitewater Bay, and Florida Bay, abound. The Flamingo Marina can accommodate boats up to 60 feet long with boat-trailer parking and free launch access. Here you can also rent small powered skiffs, houseboats, patio boats, and canoes. You'll find three marked canoe trails through the Glades. All are 14- to 22-mile round trips around Flamingo. You can rent a canoe from any of the following outfitters:

- **Chokoloskee Outdoor Resort:** ☎941-695-2881
- **Everglades National Park Canoe Rentals:** ☎941-695-2591 or ☎Toll-free 800-445-7724
- **Huron Kayak and Canoe:** ☎941-695-3666
- **North American Canoe Tours:** ☎941-695-4666

There are many canoe trails in the park, but the most comprehensive and the longest is the 99-mile Wilderness Waterway, which meanders through mangrove swamps, rivers, lakes, and bays to campsites on beaches, islands, and park-made chickees, 12-by-10-foot wooden platforms on stilts where there's no higher ground. Each comes complete with a roof and a catwalk to a chemical toilet. You'll have to make arrangements for transportation at the other end if you decide to make this trek. You'll also find the rivers near Everglades City great for canoeing. Some designated canoe trails have motor-size restrictions, and some wilderness trails prohibit motors. If you do decide to rent a motorized boat, you should make sure you obtain navigational charts, as it's easy to get lost in the maze of waterways in the Glades.

If you'd rather let someone else be your guide, you can take a sightseeing pontoon boat tour into the Ten Thousand Islands region and the mangrove swamps of the northwestern Everglades from any of the following operators out of Everglades City:

- **Captain Dan:** Chokoloskee Island, ✆813-695-4573
- **Captain Doug House's Florida Boat Tours:** ✆Toll-free 800-282-9194
- **Sammy Hamilton Boat Tours:** ✆813-695-2591
- **Totch's Island Boat Tours:** ✆Toll-free 866-626-2833

Those departing from the Flamingo Marina explore the Florida Bay and backcountry waters. Particularly beautiful are the sunset cruises, from which you can see a variety of birds heading to shore for the night.

##  TRAVEL TIP

To learn the most about the Everglades, take a one-and-a-half-hour pontoon boat tour through the park, narrated by park naturalists. Tours depart every thirty minutes from 9:30 A.M. to 4:30 P.M. from the Gulf Coast Visitor Center in Everglades City. While airboat rides can be fun, any environmental interpretation must be done while the boat is still.

And for that extra thrill, take an air tour of the Glades with Air Tours of South Florida from the Homestead Airport (305-248-1100).

Over 600 varieties of fish abound in the park's waters. You can catch game fish throughout the year, and you'll find light tackle works best when fishing in the area. Saltwater fishing requires no license. Inland and coastal waters of the Everglades are popular fishing grounds. There is largemouth-bass fishing in freshwater ponds. The saltwater species most sought after are snapper, redfish, and trout. Both Florida and special federal fishing regulations apply, so be sure to pick up a copy of the regulations at the Main Visitor Center and find out where you can't fish. You can also arrange a day fishing charter from any of the following companies:

- **Adventures in Backwater Fishing:** ✆239-643-1261
- **Captain Jay's Charters:** ✆239-417-3055
- **Dawn Patrol Charter Fishing:** ✆239-394-0608
- **Fishing Adventures Inc.:** ✆Toll-free 800-890-2312
- **Go Fish Guide Services:** ✆239-695-0687

# Dining Out and Nightlife

Other than the 200-seat dining room featuring seafood dishes over-looking Florida Bay at the Flamingo Lodge Restaurant (✆813-695-3101), you won't find any dining facilities in Everglades National Park. The closest restaurants are in Everglades City and Homestead. While most of the eateries in this area serve up the usual fried or broiled fish, you'll also want to try stone crab claws, and such delicacies as alligator tail or freshwater soft-shell terrapin, also known as *cooter*.

**Donzanti's:** Big helpings of good down-home Italian cuisine served in a family-friendly atmosphere. (255 Northeast Third Drive, Homestead, ✆305-248-5281)

**Potticker:** Anyone who loves ribs, pot pie, and fish served with a wide variety of homegrown southern vegetables will love dining in this country-style eatery. (591 Washington Avenue, Homestead, ✆305-248-0835)

**Rod and Gun Club:** Dine on local fish, stone crabs, and frogs' legs in the warm cypress-paneled dining hall of this former hunting and fishing lodge or out on the porch overlooking the yachts docked just beyond. (200 Riverside Drive, Everglades City, ✆813-695-2101)

**The Oyster House:** Serves all types of seafood, including lobster tail and "gator" in a nautical atmosphere and view of the Ten

Thousand Islands. (State Route 29, Everglades City, ☏813-695-2073, ✉ *www.oysterhouserestaurant.com*)

**The Seafood Depot:** Excellent seafood served in a historic Spanish adobe railroad depot, now the Captain's Table Inn, with magnificent views of the Glades. (102 East Broadway, Everglades City, ☏239-695-4211)

The sidewalks roll up early in the Glades, so you won't find much in the way of nightlife except the occasional motel bar. The most exciting thing to do at night in Flamingo is to stand under the stars and listen to the eerie serenade of the Glades, but only in the winter—the mosquitoes might carry you away at other times. If you crave a bit more excitement, you can drive to Florida City, or even Miami, both less than an hour away.

# CHAPTER 15

# Sarasota

WHEN PEOPLE THINK OF SARASOTA, they often think of the circus, for it was here that the Ringling Brothers and others originally wintered their shows beginning in 1927, nicknaming it "Circus Town." Today, many consider the city to be the cultural capital of Florida—"the Palm Beach of West Florida"—a concept it inherited from its main benefactor, John Ringling. Miles of beautiful beaches, as well as magnificent gardens, wildlife, interesting museums, and magnificent performing-arts centers, attract families to this sunny area along Florida's west coast.

## Getting to Know Sarasota

Sarasota lies at the beginning of what's known as the "Shell Coast," an area explored by Ponce de León in 1521. The Calusa Indians lived around Sarasota Bay until the early nineteenth century when disease decimated them. The Spanish explorers, who understood the tribal chief's name to be Calos, coined the name Caloosa, which later changed to Calusa. Originally peaceful fishermen, the Calusas turned into warriors after the Spaniards' arrival to protect themselves.

Beginning with Ponce de León, whom the Calusa severely wounded with a poison arrow and who later died of his wounds in Havana, Cuba, more Spanish explorers looking for gold, including Hernando De Soto, set up camps on the Gulf shores. Many believe

De Soto coined the name Sarasota, initially "Sara Sota." Over the next century, Cuban immigrant fishermen set up a fishing industry around Charlotte Harbor, between Sarasota and present-day Fort Myers. As the Calusa died off, Seminoles began arriving in the area.

Pirates and buccaneers, who legends say buried millions of dollars in Gulf sands, began to seek refuge in the forbidding bayous and rivers along the coast by the mid-eighteenth century. Criminals, hiding from their crimes, joined them, making for an unholy alliance.

By the mid-nineteenth century, the Seminoles had been subdued during the Seminole Wars, and the remaining ones dispersed into the Everglades. Farmers from the South moved into the area and planted citrus fruits, coffee, and coconut palms. But after the Civil War, real estate schemers invaded the area and became rich buying up "useless" swamp land.

## ☰FAST FACT

Called "Crackers" because most came from Georgia and cracked corn for corn pone and hush puppies, the southern farmers who came to Sarasota in the 1850s built wooden farmhouses with tin roofs, which today are called "Cracker" houses.

In 1885, the Florida Mortgage and Investment Company promoted Sarasota in Scotland as a place with fertile land for citrus groves and affordable housing. While those who sailed to Sarasota found it less appealing than expected and left for other areas, John Hamilton Gillespie, a Scottish lawyer and entrepreneur, made the town a tourist destination by building the De Soto Hotel.

Around 1910, coastal towns from Sarasota to Fort Myers and beyond began attracting the rich and famous, including such notables as Charles Lindbergh, Teddy Roosevelt, John Ringling, Henry DuPont, Thomas Edison, Henry Ford, and even Shirley Temple—all seeking refuge from northern winters. It was they who brought civility to the wild west coast as growth came quickly to the communities of Sarasota, Fort Myers, and Naples. But it has been the thousands of northerners, seeking a legendary land of treasure and youth, much as did Ponce de León, who have brought prosperity to the region.

# Getting Around Sarasota

The best way to explore the Sarasota area is by car. Sarasota County Area Transit (SCAT) offers dependable daily, except Sunday, bus service with discounts for children from 6 A.M. to 6 P.M. (941-951-5851). LeeTran runs trolley buses to Fort Myers Beach from Fort Myers (941-275-8726) while the Naples Trolley and Blue Trolley Line conduct sightseeing and shopping tours in the Naples area (941-262-7300).

You can also rent a bicycle for $10 a day or $25 a week from Sarasota Bicycle Center (941-377-4505). You'll have to ride on the streets or roads in town, as there are no bike paths. However, there are paths on the barrier islands.

### Best Time to Go

The best time to visit Sarasota is from February to April when temperatures range from highs in the mid-70s to lows in the mid-50s. By the end of April, daytime temperatures start to climb to the mid-80s and eventually peak in the low 90s by August. And while a good sea breeze keeps the barrier islands comfortable, Sarasota itself can get muggy. Water temperatures average 87°F year-round.

### Cautions and Safety Concerns

While the area around Sarasota and south is relatively safe, some beaches can get crowded during the winter season. The biggest danger is from red tide, a high concentration of microscopic organisms in the Gulf waters that produces a toxin that affects fish, and, down the food chain, humans, causing respiratory irritation. During a time of high "bloom," don't eat clams or oysters.

To check on red tide conditions, call the Sarasota County Beaches Red Tide Hotline (941-346-0079).

# Family-Oriented Resorts and Hotels

If you're like other visitors to the Sarasota area, you'll most likely want to stay near the beaches on the barrier islands. Here, you'll find a mix of inns, small motels, and luxury resorts. Since Sarasota underwent a renaissance of sorts in recent years, many more vacationing families are choosing to stay near or in town.

### Holiday Inn

Reservations: ☏Toll-free 888-465-4329

✐*www.holidayinn.com*

This 146-room classy high-rise sits at the northern end of Longboat Key and features regular accommodations, kitchen suites, and special family suites with a separate room within a room just for the kids, indoor and outdoor pools, whirlpool, exercise room, sailboat rentals, café, and beach bar.

### Outrigger Beach Resort

Reservations: ☏Toll-free 800-749-3131

At the quieter end of Fort Myers Beach, this 144-room family resort offers traditional and efficiency rooms with kitchens, a fenced-in pool and bar, water sports, putting green, shuffleboard, café, and live entertainment on weekends.

### Radisson Lido Beach Resort

Reservations: ☏Toll-free 800-333-3333

Located next to Lido Key's main public beach, this 116-room resort offers rooms with or without kitchens, a beachside pool and bar, plus a variety of water sports.

## House and Condo Rentals

If you'd rather have your family stay in a vacation home, you'll find a wide selection not only in Sarasota, but also on the barrier islands offshore, as well as in Fort Myers and Naples. Contact

Resort Quest Vacation Home Network (Toll-free 800-475-2892, *www.resortquestswfl.com/flausa*).

## Things to Do

You'll find plenty of activities for your family along the Shell Coast. Sarasota has the Marie Selby Botanical Gardens, a 1920s home overlooking Sarasota Bay with 10 acres of gardens full of tropical trees and bromeliads. It's world-renowned for its collection of over 6,000 orchids in a lush rainforest setting. The best time to see the orchids is in April. One of Sarasota's oldest attractions, it merges a love of nature with art and aesthetics. Before or after strolling through the gardens, take a tour of the Payne Mansion, housing the Museum of Botany. Admission $8 for adults, $4 for children. (Open 10 A.M.–5 P.M., 941-366-5731)

## ≡FAST FACT

The circus is still a thriving industry in Sarasota. Eighteen companies winter here, plus there's a clown college. Even at the local high school, circus is an extracurricular activity like sports and drama.

Another popular attraction is Bellm Cars and Music of Yesterday, with its displays of seventy-five antique cars from a 1905 horseless carriage to a 1971 Maserati, and 1,200 musical instruments under one roof. Take the thirty-minute tour, which explains the history of music boxes, player pianos, and phonographs, among other inventions. Play games in the vintage arcade—no computer games, just good old-fashioned fun. Admission $9 for adults, $5 for children 6 to 12. (Open daily 9 A.M.–6 P.M., 941-355-6228)

### For the Kids

Your kids will love getting close to sharks and other local marine life at the Mote Marine Laboratory and Aquarium, at City Island Park on the northern end of Lido Key. A 135,000-gallon tank is the centerpiece of dozens of exhibits containing sharks, lobsters, stingrays, seahorses, and other local marine life. It's more than an entertainment aquarium. In fact, it's the public arm of a marine laboratory where marine biologists have been studying the ecological problems threatening the Gulf's sea life. There's also a living sea grass and mangrove exhibit, plus a huge seashell collection. Smaller children love the "Touch Tank," filled with sea urchins and horseshoe crabs. Admission is $15 for adults, $10 for kids 4 to 17. (Open 10 A.M.–5 P.M., Toll-free 800-691-6683, *www.mote.org*)

Adjacent to the aquarium is the Dale Shields Bird Sanctuary. Shields, locally known as "the Pelican Man," has rescued and rehabilitated over 22,000 birds. Not only will your kids be able to meet some of their fine feathered friends, they'll also learn all about them. You'll find this to be a great educational experience. (Open daily 10 A.M.–5 P.M., 941-388-4444)

##  TRAVEL TIP

If you have young children who play baseball, then you must take them to Ed Smith Stadium in Sarasota to see the Chicago White Sox (☎941-954-7699) or to McKechnie Field in Bradenton to see the Pittsburgh Pirates (☎941-748-4610), both in Sarasota for Spring Training in March and early April.

Winding paths lead through 16 acres with 100 varieties of palms plus lots of local plant varieties in the Sarasota Jungle Gardens. As one of the area's favorite kiddy attractions, this zoological garden features a playground with a jungle theme, exotic bird and reptile shows, strolling peacocks, and a bird posing area. Admission $9 for adults, $5 for children. (Open daily 9 A.M.–5 P.M., Toll-free 877-861-6547)

G.Wiz is Sarasota's science fantasyland. Your children will enjoy the eighty-five interactive exhibits in this hands-on science museum (941-309-4949). And as a break from educational activities, your family can play miniature golf in caves, near rushing waterfalls, and on a shipwreck at Smugglers Cove Adventure Golf (941-351-6620, *www .smugglersgolf.com*).

### Festivals and Seasonal Events

Annually, during February and March, communities up and down Florida's west coast sponsor shell shows that draw participants from all over the world. You'll also find food, music, and wine festivals held throughout the year.

**The Medieval Fair:** Knights in shining armor, maidens, jesters, jugglers, swordsmen, magicians, and musicians all take part in a display of skills and crafts from the Middle Ages each March on the grounds of the Ringling Museum. The highlight is a human chess match, played on a giant grass chessboard. (☎941-351-8497)

**The Sanibel Shell Fair:** A showcase of shells, shell art, and marine life is held the first weekend in March. (☎941-472-2155)

**International Circus Festival and Parade:** During the last week of December, clowns, circus acts, and a carnival join together to show that Sarasota is still "Circus Town." (☎941-351-8888)

# Exploring

After you've seen the sites of Sarasota, you'll want to explore south of the city, taking in some of the coastal towns, wildlife refuges, parks, and other museums.

## Fort Myers

Known as "the City of Palms," Fort Myers began as a Calusa Indian settlement, then became a Seminole War fort. Just as Thomas Alva Edison, Fort Myers' leading resident, predicted, Fort Myers has evolved from a sleepy cow town into one of Florida's fastest-growing, most sophisticated cities. Besides its posh shopping and dining, Fort Myers' most notable attraction is the Thomas Edison Winter Home— but before visiting it, stop in at the Fort Myers Historical Museum, housed in an old Atlantic Coastline Railroad depot a few blocks up the street. One of the exhibits explains the invention of the world's greatest cure for hangovers—Alka Seltzer—by Dr. Franklin Miles, a Fort Myers resident. Admission is $2. (Open Tuesday through Friday 9:00 A.M.–4:30 P.M., Saturday and Sunday 1–5 P.M., 941-332-5955)

Wintering here for almost fifty years, Edison experimented with thousands of plants, including the bamboo he found on the site. He discovered that using carbonized bamboo fibers helped make the light bulb practical, and often used the chemicals produced by his plants in his inventions. His exotic garden, where the tour begins, provided him with a variety of tropical foliage, from the wild orchids to an extraordinary African sausage tree to fragrant frangipani. There are also beds of *solidago Edisoni*, a giant strain of goldenrod that he developed while trying to discover alternate methods of producing rubber. Pause to admire the sprawling banyan tree, which Edison grew from a two-inch-diameter seedling given to him by rubber-king Harvey Firestone in 1925. Dropping its aerial roots as it spread, the tree has grown to a perimeter of more than 300 feet, making it the largest tree in Florida.

When you enter the museum, you become aware of Edison's genius. Early on, he designed an improved ticker-tape machine, the proceeds from which helped to finance the invention of the phonograph in 1877, and two years later he discovered the electric light bulb by passing electricity through a vacuum. You'll see a variety of disc and cylinder phonographs, plus some of the first bulky light bulbs, and lots of other gadgets. Edison also invented the Kinetoscope, from which he derived the first early movie projector in 1907, which earned him over a million dollars annually in patent royalties. There's even a Model T that his friend and next-door neighbor, Henry Ford, had made especially for him. Unfortunately, you can only glimpse Edison's home through the windows.

But unlike Edison's, you can go inside the Ford Winter Home next door. Ford had been Edison's close friend since 1896, when Edison praised his concept of the automobile. So Ford bought the adjacent property in 1915. The interior has been restored to the style of Ford's time with similar furnishings. Tours of both homes begin every thirty minutes between 9 A.M. and 4 P.M. Admission is $4 for the Edison home and $8 for both homes. (Open Monday through Saturday 9 A.M.–4 P.M., Sunday 12:30–4:00 P.M., 941-334-3614)

### Sanibel and Captiva Islands

Geographically, Sanibel and Captiva islands are about 5,000 years old. Once believed to have been a single island, today they're joined by the Turner Bridge. Gulf tides and currents rolled and swept thousands of tons of seashells onto a sandbar to form the island of Sanibel. In time, vegetation and freshwater pools developed. When the Spanish arrived in the early sixteenth century, they found the Calusa fishing and living off the land. According to legend, the Spanish originally named the island Santa Isabella, which later became shortened to Sanibel.

## ≡FAST FACT

According to legend, José Gaspar, known by his pirate name of "Gasparilla," set up headquarters on Gasparilla Island fronting Charlotte Harbor. The former Spanish naval admiral gave up his position to become a pirate, but retained his love of beautiful women. He kidnapped the richest and loveliest and held them captive for ransom on another barrier island, Captiva.

While you're on Sanibel Island, you may want to visit the Sanibel-Captiva Nature Center, supported by the Sanibel-Captiva Conservation Foundation, where you can view informative live exhibits. There's also a native plant nursery and 4 miles of trails. Begin your adventure by hiking the Sabal Palm Trail to an alligator hole and continue on the Upper Ridge Trail, then the Wildflower Trail, and finally the fern-lined West River Trail, along which you may see a gopher tortoise as it makes its way to its burrow. Pause at the Sanibel River overlook and observation tower to see ospreys flying overhead.

Sanibel's fame as a prime shelling destination is world renowned. The eastward hook on the island's southern shore allows it to snag shells from the sea. You can easily scoop up scallop, turkey wing, lucina, cockle, and angle wing shells, as well as alphabet cones, fighting conches, tree tulips, junonicas, lion's paws, olives, and lightning whelks You may also find sand dollars and sea fans, especially after a storm. To help identify your finds, use one of the shell charts published in most of the free tourist magazines available in local restaurants and shops. The best place to find shells on Sanibel Island is Bowman's Beach. Captiva Beach also provides good shelling.

##  TRAVEL TIP

Plan on getting "shell bent" in Sanibel as you develop the famous "Sanibel stoop"—the classic bent-from-the-waist stance used while looking for shells. But be sure to obey the city ordinance that limits you to taking two live shells—that is, with a creature living inside—per species per person. The penalty is a stiff $500 fine or prison sentence per incident.

The shallow bays and creeks on the opposite side of Sanibel Island are the home of brown pelicans, ospreys, and the ever-present alligators of the 5,000-acre J. N. "Ding" Darling Wildlife Refuge. Stop at the Visitor's Center to learn about the preserve's flora and fauna, as well as the life of Ding Darling, the Pulitzer Prize–winning cartoonist who passionately fought to save the area's water birds. Climb the observation tower for an overview of this wild world and afterward take a ride along 5-mile-long Wildlife Drive, but do so slowly and stop frequently to observe the wildlife. Admission is $3 per car. (Open daily sunrise to sunset, 941-472-1100)

## Naples

You'll find even more opulence farther south in the sleek tropical community of Naples, the gateway to the Tamiami Trail, the route through the Everglades to Miami begun in 1918. To learn about the history of the city, stop at the Collier County Museum, which exhibits local historical artifacts, including a fine collection of the shell tools and ornaments used by the Calusa Indians. There's also a diorama of a Spanish shipwreck, with actual coins, cannonballs, and olive jars brought up from the deep, and assorted Seminole and Seminole War objects, including trade items like furs, alligator skins, and beeswax. "Old Number 2," a steam locomotive that once ran local routes for a cypress-logging firm, stands out front. You can also tour a re-creation of a Seminole village. (Open Monday through Friday, 941-774-8476)

One of the oldest structures in the city is the Seaboard Coastal Line Railroad Depot, built in 1926. It's currently a railroad museum and community art center. Another historic place is Palm Cottage, built in 1890 and one of the few houses in Florida constructed of tabby, a primitive form of cement.

Another place of special interest in the Naples area is the Koreshan State Historic Site. Cyrus R. Teed, a religious visionary, founded the Koreshan Unity and in 1894 led his followers from Chicago to this site near Naples, where they founded a settlement called Estero. The settlers built twenty buildings, including a school, and created a botanical garden of trees and shrubs. Today, you can tour twelve of the original community's frame vernacular buildings. (Open daily 8 A.M.–dusk, 941-992-0311)

## ≡FAST FACT

Cyrus Teed preached a strange gospel of reincarnation, communal ownership, celibacy, and the notion that the sun was really inside the earth. He predicted that 10 million believers would flock to the community, but they never arrived. He thought himself immortal but died in 1908.

When pioneers settled in Naples in 1887, they combed the beaches for shark teeth, which come in different shades of color depending on their age. Today, you can do the same if you can be the first to arrive at one of the more remote beaches, such as Barefoot Beach State Preserve and Delnor-Wiggins Pass Recreation Area, after a major storm.

From Naples, it's 15 miles southeast on U.S. Route 41 to the 6,423-acre Collier-Seminole State Park where Big Cypress Swamp joins the Everglades. By the 1920s, Brian Collier, a pioneer developer, had purchased almost a million acres of land in southwest Florida. He set aside 150 acres in the royal palm section of today's park, which he hoped would become the Lincoln-Lee National Park. But the federal government rejected his offer. Eventually, the county accepted his donation in 1944, then turned it over to the state.

The park, where 40 species of trees, 44 species of mammals and reptiles, and 117 species of birds thrive, is a transitional area where salt waters merge with fresh and where tropical vegetation intermingles with that of the temperate zone.

### Extra Special

Sarasota is the home of the awesome John and Mable Ringling Museum of Art, a vast display of opulence on a 66-acre estate encompassing the Ringling Mansion, Cà d'Zan, the Asolo State Theater, Museum of Art, and Museum of the Circus, plus tropical gardens with mammoth banyan trees, royal palms, and a rose garden. The complex is located off U.S. Route 41, 2 miles north of downtown.

One of the owners of the fantastically successful Ringling Brothers Circus, which toured the United States from the 1890s, John Ringling invested the circus's profits in railroads, oil, and real estate, acquiring an estimated $200 million fortune by the 1920s.

Begin your visit at Cà d'Zan, or the "House of John" in Italian, the Ringlings' fabulous thirty-room Italianate mansion, built to resemble the Doge's palace on Piazza San Marco in Venice, with columned halls, ornately tiled towers and plazas, and breathtaking views from the living areas. Ringling had architectural elements and furnishings shipped to the site from around the world to create a monument to the opulence of the Gilded Age. Workers completed the mansion in 1926 at a cost of $1.5 million. Though expensive objects and furnishings fill its rooms, Ringling and his wife, Mable, had good taste and exercised restraint. She even had her own gondola moored at the waterfront behind the house.

Next to the mansion stands the Museum of the Circus, probably the best reason to visit Sarasota. Housed in an elaborate structure patterned after a nineteenth-century Parisian circus amphitheater are priceless old photos, costumes, circus parade wagons, calliopes, and colorful posters, recalling the glory days of the Ringling Brothers Barnum & Bailey Circus. For circus fans, there's even a scale model of the Ringling Brothers' tent circus with a narration telling what went on behind-the-scenes.

On his trips to Europe to scout for new circus talent, Ringling became obsessed with baroque art, and over five years he acquired more than 500 old masters—many of them mural size—making his collection one of the finest of its kind in the country. To display his paintings, Ringling erected a museum on his estate around a reproduction of a fifteenth-century Italian palazzo, decorated with high-quality replica Greek and Roman statuary. To say that this Italian Renaissance-style villa is stunning is an understatement—the building itself is a work of art. Within its walls exists one of the country's finest collections of old master baroque, Spanish, Dutch, and Flemish paintings, including five enormous paintings by Peter Paul Rubens, commissioned by a Hapsburg archduchess in 1625. From the landscaped fountain-adorned courtyard, containing a reproduction of Michelangelo's *David*, you'll get a great view of Sarasota Bay.

Next door to the art museum stands the Asolo Theatre, a genuine eighteenth-century Italian court playhouse built in 1798 into the castle of the Italian queen, just as it once stood in the town of Asolo near Venice. As the town prepared to demolish the building, someone had the foresight to box up the sections of the rococo-style, three-level theater. Later, an architectural antique dealer purchased the theater in pieces and sold it to the Ringling Foundation, which in the 1940s had it shipped to Sarasota and reassembled. Here it served as the home of the Asolo Theatre Company until the troupe outgrew it, necessitating the construction of the larger Asolo Center for the Performing Arts, the current home of the repertory company.

Take the free guided tour of the estate that departs from the entrance. Admission to the Ringling Estate is $9 for adults, children under 12 free Sunday through Friday. Saturday is free for everyone. (Open daily 10:00 A.M.–5:30 P.M., and on Thursdays until 10 P.M., (941-351-1660)

# By Day

Besides beaches, the Shell Coast offers numerous wildlife refuges, sanctuaries, preserves, and parks to visit. Whether you choose short visits to museums and nature centers or more extended overnight adventures canoeing or boating the rivers and coastal estuaries, you'll find this area both beautiful and educational for your children.

## On the Beach

Sarasota has three barrier islands where you can enjoy white sandy beaches—Siesta Key, Longboat Key, and Lido Key. Each has its own distinct personality and style. Being only a few minutes from downtown Sarasota gives Siesta Key a tropical resort atmosphere, with shops and restaurants lining narrow streets shaded by tree branches hung with Spanish moss.

## ≡FAST FACT

On these islands, all beach is public property. All accesses, however, are not. Each island has one or more marked public access points, often with parking facilities and other provisions. There are usually no perimeters to these beaches; they run into each other along the stretch of unbroken sand.

You can walk, jog, and cycle Ocean Boulevard along Siesta Key Public Beach, which runs the length of the island. Siesta's sands come from battered quartz rock, making them the whitest in the world, and its waters are crystal clear. Experts have deemed it to be one of the finest beaches in the world, so it's often crowded. To escape the crowds, drive 6 miles farther south past Crescent Beach to Turtle Beach, a small stretch of coarser sand which, unfortunately, has no lifeguards. You can rent windsurfers by the hour from Siesta Sports Rentals (941-346-1797, *www.siestasportsrentals.com*) or you can go parasailing for $75 per person with Siesta Key Parasailing (941-586-1972, *www.siestakeyparasailing.com*).

Longboat Key, a narrow 12-mile island with million-dollar homes, exclusive golf and tennis clubs, and trendy boutiques, has been called "the Park Avenue of Sarasota." You can stay in a beach cottage or a luxurious resort and spend your days beachcombing, fishing, golfing, or just lying in a beach chair reading a novel you've checked out of the library located next to the Town Hall.

Lido Key is Sarasota's best known and most accessible barrier island. The four-lane Ringling Causeway, financed by the circus owner, crosses yacht-filled Sarasota Bay to Lido Key from the foot of Main Street. After 2 miles, it ends at South Lido Park, where a belt of dazzlingly bright sand runs beyond a large grassy park, with walking trails shaded by Australian pines. Bordered by four different water areas, it offers everything you'd want in a beach park, including barbecue grills, a playground, and a 25-meter pool with bathhouse (open daily 7 A.M.–10 P.M.).

Shell collecting is a major pastime here. Four hundred species of shells wash up on the beaches of Sanibel and Captiva islands alone.

 ## TRAVEL TIP

Johnson Shoals, on the northern tip of the barrier island Cayo Costa, and accessible only by boat, offers the best area for shelling—you can often find up to sixty different kinds of shells. You'll also find lucina, coquina, scallop, cockle, whelk, and unique murice, spiny jewel box, tulip, and nautilus shells at Cayo Costa State Park, south of the Shoals. The best time for shelling is winter or after a storm.

If you're looking for shark teeth, look no farther than Venice Beach. Most of the teeth you'll find here are prehistoric, ranging in color from black to the rarer white. You can rent shifters, called "Florida snow shovels," since digging for them isn't allowed. The beach also boasts one of the longest fishing piers on Florida's west coast, measuring 750 feet.

Wrapping around the southwestern end of Sanibel Island and its historic lighthouse is Lighthouse Beach. The sand on both the Gulf and bay side is cushiony and littered with shells. You'll find this beach the most accessible, and there's great fishing for shark, snook, and red snapper from the pier on the bayside.

### Under the Water

Though scuba diving has become popular in Sarasota, the area doesn't have the coral and interesting underwater scenery found elsewhere in southern Florida, but it does have artificial reefs. You can rent equipment from Dolphin Dive Center (941-924-2785, *www* *.floridakayak.com*).

## On the Water

If you'd like to get out on the emerald Gulf, you can take a boat trip from the docks at the South Sea Plantation on Sanibel Island. You have a choice of either a lunch or dinner cruise. The lunch cruise departs at 10:30 A.M. and returns at 3 P.M., with two hours ashore at either the Cabbage Key Inn on Cabbage Key or a gourmet restaurant on Useppa Island, for $27.50 per person; the dinner cruise goes to the same places, departing at 6 P.M. and returning at 10:30 P.M., for $38 per person. Neither price includes food while ashore. And while you don't have to order food, you cannot take your own onboard. You can also take a shorter, hour-long Continental breakfast cruise around Captiva Island, departing at 9 A.M., for $22 per person or an hour-long sightseeing cruise departing at 3:30 P.M., for $16.50 per person. No matter when you go for a sail, you're likely to see dolphins leaping above the water or turning somersaults.

 **JUST FOR PARENTS**

Sail on the emerald green sea aboard a tall three-masted schooner with Enterprise Sailing Charters while watching the sun dip below the horizon and dolphins jump playfully through the waves. (✆Toll-free 888-232-7768, ✐*www.sarasotasailing.com*)

There are lots of opportunities to go canoeing. You can go exploring the mangrove forest trail of the 7-mile-long Estero River, 10 miles south of Fort Myers, at Koreshan State Recreation Area, or you can take the 4-mile-long Hickey's Creek, 20 miles east of Fort Myers, which eventually merges into the Caloosahatchee River and which covers scenic hammocks and pinewood flatlands.

If you like to pier-fish, the Sarasota area offers seven spots to choose from. Fifteen marinas offer departures of charter fishing boats to catch big-game fish. The following companies run fishing charters:

- **Abbott's Family Charters:** ☎941-302-4734
- **CB's Saltwater Outfitters:** ☎941-349-4400
- **Flying Fish Fleet, Inc.:** ☎941-366-3373
- **Reelin & Chillin Charters, Inc.:** ☎941-228-7802
- **Rodbender Fishing Charter:** ☎941-925-8171

## On the Links and on the Courts

Golfers like to refer to Sarasota as Florida's "Cradle of Golf" since the state's first course, built by John Gillespie, opened here in 1886. There's excellent golf year-round on the following manicured golf courses. Each offers club and cart rentals, clubhouse, restaurant, driving range, practice greens, practice bunker, chipping area, and pro shop:

- **Heritage Oaks Golf & Country Club:** A semi-private eighteen-hole course. Greens fees are $64 in season, $32 off-season. (☎941-926-7600)
- **Oak Ford Golf Club:** Three 9-hole courses wind through live oak, myrtle, and palm trees, skirting ponds, swamps, and marshes on an 850-acre nature preserve. Greens fees are $60 in season, $30 off-season. (☎Toll-free 888-881-3673)
- **University Park Country Club:** There's limited outside play on this excellent course within a gated community north of Sarasota. Greens fees are $100 in season, $50 off-season. (☎941-355-3888)

If you're looking to get in some court time, you'll find facilities at these locations:

- **Gillespie Park:** Three courts, Sarasota, ☏941-316-1172
- **Hecksher Park:** Six lighted courts, Venice, ☏941-316-1172
- **Siesta Key County Beach:** Four lighted courts, Siesta Key, ☏941-346-3310

 **TRAVEL TIP**

If you've never seen a polo match and experienced the awesome power of the horses as they race up and down the field, you can see a match on Sunday afternoons at 1 P.M., December through March, at the Sarasota Polo Club (☏941-907-0000).

## Shopping

Not much has changed since Rudolph Valentino and F. Scott Fitzgerald shopped along Palm Avenue in downtown Sarasota in the 1920s. Here you'll find objets d'art from around the globe, including French and English antiques, art glass, porcelain, silver and bronzes, paintings, prints, and fine Italian jewelry. But you'd better bring your credit cards.

If you head south on John Ringling Boulevard, you'll eventually reach Saint Armand Key, a round little island on which Ringling envisioned a circle of fine shops, restaurants and Italian statuary. Today, Ringling's vision, Saint Armand's Circle, is the most upscale shopping area in Sarasota, with over 140 shops and art galleries. It's even more enjoyable if you can afford the items for sale there. (941-388-1554)

Hunt for unique shells at the Shell Factory (Toll-free 800-282-5805), 4 miles north of Fort Myers on U.S. 41. Besides a wide selection of shells from around the world, it also includes a railroad museum, lighted fountain shows, and aquariums.

# Dining Out and Nightlife

Sarasota is known for its variety of restaurants. You can eat fresh seafood by the seaside, homemade comfort food in Amish restaurants, or juicy burgers in outdoor eateries overlooking the Gulf. And there's no better taste than Florida stone crab claws.

**Barnacle Bill's Seafood:** One of Sarasota's finest fresh seafood restaurants, with outdoor seating and children's menu. (1526 Main Street, Sarasota, ☎941-365-6800)

**Bella Cucina Italian Buffet:** Family-style Italian gourmet buffet for dinner and Sunday brunch. (3811 Kenny Dr., Sarasota, ☎941-379-8158)

**El Greco Café:** Inexpensive Greek dishes, plus American breakfast and lunch selections. (1592 Main Street, Sarasota, ☎941-365-2234)

**Sugar & Spice:** Local Mennonite restaurant, serving homemade food at reasonable prices, with kids' menu. (4000 Cattlemen Road, Sarasota, ☎941-342-1649)

**Surfrider:** Outstanding seafood dinners for under $15. (6400 Midnight Pass Road, Lido Key, ☎941-346-1199)

You'll find a wide variety of arts events to keep you entertained at night. The largest venue is the Asolo Center for the Performing Arts, with three theaters. One incorporates parts of the historic turn-of-the-century Scottish Dunfermline Opera House; another hosts the Asolo Theater Company, a repertory group; and yet another intimate one is home to the Florida State University's graduate actor training program (941-351-8000). The Florida West Coast Symphony and Florida Symphonic Band both perform at the purple eye-catching Van Wezel Performing Arts Hall, designed by the Frank Lloyd Wright Foundation in the style of Wright (941-953-3366).

And if you're in Sarasota in December, you absolutely must see the season premiere of the Ringling Brothers Barnum & Bailey Circus, held in Venice, 17 miles south of the city (941-484-0496). In 1960, the Ringlings moved their circus's winter base 20 miles south from Sarasota to this small town modeled on its European namesake.

Unlike some of Florida's west coast resorts, Sarasota, Fort Myers, and Naples cater to an older crowd. If you're wishing for a good beer, head to Sarasota Brewing Company Bar & Grill, which home-brews beers to traditional German specifications, or to the Old Salty Dog, which offers British ales with "English-style" fish and chips.

# CHAPTER 16

# *Tampa*

TO MANY, TAMPA MEANS Busch Gardens and Buccaneer football, but there's so much more. The area stretching from Tampa and Saint Petersburg northward has nesting sea turtles, colorful sea-shells on snow white beaches, spectacular golf courses, seemingly unlimited tennis courts, marinas with luxurious yachts, magnificent art and science museums, Greek and Scottish villages, all types of water sports, and nearly 361 days of sunshine. What better place for a family vacation?

## Getting to Know Tampa

Tampa, whose name means "stick of fire" in the Calusa language, began as an Indian fishing village beside Fort Brooke, established in 1824 to keep a watchful eye on the local Seminole Indians. Located at the head of Tampa Bay, it remained a small and isolated trading post until 1884 when Henry B. Plant brought his railroad to town and started a steamship line between Tampa, Key West, and Havana, Cuba.

After the railroad arrived, Plant dredged the Hillsborough River, on which the city stands, to allow seagoing vessels to dock and Tampa became a booming port. Two years later, Cuban cigar-makers led by Don Vincente Martinez Ybor migrated from fire-ravaged Key West to Tampa and founded Ybor City, a neighborhood of Tampa. Not satisfied to just build a railroad to Tampa, Plant, like his rival Henry

Flagler on the east coast, built elaborate resort hotels that attracted rich vacationers to Tampa's sunny climate. Even though Tampa's economic boom slowed during the Great Depression, Tampa's port remained one of the busiest in the country.

## ≡FAST FACT

Tampa has been touted as "the Sports Capital of the U.S.A." The Cincinnati Reds and the New York Yankees do their spring training here in March. The Tampa Bay Buccaneers play football from August to December, National Hockey League's Tampa Bay Lightning plays hockey in winter, and jai-alai plays all year.

Today, the Tampa Bay area has become the busiest and most congested part of Florida's west coast. The city thrives as corporate towers rise almost overnight next to restored historic buildings. But even with the hustle and bustle of business, the blue-green waters of Tampa Bay provide a serene backdrop for the city itself.

## Getting Around Tampa

There's a good working public transit system in Tampa, but you may still prefer to use a car to see the sights and get to the beaches. Beware of the one-way streets downtown. Buses, streetcars, and trolleys run throughout the county (813-254-4278). The streetcar line connects the waterfront to Ybor City, with stops at major attractions in between.

### Best Time to Go

With an annual temperature of just 73°F, almost any time is a good time to visit the Tampa Bay area. Spring and fall days are warm, with nights comfortably cool. Daytime temperatures rise in the summer but not by much, and are usually cooled off by afternoon showers.

## Cautions and Safety Concerns

The Tampa area is a relatively safe place, making it a great destination for families. About the only precaution is to make sure not to get overexposed to the intense Florida sun, especially in the summer. Ocean breezes can make it seem comfortable, but, at the same time, you could be getting a severe sunburn if not properly protected. Use sunblock with an SPF of at least 15 at all times when in the sun.

# Family-Oriented Resorts and Hotels

Most of Tampa's hotels are chain properties catering to the business traveler. If you're looking for a fun-in-the-sun resort or are on a budget, head to Saint Petersburg and the beaches.

### DoubleTree Guest Suites Tampa Bay

Reservations: ✆813-888-8800

✍*www.doubletreetampabay.com*

Built to look like a Mayan temple, this contemporary 203-unit hotel offers spacious two-room suites with all modern conveniences, including breakfast, plus a restaurant, outdoor heated pool, health club with Jacuzzi, sauna, and weight training and cardiovascular equipment.

### Hampton Inn & Suites Tampa/Ybor City

Reservations: ✆813-247-6700

Located in Ybor City, this 138-suite hotel offers a contemporary base in the most historic part of Tampa, featuring one-bedroom suites with a king or two double beds, sleeper sofa, bar sink, refrigerator, and microwave oven, plus complimentary hot breakfast and high-speed Internet access.

### Radisson Bay Harbor Inn

Reservations: ✆813-281-8900

✍*www.radisson.com/tampafl*

Overlooking the Intracoastal Waterway, this 257-room hotel is the only one in Tampa with a beach. Amenities include private balconies, restaurant, lounge, sailing and windsurfing rentals, tennis courts, and a pool.

You'll find a variety of condominium and villa rentals, ranging in price from $600 to $1,600, in and around Tampa. To make a reservation, visit the Web sites of either Value Vacation Rentals (*www .valuevacationrentals.com/FL/Tampa.cfm*) or Vacation Home Rentals (*www.vacationhomerentals.com/vacation-rentals/Tampa-gulf Creek-Central-Florida.htm*).

## Things to Do

Because Tampa itself is a relatively small city, you only need a day or two to explore it. Many visitors never see downtown Tampa but head directly to Busch Gardens, a theme park on the fringe of the city, and the Gulf coast beaches half an hour's drive west. Be sure not to make this mistake.

With its high-rise office buildings, downtown Tampa seems just like any other modern city, but hidden among them are some treasures that you should explore. To get an overall view, take your kids for a ride on the 25-cent PeopleMover monorail from the terminal on top of the Fort Brooke Parking Garage on Whiting Street to Harbor Island, a large shopping mall on an island dredged from Hillsborough Bay. You can browse the shops for a while there, or head back to downtown.

 **JUST FOR PARENTS**

If you like to a gamble, take time out to play over 2,000 slot machines and fifty live-action poker tables at the 24-hour Seminole Hard Rock Hotel and Casino, then attend the show in Floyd's nightclub. (☎866-ROCK4ME, *www.seminolehardrock.com*)

Take several hours to wander through the contemporary Tampa Museum of Art, viewing its impressive collection of Greco-Roman antiquities and twentieth-century American art. Standing on the banks of the Hillsborough River, it has become a symbol of the city's cultural scene. Admission is free. (Open Tuesday, Thursday, and Saturday 10 A.M.–6 P.M., Wednesday 10 A.M.–9 P.M., and Sunday 1–5 P.M., 813-223-8130)

Then head over to the awesome Tampa Bay Hotel, one of the few reminders of Tampa's early days. This hotel, built by Henry Plant in 1891 to house the social elite arriving on his trains, is a Moorish fantasyland of silver minarets, cupolas, domes, keyhole arches, and ballrooms. The quarter-mile-long building cost $3 million to build—a lot of money in its day. Plant spent another half-million on furnishings but the effect all of this had on promoting Tampa as a vacation destination for the rich was far beyond what Plant had expected. Before he built the hotel, he vowed to "turn this sand heap into the Champs-Élysées, the Hillsborough into a Seine." And his monument to the Gilded Age did just that.

##  RAINY DAY FUN

If it rains while you're in Tampa, and you like to watch old movies like *Gone with the Wind* in a classic movie house, take in the 3 P.M. weekend matinee for $7 per person at the restored Tampa Theatre. You not only get to see the theater's magnificently restored interior but get to watch a movie, too.

Stand on the hotel's front veranda and imagine America's industrial barons and their refined wives taking afternoon tea. Then suddenly you're jolted back to the present as you hear students conversing in various languages, for today the hotel houses the administrative offices of the University of Tampa. Wander through its hallways, ballrooms, and gardens before ending up in the Henry B. Plant Museum, which occupies the south wing of the hotel. You'll see some of the hotel's original furnishings and decorations on display, along with collections of English and French antiques and a replica of Plant's own private train. Admission $5 for adults, $2 for children.

(Open Tuesday through Saturday 10 A.M.–4 P.M., Sunday noon–4 P.M., 813-254-1891, *www.plantmuseum.com*)

Though there isn't much visible history in Tampa, there's one building that's still standing—the Tampa Theatre, one of the few surviving "atmospheric theaters" erected by Mediterranean-mad designer John Eberson in 1926. When silent movies were at their peak, Eberson's movie theaters heightened the mood with star-studded ceilings, Moorish arched balconies, gargoyles, and repro-ductions of Greek and Roman statuary. When television came along, the Tampa Theater, like so many other old movie houses, fell into disuse. It's been restored to the original glamour that once earned it the reputation of "the Pride of the South." Today, it houses the Tampa Film Club. For a $5 donation, you can take one of the occa-sional behind-the-scenes backstage tours of the theater. (813-274-8982, *www.tampatheatre.org*)

### Hillsborough River State Park

At Hillsborough River State Park, 12 miles north of Tampa, you can experience one of the few rapids outside of a theme park in Florida. Beneath a shady overhang of magnolias, live oaks, and sable palms, the Hillsborough River tumbles over limestone outcrops before resuming its normal meandering course.

 **TRAVEL TIP**

Explore the Hillsborough River through the 16,000-acre Hillsbor-ough River State Park and discover the natural Florida on a two-hour to full-day downstream paddling excursion with Canoe Escape. Cost is $19.50 to $27.50 per paddler in a tandem canoe or $35 to $45 per kayak, depending on which of six trips you choose. Shuttles and life vests are included. (813-986-2067, *www.canoeescape.com*)

Plan to spend the day, especially on the weekends. In the morning, you can hike the park's walking trails or canoe the calmer parts of the river; in the afternoon you should visit Fort Foster Historic Site, a reconstructed 1836 Seminole War fort. You can only view the fort on one of the guided tours at 1, 2, and 3 P.M. for $1.50 per person. Costumed re-enactors, representing soldiers of the U.S. Second Artillery, occupy the fort and tell how more soldiers died from tropical diseases than in battle. On the opposite side of the river, similar re-enactors, dressed as Seminole Indians, tell their side of the conflict. To truly understand the nineteenth-century history of South Florida, you must see this. Admission $5 per car. (Open daily 8 A.M.–sunset, 813-987-6771)

### Ybor City

Though you won't find much history or atmosphere in downtown Tampa, you'll find plenty of both in Ybor City (pronounced *E-bore*), 3 miles to the northeast. Bordered by Nebraska Avenue, Twenty-second Street, Fifth Avenue, and Columbus Drive, this turn-of-the-twentieth-century neighborhood looks much as it did when workers rolled cigars in its 200 giant factories.

In 1886, as soon as Henry Plant improved port facilities and could bring in a regular supply of Havana tobacco to Tampa, cigar magnate Don Vincente Martinez Ybor purchased 40 acres two miles north of Tampa and had workers clear the palmettos to lay the foundations for Ybor City. Around 20,000 Cuban cigar-makers, drawn from the stricken Key West cigar industry, plus Italian, German, and Jewish immigrants came to work in the cigar factories. They moved into boarding houses and casitas and formed social clubs, which gave them cradle-to-grave health care, death benefits, and recreational facilities. They produced first-class hand-rolled cigars that eventually made Tampa "the Cigar Capital of the World" for the next forty years. But mass-production techniques and the popularity of cigarettes began to take their toll. That and the onset of the Great Depression put many skilled cigar-makers out of work. Though revived somewhat, the death knell came with the embargo against Cuban tobacco in the 1960s.

In recent years, Ybor City has been turned into a tourist attraction. Begin your exploration at Ybor City Museum State Park. Located on Seventh Street in the 1923 Ferlita Bakery, with its original brick oven from 1896, the museum tells the story of the immigrants who worked in the cigar factories, as well as the creation of Ybor City, through photographic murals of the cigar rollers at work. Thousands sat in long rows at bench-tables working at a 25-cent-per-cigar piece-work rate, cheering or heckling the lector, who read the news from Spanish-language newspapers while they worked. A cigar-roller demonstrates the skill needed to roll cigars from 11 A.M. to 1 P.M. on weekends. After visiting the museum, walk a short distance down Ninth Avenue to the six restored workers' houses, called Las Casitas, built of Florida pine and cypress around 1895 and moved here in 1976. You can visit one daily 10 A.M. to 3 P.M. to see how the workers lived in simple surroundings. Admission to the museum and house is $3 per person. (Open Tuesday through Saturday 9 A.M.–5 P.M., 813-247-1434, *www.ybormuseum.org*)

From the museum you can take a one-and-half-hour guided walking tour on Saturdays at 10:30 A.M. for $6 per person (including museum admission)—walk past the factories where workers hand-rolled cigars, see the Cuban and Italian clubs where cigar workers socialized, and visit the homes where they lived. The tour ends in front of the Columbia Restaurant (see page 313).

## ═FAST FACT

You'll find Cuban sandwiches, known as *cubanos*, everywhere in Tampa. They're made with Cuban bread, ham, pork, and pickles, then pressed in a *plancha* until the meats have warmed in their own steam. Cuban bread, baked in 3-foot-long loaves, with washed palmetto fronds laid down the middle during baking to make the crust split, is crispy and makes eating a Cuban sandwich a memorable culinary experience.

After viewing the Casita, stroll to Ybor Square on Thirteenth Street. A Latin ambiance permeates the neighborhood. You'll discover shops selling hand-rolled cigars, and the smell of newly baked Cuban bread and freshly brewed coffee wafts through the streets. Spanish Talavera tiles adorn many buildings containing arts and crafts galleries, bookstores, antique shops, and intimate cafés—all making Ybor City one of Tampa's hippest neighborhoods.

Ybor Square, one of the former cigar-rolling factories, now houses shops and restaurants directed at tourists and has become the center of activity in the area. Stop here for a cup of strong Cuban coffee—if you're a coffee lover, you'll be drawn in by the heady aroma. As you sip your coffee, take a look at the cavernous interior of the former factory, its three stories supported by sturdy oak pillars. You can almost imagine the workers you saw in the museum murals sitting at tables rolling cigars. In 1893, Cuban poet and independence fighter José Martí spoke to thousands of workers from the factory's iron steps. He asked them for pledges of money, machetes, and manpower for Cuba's pro-independence struggle. It's said that the workers pledged 10 percent of their earnings, most of which went for the purchase and shipment of arms to rebels in Cuba. You'll see a stone marker at the foot of the steps that records the event. A statue of José Martí stands in the park across the street. After your tour of Ybor City, have lunch at the Columbia, the world's largest Spanish restaurant. Tampa Rico (813-247-6738) hand-rolls and sells cigars.

## Busch Gardens

When you hear the name Tampa, you most likely associate it with Busch Gardens, a theme park on the grounds of a brewery. It's the prime attraction in the Tampa Bay area and the second most popular in Florida. Now known as Busch Gardens Africa, it takes you on a journey through colonial Africa. You can either walk or take the little steam train through the 300-acre gardens divided into several areas.

**TRAVEL TIP**

If you plan to take in Adventure Island, Busch Gardens' 10-acre water park across the road—featuring water slides, an endless surf pool with simulated waves, inner-tubing chutes, plus beaches and picnic areas, all set in a tropical garden environment—you'd better allow two days and save up. Admission is $34.95 for adults, $32.95 for kids 3 to 9. (*www.buschgardens.com*)

You'll first enter a typical Moroccan souk where you'll find crafts for sale as belly dancers and snake charmers weave through the crowd. By following the signs to Nairobi, you'll discover alligators, crocodiles, and monkeys, as well as the animal hospital and petting zoo. Straight ahead in Timbuktu, you'll see fewer animals and more rides, including a hair-raising switchback and a simulated ride through a desert sandstorm. If the Ubanga-Banga bumper cars in the Congo don't thrill you, take the raft trip around the Congo River Rapids and then cross Stanleyville Falls on a roller coaster, in the Stanleyville section of the park. The Serengeti Plain, roamed by giraffes, buffaloes, zebras, antelopes, black rhino, and elephants, is the largest section of the park and comes closest to showing you a simulated African environment, which you'll see from a short monorail ride. After all this excitement, you can spend time in the Hospitality House of the Anheuser-Busch Brewery, where you can down up to three free cold beers. High-priced admission is $57.95 per adult, $47.95 per child 3 to 9, and includes all rides. (Open daily 9:30 A.M.–6 P.M. with longer hours in summer, Toll-free 888-800-5447, *www.buschgardens.com*)

## For the Kids

You'll find plenty to keep your children interested in the Tampa area. In fact, the Tampa area probably offers more attractions aimed at kids than any other Coastal Florida destination, making it a prime destination if you have little ones.

There are science museums, and there are science museums. But the Museum of Science and Industry (MOSI) in Tampa, the largest in the southeastern United States, features Kids-in-Charge, the biggest children's science center in the country and the only domed IMAX theatre in Florida. (Open daily 9 A.M.–6 P.M., 813-987-6000, *www.mosi.org*)

The state-of-the-art 120,000-square-foot Florida Aquarium contains over 10,000 aquatic animals and plants, including fish from the ocean, exotic sea dragons, plus alligators and otters and wading birds. You can also see animal and dive shows and experience Explore-a-Shore, an outdoor water adventure exhibit. Admission is $23.95 per adult, $19.95 per child 2 to 12. A special DolphinQuest Ecotour costs $18.95 per adult, $17.95 per child. (Open daily 9:30 A.M.–5:00 P.M., Toll-free 800-353-4741, *www.flaquarium.org*)

And what kid doesn't like to play pirate? Your kids will be Yo-Ho-Hoing when they board the 300-ton *José Gasparilla*, the world's only full-rigged pirate ship, docked on Bayshore Boulevard. (813-223-8130)

At Lowry Park Zoo, the area's only dedicated zoological garden, your kids can see giant manatees in the Pepsi Manatee and Aquatic Center. A guide explains how they live, why they have become endangered, and what you can do to protect them as your kids stand transfixed in amazement inside a cool, dimly lit underwater viewing room, watching these two-ton "sea cows" flirt, play, and swim up for air. What makes this so unique is that this zoo is one of the few places in Florida where your kids can see manatees close-up swimming underwater. In fact, the zoo, with its 1,600 animals, has been designated the family-friendliest zoo in the country. It also features a Wallaroo Station Australian exhibit, a Safari Africa, a Primate World, a free-flight aviary, and a Florida Boardwalk, showcasing the state's native animals. (813-935-8552, *www.lowryparkzoo.com*)

Young kids have an inborn curiosity about life, and the Great Explorations Museum, 2 miles northeast in Saint Petersburg, lets them explore it. This interactive, hands-on museum for those 7 and under challenges kids to explore other worlds, their own perceptions, their creativity, and their feelings. You'll find it time well spent—and your children will thank you for it. Among the thirty-two major exhibits, kids can explore a firehouse, a veterinary office, a pizza restaurant, a working lie detector, water, and sounds, plus Puppets on Parade. Admission is $9 per person. (Open daily 10:00 A.M.–4:30 P.M., Sunday noon–4:30 P.M., Toll-free 800-444-6674, *www.greatexplorations.com*)

Big Cat Rescue, an educational sanctuary devoted to rescuing thirty-five species of exotic big cats that have been abused or abandoned, offers a special one-hour tour for children under 10 on Saturdays at 9 A.M. for $12 per person. The regular hour-and-a-half tour Monday through Friday at 9 A.M. and 3 P.M. and Saturdays at 9:30 A.M., 11:30 A.M., and 1:30 P.M. costs $22 per person. (813-920-4130, *www.bigcatrescue.org*)

## Festivals and Seasonal Events

Tampa's multiple cultures offer many opportunities for festivals and special events. The following are the most notable:

**Gasparilla Pirate Fest:** Hundreds of costumed pirates, with cannon and guns blazing, "invade" Tampa's waterfront for a grand celebration at the end of January from the pirate ship *José Gasparilla*. A Children's Gasparilla Parade and fireworks display is held the Saturday before. (☎813-353-8108, ✐*www.gasparillapiratefest.com*)

**Guavaween:** A zany Latin-style one-day Halloween celebration, held in Ybor City in October, featuring a daytime Family Fun-Fest, followed by "the Mama Guava Stumble," a night parade and costume contest, and a street party with multiple entertainment stages. Admission is $3 to $12. (☎Toll-free 877-9FIESTA, ✐*www.cc-events.org/gw*)

**Tampa Cigar Heritage Festival:** Held in November at the Ybor State Museum, this festival celebrates the Tampa cigar tradition, with music, cigars, and cultural demonstrations, including a pig roast. (☎813-247-1434, ✐*www.ybormuseum.com*)

**Ruskin Seafood and Arts Festival:** Seafood is king on the first weekend of November in Ruskin on the eastern shore of Tampa Bay as twenty vendors and restaurants offer tastes of their seafood specialties, along with a boat show, children's area, and exotic animals. Adults pay $3 and kids 5 to 12 pay $1. (✆813-645-3808, ✐*www.ruskinchamber.org*)

# Exploring

Though Tampa has a lot to see and do, you'll find some of the best attractions in surrounding communities as far north as Tarpon Springs.

##  TRAVEL TIP

For a different perspective on the Gulf Coast, take a hot-air balloon ride with 18th Century Aviation and ride the breezes over subtropical Florida for $179 per person. (✆Toll-free 877-256-1937, ✐*www.18thcenturyaviation.com*)

### Saint Petersburg

Named the healthiest place in the country, Saint Petersburg, located 20 miles from Tampa on the eastern edge of the Pinellas peninsula, attracted the recuperating and the retired to its subtropical climate as early as 1885. By the mid-twentieth century, the city placed 5,000 green benches along its streets so the elderly would have a place to rest. It's no wonder it became the setting for the hit film *Cocoon*. But that's all changed, as the average age has fallen to thirty-something.

And though Saint Petersburg became known as a retirement mecca, it's perfect for a family vacation, with beaches on three sides and subtropical keys nearby. Like Tampa, it remained sparsely populated for over 100 years until entrepreneur Hamilton Disston founded Disston City, which is now Gulfport, on the peninsula's southern tip. In 1887, Russian émigré Peter Demens and two partners ran their Orange Belt Railroad to Disston City, naming one of the stops along the way Saint Petersburg in honor of Demens's home in Russia.

By the time Henry Plant took over Demens's Orange Belt Railroad, severely hurt financially in the citrus freeze of 1893, Saint Petersburg had grown to a village of 300 inhabitants. After several real-estate booms, the town became a center for retirees and the most popular location for baseball Spring Training camps. Troops trained there during World War II, something the area had already experienced when Plant's Tampa Bay Hotel became a training center for Teddy Roosevelt's Rough Riders during the Spanish-American War. After the war, Saint Petersburg developed its aerospace industry, which continues today.

The center of the action in Saint Petersburg is The Pier, a quarter-mile-long pedestrian extension of Second Avenue. To see what the city looked like in the past, visit the Saint Petersburg Historical Museum at its foot, where exhibits with photos and memorabilia tell you about Spring Training and the green benches. There's also a 3,000-year-old mummy given to the city in the 1920s by a ship's captain in exchange for port fees, plus a working model of the Benoist Airboat. Admission is $5 per adult, $3 per child. (Open Monday through Saturday 10 A.M.– 5 P.M., Sunday noon–5 P.M., 813-894-1052, *www.spmoh.org*)

## ≡FAST FACT

Aviation pioneer Tony Jannus flew the Benoist Airboat from Saint Petersburg to Tampa on New Year's Day, 1914, marking the world's first scheduled passenger flight. Saint Petersburg's mayor was the passenger and paid $400 for his ticket. And you thought air travel was expensive today!

Restaurants and fast-food outlets, shops, and an observation deck pack an entertainment complex on the Saint Petersburg Pier. The complex of various restaurants and entertainment venues is known simply as the Saint Petersburg Pier. Be sure to take in the view of the city and bay from here, especially at night. (813-821-6164)

A group of Mediterranean Revival buildings houses the Saint Petersburg Museum of Fine Arts, in which you can view works by Renoir, Gauguin, Monet, and other masters. The museum also contains pre-Columbian pieces, art glass, ceramics, and antiquities from Europe and Asia, plus drawings by Kandinsky and works by Georgia O'Keeffe and George Luks. Take the free guided tours offered Tuesday through Friday at 11 A.M. and 2 P.M. and weekends at 2 P.M. Admission is $8 per adult, $4 per child. (Open Tuesday through Saturday 10 A.M.–5 P.M., Sunday 1–5 P.M., 727-896-2667, *www.fine-arts.org*)

If you're not that interested in art but like gardening, you'll enjoy the jungle-like atmosphere of the Sunken Gardens, a mile north of the museum. In 1903, George Turner drained a sinkhole and began planting thousands of tropical trees and plants that now make up these sweet-scented gardens. Read the plaques along the way describing the plants to truly understand South Florida's tropical environment. As you descend through sweet-smelling hibiscus, bougainvillea, and lush staghorn ferns, monkeys and rare birds flitter about. Admission is $8 per adult, $4 per child. (Open Monday through Saturday 10 A.M.–4:30 P.M., 727-551-3100, *www.stpete.org/fun/parks/sunken*)

With so many theme parks and other tourist sites, you'll be surprised to know that Saint Petersburg is also the home of the Salvador Dali Museum, which stores and exhibits more than 1,000 works by the Spanish surrealist, including 93 oils created between 1914 and 1980. The works came from the collection of a Cleveland industrialist who became friends with Dali in the 1940s. He bought lots of Dali's paintings and ran out of space to show them, so he built this museum in 1982 to house them. Take one of the free guided tours to truly understand Dali's genius. Beginning with his early experiments in Impressionism and Cubism, then moving on to his classic period in the 1940s, you see a chronological representation of Dali's life's work. Some of his works, such as the awesome *Discovery of America by Christopher Columbus*, are so large they're hung in a special section of the gallery. A new museum is currently under construction. Admission is $5. (Open Tuesday through Saturday 10 A.M.–5 P.M., Sunday noon–5 P.M., 727-823-3767, *www.salvadordalimuseum.org*)

### Tarpon Springs

Tarpon Springs, 10 miles north of Clearwater, owes its beginnings to real estate businessman John Cheyney, who invested in sponge harvesting here around 1900. Greek sponge buyer John Corcoris and his two brothers were the first of several thousand Greek sponge fishermen who helped Tarpon Springs become "the Sponge Capital of the World" by 1936.

It was originally founded by a few early settlers, who named their village Tarpon Springs because they thought that tarpon spawned in Spring Bayou, a crescent-shaped lake nearby. But it wasn't until 1905, when 2,000 Greek sponge fishermen, driven out by protectionist-minded residents, emigrated from Key West, that Tarpon Springs' sponge industry really began. The Greeks stuccoed over the turn-of-the-century bungalows in the old sponge dock area on Athens and Hope streets, which today have been converted to antique shops, cafés, art studios and galleries, and souvenir shops. Tree-lined brick sidewalks, banners, and old-fashioned street lamps brighten Tarpon Springs' downtown streets.

##  TRAVEL TIP

You can climb aboard the Mediterranean-style sponge boat *Saint Nicholas VI* along Dodecanese Boulevard for a thirty-minute cruise and sponge demonstration. You'll witness a diver twist on his heavy helmet, have his suit pumped up with air, and slowly be lowered to the sea floor where he tediously spears the sponges, puts them in a basket, and passes it up to the waiting boat.

Back at the dock, boats unload bundles of sponges from giant green nets into bins on the dock as the heady aroma of garlic wafts over from a nearby restaurant, telling you that delicious Greek food— fried squid, pickled octopus, moussaka, shrimp in garlic, and ever-so-sweet baklava for dessert—isn't far away.

You can learn more about Tarpon Springs and the perils of sponge diving at the Sponge Factory, a shop with a special Spong-erama museum, which traces the roots and growth of Tarpon Springs' Greek sponge divers and the primitive techniques used in the industry. (Open daily 10 A.M.–6 P.M., 727-938-5366)

The beautiful Byzantine Revival Saint Nicolas Orthodox Cathedral stands as the symbol of this close-knit Greek community, partly funded by a half-percent levy on local sponge sales and finished in 1943. Beautifully painted icons and sculptured Greek marble adorn the cathedral's interior, and the intense aroma from slow-burning incense creates an atmosphere of reverence. (Open daily 9 A.M.–5 P.M., 727-937-3540)

After visiting the cathedral, stop into the neighboring Tarpon Springs Cultural Center, housed in the former City Hall from 1915. Imaginative exhibitions show Tarpon Springs when Tarpon Avenue was a bustling commercial strip with shops of butchers and bakers.

## ═FAST FACT

The Tsalickis family built the Shrine of Saint Michael in 1939 as a result of a miracle they supposedly experienced. Their son, Steven, almost died from a childhood illness. While praying to Saint Michael, Steven received divine instructions to have his mother build a shrine to him. She did, and Steven was healed.

Walking west along Tarpon Avenue leads downhill to Spring Bayou, the body of water around which many early residents built their homes. As you stroll along the lakeside path, you'll see the gabled roofs, shady verandas, and latticework of these late nineteenth-century houses. George Innes, the noted American landscape painter, rented one of them. His son, George Jr., himself a famous artist, purchased it. Inspired by the tropical landscape around him, he painted some of his best works here. When a hurricane blew out the stained-glass windows of the nearby Universalist Church, George Jr. created six mural-sized paintings showing Florida flora and biblical scenes to replace them (open for tours Tuesday through Sunday 2–5 P.M., November through April). Not far from the Universalist Church, you'll come upon the Shrine of Saint Michael Taxiarchis, a small Greek Orthodox chapel with beautiful stained-glass windows, religious portraits, and a simple altar.

### Extra Special

In the middle of the Pinellas peninsula, in the town of Largo, stands Pinewood Cultural Park, a complex of museums dedicated to history and the arts. Heritage Village is a village of twenty historic structures gathered from around Pinellas County. Furnishings of the appropriate period fill all but two. The oldest is the McMullen-Coachman log house from 1852, but most date from around 1900, when the first settlers arrived via Plant's railroad. You'll also see a Victorian gazebo, bandstand, barn, and a train depot with a 1926 caboose parked in front. (727-582-2123)

The complex also includes the Gulf Coast Museum of Art, with nine permanent collections and galleries featuring artwork by Florida artists, along with sculpture gardens. Admission is $8 for adults, $4 for children (open Tuesday through Saturday, 10 A.M.–4 P.M., Sunday noon–4 P.M., 727-518-6833, *www.gulfcoastmuseum.org*).

## By Day

You had better plan on staying at least a week in the Tampa Bay area to take advantage of all there is to do here. Besides great museums, historic districts, and entertainment, you can spend part of your vacation just lying on some of the best beaches on the planet.

## On the Beach

The Ben T. Davis Municipal Beach, fronting Tampa Bay along the Courtney Campbell Causeway between Tampa and Clearwater, is Tampa's only saltwater beach. Locals love the soft white sand and flock here on weekends. But Saint Petersburg has even better beaches.

Any trip to Saint Petersburg calls for plenty of time at the beach. The beaches, 9 miles west of town on the Gulf coast, stretch for 25 miles, through the communities of Clearwater Beach, Saint Petersburg Beach, Treasure Island, and Madeira Beach. Together, they're known as the Saint Petersburg Beaches. When Miami Beach lost its charm in the 1970s, vacationers headed here.

Besides sunning and people-watching, you can spend several days snorkeling, windsurfing, surfing, parasailing, Jet-Skiing, water-skiing, sailing, and scuba diving. If you want to go bicycling, you can rent a bike from the Beach Cyclist on Saint Petersburg Beach (813-367-5001).

One of the best spots on the coast is Pass-a-Grille. Settled by fishermen in 1911, it was one of the first beach communities on the west coast. Today, it's a quiet community of manicured lawns, tidy houses, small shops, and restaurants. Locals head for Pass-a-Grille's beach on weekends to enjoy unobstructed views of the tiny islands lying at the entrance to Tampa Bay.

If you'd rather do some exploring, stay on the Pinellas County Bayway to Fort de Soto Park, a grouping of five islands. Historians believe Ponce de León anchored here in 1513 and again in 1521. Centuries later, the islands became an important Union base during the Civil War, and in 1898 the U.S. Army constructed a fort to defend Tampa against attacks during the Spanish-American War. You can wander around the remains of the uncompleted fort on one of several walking trails that wind beneath Australian pines and live oaks hung with Spanish moss. Although there are 3 miles of good swimming beaches in the park, the sand is coarse, with lots of shells and sand spurs. Midweek there's virtually no one there, giving you a Robinson Crusoe feeling since there's no development to hinder the view.

## On the Water

If you're in the mood, take a forty-five-minute gondola ride around Tampa's rivers and bays from Harbour Island's waterside, departing Monday through Saturday noon–6 P.M. and Sunday noon–9 P.M., cost $20 for two people. (813-888-8864)

Captain Memo's Original Pirate Cruise takes your family into the fantasy world of swashbucklers aboard the ship *Pirate Ransom*. Two-hour cruises at 10 A.M., 2 P.M., 4:30 P.M., and 7 P.M. cost $32 per adult, $22 for children under 12. (727-446-2587, *www.captainmemo.com*)

For a more elegant cruise, sail aboard the *Yacht Starship*, an $8 million, 600-passenger vessel offering lunch and dinner cruises with fine wines and champagnes on Tampa Bay. A typical weeknight dinner cruise runs $69.95 per adult and $39.95 per child. On weekends the price climbs to $79.95 per adult and $44.95 per child. You can go on a sightseeing cruise for $15.95 per person.

Are you looking to chase tarpon or catch a snook in Tampa Bay? If so, you'll find the following charter outfitters in the Tampa Bay area:

- **Light Tackle Adventures:** Odessa (Toll-free 800-259-9010, *www.lighttackleadventures.com*)
- **Tampa Bay Sportfishing Adventures:** Palm Harbor (727-784-0098, *www.tampabaysportfishing.com*)
- **Tightlines Tackle Charter Service:** Tampa (813-932-4721, *www.tightlinesfishingcharters.com*)

## On the Links and on the Courts

You'll find superb public golf courses in the Tampa area. Each offers eighteen holes in a tropical setting. Greens fees vary depending on the time of day and season and whether you walk or use a cart.

- **Babe Zaharias Golf Course:** The shortest of the city courses, it has tight fairways and small greens. Greens fees range from $8.41 to $20.56. (Tampa, ☎813-631-4374, ✍*www.babezahariasgc.com*)

- **Bardmoor Golf & Tennis Club:** You'll have fun on this PGA Tournament course even though it presents challenges for professionals. Facilities include practice greens, driving range, and pro shop. Greens fees are $29.91 to $89.72. Club rentals are available for $40. (Largo, ☎727-392-1234, ✍*www.bardmoorgolf.com*)
- **The Claw at USF:** One of Tampa's most challenging courses, it features elevated greens on defined layout. Greens fees range from $17 to $53. (Tampa, ☎813-632-6893, ✍*www.theclawatusf.org*)
- **Heritage Harbor Golf & Country Club:** A beautiful course laid out between cypress trees and natural water areas that golfers of all levels can enjoy. Greens fees range from $25 to $45. (Lutz, ☎813-949-6841, ✍*www.heritageharbor golf.com*)
- **Rogers Park Golf Course:** Originally built in 1952 and renovated in 2000, this course is the home of the Tampa City Amateur Medal Championship and features a three-hole short course and driving range. Greens fees are $8.41 to $20.56. (Tampa, ☎813-356-1670, ✍*www.rogersparkgc.com*)
- **Tournament Players Club of Tampa Bay:** This PGA Tournament course is Tampa's best public course, offering a challenging course with up to sixty days' advance tee-time reservations. Greens fees, including cart rental, are $59 to $155. (Lutz, ☎813-949-0090, ✍*www.tpc.com*)
- **Westchase Golf Club:** Close to Tampa Airport, this eighteen-holer, carved out of a cypress forest, offers long, narrow fairways, fast, smooth greens, and a clubhouse. Greens fees, including cart with GPS, are $18 to $45. (Tampa, ☎813-854-2331, ✍*www.westchase.com*)

Several public tennis courts are located along the west coast. Tampa's Riverfront Park (813-253-6038) offers tennis, racquetball, and handball courts. You'll also find tennis courts at City of Tampa Courts (813-253-3782).

### Shopping

If you like to shop, Tampa, with its many restored areas and malls, is perfect for you. Two shopping areas stand out—Harbour Island Market and Old Hyde Park Village. Both cater to the upscale market with exclusive shops and luxury boutiques. The first is an indoor marketplace on its own island (813-223-9898). The second is an outdoor shopping center in a restored village setting (813-251-3500).

For the best bargains in Tampa, head to Fairground Outlet Mall on Buffalo Avenue, where wholesale outlets sell clothing, shoes, jewelry, and other items. Or browse the over 1,000 dealers at the Big Top Flea Market in Thonotosassa every weekend from 9 A.M. to 4:30 P.M. (813-986-4004). If your taste leans to antiques, you'll find twenty shops at the El Prado Antique Center, a three-block area offering everything from nineteenth-century furniture and art to ceramics and silver.

# Dining Out and Nightlife

You can choose from a wide assortment of cuisines and restaurants in the Tampa area. Chain restaurants are a dime a dozen in downtown Tampa. But while in town sightseeing, there are plenty of delicatessens and sandwich shops to provide your family with a good lunch at moderate prices. Though local seafood tops most menus, the influence of Cuban, Spanish, and Greek cultures is apparent. To experience some of the best food in the Tampa area, try any of the following:

**The Castaway:** Saltwater aquariums, exotic music, and articles that have washed ashore give this casual restaurant its South Seas ambience, but the food is mainly steak and seafood. (7720 Courtney Campbell Causeway, Tampa, ☎813-281-0770)
**The Columbia:** An Ybor City institution, which opened in 1905 as a humble coffee shop for cigar workers, it is *the* restaurant in

Tampa. As musicians serenade you, waiters wearing dinner jackets serve moderately priced traditional Spanish dishes while you gaze at newspaper clippings about the restaurant's history on the wall. (2117 East Seventh Avenue, Tampa, ☎813-248-4961)

**Tampa's Silver Ring Café:** Holding the reputation as the maker of the best Cuban sandwich, produced in a showcase window for all to see, this café's luncheonette decor has you sitting either at a long Formica counter, at tables, or on stools facing shelves along the wall. (206 North Morgan Street, Tampa, ☎813-301-0200)

 **JUST FOR PARENTS**

Treat yourself to a night out without the kids at Bern's Steak House. After choosing a steak from the largest selection in Tampa, accompanied by organic home-grown herbs and vegetables, you'll think you're in heaven when you enjoy dessert from a sixty-five-page menu upstairs in a glass booth equipped with radio and television for after-dinner relaxation. (1208 South Howard Avenue, ☎813-251-2421)

When the sun goes down, things heat up in Tampa as bands in clubs and bars play everything from rock to reggae and blues to country. The center of nighttime action is Seventh Avenue in Ybor City, which becomes a pedestrian thoroughfare on weekend nights. The main entertainment center here is Centro Ybor (813-242-4660), a mix of shops, restaurants, and entertainment centers. Don't miss Gameworks, featuring over 180 games for adults and kids (813-241-9675), arranged around a palm-lined plaza. The city also has several comedy clubs, including the Tampa Improv Comedy Theater and Restaurant (813-864-4000) and Comedy Works (813-875-9129). Both feature top-name comedians. If you prefer to listen to blues and reggae, go to Skipper's Smoke-house (813-971-0666).

But Tampa has its cultural side, too. The Tampa Bay Performing Arts Center, one of the largest arts complexes in the country, houses three theaters, offering opera, classical music, and ballet programs plus Broadway road shows (813-229-2787). The city is also home to the Florida Orchestra (813-286-2403), as well as theatrical groups, such as the New Playmakers (813-972-1177), the Spanish Lyric Theater (813-223-7341), and The Tampa Players (813-229-3221). For nightlife listings, pick up a copy of *Creative Loafing* or *Tampa Tonite*, or buy the Friday edition of the *Tampa Tribune*.

# CHAPTER 17

# Panama City

PANAMA CITY IN NORTHWESTERN FLORIDA is known for its Southern hospitality. The pace of life is slower here than in the hectic tourist cities farther south. That, together with the rolling dunes on its powdery white beaches kissing the emerald green water of the Gulf of Mexico against a background of swaying palms and moss-draped oaks and magnolias, makes it an ideal place for a quiet family vacation—a place to get away from it all.

## Getting to Know Panama City

Panama City, one of the smaller cities on Florida's Panhandle, lies on the land side of the lagoon separating it from a strip of barrier islands on which is Panama City Beach, a 27-mile-long strip of white sand some call "the World's Most Beautiful Beach." Though it lacks the glamour of Florida's southern beaches, it's nevertheless a favorite with southern folks, who flock to it throughout the summer.

Panama City grew as a result of the lumbering industry in the area. Its founders named it for the Panama Canal, which is on the same latitude. Eventually, the smoke from paper mills clouded the sky and the city became an industrial center. In the late nineteenth century, as people looked forward to going to the beach for fun, Panama City Beach came into existence on the barrier island 8 miles away. Today, the Hathaway Bridge connects the two.

# Getting Around Panama City

Panama City Beach stretches for 27 miles, so getting your bearings is relatively simple. Locals refer to Front Beach Road, beginning at the end of Hathaway Bridge, as "the Strip." Cars filled with young people jam it on weekends. Two piers—the eastern County Pier and the western City Pier—anchor the Strip. If you want to make better time, use U.S. Route 98, also known as Back Beach Road.

##  TRAVEL TIP

For a family, it makes more sense to rent a car since you can also explore the coast beyond the beach as far east as Cedar Key. You'll find several of the major rental car companies—Hertz, Budget, and Avis—in Panama City.

Because of the extreme distances, it's not easy to walk here. There's no public transportation to speak of, except hourly shuttle buses that carry beachgoers over the bridge from Panama City (850-234-5571) and then run along Front Beach Road. One-way tickets cost $1, or you can buy a weekly pass for $10. You can also rent a bicycle for about $10 per day from a number of shops along Front Beach Road, including Aquatic Adventures Moped and Bicycle Rentals (850-235-8051). However, these are better for getting around the beach itself than for traveling longer distances in heavy traffic.

### Best Time to Go

Unlike southern Florida, the area around Panama City receives over 320 days of sunshine a year. Temperatures, however, do differ, especially during the winter, with January highs only reaching the lower 60s. Summer is a different story. With highs reaching the upper 80s and with this area receiving the most rain of any region in Florida, summer days tend to be hot and humid.

## Cautions and Safety Concerns

The glare of the ultrawhite sands on the beaches around Panama City can be blinding. Be sure to wear dark sunglasses and use appropriate sunscreen often. Colored beach flags indicate the safety or relative danger on the beach—red flags mean high surf and/or strong currents, yellow flags mean medium surf, dark green flags mean low hazard, and dark blue flags mean dangerous marine life is lurking in the waters. Be sure to heed these warnings. Beaches on the Apalachicola barrier islands have no lifeguards on duty.

# Family-Oriented Resorts and Hotels

Throughout the lively 100 days of summer, you'll find accommodation costs high—in fact, higher than other destinations on Florida's Panhandle—with advance reservations required. However, prices drop in winter. Typical of most seasonal seaside resorts, visitors to Panama City Beach outnumber residents in summer. Weekends are especially crowded with young people. It may pay you to stay in Panama City and drive or take the shuttle to the beach. Generally, the motels at the beach's eastern end are newer and more expensive than in the center. You'll find the family-oriented hotels at the western end of the beach.

### Bay Point Marriott Resort
Reservations: ☎Toll-free 800-874-7105
✍*www.marriottbaypoint.com*

An ultradeluxe 356-room complete resort on Saint Andrews Bay with a hotel overlooking the Grand Lagoon, plus villas. Facilities include a number of restaurants and lounges, pools, tennis courts, two golf courses, and shops. Though there's no beach, the resort's paddlewheel boat can take you to Shell Island.

### Bikini Beach Resort Motel
Reservations: ☎Toll-free 800-451-5307
✍*www.bikinibeachresort.com*

A resort motel located in the middle of Panama City Beach, with efficiency units and one-bedroom suites with fully equipped kitchens if you're on a budget.

### Edgewater Beach Resort
Reservations: ✆Toll-free 800-874-8686
✐*www.edgewaterbeachresort.com*
A classy, luxurious 550-unit condominium resort with both tower and mid-rise condominiums, each individually decorated, overlooking a wide beach and the Gulf of Mexico. Villas on the golf course closer to the beach offer more intimacy. Other facilities include several restaurants, tennis courts, and swimming pools.

### Holiday Inn Sunspree Resort
Reservations: ✆Toll-free 800-633-0266
✐*www.hipcbeach.com*
A family-oriented beach resort with 340 oceanfront rooms with balconies, restaurants, seaside pool and Jacuzzi, kids' activity program, fitness center, and game room.

### Osprey Motel
Reservations: ✆Toll-free 800-338-2659
✐*www.ospreymotel.com*
A five-story motel popular with families for its convenient location near the action on Panama City Beach. Large rooms feature fully equipped kitchens and balconies, and there's a heated pool and sun deck, barbecue, volleyball, and shuffleboard.

## House and Condo Rentals
If you're looking to rent a vacation home or condominium, you'll find many along Panama City Beach and on Saint George Island. The following rental agencies are able to make all the arrangements:

- **Collins Vacation Rentals, Inc.:** ✆Toll-free 800-423-7418, ✐*www.collinsvacationrentals.com*

- **Pinnacle Port Vacation Rentals:** ✆Toll-free 800-874-8823, 🖱*www.pinnacleportrentals.com*
- **Resort Vacation Properties of Saint George Island, Inc.:** ✆Toll-free 866-332-2934, 🖱*www.resortvacationproperties .com/usa*

# Things to Do

While the beaches and the clear, turquoise-green waters of the Gulf of Mexico are Panama City's biggest attraction, you'll find plenty of other affordable things to do. The exhibits at the Museum of Man-in-the-Sea tell the history of diving. Here, you'll see early animal bladders plus nineteenth-century diving equipment, like bulky helmets and diving suits, torpedo-like propulsion vehicles, and underwater cutting devices, which will bring back images from Jules Verne's classic *20,000 Leagues under the Sea.* There are also sea-lab chambers, like the type used in modern undersea exploration, plus an excellent exhibit on underwater oil drilling. The U.S. Navy outfitted the first SEALAB, an underwater research vessel in Panama City. Other exhibits display treasures from Spanish galleons found off the Florida coast. Admission is $5 per adult and $2.50 per child, 6 to 16. (Open 9 A.M.–5 P.M., 850-235-4101)

## For the Kids

You'll find the Panama City area a great place to entertain kids, especially active ones. Panama City Beach is a true all-American beach resort, with miniature golf courses, amusement parks, water parks, and go-cart raceways. While they'll enjoy playing in the sand during the day, you can also be sure they'll have fun at night.

One of the top attractions here is Gulf World Marine Park, featuring the usual dolphin and sea lion shows and also unique penguin shows. The marine park's aquarium displays giant stingrays, and your younger children will hold on tightly to your hand as you lead them through the walk-through shark tank. Meanwhile, talking parrots squawk loudly as you make your way through the jungle-like environment. Kids at least 5 years old and 48 inches tall can swim with a dolphin for an hour and fifteen minutes for $150 in summer, $125 in winter. Admission is $24 for adults and $15 for kids 5 to 11. (Open 9:00 A.M.–9:30 P.M., 850-234-5271, *www.gulfworldmarinepark.com*)

## ☔ RAINY DAY FUN

A great way to wile away a few hours on a rainy afternoon is to take the kids roller skating at either Silver City East (☎850-763-8551) or the Skate Factory (☎850-785-2261). Both have urethane skating areas with a separate section for beginners, as well as speed and in-line skate rentals.

With more than thirty rides, including a rattling 2,000-foot roller coaster and a 40-foot swinging sea dragon, the Miracle Strip Amusement Park will provide your children with hours of fun. From atop the Top of the Strip, a 203-foot-high observation tower, they'll be able to see down the entire beach and out into the Gulf of Mexico.

Across from the amusement park stands Shipwreck Island Water Park, northwest Florida's largest, complete with a wave pool, a "Rapid River Run," and a kiddy pool called the "Tadpole Hole" (850-234-3333). Nearby, Fun Land Arcade will lure them in with a video arcade, go-carts, and bumper boats (850-234-3693).

If you want to include some educational fun in your kids' itinerary, visit the Junior Museum of Bay County where they'll learn how early pioneers in Florida lived and worked. They'll get to explore a log homestead and an interactive exhibit that teaches them about Florida's history. Indoor exhibits focus on the environment, science, and culture. Suggested donations are $5 for adults and $3 for children under 12. (Open Monday through Friday 9:00 A.M.–4:30 P.M., Saturday 10 A.M.–4 P.M., 850-769-6128, *www.jrmuseum.org*)

# 💼 TRAVEL TIP

If your kids like to play miniature golf, they'll love Coconut Creek Family Fun Park. They'll set out on an adventure under waterfalls and through caves as they keep their ball in motion. Adjacent to the mini–golf course is Gran Maze where they'll race against time to find their way through a giant maze. (📞850-234-2625, *www.coconut creekfun.com*)

## Festivals and Seasonal Events

As a popular southern beach destination, Panama City Beach offers a host of events throughout the year to add to the fun. Here are a few of them:

**Saint Andrews Mardi Gras:** The Krewe of Saint Andrews hosts this two-day pre-Lenten celebration in mid-February, with parades, live bands, food, and crafts. (*www.saintandrewsmardigras .com*)

**Indian Summer Festival:** This highlight of the fall season in Panama City Beach features local food, art, and music on two stages for three days in mid-October. (📞Toll-free 800-722-3224)

# Exploring

There's plenty to explore beyond Panama City's beaches. While most of the area's attractions lie along the coast, you'll find the expanse of Apalachicola National Forest as you head inland.

## The Coast

If you drive east along the coast from Panama City on U.S. Route 98, you eventually come to the Florida Panhandle's Apalachicola Bay region—a coast without beaches. You probably thought that beaches lined all the coasts of Florida, but a distant barrier reef protects this stretch. In fact, this is what Florida, with its quiet fishing villages, marshes, and bayous, looked like before all the development.

## Saint Joseph Peninsula State Park and Port Saint Joe

The first stop off U.S. Route 98 after Panama City is Saint Joseph Peninsula State Park (850-227-1327). This long finger of sand, with a 9-mile hiking trail at one end and a short nature trail at the other, protectively cradles Port Saint Joe on the mainland, a small fishing town whose only claim to fame is that signers of a liberal constitution calling for Florida statehood met here in 1838. Unfortunately, their ideas were a bit too radical, and the legislature voted it down. However, you can visit the Constitution Convention State Museum where you'll see audio-animated mannequins debate the proposed constitution in a reproduction of the original convention hall, plus other memorabilia showing how the town earned the title "wickedest city in the Southeast." Admission is $1 per person. (Open Thursday through Monday 9 A.M.–noon and 1–5 P.M., 850-229-8029)

### Apalachicola

Eighteen miles beyond Port Saint Joe, you'll approach Apalachicola, whose name means "friendly people"—but to many it means oysters, because Apalachicola Bay produces 90 percent of Florida's oysters in more than 10,000 acres of carefully tended oyster beds.

Following U.S. Route 98, you cross the Gorrie Bridge—moving from Eastern to Central Time—which leads into Apalachicola, a charming old riverboat town that sits on a lagoon-like bay, protected by three offshore barrier islands. It made its past fortunes on cotton, lumber, and sponges. Little remains of the town's cotton business, dating back to the 1820s, except a couple of old warehouses and some historical markers. But you can't help but notice the stately old antebellum mansions built by men who made their fortunes when riverboat trade was at its peak. Stop into the Raney House on

Market Street, built in the temple-pediment style with four tall columns across the front. Its wide hallways, displaying antiques, once served as breezy rooms on hot summer days. Once belonging to a cotton commission merchant, it now houses the Apalachicola Chamber of Commerce, from which you can obtain a self-guided walking tour brochure. (Open daily 9 A.M.–5 P.M., 850-653-9419)

## ≡FAST FACT

When a flower on a cotton plant blossoms, it develops into an oval boll that splits open, revealing a mass of long white seed hairs called lint. The invention of the cotton gin enabled the lint to be separated from the seed. After separation, it's compressed into bales for processing into cloth and string.

Originally, forty-three warehouses serviced Apalachicola's cotton industry. Large bales stood in huge piles on the wharves, waiting for shipment around the world. You can imagine the beehive of activity along docks at the end of a prosperous growing season. Next door, you'll see what remains of the old sponge exchange, a memorial to the days when Apalachicola's sponge trade was the third largest in Florida.

The bridge leading into town commemorates Dr. John Gorrie, who invented an ice machine. After arriving in 1833, young Dr. Gorrie sought a way to keep the rooms of yellow fever patients cool and stumbled on the idea of making ice. Previously, riverboats transported blocks of ice from the north. He received the first U.S. patent for mechanical refrigeration in 1851, and his idea became the basis of the modern refrigeration compressor and air-conditioner—something many Floridians cannot live without. Unfortunately, he died penniless before his idea caught on. You can visit the John Gorrie Museum to see a replica of his cumbersome ice-making machine—the original stands in the Smithsonian Institution in Washington, D.C.

Admission is $1 per person. (Open Thursday through Monday 9 A.M.–noon and 1–5 P.M., 850-653-9347)

 **TRAVEL TIP**

Take your kids down to the old waterfront where they can watch the oystermen returning from harvesting oysters. Oysters attach themselves to rocks or lie on the sea bottom. The oystermen use specially made long tongs to pry them loose. Once the oysters are collected, they have to be pried open with a knife since a strong muscle keeps the shell tightly closed.

On the way back, stop at Trinity Episcopal Church. Shipped in pieces from New York and assembled with wooden pegs in 1837 and 1838, this Greek revival building displays antique stained-glass windows plus hand-stenciled designs on its curved wooden ceiling, and houses two historic organs. It also features a special gallery where slaves sat during services.

### The Barrier Islands of Saint George, Saint Vincent, and Dog

If you gaze across the blue-green waters of Saint George Sound and Apalachicola Bay, you'll see several long islands hovering on the horizon. Guarding some of the most productive fishing waters in the state while protecting the mainland from wind and storm, the barrier islands of Saint George, Saint Vincent, and Dog provide nesting grounds for thousands of birds. Raccoons, salt marsh snakes, diamond back terrapins, and ghost crabs call the islands home. And the brilliantly white beaches attract visitors in search of seashells and solitude. Though each has a distinctive character, you can only reach the largest, Saint George, by road.

You can easily get to Saint George Island, a narrow 25-mile-long strip of mostly developed land, by crossing the Saint George Island Bridge and Causeway, off Route 98 at Eastpoint. Nine miles of undeveloped beaches and dunes, shady pine and live oak hammocks, bay shore and sandy coves, and salt marshes on the eastern end of the island have been preserved as the beautiful 1,882-acre Dr. Julian G. Bruce Saint George Island State Park. A two-and-a-half-mile hiking trail leads through a pine woods and coastal plain to Gap Point beside the bay. The park offers picnic areas and observation decks, and 9 miles of undeveloped beaches and dunes, the longest coastal park in the state. Fishing for bluefish, redfish, Spanish mackerel, pompano, and ladyfish is also excellent. (850-927-2111)

Originally Little Saint George Island was part of the main island, but it's now separated by an artificial channel. Little Saint George Light, a historic 78-foot lighthouse, is the only building on this state reserve, and you can only reach it by boat.

Saint Vincent National Wildlife Refuge covers the entire 12,358 acres of a triangular-shaped island, accessible only by boat, a stone's throw from the western end of Saint George. But the island is unlike most barrier islands. At its widest, it's 4 miles from shore to shore, with 14 miles of beaches and 80 miles of crisscrossing sand roads, plus several swamps and freshwater lakes. Alligators lazily bask in the sun while bald eagles nest in the pines and loggerhead turtles lay eggs on the beaches. Today, wild hogs and deer roam on what was once a private hunting ground. Bird watchers have spotted over 200 species of birds, including wild turkeys. You can take a guided wildlife tour to the island in November. (850-653-8808)

The easternmost of these barrier islands is Dog Island, a couple miles east of Saint George. Here, you can climb some of the highest and most unspoiled dunes in Florida. Scattered among them are a handful of cottages belonging to more than 100 residents who live here year-round.

Today, most of the island is a wildlife preserve, protecting thirty species of endangered plants, birds, and animals. Narrow footpaths enable you to walk among ancient sand pines, reindeer moss, and rosemary at the higher points while live oak, slash pine, dune goldenrod, sea laven-der, and morning glory cover the lower ridges. The rich estuaries on the island's bay side support marsh grasses and black mangrove trees.

### Apalachicola National Forest

Several roads lead inland off Route 98 toward Apalachicola National Forest, a vast preserve with swamps, savannahs, and springs dotted liberally about its half-million acres. As the largest of Florida's national forests, it encompasses four state parks and recre-ation areas, plus the Ochlockonee River. Black bears and panthers roam its interior, and abundant fish swim in its lakes. You can take a leisurely drive through it and stop for a picnic at one of its many road-side picnic areas. Whether you enter the park via Florida Highway 65 or U.S. Route 319, you'll eventually pass Tate's Hell Swamp State Forest (850-487-3766).

# ≡FAST FACT

According to the legend of Tate's Hell Swamp, a panther had killed the livestock of Cebe Tate, so he pursued it into the swamp with his shotgun and hunting dogs. A snake bit him after he wandered around for a week, surviving by drinking the murky waters. Emerg-ing near town, he uttered, "My name is Cebe Tate, and I just came through Hell!"—then promptly died.

Just before entering the national forest on Route 65, you'll come to Fort Gadsden State Historical Site, a 76-acre park on the site of a British fort built to recruit blacks and Indians during the War of 1812, destroyed by American forces in 1816 and later rebuilt by Lieutenant James Gadsden under orders from Andrew Jackson, who established a supply base there in 1818. Confederate forces occupied it during the Civil War. Though little remains of the fort today, you'll find a model of it, plus historical exhibits and a picnic area (850-670-8988).

To see the Apalachicola National Forest more closely, you can hike one of several trails or paddle a canoe up the Ochlockonee River, its main waterway. If you're an experienced hiker, you can try the 30-mile Apalachicola Trail, the forest's main trail beginning near Crawfordville on U.S. Route 319. You'll pass through the heart of the forest along a trail across the isolated swamp of Bradwell Bay Wilderness. Before doing so, however, be sure to pick up maps and advice at the Rangers' Office in Crawfordville.

### Cedar Key

While following U.S. Route 98 and turning south along the coast, you'll come to a cluster of islands that includes the quaint fishing village and artists' colony of Cedar Key, on the Gulf of Mexico. During the week, it remains quiet and secluded, but on weekends, it bustles with crowds out for the day.

Though Cedar Key doesn't have the glamour of other artist colonies, its residents are just down-home folks who have weathered many a storm. The necessity for deeper harbors resulted in the decline of Cedar Key as a port. First settled in the early 1840s, the island developed into a major port for lumber and turpentine with the completion of the railroad from Fernandina. The Civil War brought more trade as ships dropped supplies and salt for the Southern troops. Lumber shipment continued until the 1880s when fishing became the main industry.

## ══FAST FACT

Today, Cedar Key is the home to Project OCEAN (Oyster Clam Educational Aquaculture Network), begun in 1991, which provides training through the Federal Job Training Partnership Act to teach the techniques of shellfish farming in which fishermen can raise clams and oysters from seed to harvest under protective conditions.

Today, you can learn about Cedar Key's historic past by visiting the Cedar Key Museum, just north of town. Besides historic exhibits, the museum also displays a large shell collection (850-543-5600). Afterward, head over to the Cedar Key National Wildlife Refuge, encompassing a series of offshore islands and established by President Herbert Hoover in 1929. Here, you'll see hundreds of nesting birds, including egrets, white herons, cormorants, pelicans, and osprey, plus scores of species of flora native to northern Florida. To get to the refuge, you have to hire a boat from the Cedar Key City Marina. Boats will drop you for a day of shelling and come back to pick you up.

# By Day

Your entire family will have fun during the day. The beach buzzes with activity, from lively volleyball games on the beach to Jet-Skiing, windsurfing, and boating on the water. You'll find lots of opportunities for fun in the sun. And at the end of the day, you'll join others in marveling at breathtaking sunsets, as the sun dips into the emerald sea.

### On the Beach

The sand on Panama City Beach is fluffy and powdery like confectioner's sugar, its oval-shaped grains squeak beneath your feet. Over the centuries, it washed down from the Appalachian Mountains, became bleached, ground, smoothed, and polished until being washed up on shore. Since the whiteness of the sand reflects the heat of the sun, it stays cool even on hot days making walking without shoes a dream. As you walk along the shore, shore birds dart into the waves as they scurry to and fro along the water's edge. The clarity and the blue-green color of the warm water is irresistible, and you can't wait to try it yourself. Around you sun worshipers lie in low-rise beach chairs, reading books and chatting, while others bob in the waves.

While on the beach, you float high above the sea suspended from a parachute with Coastal Parasailing (850-233-0914). Or you can rent WaveRunners from the Original Island Wave Runner Tours (850-234-7245). Hydrotherapy Kiteboarding and Windsurfing offers rentals and lessons to get you out on the waves (850-236-1800). You'll find Jet Ski rentals available all along Front Beach Road.

##  TRAVEL TIP

Play Robinson Crusoe and take the thirty-minute ferry to 700-acre Shell Island, a one-mile wide, seven-and-a-half-mile long barrier island just south of Panama City Beach. On this idyllic slice of deserted sandy beach, you can swim or search for exotic shells, or just relax. Be sure to bring along a cooler of drinks and snacks as there are no facilities on the island.

When you get overloaded from typical seashore activities, you can find peace and contentment on the snow-like sand of Saint Andrews State Recreation Area—1,062 acres of rolling sand dunes covered in sea oats and wide beaches, marshes, pinewood, and the wildlife that inhabits them. Bordered by the Gulf of Mexico, the Grand Lagoon, and the ship channel, it offers a variety of water sports. To provide some variation on lying in the sun or swimming in the ultraclear warm waters, bring along a bucket to collect scallops from the grass flats on the bay side of the park. Or, using a net, walk out into the bay and scoop up the blue crabs running through the grassy flats. If you seek shade, follow the nature trails through the park, but keep your eyes peeled for sleeping alligators and exotic water birds. Remember to be quiet. Admission is $2 per car (open daily 8 A.M.–sunset).

If you like to fish, the park offers freshwater Gator Lake and the saltwater bay. During spring, you can reel in speckled trout, flounder, redfish, bluefish, pompano, and Spanish and king mackerel. Later, during the summer and autumn months, bonito and schoolie, as well as both mackerels, trout, and flounder, are plentiful. There's also a restored old-time "Cracker" turpentine still, plus picnicking, swimming, and scuba-diving facilities for your family to enjoy (850-234-2522).

## On the Boat

Take a glass-bottom boat tour with The Glass Bottom Boat. While on board you can learn to bait crab traps, feed dolphins, and observe how a shrimp net is reeled in. Special shelling trips to the best spots on Shell Island are popular (850-234-7245). Or you can take a snorkel and narrated sightseeing trip of Saint Andrews Bay with Island Star Cruises (850-235-2809). Or perhaps you'd rather take a four-hour narrated harbor cruise aboard the *Ashley Gorman*, passing Audubon Island where you can observe pelicans (850-785-4878).

Whether you choose to fish from Panama City's 1,642-foot pier, the longest in Florida, or two other piers, or from a bridge or jetty, or from the back of a charter fishing boat, you'll find the Gulf waters offer as much as you can handle.

From March to November, fishermen from around the world troll the bay off the beach for barracuda, bonito, king and Spanish mackerel, and dolphinfish. Some try fly-fishing for redfish in Saint Andrews Bay. Or you may wish to join a party boat with a larger group of people, trying to reel in grouper, red snapper, or amberjack. Choose from any of the following to make arrangements:

- **Captain Anderson's Marina:** 850-234-3435
- **Captain Blood Light Tackle Fishing:** 850-785-6216
- **Osprey Charters:** 850-233-1959
- **Pirate's Cove Marina:** 850-234-3939
- **Treasure Island Marina:** 850-234-8533

## Under the Water

Whether you enjoy snorkeling or diving, you'll find some good spots here. A favorite snorkeling spot is the jetties at Saint Andrews State Recreation Area. Divers prefer either the wreck of the tugboat *Grey Ghost*, lying on its side 100 feet below the surface, or by the old spans of the Hathaway Bridge. While not as popular a diving destination as some coastal spots farther south, you'll find what you need at the following dive shops:

- **Hydrospace Dive Shop:** ☏850-234-3063
- **Dive Locker:** ☏850-230-8006
- **Diver's Den:** ☏850-234-8717
- **Panama City Dive Center:** ☏850-235-3390

## On the Links and on the Courts

Even though Panama City Beach is a honky-tonk kind of place, you'll find five good golf courses to play in the area. With moderate year-round temperatures and lots of sunshine, there's never a bad time to play golf. Reservations for tee times, up to seven days in advance, are a necessity as slots fill quickly.

**The Bay Point Resort:** One of Florida's top golfing destinations, this resort offers two courses—an eighteen-hole championship course designed by Jack Nicklaus and a nine-hole resort course—plus pro shop, practice range, and restaurant. (☏850-236-6950)

**Holiday Gold Club:** An eighteen-hole championship course with newly installed greens, offering challenging play. (☏850-234-1800)

**Hombre Golf Club:** A twenty-seven-hole course, designed by Wes Burnham, with challenges on each set of nine named The Good, The Bad, and The Ugly. You can take half-day, two-, three-, and five-day golf lessons at the Martin Green Golf Academy on site. (☏850-234-3673, ✐*www.hombregolfclub.com*)

**Signal Hill Golf Course:** As the original course on Panama City Beach, it features well-groomed fairways and large manicured greens set atop white sand dunes. (☏850-234-3218)

## Shopping

Panama City Beach has all the types of stores to keep teens occupied for hours. If they can't find just the right seashore souvenir or swimsuit, then it just isn't made. One shop carries over 25,000 swimsuits. Shops by the dozens sell everything from designer sunglasses to beach toys, hats, bikinis, and, of course, silk-screened and airbrushed T-shirts. One of the most popular shopping places is the

Promenade Mall. And there's also the Panama City Mall. If you're a golf enthusiast, you'll find bargains on discounted equipment at outlets here.

# Dining Out and Nightlife

Most of the restaurants in the Panama City area serve basic home-style food and lots of it. Many chefs prepare freshly caught seafood like Gulf scallops and swordfish Cajun style. You'll find the buffet restaurants to be the least expensive eateries, especially for families. Most charge around $15 per adult, and less for kids, for all you can eat. Both Bishop's (12628 Front Beach Road, ☎850-234-6457) and the Mariner Restaurant, Seafood Buffet, and Oyster House (9104 Front Beach Road, ☎850-234-8450) are favorites.

> **Captain Anderson's:** An award-winning landmark seafood restaurant where you can watch the fleet come in while you eat. (5551 North Lagoon Drive, Panama City Beach, ☎850-234-2225)
> **Pineapple Willy's Beachside Restaurant and Sports Bar:** Dine on prime rib, oysters, and shrimp by the beach. (9875 S. Thomas Drive, ☎850-235-0928)
> **Sweet Basil's Bistro:** An affordable family restaurant, serving fresh pasta and pizza. (11208 Front Beach Road, ☎850-234-2855)
> **The Treasure Ship:** Your kids will love this seafood restaurant complex built to resemble a wooden sailing ship, complete with pirates. Three restaurants serve a variety of beef and seafood dishes. (3605 Thomas Drive, ☎850-234-8881)

As with any typical seaside resort along the east coast of the United States, nightlife in Panama City Beach is most active during the summer. If you love country music and the Grand Ole Opry, then head straight for Ocean Opry, an imitation show put on by the Rader family in Panama City Beach. Singing, dancing, and good old country humor make for a couple of hours of fun (850-234-5464).

**JUST FOR PARENTS**

After the workout you and your spouse have gotten keeping tabs on your kids in this kiddy playland, take some time for yourselves and board a moonlight dinner cruise with dancing out on Saint Andrews Bay aboard the *Lady Anderson* on Monday, Wednesday, and Friday—that's right, the same Anderson with such delicious food in his restaurant. (Toll-free ✆800-360-0510)

If you prefer to stay out late and listen to music under the stars while overlooking the bay, you'll find Pineapple Willy's, with its Caribbean ambiance, to be just the place. If you're a bit younger, you'll enjoy the raucous crowd of the twenty bars at Spinnaker where '70s and '80s rock groups sometimes perform. Both have a cover charge. Whatever type of music you like—rock 'n' roll, country, jazz, or blues—you'll find it here.

# CHAPTER 18

# Pensacola

PENSACOLA IS A CITY of traditional Southern hospitality, elegance, and charm. Located at the western end of Florida's Panhandle on the northern bank of the broad Pensacola Bay and 5 miles inland from the nearest beaches, it's a historic city first occupied by the Spanish, then exchanged among the Spanish, French, and British thirteen times before becoming the place where Spain ceded Florida to the United States in 1821. With its complement of just about everything Florida has to offer—alligators, spectacular beaches, and Hispanic landmarks—you'll enjoy its Dixie atmosphere and its Gulf islands.

## Getting to Know Pensacola

Pensacola, a city of over a quarter-million people, overlooks 15-mile-wide Pensacola Bay. Named for the Panzacola Indians, the city has over 400 years of history, dating back to Diego Miruelo who discovered the bay in 1516. Tristán de Luna established a colony with 1,400 settlers, mostly from Mexico, on its shores in 1559. It lasted until a hurricane wiped it out two years later.

Though the Spanish established a second settlement in Pensacola in 1698, the French captured it in 1719. Possession bounced back and forth until the city officially returned to Spanish rule in 1722. For better defense, the Spaniards moved the settlement to Santa Rosa

Island, but a hurricane flattened it in 1752, so they moved the settlement to its present location on the mainland later that year. A decade later, the British took over Florida, so the Spaniards in Pensacola fled to Mexico. The town filled with Tories fleeing the American Revolution and became very prosperous. In 1781 the Spanish recaptured the town in the Battle of Pensacola and routed the British, but two years later the Treaty of Paris ceded all of Florida back to the Spanish.

## ≡FAST FACT

Andrew Jackson has a direct connection to Pensacola. During the War of 1812, a British detachment began to drill there even though the Spanish controlled it. Andrew Jackson attacked the town and forced the British to withdraw. In 1818, Jackson took Pensacola and in February 1821, President James Monroe appointed Jackson provisional governor when Florida became a U.S. territory.

The U.S. Navy established a naval yard in well-sheltered Pensacola Bay in 1825. By the time of the Civil War, Pensacola had become the largest city in Florida, siding with the Confederacy. It fell to Union forces early in the war, and the town sank into a depression that lasted until the late nineteenth century when new railroad lines from Alabama and Georgia helped revitalize the naval industry. With better rail connections and a well-developed network of river steamboats, the city became an important port of call. The Navy helped boost Pensacola's economy again in 1914, when it established the first flight-training center at the Naval Air Station. Today, the Navy is still the city's biggest employer.

## Getting Around Pensacola

Except for walking the historic area downtown, you'll need a car to get around Pensacola. Renting a car will also allow you to explore the Gulf Islands National Seashore, as well as the neighboring resort towns of Fort Walton Beach and Destin.

## Best Time to Go

Since the Pensacola area receives over 320 days of sunshine a year, just about any time is a good time to visit. However, temperatures during the winter season tend to be slightly lower, with highs in the mid-50s to mid-60s. Summer highs reach the low to mid-80s, and the air feels humid even though there are breezes off the Gulf.

## Cautions and Safety Concerns

Though the blue-green Gulf waters seem relatively calm on the surface, dangerous currents can lurk underneath. Be sure to heed the warnings of the flag system used on area beaches:

**Green:** calm conditions, low hazard
**Yellow:** moderate surf, medium hazard
**Red:** high surf, high hazard
**Double red:** dangerous surf, closed to public use
**Purple:** dangerous marine life
**No flag:** no lifeguard on duty

Surf conditions can be deceiving. To receive the latest surf advisory, call 850-932-7873 for Pensacola beaches and the Gulf Islands National Seashore for beaches within its boundaries (Opal Beach on Santa Rosa Island and Rosamund Johnson Beach on Perdido Key).

# Family-Oriented Resorts and Hotels

You have a variety of accommodations to choose from in the Pensacola area. Most of the larger family resorts and activities are along the sands of Pensacola Beach. You'll find a larger number of resorts catering to families in this area than farther east.

### Crowne Plaza Pensacola Grand Hotel

Reservations: ✆Toll-free 800-348-3336

✍*www.pensacolagrandhotel.com*

Incorporated into the 1912 L&N train depot, this 212-room classic hotel features regular rooms plus suites with kitchenettes, and elegant dining rooms decorated with antiques to recall the early days of train travel; the higher-story rooms above the old station offer magnificent views.

### Hampton Inn Pensacola Beach

Reservations: ✆Toll-free 800-426-7866

✍*www.hamptoninn.com*

This 181-room beachfront hotel has just undergone a major renovation and features suites with kitchenettes, free continental breakfast, pool, and exercise room.

### Holiday Inn Express Pensacola Beach

Reservations: ✆800-833-8637

This high-rise art deco–style hotel, overlooking the beach, has a café, outdoor and indoor pools, exercise room, penthouse suites, free continental breakfast, and a kids' program in summer.

## House and Condo Rentals

Condominiums, such as Sea Spray on Perdido Key (Toll-free 800-336-7263, *www.seasprayperdido.com*), featuring two- and three-bedroom apartments for family groups only, have sprung up along beaches in Destin and on Perdido Key. Stays are usually for a minimum of four nights, but shorter times are available off-season. For rental possibilities, contact Key Concepts Realty, Inc. (Toll-free 800-955-5462, *www.gulfcoastarea.com*) or Paradise Beach Homes/Coastal Realty (Toll-free 800-860-0067, *www.paradisebeachhomes.com*).

# Things to Do

All sorts of adventures await you and your family along the Emerald Coast, as this strip of coastline is known because of the emerald green color of the Gulf waters. Whether you choose to visit the historic sites in Pensacola, hike the pristine beaches of the Gulf Islands National Seashore, explore under the water or canoe on top of it, you're sure to find many activities to interest your entire family.

Pensacola has had a lively past, and virtually everything worth seeing lies within three adjoining districts downtown. Begin your exploration at the old Spanish plaza, the heart of the city. The Pensacola Historical Museum, operated by the Pensacola Historical Society and housed in Old Christ Church (the oldest Protestant church in Florida, built in 1832), divides the plaza into two halves, Plaza Ferdinand VII and Seville Square. Union forces used the old church as a prison, barracks, and hospital during the Civil War, and later in the nineteenth century, it acquired its stained-glass windows and Gothic arches. As you wander through it, you'll see a collection of Indian and Civil War artifacts, art glass, Victorian clothing, old photos, and memorabilia of the city's shipping industry. (Open Tuesday through Thursday, Saturday, and Sunday 9:00 A.M.–4:30 P.M., 850-433-1559, *www .pensacolahistory.org*)

 **TRAVEL TIP**

What better place to have an old-fashioned family photograph taken than in the Pensacola Historical Museum. After viewing the exhibits, stop in at the Old Time Photo Studio, a project of the Pensacola Historical Society, where your family can dress in period costumes to have their portrait taken (✆850-434-5455).

As you walk the oak-lined streets of the twenty-block Seville Square Historic District—bounded by Bayfront Parkway, Tarragona, Romana, and Cevallos streets—you'll discover a number of smaller museums and important historic houses (850-595-5985, *www.seville-district.com*). The Museum of Commerce and the Museum of Industry occupy two restored fish warehouses. The former includes a re-creation of Palafox Street at the turn of the twentieth century, with many of the storefronts and shop fittings of the time and a collection of antique buggies. The latter includes a working sawmill, for it was lumber that made the city prosper, and memorabilia of the fishing industry.

After visiting the museums, cross Church Street to the Pensacola Colonial Archaeological Trail, a series of outdoor exhibits along a marked path that features ruins of the British colonial commanding officer's house and its refuse pits. The foundations of the officer of the day's building lie just inside the western gate of the eighteenth-century British fort—the only one built on American soil—and the remains of what appears to have been a trader's home and warehouse sit just outside the western gate. You can pick up a map brochure at the Tivoli House in Historic Pensacola Village. Next door stands the Julee Cottage, the 1809 home of Julee Panton, a "freewoman of color," who had her own land and business and even her own slave; it now shows an exhibit of local black history (850-595-5985).

In front of the Archaeological Trail stands the T. T. Wentworth, Jr. Florida State Museum, housed in the 1908 Pensacola City Hall within the Seville District and the oldest museum in town. Inside the yellow-brick Renaissance Revival building, 35,000 pictures, documents, and historical objects, arranged categorically, will show you more about Pensacola's fascinating history. Your kids will love the unusual collection of Coca-Cola memorabilia, plus over 100,000 of Wentworth's personal artifacts, including a bizarre petrified cat and shrunken head, as well as the third-floor Discovery Gallery with its giant aquarium, room of mirrors, and an old ship. (850-595-5985)

Pensacola gained prominence as a commercial center in the late eighteenth century. A mix of early settlers, Native Americans, and traders regularly gathered to sell and barter on the waterfront of the Seville District, about half a mile east of present-day Palafox Street. The wealthier ones built fine homes that today, together with several museums, form Historic Pensacola Village, bounded by Alcaniz, Government, Jefferson, and Zaragoza streets. A $3 per person admission gets you into all of the historic houses and museums in the Village. Stop first at the Hispanic Museum to see exhibits of sixteenth-century Spanish armor and household furnishings, and while you're there, sign up for the village tour led by costumed docents. (Open Easter to Labor Day, Monday through Saturday 10:00 A.M.–4:30 P.M., Sunday 1:00–4:30 P.M., and the rest of the year Monday through Saturday 10:00 A.M.–4:40 P.M., 850-595-5985, *www.historicpen sacola.org*)

## ≡FAST FACT

The West Florida Historic Preservation, Inc., a direct support organization of the University of West Florida, operates Historic Pensacola Village, consisting of twenty buildings in the Pensacola National Register Historic District. Costumed docents staff ten of these buildings, all within a four-block area.

On the tour you'll see three fine old houses, restored and furnished in the style of the time, recalling the days Seville Square was Pensacola's most fashionable neighborhood. The first is a restored and furnished Creole cottage belonging to Charles LaValle, who moved to Pensacola from New Orleans with his mistress and built this one-story frame house in 1815. The second, the Quina House (850-434-3050), provides a look at a furnished Creole cottage of the 1840s, while the third, the Clara Barkley Dorr House, the late Greek

Revival home of a lumber magnate's family, overflows with opulent mid-Victorian furnishings.

Be sure to visit the 8-acre Saint Michael's Cemetery, the oldest surviving cemetery in town, dating back to 1822 when the king of Spain deeded it to the city. Here, among the 3,200 marked burials you'll find old Spanish graves, plus the tombstone of Dorothy Walton, whose husband, Judge George Walton, signed the Declaration of Independence, and a replica of Napoleon's tomb. (850-436-4643, *www.stmichaelscemetery.org*)

If you have the time, you'll find more houses built by Pensacola's late-nineteenth-century lumber barons in the North Hill Historic District, the city's first elegant suburb, bounded by LaRue, Palafox, Blount, and Reus streets. Over 400 historic private homes, constructed of yellow pine, stand along the tree-lined and brick-paved streets, including examples of Tudor, Queen Anne, Mediterranean Revival, and Southern Vernacular styles. Though none is open for public tours, you'll be able to appreciate the craftsmanship of gifted artisans and the wealth of the lumber barons. (850-439-3384, *www .historicnorthhill.com*)

 **TRAVEL TIP**

The Pensacola area provides you with lots of opportunities for bird watching—while strolling along downtown Pensacola's waterfront where Project Greenshores, a habitat-restoration project, attracts large numbers of water birds, or while playing a round of golf at Lost Key Golf Club on Perdido Key Beach, or while simply walking through Avian Alley at the zoo in Gulf Breeze.

In the converted cells of the old city jail, you can view changing exhibits at the Pensacola Museum of Art. (850-432-6247, *www.pen sacolamuseumofart.org*)

While it's better to see the Seville District by walking, you'll learn more about the Palafox and North Hill districts by taking the hour-long historical van tour for $7.50 per person, departing at 10 A.M. and 1 P.M. Monday through Saturday from the visitor information center.

Pensacola's merchants saw a potential boost to their fortunes with the opening of the Panama Canal. Many new buildings appeared in the southern part of Palafox Street during the early twentieth century. Though their wrought-iron work and ornate detail reflected their optimism, the boom in business never came.

##  TRAVEL TIP

Stop at the Pensacola Area Convention and Visitor Bureau at 1401 East Gregory Street for helpful brochures, including a self-guided tour map of the Seville and Palafox historic districts, brochures on local flora and fauna, theater, and local events schedules.(☎850-434-1234 ⌕ *http://visitpensacola.com/*)

Take a look at the County Court House, which also served as a customs house, a post office, and tax offices. Opposite it, the Empire Building's slender form and vertically aligned windows exaggerate its height. In 1909, it was Florida's tallest building. A block farther stands the Spanish baroque Saenger Theater, now the home of Pensacola's Symphony Orchestra. If the door's open, be sure to peek inside for a look at its magnificent interior.

### Pensacola Naval Air Station

Eight miles southwest of downtown Pensacola lies the vast U.S. Naval Air Station, home of the famous flying Blue Angels; the U.S.S. *Lexington*, a World War II carrier now used for training; and the Naval Aviation Museum. The Museum of Naval Aviation is one of the most comprehensive air museums in the nation, containing a collection of over 140 restored aircraft representing Navy, Coast Guard, and Marine Corps aviation. The aircraft ranges from a replica of the first seaplane, purchased in 1911, to an actual Skylab command vehicle, and the latest Hornet and Phantom jets displayed both inside the 291,000-square-foot building and outdoors on 37 acres of airfield. Both you and your kids will enjoy gazing up at four A-4 Skyhawks suspended in a diving-diamond formation in the museum's seven-story glass and steel atrium. To get an eye-level view, ascend to the mezzanine level. Afterward, view the special IMAX film *The Magic of Flight* from a seven-story-high screen. You'll feel as if you're right in the cockpit with the pilot of a Blue Angels jet.

 **JUST FOR PARENTS**

If you're a Vietnam veteran, you won't want to miss the Wall South, a one-half-scale replica of the design of the Vietnam Memorial in Washington, D.C., at Veterans Memorial Park on Bayfront Parkway in Pensacola (✆850-455-0906, ✉*www.pensacolawallsouth.org*). World War II naval veterans will enjoy reminiscing on the flight deck of the aircraft carrier U.S.S. *Cabot* at the Museum of Naval Aviation.

What child won't find it a thrill to fly an F/A 18 mission in Desert Storm via a motion-based flight simulator—the ultimate computer game—then climb into one of the full-size training cockpits to tug on the controls. The museum also has memorabilia from important naval air battles, flight clothing and logs, and old equipment, plus missiles and bombs. You can take the Flight Line Bus for a free twenty-minute tour of the aircraft displayed outdoors, as well as a number of historic structures including an 1845 octagonal armory and chapel and some seaplane hangars from the first years of the base. Admission is free. (Open daily 9 A.M.–5 P.M., Toll-free 800-327-5002, *www.naval-air.org*)

## For the Kids

About 10 miles east of Gulf Breeze on Route 98 lies The Zoo Northwest Florida, the only accredited zoo in the Panhandle. You'll find over 700 animals, a petting zoo for children, and a small botanical garden (850-932-2229, *www.the-zoo.com*). Across the road, the folks at the Wildlife Rescue & Sanctuary Park will introduce your children to pelicans, alligators, raccoons, owls, and other wildlife (850-433-9453).

 **RAINY DAY FUN**

If it rains, you can take the kids to Sam's Fun City & Surf City. Located in the heart of Pensacola, this family fun park offers a great arcade with over fifty games, a 1,600-square-foot Laser Tag arena, plus a new water park that's sure to keep your children occupied for hours. (850-505-0800, *www.samsfuncity.com*)

The Gulfarium at Fort Walton Beach offers entertaining live dolphin and sea lion performances, as well as giant sea turtles and other marine life. The activities here should keep your little ones happy for about three hours (Toll-free 800-247-8575, *www.gulfarium.com*).

For go-cart enthusiasts, Fast Eddie's Fun Center in Pensacola offers four tracks, including a figure eight with a bridge and wild turns. Younger children can race Junior Racers, or they can ride with an adult in a double go-cart. There's also miniature golf. (850-433-7735, *www.fasteddiesfunctr.com*)

## Festivals and Seasonal Events

When it comes to festivals and events, the Pensacola area has a flavor all its own. Celebrations of seafood, folk music, fishing, history, and pirate revelry are all a part of the area's more than sixty festivals and events celebrated annually. Here is a selection of some of the most popular:

**The Great Gulfcoast Arts Festival:** Held the first weekend of November, this festival features both visual and performing artists from around the country, plus a special children's art festival with hands-on activities. (✑*www.ggaf.org*)

**Fiesta of Five Flags:** For the first ten days of June, Pensacola celebrates its history with a costumed fiesta and the arrival of a heritage four-masted sailing vessel to mark de Luna's colonization attempt. (✆850-433-6512, ✑*www.fiestaoffiveflags.org*)

**Pensacola Beach Air Show:** Held in mid-July, this spectacular event showcases the Blue Angels. (✆850-932-1500)

# Exploring

Beyond Pensacola, you have a full range of interesting places to explore. Towns like Fort Walton Beach and Destin on Pensacola's barrier islands are just the beginning. You also have the vast expanse of Gulf Islands National Seashore, with its remote beaches, old forts, and nature trails, as well as the Eden State Gardens.

## Fort Walton Beach

It's difficult to tell from the neon motel signs in Fort Walton Beach that it was once a major Indian religious and social center some 10,000 years ago. A 12-foot high temple mound from the Mississippian Period stands beside the highway, and the small but excellent Indian Temple Mound Museum nearby contains more than 4,000 artifacts taken from mounds in the area, ranging from 10,000-year-old projectile points to artifacts of the Mississippian Period. In fact, so much pottery has been found from this era (around 1200 A.D.) that archaeologists have dubbed it "Fort Walton Period" pottery.

Visit the Air Force Armaments Museum, 6 miles north of Fort Walton Beach, to see its vast collection of missiles, bombs, guns, and war planes. Admission is free. (Open Tuesday through Sunday 9:30 A.M.–4:30 P.M., 850-243-6521)

## ≡FAST FACT

Elgin Air Force Base, the country's biggest Air Force base, dominates Fort Walton Beach. It was here that the U.S. Air Force assembled the first guided missiles in the 1940s, and it's here that work on developing and testing non-nuclear airborne weaponry continues today.

Within the base's boundaries, you can canoe 52 miles of marked trails through eight bayous and rivers. It also has some of the largest and most impressive sand dunes in Florida on its white sand beaches, as well as miles of backcountry hiking, mountain biking, or horseback riding. During the summer, the base sponsors a free two-hour tour; otherwise, you'll need to obtain permits from the Jackson Guard office for all other activities. (Open Monday through Friday 7:00 A.M.–3:15 P.M.)

### Destin

Called "the luckiest fishing village in the world" for its legendary fishing for more than a century, Destin today—at least the western part—is covered with high-rise condos. Unfortunately, these are the result of unrestrained development that has changed the town's once picturesque character.

If you're looking for Destin's beaches, you'll find the first one 2 miles east of town on Beach Road at Henderson Beach State Recreation Area, a 208-acre natural beach popular with families for its excellent swimming. Ten miles farther along U.S. Route 98, you'll come to Grayton Beach State Recreation Area, a world of windswept white dunes that reach almost to the tops of the slash pines and oaks.

### Eden State Gardens

Farther east, along the coast beyond Destin in Point Washington, overlooking Choctawhatchee Bay, stands the white-columned mansion by legendary swamp lumber entrepreneur William Henry

Wesley. Built in 1897 at the height of the lumber boom, it has been restored with eighteenth- and nineteenth-century furnishings. Take a tour of the house and azalea-filled gardens, sheltered by moss-draped oaks, to feel what it was like to live in the antebellum South. (The gardens are open daily 8 A.M.–dusk, the mansion from Thursday through Monday)

### Extra Special

Of all the areas of natural beauty around Pensacola Bay, the Gulf Islands National Seashore merits special praise. It includes six distinct areas—Perdido Key, the western part of Santa Rosa Island, the Historic Forts section within Pensacola Naval Air Station, Navarre Beach on Santa Rosa, a small island east of Fort Walton Beach, and the Naval Live Oaks area, site of the Seashore's Visitor Center, 2 miles east of Gulf Breeze on U.S. Route 98. Before exploring the park, stop at the Visitor Center for information and a map, plus a copy of the *Barnacle*, a free newspaper with details on daily events and tours. Natural and Indian history exhibits, as well as an orientation film, will prepare you for what you'll see and do in the park.

## ≡FAST FACT

When the U.S. Congress established the 137,598-acre Gulf Islands National Seashore as the second one in 1971, this preserve of islands, sounds, and mainland tracts, stretching from the east end of Santa Rosa Island in Florida west to West Ship Island in Mississippi, became the largest tract of protected coastline in the country.

While at Naval Live Oaks, you can wander through 1,378 acres of live oaks, southern magnolias, pines, sweet bays, and myrtles situated within the Pensacola Naval Base. In 1827, the U.S. Congress passed a resolution requiring the U.S. Navy to increase its reserve of live oaks for shipbuilding, and President John Quincy Adams inaugurated the first federal timber conservation program. Live oak, the heaviest of oaks, resists disease and decay. The U.S.S. *Constitution*, also known as "Old Ironsides" and now moored north of Boston, is one of the ships built of live oak. Unfortunately, problems arose, as the wood was too heavy to haul by wagon, then timber rustlers cut down trees and sold them to foreign navies, and finally the need for the tall, tough trees diminished after the introduction of iron and steel warships. The Visitor Center shows exhibits about the forest. Stroll along one of the short but shady forest trails, which include a 2-mile section of what was, during the early nineteenth century, Florida's major roadway linking Pensacola and Saint Augustine. (The forest is open daily 8 A.M.–sunset and the Visitor Center is open daily 8:30 A.M.–5:00 P.M.)

The National Seashore extends west of Pensacola Beach for 10 miles. At the western end of Santa Rosa Island stands Fort Pickens, a nineteenth-century fortification built by slaves between 1829 and 1834 using 21.5 million bricks to protect Pensacola from attack by sea. This moated pentagonal brick fort has walls 40 feet high and 12 feet thick. The big guns you'll see on display in the batteries date from the 1890s to the 1930s. A national park surrounds the intricate ruins of the ancient fort, which has seen action in every major U.S. military conflict from the Civil War to World War II. The large fort of brick and earth became obsolete by the turn of the twenty-first century, but it has been preserved so that you can explore a labyrinth of extensive passageways, chambers, dark gunpowder storage rooms, and pits for disappearing cannon. The U.S. Army held the exiled Apache chief Geronimo prisoner here in the 1880s. Try to go on one of the free guided tours, departing at 2 P.M. Monday through Friday and 11 A.M. and 2 P.M. on Saturday. Fort Pickens National Park suffered severe damage from recent hurricanes, so call ahead to make sure all facilities are operational.

Beside Fort Pickens, some crumbling concrete walls remain from another fort erected in the 1940s, which, together with the pillboxes and observation posts that litter the area, is a reminder that the fort's defensive function lasted until the end of World War II, only becoming obsolete with the advent of guided missiles. (Open daily 10 A.M.–4 P.M., Toll-free 800-365-2267)

The National Seashore's other forts are on Perdido Key, which in Spanish means "Lost" Key. The Spaniards built Fort San Carlos de Barrancas in 1698. The French captured it, then the British, then the French took it back, and finally the Spanish reclaimed it 100 years later. It was restored between 1839 and 1845 and last saw military action during the Civil War. You can take a guided tour daily at 2 P.M. Admission to the National Seashore is $8 per car per week. (Open 7:30 A.M.–sunset, 850-934-2600)

 **TRAVEL TIP**

Though you cannot walk over the dunes along the 9-mile-long stretch of high, rugged dunes that wall in a beach with vibrant white sands at this end of Santa Rosa Island, there are many places to cross them on boardwalks or paths to enjoy the pristine beach. To learn more about the dunes and the curious ecology of the island, join one of the ranger-led walks.

## By Day

Pensacola overflows with daytime activities. With so many beaches and so much coastline, you'll have hours of fun swimming, sunbathing, canoeing, or fishing. Add to that the historic sites within the Pensacola Naval Air Station and the Gulf Islands National Seashore, and you'll have more than enough to fill out your family vacation.

### On the Beach

The most powerful lure of Florida's western Panhandle lies within the 50-mile stretch of quartz-sand beaches that winds its way from Pensacola through Fort Walton Beach. You'll find just about everything you want at Pensacola Beach on Santa Rosa Island—mile after mile of fine white sands, water sports rentals, a fishing pier, and the usual hotels, snack stands, and beach bars.

## ≡FAST FACT

Casino Beach, located in the center of Pensacola Beach and named for the old casino building that held dances and special events there, stretches beneath the famous beach-ball water tank and is home to Gulfside Pavilion, where you can attend free concerts during the summer season.

The glistening beaches of Santa Rosa Island, across the bay from Pensacola, offer ideal sunbathing and swimming, plus two protected areas: a dense prehistoric forest and a long line of windswept sand dunes. Quietwater Beach is not only safe but is also shallow enough for toddlers to enjoy the surf.

Another nearby park is Big Lagoon State Recreation Area, 698 acres of lagoon beaches, salt marshes, dunes, and pine woods. It's an excellent place for observing birds and animals. Though board-walks make many areas accessible, you'll find a total sense of seclusion beyond the crowds of Pensacola Beach. A short nature trail will introduce you to some of the plants—Florida rosemary, black rush, sawgrass, milkweed, live oak, and slash pine. Three nature trails—Long Pond, Yaupon, and Grand Lagoon—will take you by board-walk along a mystical route of flatwoods, swales, and salt marshes, where you'll see mammals and reptiles and a myriad of birds. A 40-foot observation tower at East Beach, honoring ornithologist Francis M. Weston, will provide you with a panoramic view of Big Lagoon and Perdido Key (open 8 A.M.–sunset, 850-492-1595).

## On the Boat

With so many miles of coastline, as well as rivers, sounds, and bays, it's only natural that Pensacola would offer good opportunities for saltwater fishing. Offshore waters from Pensacola to Destin teem with blue and white marlin, sailfish, dolphin, black-fin tuna, barracuda, and king mackerel. Excellent fleets of charter boats serve Pensacola, Pensacola Beach, Fort Walton Beach, and Destin. Though rates vary, you'll pay about $200 and up for a boat carrying up to six anglers. You'll also find good surf and bay fishing and crabbing along the Gulf Islands National Seashore, or perhaps you'd rather fish off the city's 3-mile fishing bridge, the world's longest. To arrange a fishing charter, contact any of the following:

- **A Reel Eazy Charters:** Pensacola Beach, ✆Toll-free 877-733-5329
- **Big Fish Charters:** Pensacola, ✆Toll-free 866-246-2442
- **Chulamar Inc. & Fishing Fleet:** Pensacola Beach, ✆850-934-8037
- **Gulf Breeze Guide Service:** Gulf Breeze, ✆850-934-3292

 **TRAVEL TIP**

Learn to sail with Lanier Sailing Academy, which offers sailing lessons from beginning to advanced certification. Or if you already know how to sail, rent sailboats by the hour or charter a 33- to 39-foot yacht for an overnight trip on the inland waterway. (✆Toll-free 800-684-9463, ✎*www.laniersail.com*)

Canoeing is popular throughout the Pensacola area, with many navigable streams and spring-fed rivers. Rent canoes or kayaks from Adventures Unlimited (Toll-free 800-239-6864, *www.adventuresun limited.com*).

## Under the Water

If you're a certified diver, you can explore the U.S.S. *Massachusetts*, commissioned in 1896, which rests in 26 feet of water. To rent equipment or take dive classes, contact Scuba Shack/Wet Dream Charters, Inc.( 850-433-4319, *www.scubashackpensacola.com*).

## On the Links and on the Courts

Golf and tennis facilities abound all along the coast. With seven major golf courses, you can play a different course every day for a week. Here are some of the major courses:

**The Club at Hidden Creek:** This eighteen-holer is challenging enough to host the U.S. Open and features a clubhouse, pro shop, and restaurant overlooking the course. (Navarre, ☏Toll-free 888-248-8463, *www.hiddengolf.com/hiddencreek*)

**Lost Key Golf Club:** With a multiple teeing system, you'll be able to play a challenging round every time on this eighteen-hole championship course, designed by Arnold Palmer. (Perdido Key Beach, ☏Toll-free 888-256-7853, *www.lostkey.com*)

**Marcus Pointe Golf Club:** This eighteen-hole course features sand bunkers and trees, but few water hazards. Its well-manicured greens have been designed for beginning to advanced golfers. (Pensacola, ☏850-484-9770, *www.marcuspointe.com*)

**Osceola Municipal Golf Course:** A public eighteen-hole course, offering fine Bermuda-grass greens. Electric and pull carts are available for rental, plus there's a pro shop and restaurant. (Pensacola, ☏850-453-7599)

**Perdido Bay Golf Club:** After a multi million-dollar overhaul, this eighteen-hole PGA Tournament course has been converted into a fine links-style layout, featuring artificial dunes and lakes and a new type of grass providing a lush playing surface. (Perdido Key Beach, ☏Toll-free 866-319-2471, *perdidobaygolf.com*)

**Scenic Hills Country Club:** Redesigned by former U.S. Open Champion Jerry Pate, this eighteen-hole championship course, with multiple tees, mixes a dynamic layout with scenic beauty to offer you a challenging round every time. Facilities include a putting green and driving range, plus pro shop. (Pensacola, ✆Toll-free 888-248-8463, ✑*www.scenichills.com*)

**Tiger Point Country Club:** A pleasant round awaits you at this renovated eighteen-hole course, with clubhouse, restaurant, pro shop, two practice greens, driving range, and pool. (Gulf Breeze, ✆Toll-free 888-248-8463, ✑*www.meadowbrookgolf.com*)

You can learn to play tennis at the Roger Scott Municipal Tennis Center in Pensacola. (850-595-1260, *www.rogerscott.org*)

## Shopping

A number of small shops reside in restored cottages and mansions in the Seville Historic District. If you like pecans, you can get your fill at J. W. Renfroe Pecan Company (toll-free 800-874-1929, *www .renfroepecan.com*). If your family loves malls, take them to the Cordova Mall, the largest in Pensacola, or the University Mall.

 **JUST FOR PARENTS**

Being a historic city, Pensacola has an abundance of antique shops—obtain a list from the Convention and Visitors Bureau. Besides the shops, you can browse for china, glass, and memorabilia at the Ninth Avenue Antique Mall with its thirty-eight shops under one roof (✆850-438-3961) or at the Blue Moon, another indoor antiques mall with sixty-five dealers (✆850-455-7377).

Florida is known for its winter flea markets. You'll find plenty of them in the Pensacola area. The Flea Market in Gulf Breeze is one of the largest, with 500 vendor spaces under one roof (open Saturday and Sunday, year-round, 9 A.M.–5 P.M., 850-934-1971).

# Dining Out and Nightlife

Throughout the Pensacola area, you can taste a variety of cuisines from fresh seafood to Southern barbecue to Cajun specialties, steaks, or juicy burgers. The variety of local restaurants complements the city's cultural heritage.

**Barnhill Buffet:** If your brood is hungry, take them to this afford- able all-you-can-eat Southern-style buffet. (3075 Gulf Breeze Parkway, Gulf Breeze, ☎850-932-0403, ✑www.barnhills.com)

**Crabs—We Got 'Em:** If you like to eat crabs, you can choose from the largest selection on Pensacola Beach while overlooking the Gulf of Mexico. (6 Casino Beach Boulevard, Pensacola Beach, ☎850-932-0700, ✑www.crabswegotem.com)

**Flounder's Chowder and Ale House:** The menu at this family res- taurant offers a wide variety of hickory-grilled seafood, served in a fun atmosphere. (800 Quietwater Beach Road, Pensacola Beach, ☎850-932-2003, ✑www.flounderschowderhouse.com)

**Patti's Seafood Deli:** It attracts local folks to its bare-bones store by offering seafood in terrific sandwiches known as "Po-Boys," as well as gumbos, creole, and platters. No hamburgers or chicken here, just fish right off the boats. (610 South C Street, Pensacola, ☎850-434-3193)

**Skopelos on the Bay Seafood & Steak Restaurant:** It has proven for over three decades that a restaurant doesn't have to be next to the water to serve some of the best seafood possible. They also offer lamb, veal, and steak, and add Greek touches to many of their entrées (670 Scenic Highway, Pensacola, ☎850-432-6565)

**The Fish House:** The city's best seafood restaurant, serving sushi and seafood prepared in a variety of ways by an award-winning chef. (600 South Barracks Street, Pensacola, ☎850-470-0003, ✑www.pensacolafishhouse.com)

Though there are things to do at night in Pensacola, it's consid- ered quiet and sedate, especially for a Navy town. To see what's going on, check the "Weekender" section of *Pensacola News Journal*.

One of the most popular family nightspots is McGuire's Irish Pub, serving home-brewed ale, steaks, and seafood to the accompaniment of toe-tapping Irish music. McGuire cooked and tended bar and his wife, Molly, waited tables. When she made her first tip of one dollar, she tacked it to the back bar for good luck. Soon it became a tradition, and today over $250,000 in one-dollar bills hangs from the ceiling, all signed by "Irishmen" of all nationalities. (Toll-free 800-224-7474, *www.mcguiresirishpub.com*)

Since the late 1960s, the Seville Quarter, home of the original Rosie O'Grady's Goodtime Emporium, has been one of Pensacola's most happening nighttime places. This family entertainment center features music, dancing, darts, pool, and electronic games, and serves fresh seafood. Located in the historic district, it boasts seven clubs and two courtyards with a wide variety of live music, from country and western to Dixieland to rock-and-roll. One admission gets you into all of them. (850-434-6211, *www.rosies.com*)

 **TRAVEL TIP**

You can attend free Blues on the Beach concerts from May through October on Tuesdays from 7–9 P.M. at the Gulfside Pavilion on Pensacola Beach (☎Toll-free 800-635-4803). The Evenings in Olde Seville Square series in downtown Pensacola presents concerts on Thursdays at 7 P.M. during the summer (☎Toll-free 800-874-1234).

The Pensacola Symphony Orchestra (850-435-2533) also offers family pops concerts on Sunday afternoons. For traditional theater, there's the Pensacola Little Theatre (850-432-2042) and the University of West Florida Repertory Theatre (850-474-2405), which offer performances during the winter. The handsomely restored Spanish baroque Saenger Theatre, opened in 1925, hosts opera, dance, and musical performances, including some major Broadway shows (850-444-7686, *www.pensacolasaenger.com*).

# *Coastal Florida Destination Directory*

## Miami Area
### Greater Miami Convention & Visitors Bureau
✍*www.gmcvb.com*
✆Toll-free 800-933-8448

### Coral Gables Chamber of Commerce
✍*www.coralgableschamber.org*
✆305-446-1657

### Coconut Grove Chamber of Commerce
✍*www.coconutgrove.com*
✆305-444-7270

## Miami Beach Area
### Miami Beach Visitor & Convention Authority
✍*www.miamibeachvca.com*
✆305-673-7050

### Miami Beach Visitors Center at the Miami Beach Chamber of Commerce
✍*www.miamibeachchamber.com*
✆305-672-1270

**City of Miami Beach**
✍www.miamibeachfl.gov
☎305-673-7577

**Key Biscayne Chamber of Commerce & Visitors Center**
✍www.keybiscaynechamber.org
☎305-361-5207

## Fort Lauderdale Area
**Greater Fort Lauderdale Convention & Visitors Bureau**
✍www.sunny.org
☎Toll-free 800-22-SUNNY

**Greater Fort Lauderdale Chamber of Commerce**
✍www.ftlchamber.com
☎954-462-6000

**Greater Boca Raton Chamber of Commerce**
✍www.bocaratonchamber.com
☎561-395-4433

**Chamber of Commerce of the Palm Beaches**
✍www.palmbeaches.org
☎561-833-3711

**Palm Beach Chamber of Commerce**
✍www.palmbeachchamber.com
☎561-655-3282

**Palm Beach County Convention & Visitors Bureau**
✍www.palmbeachfl.com
☎Toll-free 800-833-5733

**Palm Beach County Cultural Council**
✍www.palmbeachculture.com
☎Toll-free 800-882-2787

## City of West Palm Beach
✎*www.clematisbynight.net*
✆561-822-1515

# Cocoa Beach Area
## Cocoa Beach Area Chamber of Commerce/
## Convention and Visitors Bureau
✎*www.visitcocoabeach.com*
✆877-321-8474

## Florida's Space Coast Office of Tourism
✎*www.space-coast.com*
✆Toll-free 800-572-3224

## Canaveral National Seashore
✎*www.nps.gov/cana*
✆321-267-1110

## City of Titusville
✎*www.titusville.com*
✆321-383-5775

## Titusville Area Visitors Council
✎*www.spacecityflusa.com*
✆321-267-3036

## Indian River County Chamber of Commerce,
## Tourism Division
✎*www.indianriverchamber.com*
✆772-567-3491

## Cultural Council of Indian River County
✎*www.cultural-council.org*
✆772-770-4857

**Stuart/Martin County Chamber of Commerce**
*www.goodnature.org*
772-287-1088

**Melbourne/Palm Bay Area Chamber of Commerce**
*www.melpb-chamber.org*
Toll-free 800-771-9922

**The Sebastian River Area Chamber of Commerce**
*www.sebastianchamber.com*
Toll-free 888-881-7568

**Saint Lucie County Chamber of Commerce**
*www.stluciechamber.org*
Toll-free 888-785-8243

**The Saint Lucie County Tourist Bureau**
*www.visitstluciefla.com*
Toll-free 800-344-8443

## Jacksonville Area
**Jacksonville & The Beaches Convention & Visitors Bureau**
*www.visitjacksonville.com*
Toll-free 800-733-2668

**City of Jacksonville Beach**
*www.jacksonvillebeach.org*
Toll-free 866-JAXBCHS

**Cultural Council of Greater Jacksonville**
*www.culturalcouncil.org*
904-358-3600

**Amelia Island Tourist Development Council**
*www.ameliaisland.org*
Toll-free 888-265-5845

### WVTAA/Saint Johns River Country
✍*www.stjohnsrivercountry.com*
☎Toll-free 800-749-4350

### Saint Augustine, Ponte Vedra & The Beaches Visitors & Convention Bureau
✍*www.getaway4florida.com*
☎Toll-free 800-653-2489

### Saint Augustine and Saint John's County Chamber of Commerce
✍*www.staugustinechamber.com*
☎904-829-5681

### City of Ormond Beach
✍*www.ormondbeach.org*
☎386-677-0311

### Daytona Beach Area Convention & Visitors Bureau
✍*www.daytonabeach.com*
☎Toll-free 800-854-1234

### City of Daytona Beach, Cultural Arts/Tourism
✍*www.codb.us*
☎Toll-free 866-605-4276

## Florida Keys
### Florida Keys and Key West Tourist Development Council
✍*www.fla-keys.com*
☎Toll-free 800-352-5397

### Key Largo Chamber of Commerce/Florida Keys Visitor Center
✍*www.keylargochamber.org*
☎Toll-free 800-822-1088

**Greater Marathon Chamber of Commerce & Visitor Center**
✐*www.floridakeysmarathon.com*
✆Toll-free 800-262-7284

**Islamorada Chamber of Commerce**
✐*www.islamoradachamber.com*
✆Toll-free 800-322-5397

**Lower Keys Chamber of Commerce**
✐*www.lowerkeyschamber.com*
✆305-872-2411

## Key West
**Key West Information Center**
✐*www.keywestinfo.com*
✆Toll-free 888-222-5090

**Key West Chamber of Commerce**
✐*www.keywestchamber.org*
✆Toll-free 800-LAST-KEY

## Everglades Area
**Everglades Area Chamber of Commerce**
✐*www.evergladeschamber.com*
✆Toll-free 800-914-6355

**Tropical Everglades Visitor Association**
✐*www.tropicaleverglades.com*
✆Toll-free 800-388-9669

**Everglades National Park**
✐*www.nps.gov/ever*
✆305-242-7700

## Florida Gulf Islands
✐*www.floridagulfislands.com*
☎Toll-free 800-462-6283

## Sarasota Area
### Sarasota Convention & Visitors Bureau
✐*www.sarasotafl.org*
☎Toll-free 800-522-9799

### Siesta Key Chamber of Commerce
✐*www.siestakeychamber.com*
☎Toll-free 888-837-3969

### Venice Area Chamber of Commerce
✐*www.venicechamber.com*
☎941-488-2236

### Greater Fort Myers Beach Area Chamber of Commerce
✐*www.fmbchamber.com*
☎Toll-free 800-782-9283

### The Greater Fort Myers Chamber of Commerce
✐*www.fortmyers.org*
☎Toll-free 800-366-3622

### The Beaches of Fort Myers & Sanibel
✐*www.FortMyers-Sanibel.com*
☎Toll-free 888-231-7073

### Sanibel and Captiva Islands Chamber of Commerce
✐*www.sanibel-captiva.org*
☎239-472-1080

### Charlotte Harbor & the Gulf Islands Visitor's Bureau
✐*www.pureflorida.com*
☎Toll-free 888-4PURFLA

**Greater Pine Island Chamber of Commerce**
✐*www.pineislandchamber.org*
✆239-283-0888

**Longboat Key Chamber of Commerce**
✐*www.longboatkeychamber.com*
✆941-383-2466

**Naples, Marco Island, Everglades Convention & Visitors Bureau**
✐*www.paradisecoast.com*
✆Toll-free 800-237-2273

## Tampa Bay Area

**Tampa Bay Beaches Chamber of Commerce**
✐*www.tampabaybeaches.com*
✆Toll-free 800-944-1847

**Official Tampa Bay Visitor Information Center**
✐*www.VisitTampaBay.com*
✆Toll-free 800-44TAMPA

**Ybor City Chamber of Commerce Visitor Information Center**
✐*www.ybor.org*
✆813-248-3712

**Saint Petersburg/Clearwater Area Convention & Visitors Bureau**
✐*www.floridasbeach.com*
✆877-352-3224

**Saint Petersburg Area Chamber of Commerce**
✐*www.stpete.com*
✆727-821-4069

## City of Saint Petersburg
✍ *www.stpete.org*
☎ Toll-free 800-874-9007

## Clearwater Beach Chamber of Commerce & Visitor Information Center
✍ *www.beachchamber.com*
☎ Toll-free 888-799-3199

## Ruskin Chamber of Commerce
✍ *www.ruskinchamber.org*
☎ 813-645-3808

## Tarpon Springs Chamber of Commerce
✍ *www.tarponsprings.com*
☎ 727-937-6109

# Panama City Area

## Panama City Beach Convention & Visitors Bureau
✍ *www.thebeachloversbeach.com*
☎ Toll-free 800-722-3224

## Panama City Beaches Chamber of Commerce
✍ *www.pcbeach.org*
☎ 850-234-3193

## Perdido Key Area Chamber of Commerce
✍ *www.perdidochamber.com*
☎ Toll-free 800-328-0107

## Gulf County Tourism Development Council (Port Saint Joe)
✍ *www.visitgulf.com*
☎ 850-267-1216

## Apalachicola Bay Chamber of Commerce
*www.apalachicolabay.org*
℡ 850-653-9419

## Cedar Key Chamber of Commerce
*www.cedarkey.org*
℡ 352-543-5600

# Pensacola Area
## Pensacola Bay Area Convention & Visitors Bureau
*www.visitpensacola.com*
℡ Toll-free 800-874-1234

## Gulf Islands National Seashore
*www.nps.gov/guis*
℡ 850-934-2600

## Beaches of South Walton
*www.beachesofsouthwalton.com*
℡ Toll-free 800-822-6877

## Destin Area Chamber of Commerce
*www.destinchamber.com*
℡ 850-837-6241

## Emerald Coast Convention & Visitors Bureau, Inc./ Destin–Fort Walton Beach–Okaloosa Island
*www.destin-fwb.com*
℡ Toll-free 800-322-3319

## Greater Fort Walton Beach Chamber of Commerce
*www.fwbchamber.org*
℡ 850-244-8191

## Gulf Breeze Area Chamber of Commerce

✍*www.gulfbreezechamber.com*

✆850-932-7888

# *Books to Read on Coastal Florida*

Akin, Edward N. *Flagler: Rockefeller Partner and Florida Baron.* Gainesville: University Press of Florida, 1992.

Allman, T. D. *Miami: City of the Future.* New York: Grove/Atlantic Press, 1988.

Anderson, Robert. *Guide to Florida's Vanishing Wildlife.* Altamonte Springs, Florida; Winner Enterprises, 1988.

Bartram, William. *Travels.* New Haven, Connecticut: Yale University Press, 1958.

Bethel, Rodman. *A Slumbering Giant of the Past: Fort Jefferson, U.S.A. on the Dry Tortugas.* Hialeah, Florida: W. L. Litho, 1979.

Bloodworth, Bertha E. and Alton C. Morris. *Place in the Sun: The History and Romance of Florida Place Names.* Gainesville: University Press of Florida, 1978.

Capitman, Barbara Baer. *Deco Delights.* Miami, Florida: Studio Publishing, 1988.

Cline, Howard. *Florida Indians, Volume II.* New York: Garland Publishing Company, 1974.

DeGolia, Jack. *Everglades: The Story Behind the Scenery.* Las Vegas, Nevada: K. C. Publications, 1986.

Didion, Joan. *Miami.* New York: Simon and Schuster, 1987.

Douglas, Marjory Stoneman. *The Everglades: River of Grass.* Sarasota, Florida: Pineapple Press, 1997.

Greenberg, Jerry and Idaz. *The Living Reef.* Miami, Florida: Seahawk Press, 1985.

Griswold, Oliver. *The Florida Keys and the Coral Reef.* Miami, Florida: Graywood Press, 1965.

Hall, F. W. *Birds of Florida.* Saint Petersburg, Florida: Great Outdoors Publications, 1979.

Hatton, Hap. *Tropical Splendor: An Architectural History of Florida.* New York: Knopf, 1987.

McIver, Stuart B. *Dreamers, Schemers and Scalawags.* Saint Petersburg, Florida: Pineapple Press, 1994.

Muir, Helen. *Miami, USA.* Gainesville: University Press of Florida, 2000.

Neal, Julie and Mike. *Sanibel & Captiva: A Guide to the Islands.* Sanibel, Florida: Coconut Press, 2002.

Oppel, Frank. *Tales of Old Florida.* Secaucus, New Jersey: Castle (Book Sales), 1991.

Parks, Arva Moore and Klepser, Carolyn. *Miami Then and Now.* San Diego, California: Thunder Bay Press, 2003.

Rieff, David. *Going to Miami: Exiles, Tourists and Refugees in the New America.* Gainesville: University Press of Florida, 2000.

Rothchild, John. *Up for Grabs: A Trip Through Time and Space in the Sunshine State.* Gainesville: University Press of Florida, 2000.

Standiford, Les. *Last Train to Paradise: Henry Flagler and the Spectacular Rise and Fall of the Railroad That Crossed an Ocean.* New York: Crown Publishers, 2003.

Unterbrink, Mary. *Manatees: Gentle Giants in Peril.* Saint Petersburg, Florida: Great Outdoors Publications, 1984.

Weber, Jeff. *Visitor's Guide to the Everglades.* Miami, Florida: Florida Farm Books, 1986.

Williams, Joy. *The Florida Keys.* New York: Random House, 1997.

Williams, Winston. *Florida's Fabulous Seashells: And Other Seashore Life.* Tampa, Florida: World Publications, 2001.

# Coastal Florida Lodging, Transportation, and Attractions

## Miami Area Lodging, Transportation, and Attractions

Bayside Cruises: ☎305-888-3002

Bayside Marketplace: ☎305-577-3344

Biltmore Hotel: ☎Toll-free 800-727-1926

Boutique Spa at the Ritz-Carlton Coconut
   Grove: ☎305-644-4684

Captain Jimmy's Fiesta Cruises: ☎305-371-3033

Captain's Tavern: ☎305-666-5979

Carnaval Miami: ☎305-644-8888

Chuck Smith Charters: ☎305-378-2332

Coconut Grove Art Festival: ☎305-447-0401

Coral Castle: ☎305-248-6345

Coral Gables House: ☎305-460-5361

Coral Gables Tennis Center: ☎305-460-5360

Crooked Creek: ☎305-274-8308

Days Inn Civic Center: ☎305-324-0200

Easy Sailing in the Dinner Key Marina: ☎305-858-4001

Edwin Link Children's Railroad: ☎305-253-0063

The Fairchild Tropical Botanical Garden: ☎305-667-1651

Flamingo Park Capital Bank Tennis Center: ☎305-673-7761

Golf Club of Miami: ☎305-821-0111

Greater Miami Calendar of Events: ☎305-375-4634

Greater Miami Opera: ☎305-854-7890

The Gusman Center for the Performing Arts: ☎305-372-0925

The Heritage of Miami: ☎305-442-9697

Hialeah Roller Rink: ☎305-887-9812

Historical Museum of Southern Florida: ☎305-375-1492

Holiday Inn Marina Park Port of Miami: ☎Toll-free 800-356-3584

Improv Comedy Club and Restaurant: ☎954-342-2898

InterContinental Miami: ☎Toll-free 877-314-2424

Kendale Lakes: ☎305-279-3130

La Tasca: ☎305-642-3762

Lowe Art Museum: ☎305-284-3535

Malaga: ☎305-858-4224

Metro-Dade at the International Tennis Center: ☎305-361-8633

Miami Art Museum: ☎305-375-3000

Miami Children's Museum: ☎305-373-5437

Miami City Ballet: ☎305-532-4880

Miami-Cuba USA and Hispanic Florida Tours: ☎305-491-5884

Miami-Dade Yellow Cab: ☎305-633-0503

The Miami Free Zone: ☎305-591-4300

The Miami Lakes Golf Club: ☎305-821-1150

Miami Metro Zoo: ☎305-251-0400

Miami Shores Country Club: ☎305-795-2366

Miami Skylift: ☎305-444-0422

Morningside Park: ☎305-754-1242

Museum of Science and Space Transit Planetarium: ☎305-854-2222

Opalocka/Hialeah Flea Market: ☎305-688-0500

Palmetto Golf Course: ☎305-238-2922

Parrot Jungle Island: ☎305-400-7000

Polar Palace ice skating rink: ☎305-634-3333

Richmond Cottage Inn: ✆305-235-1668

River Park Hotel and Suites Miami: ✆305-374-5100

S & S Diner: ✆305-373-4291

Salvadore Park Tennis Center: ✆305-460-5333

Shorty's Bar-B-Q: ✆305-665-5732

Spa at Mandarin Oriental: ✆305-913-8288

Spa Internazionale: ✆305-535-6030

Tropical Roller Skating Center: ✆305-667-1149

The Venetian Pool: ✆305-460-5357

Vizcaya Museum and Gardens: ✆305-250-9133

Willow Stream Spa: ✆305-932-6200

## Miami Beach Area Lodging, Transportation, and Attractions

American Watersport Clubs, Inc.: ✆305-538-7549

Aquasports Unlimited: ✆305-458-3133

Bal Harbour Shops: ✆305-866-0311

Bass Museum of Art: ✆305-673-7530

Beach Boat Rentals: ✆305-534-4307

Cardozo Hotel: ✆Toll-free 800-872-6500

Club Nautico South Beach: ✆305-361-9217

Club Tropigala: ✆305-672-7469

CoCo's Sidewalk Café: ✆305-864-2626

Crandon Park Beach on Key Biscayne: ✆305-361-5421

Crawdaddy's: ✆305-673-1708

Crescent Resort and Spa on South Beach: ✆305-531-9954

Days Inn Oceanside: ✆Toll-free 800-356-3017

Energy Fitness Center Spa Studio: ✆305-695-4200

Flamingo Park Tennis Center: ✆305-673-7761

Flashbacks: ☎305-674-1143

Florida Sunbreak: ☎Toll-free 800-786-2732

Fontainebleau Hilton Resort & Towers: ☎Toll-free 800-548-8886

Haulover Beach Park: ☎305-947-3525

The Island Club: ☎305-538-1213

Jackie Gleason Theater of the Performing Arts: ☎305-673-7300

Joe's Stone Crab: ☎305-673-0365

Kafka's Cybernet Kafe: ☎305-673-9669

Le Spa Lancôme: ☎305-674-6744

Lincoln Road Arts District: ☎305-674-8278

The Links at Key Biscayne: ☎305-361-9129

Lulu's: ☎305-532-6147

Miami Beach Botanical Garden Center and
   Conservatory: ☎305-673-7256

Miami Beach Golf Club: ☎305-532-3350

Miami-Dade County Metrobus: ☎305-770-3131

Miami Habitat: ☎Toll-free 800-385-4644

Miami Seaquarium: ☎305-361-5705

Newport Beach Pier: ☎305-949-1300

News Café: ☎305-538-6397

Normandy Shores Golf Club: ☎305-868-6502

Penrod's: ☎305-538-2604

Reward Fishing Fleet: ☎305-372-9470

Sanctuary Salon and Spa: ☎305-674-5455

Sissy Baby Sport Fishing: ☎305-531-4223

South Beach Cigar Factory: ☎305 604 9694

South Beach Local Shuttle: ☎305-673-7275

The Strand: ☎305-532-2340

Sugar 'n Spice: ☎305-865-5265

Tarpoon Lagoon Dive Center: ☎305-532-1445

Traymore Hotel: ☎Toll-free 800-445-1512

Washington Square: ☎305-534-1403

Wolfe Cohen's Rascal House: ☎305-947-4581

## Fort Lauderdale Area Lodging, Transportation, and Attractions

15th Street Fisheries: ☎954-763-2777

Action Sportfishing: ☎954-423-8700

All-Inclusive Sportfishing: ☎954-761-1066

Aloha Watersports: ☎954-462-7245

American Boat Rental: ☎954-761-8845

American Golfers Club: ☎954-564-8760

Anglin's Fishing Pier: ☎954-491-9403

Anhinga Indian Museum and Art Gallery: ☎954-581-0416

The Atlantic: ☎954-567-8020

BC Surf & Sport: ☎954-564-0202

Bill's Sunrise Boat Rental: ☎ 954-763-8882

Boca Raton Hotel and Club: ☎561-395-8655

Bonaventure Country Club: ☎954-389-2100

Bonnet House: ☎954-563-5393

The Breakers: ☎Toll-free 888-273-2537

Children's Museum of Boca Raton at Singing Pines: ☎561-368-6875

Club Nautico: ☎954-779-3866

Deerfield Island Park: ☎954-428-3463

Doubletree Guest Suites Galleria: ☎Toll-free 866-613-9330

Downtown Bicycles: ☎Toll-free 866-813-7368

Elizabeth Arden Red Door Spa: ☎954-564-5787

Esplanade Park: ☎954-561-7362

Ernie's Bar B Que and Lounge: ☎954-523-8636

Everglades Holiday Park:  954-434-8111

Flamingo Gardens and Wray Botanical Collection:  954-473-2955

Florida Bicycle:  954-763-6974

Fort Lauderdale Ghost Tour:  954-290-9328

Frank Stranahan Cottage:  954–524–4736

Fun Boards:  561-272-3036

George English Park tennis courts:  954-566-0622

Ghosts, Mysteries & Legends of Old Fort Lauderdale:  954-523-1501

Gondola Servizio:  954-561-7650

Grand Palms Golf Country Club:  954-437-3334

The Gumbo-Limbo Environmental Education Center:  561-338-1473

Holiday Park tennis courts:  954-761-5378

Hyatt Regency Sixty-Six Resort & Spa:  Toll-free 800-327-3796

John U. Lloyd Beach State Recreation Area:  954-923-2833

International Bike Shop:  954-764-8800

International Swimming Hall of Fame Museum
  and Aquatic Complex:  954-462-6536

Island Water Sports:  954-491-6229

Jungle Queen cruises:  954-462-5596

Lago Mar Hotel Resort and Club:  Toll-free 800-524-6627

Lauderdale Diver:  Toll-free 800-654-2073

Lauderdale Sandblast:  954-472-3755

Lion Country Safari:  561-793-1084

Loggerhead Marinelife Center of Juno Beach:  561-627-8280

Marriott's Harbor Beach Resort & Spa:  Toll-free 800-222-6543

Memorial Park tennis courts:  561-393-7978

Morikami Museum and Japanese Gardens:  561-495-0233

Museum of Discovery & Science and
  3-D IMAX Theater:  954-467-6637

Old Fort Lauderdale Village and Museum:  954-463-4431

Palm Beach Bicycle Trail Shop: ☎561-659-4583

Palm Beach Jai Alai: ☎561-844-2444

Palm Beach Polo & Country Club: ☎561-793-1400

Pro Dive: ☎954-776-3413

Royal Palm Polo Sports Club: ☎561-994-1876

Sabal Palms Golf Course: ☎954-731-2600

Sawgrass Recreation Marina: ☎954-389-0202

Shirttail Charlie's Restaurant: ☎954-463-3474

Singer Island Sailboard Rental: ☎561-848-2628

The Southport Raw Bar: ☎954-525-2526

Swap Shop: ☎954-791-7927

Undersea Sports: ☎ Toll-free 800-842-9798

United States Croquet Association: ☎561-627-3999

Watersports Unlimited: ☎954-467-1316

West Lake Park tennis courts: ☎954-926-2410

Whitehall Mansion: ☎561-655-2833

Wind Dancer Charters: ☎954-895-5408

Windsurfing Madness: ☎954-525-9463

## Cocoa Beach Area Lodging, Transportation, and Attractions

Adventure Kayak of Cocoa Beach: ☎321-480-8632

American Police Hall of Fame and Museum: ☎321-264-0911

Andretti Thrill Park: ☎321-956-6707

The Astronaut Hall of Fame: ☎321-449-4444

Baytree National Golf Links: ☎321-259-9060

BCCP Astronaut Memorial Planetarium
  and Observatory: ☎321-631-7889

Beach Island Resort: ☎321-784-5720

Bernard's Surf: ☏321-783-2401

Best Western Oceanfront Resort: ☏Toll-free 800-962-0028

Brassy's Take II: ☏321-784-1277

Brevard Museum of History and Natural Science: ☏321-632-1830

Brevard Turtle Preservation Society: ☏321-676-1701

Brevard Zoo: ☏321-254-9453

City News Books: ☏407-725-0330

Cocoa Beach Country Club: ☏321-868-3351

Cocoa Beach Scuba Odyssey: ☏321-537-9751

Coconuts on the Beach: ☏321-784-1422

Desperadoes: ☏321-784-3363

Dino's Jazz Piano Bar: ☏321-784-5470

Dixie Crossroads: ☏321-268-5000

Doubletree Cocoa Beach Oceanfront: ☏321-783-9222

The Elliott Museum: ☏772-225-1961

Florida Dolphin Watch: ☏772-466-4660

Gettin' There II Sportfishing Charters: ☏321-631-5055

Gilbert's Bar House of Refuge: ☏772-225-1875

Grasshopper Airboat Ecotours: ☏321-631-2990

The Habitat at Valkaria: ☏321-952-4588

Harvey's Indian River Groves: ☏321-636-6072

Heathcote Botanical Gardens: ☏407-464-4672

Herbie K's Diner: ☏321-783-6740

Holiday Inn Cocoa Beach Oceanfront Resort: ☏Toll-free 888-465-4329

Indian River Cruises: ☏321-223-6825

Island Boat Lines: ☏321-302-0544

Kennedy Space Center: ☏321-449-4444, 877-893-6272

Kountry Kitchen: ☏321-459-3457

Little Dixie River Queen: ☏Toll-free 888-755-6161

Lone Cabbage Fish Camp: ✆321-632-4199

McClarty State Museum: ✆772-589-2147

Melbourne Greyhound Park: ✆772-259-9800

Merritt Square Mall: ✆321-452-3272

Nannie Lee's Strawberry Mansion: ✆321-724-8078

North Hutchinson Island: ✆772-595-5845

Obsession Fishing Charters: ✆321-453-3474

Oceansports World: ✆321-783-4088

Olde Cocoa Village: ✆321-433-0362

Refuge's Visitor Information Center: ✆321-861-0667

Saint Lucie County Historical Museum: ✆772-468-1795

The Savannahs on Merritt Island: ✆321-952-4588

Schooner Sails: ✆321-783-5274

Sebastian Inlet State Recreation Area: ✆772-984-4852

Space Coast Association of Realtors: ✆321-452-9490

Space Coast Nature Tours: ✆321-267-4551

Spessard Holland at Melbourne Beach: ✆321-952-4588

The Super Flea and Farmer's Market: ✆321-242-9124

Tico Warbird Air Show: ✆321-268-1941

Tropicana: ✆321-799-3800

Valiant Warbird Museum: ✆321-268-1941

## Jacksonville Area Lodging, Transportation, and Attractions

A1A Beachside Trolley: ✆386-761-7700

Adventure Landing: ✆904-246-4386

The Alhambra Dinner Theater: ✆904-641-1212

All South Realty, Inc: ✆904-241-4141

Amelia Island Plantation: ✆904-261-6161

Aqua East Surf Shop: ✆904-246-2550

Blue Sky Surf Shop: ☎904- 824-2734

Bombay Bicycle Club: ☎904-737-9555

Boone Park: ☎904-384-8687

Bukkets Baha: ☎904-246-7701

Bulow Plantation Ruins Historic Site: ☎386-517-2084

Chiang's Mongolian Bar-B-Q: ☎904-241-3075

Conch House Marina: ☎904-824-4347

Crab Pot Restaurant: ☎904-241-4188

The Cummer Museum of Art and Gardens: ☎904-356-6857

Cypress Courts: ☎904-258-9198

Daytona Beach and Country Club: ☎904-258-3119

Daytona Beach Surf Shops: ☎904-253-3366

Daytona International Speedway: ☎386-253-7223

Daytona's Museum of Arts and Sciences: ☎386-255-0285

Daytona Recreational Sales and Rentals: ☎904-672-5631

The Doctor Peck House: ☎904-829-5064

Fort Caroline National Monument: ☎904-641-7155

Hendricks Avenue Courts: ☎904-399-1761

The Homestead: ☎904-249-5240

Hotel Ponce de León: ☎904-819-6400

Huguenot Park: ☎904-249-9407

Isle of Eight Flags Shrimp Festival: ☎Toll-free 866-426-3542

The Jacksonville Art Museum: ☎904-398-8336

Jacksonville Beach Golf Club: ☎904-247-6184

Jacksonville Kennel Club: ☎904-646-0001

Jacksonville Symphony Orchestra: ☎Toll-free 877-662-6731

King Neptune Deep-Sea Fishing: ☎904-246-0104

Kingsley Plantation Historic Site: ☎904-251-3537

Lightner Museum: ☎904–824–2874

Manucy Museum: ✆904–824–2872

The Marina Restaurant: ✆904-261-5310

Marineland's Dolphin Conservation Center: ✆Toll-free 888-279-9194

Okavango Village Petting Zoo: ✆904-757-4463

Old Saint Augustine Village: ✆904-823-9722

Oldest Wooden Schoolhouse: ✆904-829-6545

Ormond Beach Tennis Center: ✆904-677-0311

Pappa's: ✆904-641-0321

Perry's Ocean Edge Hotel: ✆386-255-0581

Pine Lakes Golf Club: ✆904-757-0318

Ponce de León Inlet Lighthouse: ✆386-761-1821

Ponte Vedra Beach Realty: ✆Toll-free 888-575-0077

Queen's Harbor Yacht and Country Club: ✆904-220-2118

The River City Playhouse: ✆904-388-8830

Saint Augustine Alligator Farm: ✆386-824-3337

Saint Augustine Sightseeing Trains: ✆904-829-6545

Sandy Point Sailboards: ✆904-255-4977

Sea Love Charters: ✆904-824-3328

Sea Love Marina: ✆904-767-3406

Sea Turtle Inn: ✆Toll-free 800-874-6000

Suncastle Properties, Inc.: ✆Toll-free 800-386-5585

Surf Station: ✆904-471-9463

Tradewinds: ✆904-261-9486

Tournament Players Club at Sawgrass: ✆904-273-3230

Washington Oaks State Gardens: ✆904-445-3161

Windsor Parke Golf Club: ✆904-223-4971

World Golf Hall of Fame: ✆Toll-free 800-948-4653

## Florida Keys Area Lodging, Transportation, and Attractions

American Diving Headquarters: ☎Toll-free 800-322-3483

Bahia Honda State Recreation Area: ☎305-872-2353

Big Pine Vacation Rentals: ☎305-872-9863

Big Pine Winterfest: ☎Toll-free 800-372-3722

Bounty Hunter Charters: ☎305-743-2446

Brian's in Paradise: ☎305-743-3183

Cabaña Bar: ☎305-664-4338

Captain Slate's Atlantis Dive Center: ☎305-451-3020

Caribbean Club: ☎305-451-9970

Castaway: ☎305-743-6247

Charters Unlimited: ☎305-451-9289

Choice Backcountry Charters: ☎305-664-2972

Coconuts: ☎305-451-4107

Coral Grill: ☎305-664-4803

Dip 'N Deli: ☎305-872-3030

The Diving Site: ☎Toll-free 800-634-3935

Dolphins Plus on Key Largo: ☎305-451-1993

Flipper's Sea School: ☎305-289-0002

The Florida Keys Children's Museum: ☎305-743-9100

Florida Keys Island Festival: ☎Toll-free 800-322-5397

The Green Turtle Inn: ☎305-664-9031

Harbor Bar: ☎305-664-9888

Holiday Isle Resorts and Marina: ☎Toll-free 800-327-7070

Hurricane: ☎305-743-5755

Islamorada Tennis Club: ☎305-664-5340

Jules Undersea Lodge: ☎305-451-2353

Key Colony Beach Golf Course: ☎305-289-1533

Looe Key Dive Center: ☎Toll-free 800-942-5397

Marathon Seafood Festival: ☎Toll-free 800-262-7284

Marina del Mar Resort: ☎Toll-free 800-451-3483

Monte's Restaurant and Fish Market: ☎305-745-3731

Mrs. Mac's Kitchen: ☎305-451-3722

Museum of Natural History of the Florida Keys: ☎305-743-3900

National Key Deer Refuge: ☎305-872-2239

Nautical Flea Market: ☎305-453-3802

No Name Pub: ☎305-872-9115

Quay: ☎305-289-1810

Sheraton Key Largo Beach Resort: ☎888-627-8545

Snook's Bayside Club: ☎305-451-3847

Sombrero Country Club: ☎800-433-8660

Sombrero Resort and Lighthouse Marina: ☎Toll-free 800-433-8660

Stull Bowling Lanes: ☎305-743-0288

The Theatre of the Sea: ☎305-644-2431

Tilden's Pro Dive: ☎305-743-5422

Two Conchs Charters: ☎305-743-6253

Vagabond Charters: ☎305-310-1962

Yellowfin Charters: ☎305-664-5333


## The Everglades Area Lodging, Transportation, and Attractions

Adventures in Backwater Fishing: ☎239-643-1261

Air Tours of South Florida from the Homestead Airport: ☎305-248-1100

Captain Dan: ☎813-695-4573

Captain Doug House's Florida Boat Tours: ☎Toll-free 800-282-9194

Captain Jay's Charters: ☎239-417-3055

Captains Table Inn: ☎239-695-4211

Chokoloskee Outdoor Resort: ☎941-695-2881

Corkscrew Swamp Sanctuary: ☎239-348-9151

Dawn Patrol Charter Fishing: ☎239-394-0608

Ernest C. Coe Visitor Center of Everglades
  National Park: ☎305-242-7700

Everglades National Park Canoe Rentals:
    ☎941-695-2591 or ☎Toll-free 800-445-7724

Fakahatchee Strand Preserve State Park: ☎239-695-4593

Fishing Adventures Inc.: ☎Toll-free 800-890-2312

Flamingo Lodge, Marina, and Outpost Resort: ☎305-253-2241

Flamingo Lodge Restaurant: ☎813-695-3101

Go Fish Guide Services: ☎239-695-0687

Gulf Coast Visitor Center: ☎239-695-3311

Huron Kayak and Canoe: ☎941-695-3666

Museum of the Everglades: ☎239-695-0008

North American Canoe Tours: ☎941-695-4666

River Wilderness Waterfront Villas: ☎239-695-4499

Sammy Hamilton Boat Tours: ☎813-695-2591

Smallwood Store and Museum: ☎239-695-2989

Totch's Island Boat Tours: ☎Toll-free 866-626-2833

## Sarasota Area Lodging, Transportation, and Attractions

Abbott's Family Charters: ☎941-302-4734

Barnacle Bill's Seafood: ☎941-365-6800

Bella Cucina Italian Buffet: ☎941-379-8158

Bellm Cars and Music of Yesterday: ☎941-355-6228

CB's Saltwater Outfitters: ☎941-349-4400

Collier County Museum: ☎941-774-8476

Dale Shields Bird Sanctuary: ✆941-388-4444

Dolphin Dive Center: ✆941-924-2785

Ed Smith Stadium: ✆941-954-7699

El Greco Café: ✆941-365-2234

Enterprise Sailing Charters: ✆Toll-free 888-232-7768

Flying Fish Fleet, Inc.: ✆941-366-3373

Fort Myers Historical Museum: ✆941-332-5955

G.Wiz: ✆941-309-4949

Holiday Inn: ✆Toll-free 888-465-4329

J. N. "Ding" Darling Wildlife Refuge: ✆941-472-1100

Koreshan State Historic Site: ✆941-992-0311

LeeTran: ✆941-275-8726

McKechnie Field: ✆941-748-4610

Mote Marine Laboratory and Aquarium: ✆Toll-free 800-691-6683

Museum of Botany: ✆941-366-5731

Outrigger Beach Resort: ✆Toll-free 800-749-3131

Radisson Lido Beach Resort: ✆Toll-free 800-333-3333

Reelin & Chillin Charters, Inc.: ✆941-228-7802

Resort Quest Vacation Home Network: ✆Toll-free 800-475-2892

Ringling Estate: ✆941-351-1660

Rodbender Fishing Charter: ✆941-925-8171

Sarasota Bicycle Center: ✆941-377-4505

Sarasota County Area Transit (SCAT): ✆941-951-5851

Sarasota County Beaches Red Tide Hotline: ✆941-346-0079

Sarasota Jungle Gardens: ✆Toll-free 877-861-6547

Siesta Key Parasailing: ✆941-586-1972

Siesta Sports Rentals: ✆941-346-1797

Smugglers Cove Adventure Golf: ✆941-351-6620

Van Wezel Performing Arts Hall: ✆941-953-3366

## Tampa Area Lodging, Transportation, and Attractions

Big Cat Rescue:  ☎813-920-4130

Busch Gardens Africa:  ☎Toll-free 888-800-5447

The Castaway:  ☎813-281-0770

Centro Ybor:  ☎813-242-4660

The Columbia:  ☎ 813-248-4961

DoubleTree Guest Suites:  ☎813-888-8800

Florida Aquarium:  ☎Toll-free 800-353-4741

Fort Foster Historic Site:  ☎813-987-6771\

Gameworks:  ☎813-241-9675

Great Explorations Museum:  ☎Toll-free 800-444-6674

Gulf Coast Museum of Art:  ☎727-518-6833

Hampton Inn & Suites:  ☎813-247-6700

Henry B. Plant Museum:  ☎813-254-1891

Hillsborough River State Park:  ☎813-986-2067

Museum of Science and Industry:  ☎813-987-6000

Pinewood Cultural Park:  ☎727-582-2123

Radisson Bay Harbor Inn:  ☎813-281-8900

Saint Petersburg Museum of Fine Arts:  ☎727-896-2667

Saint Petersburg Pier:  ☎813-821-6164

Salvador Dali Museum:  ☎727-823-3767

Seminole Hard Rock Hotel and Casino:  ☎866-ROCK4ME

The Tampa Bay Performing Arts Center:  ☎813-229-2787

Tampa Museum of Art:  ☎813-223-8130

Tampa's Silver Ring Café:  ☎813-301-0200

Trolleys of HART (Hillsborough Area Regional Transit):  ☎813-254-4278

Ybor City Museum State Park:  ☎813-247-1434

## Panama City Area Lodging, Transportation, and Attractions

Aquatic Adventures Moped and Bicycle Rentals:  ☏850-235-8051

Bay Point Marriott Resort:  ☏Toll-free 800-874-7105

The Bay Point Resort:  ☏850-236-6950

Bikini Beach Resort Motel:  ☏Toll-free 800-451-5307

Captain Anderson's:  ☏850-234-2225

Captain Anderson's Marina:  ☏850-234-3435

Captain Blood Light Tackle Fishing:  ☏850-785-6216

Coastal Parasailing:  ☏850-233-0914

Coconut Creek Family Fun Park:  ☏850-234-2625

Constitution Convention State Museum:  ☏850-229-8029

Edgewater Beach Resort:  ☏Toll-free 800-874-8686

Fun Land Arcade:  ☏850-234-3693

Holiday Gold Club:  ☏850-234-1800

Holiday Inn Sunspree Resort:  ☏Toll-free 800-633-0266

Hombre Golf Club:  ☏850-234-3673

Hydrotherapy Kiteboarding and Windsurfing:  ☏850-236-1800

John Gorrie Museum:  ☏850-653-9347

Junior Museum of Bay County:  ☏850-769-6128

Museum of Man-in-the-Sea:  ☏850-235-4101

Original Island Wave Runner Tours:  ☏850-234-7245

Osprey Charters:  ☏850-233-1959

Osprey Motel:  ☏Toll-free 800-338-2659

Pineapple Willy's Beachside Restaurant and Sports Bar:
     ☏850-235-0928

Pirate's Cove Marina:  ☏850-234-3939

Saint Andrews Bay with Island Star Cruises:  ☏850-235-2809

Saint Joseph Peninsula State Park:  ☏850-227-1327

Shipwreck Island Water Park: ☎850-234-3333

Signal Hill Golf Course: ☎850-234-3218

Silver City East: ☎850-763-8551

Skate Factory: ☎850-785-2261

Sweet Basil's Bistro: ☎850-234-2855

Tate's Hell Swamp State Forest: ☎850-487-3766

Treasure Island Marina: ☎850-234-8533

The Treasure Ship: ☎850-234-8881

## Pensacola Area Lodging, Transportation, and Attractions

Barnhill Buffet: ☎850-932-0403

Big Fish Charters: ☎Toll-free 866-246-2442

Big Lagoon State Recreation Area: ☎850-492-1595

Chulamar Inc. & Fishing Fleet: ☎850-934-8037

The Club at Hidden Creek: ☎Toll-free 888-248-8463

Crabs—We Got 'Em: ☎850-932-0700

Crowne Plaza Pensacola Grand Hotel: ☎Toll-free 800-348-3336

Fast Eddie's Fun Center: ☎850-433-7735

Fiesta of Five Flags: ☎850-433-6512

The Fish House: ☎850-470-0003

Flounder's Chowder and Ale House: ☎850-932-2003

Gulf Breeze Guide Service: ☎850-934-3292

Hampton Inn Pensacola Beach: ☎Toll-free 800-426-7866

Holiday Inn Express Pensacola Beach: Reservations: ☎800-833-8637

Lost Key Golf Club: ☎Toll-free 888-256-7853

Marcus Pointe Golf Club: ☎850-484-9770

Osceola Municipal Golf Course: ☎ 850-453-7599

Patti's Seafood Deli: ☎850-434-3193

Pensacola Area Convention and Visitor Bureau: ☎850-434-1234

Pensacola Beach Air Show: ☎850-932-1500

Pensacola Historical Museum: ☎850-433-1559

Pensacola Museum of Art: ☎850-432-6247

Perdido Bay Golf Club: ☎Toll-free 866-319-2471

A Reel Eazy Charters: ☎Toll-free 877-733-5329

Roger Scott Municipal Tennis Center: ☎850-595-1260

Sam's Fun City & Surf City: ☎850-505-0800

Scenic Hills Country Club: ☎Toll-free 888-248-8463

Skopelos on the Bay Seafood & Steak Restaurant: ☎850-432-6565

Tiger Point Country Club: ☎Toll-free 888-248-8463

T. T. Wentworth, Jr. Florida State Museum: ☎850-595-5985

Wildlife Rescue & Sanctuary Park: ☎850-433-9453

The Zoo Northwest Florida: ☎850-932-2229

# Maps

Atlantic Ocean

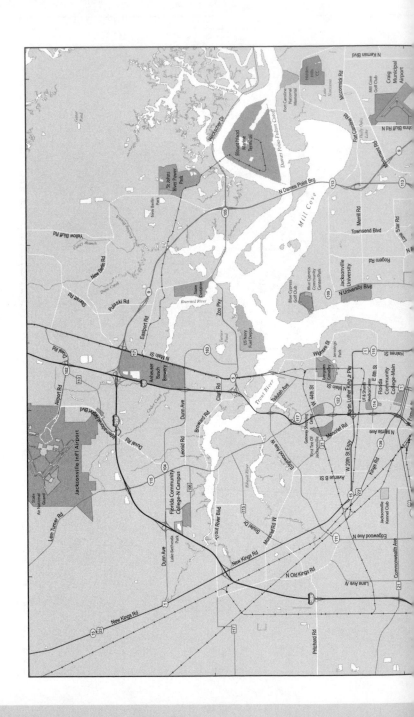

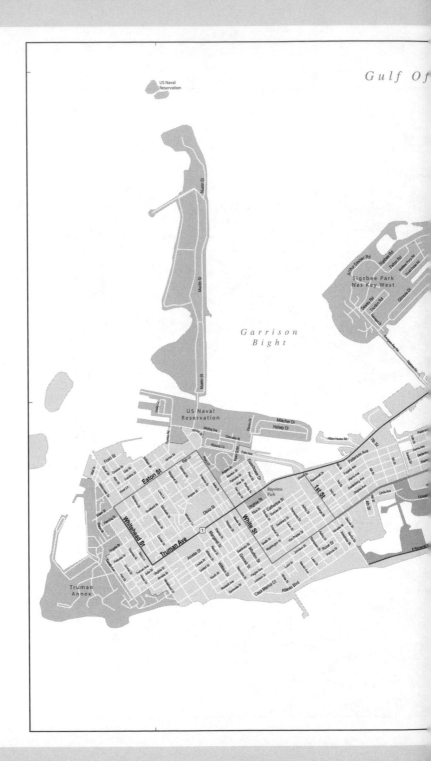

*ico*

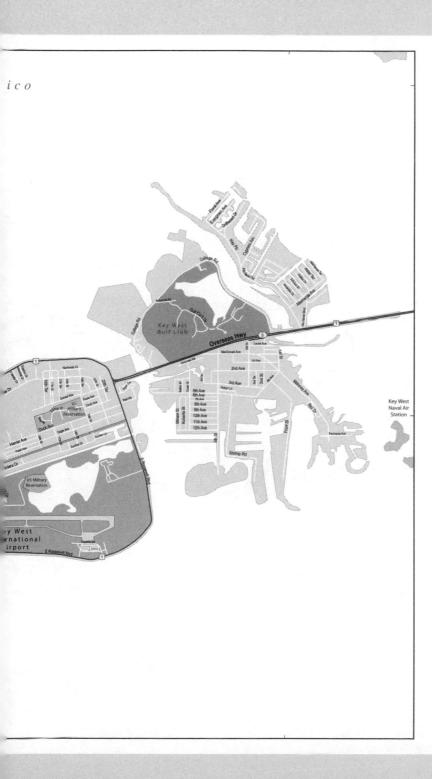

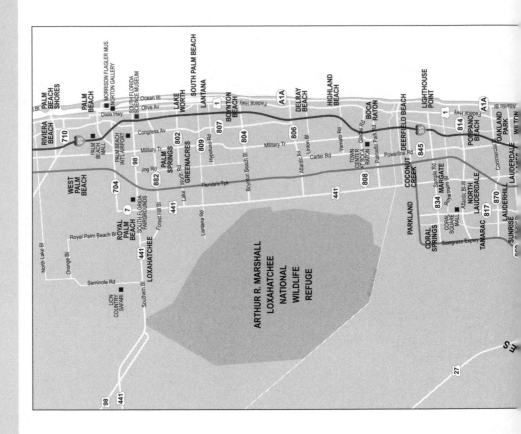

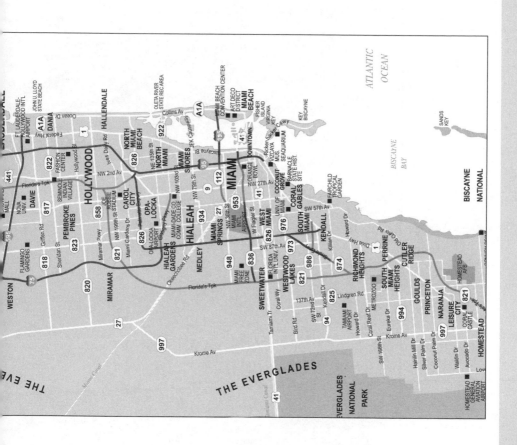

# Pensacola

# Tampa

# Index

# Everything® You Need for a Family Vacation to Remember

**The Everything® Family Guide to the Caribbean**
ISBN 10: 1-59337-427-5
ISBN 13: 978-1-59337-427-3
$14.95

**The Everything® Family Guide to Coastal Florida**
ISBN 10: 1-59869-157-0
ISBN 13: 978-1-59869-157-3
$14.95

**The Everything® Family Guide to Cruise Vacations**
ISBN 10: 1-59337-428-3
ISBN 13: 978-1-59337-428-0
$14.95

**The Everything® Family Guide to Hawaii**
ISBN 10: 1-59337-054-7
ISBN 13: 978-1-59337-054-1
$14.95

**The Everything® Family Guide to Las Vegas, 2nd Ed.**
ISBN 10: 1-59337-359-7
ISBN 13: 978-1-59337-359-7
$14.95

**The Everything® Family Guide to Mexico**
ISBN 10: 1-59337-658-8
ISBN 13: 978-1-59337-658-1
$14.95